Langenscheidt's
Pocket Italian
Grammar

Langenscheidt's Pocket Italian Grammar

LANGENSCHEIDT

NEW YORK · BERLIN · MUNICH

Contents

Contents

Introduction

This new series of Language Guides is designed to meet the needs of English-speaking learners and users of Italian. We are assuming that you, the reader, have some grasp of the basics of Italian, and want to improve your command of the spoken and written language. You may be studying Italian as part of your education, or it may be that in your professional capacity you have dealings with Italian-speaking colleagues or customers, or you may simply enjoy using your Italian when on holiday abroad. We believe that the unique three-part structure of our series is equipped to meet your needs.

Part 1 provides a concise reference grammar. We include all the main areas treated in full-length reference grammars, with a particular focus on those areas which cause problems to the English-speaking learner. Explanations are followed by examples from contemporary usage, and we make a point of indicating differences of usage between formal and informal Italian. The index to the book enables you to locate sections on specific points easily.

Part 2 demonstrates how to use the contemporary language in specific contexts. There are fourteen sections on key functions of language, such as giving advice, expressing agreement, making apologies. These sections aim to make you aware of the importance of the sociolinguistic context in which you are speaking, i.e. that we adapt the way we express ourselves according to the situation we are in and the person to whom we are speaking. If you were asking for advice in English, you would be likely to express yourself differently when talking to a friend as opposed to an official whom you had never met before. Of course, similar nuances exist in Italian, and for the foreign speaker it is important to develop sensitivity to the right expression for a particular context. So the 'register' or degree of formality of expression is indicated. The last six sections of Part 2 look at the language required for specific tasks: telephoning, writing letters, essays and reports. Generous illustrations are given, again with attention to the context in which you are speaking or writing.

Part 3 concentrates on building up your word power in Italian. It offers a convenient bank of important idioms based on verbs, nouns, adjectives and adverbs. Other sections focus on particularly rich areas of vocabulary (synonyms, slang, false friends, proverbs), or deal with key thematic areas relevant to various groups of readers (e.g. travel, finance, literature). Part 3 can be used for reference, if you come across a particular expression and want to track down its meaning, or as a basis from which to build up your own active vocabulary.

Since the series is aimed at English-speaking learners of Italian, one essential feature is the bilingual nature of the Language Guide. All examples, from short phrases to whole letters, are translated into English, so you can see at a glance what is being illustrated. Finally, all our examples are drawn from authentic contemporary situations. This is the 'real' Italian that is spoken and written in Italy. To remind you of this, we include a number of illustrations which show Italian in action.

We hope you enjoy using this book; *buona fortuna*!

VALERIE WORTH-STYLIANOU
Series Editor

Note to the reader

If you want to find out more about Italian pronunciation in general, or to check the pronunciation of a word in one of our examples, we suggest you consult *Langenscheidt's Universal Italian–English / English–Italian Dictionary*, which offers a Key to Pronunciation and gives the transcription of words according to the symbols of the International Phonetic Association.

English grammatical terms are kept to a minimum, but for further information consult *Cassell's English Usage*, edited by Tim Storrie and James Matson, which contains a grammatical survey of parts of speech and the rules of syntax.

The material presented in all three parts provides you with illustrations of key aspects of grammar, current usage and word power. If you would like to find out more about a particular topic, the list of books under 'Suggestions for further reading' (p.511) will be useful.

Abbreviations and symbols used

f.	feminine
m.	masculine
pl.	plural
sg.	singular
subj.	subjunctive
coll.	colloquial
< >	indicates the register of language, e.g. < formal >
X——X	indicates an incorrect usage, not to be followed
★	indicates an important note
!!	indicates vulgar or slang words or usage
*	irregular verbs

Acknowledgements

I would particularly like to thank Maria Rosser and Giulia Sokota for their thorough work on the drafts, and Victoria Campanaro, Serena Conti and Sergio Seregni for their suggestions in compiling the youth slang. I am equally grateful to the editor of the series, Valerie Worth-Stylianou, and to Steve Cook, Cassell's reference publisher, and Sandra Margolies, of house editorial, for their most valuable advice.

N.M.
1992

PART 1

A concise
reference grammar

NOUNS

Every Italian noun is characterized by its gender. This is indicated in dictionaries by the abbreviations *m.* (masculine) or *f.* (feminine). In a written text or speech, gender is clear from the article and adjective ending.

Noun endings in Italian can be modified for two reasons:

- to mark singular and plural. Grammatically, this is referred to as agreement in number:

  un biscotto a biscuit *due biscotti* two biscuits

- to differentiate between a man and a woman or a male and a female animal. Grammatically, this is referred to as gender agreement:

  un amico a male friend *un'amica* a female friend
  un gatto a male cat *una gatta* a female cat

There are no cast-iron rules to help foreign students know the gender of an Italian noun. However, one may use two types of guidelines, one according to meaning and origin, the other according to the noun ending.

1 Gender according to meaning

(a) Masculine nouns

(i) Months and days

il venerdì successivo the following Friday

(EXCEPTION: *la domenica* Sunday)

il giugno scorso last June

(ii) Languages

il russo Russian *lo spagnolo* Spanish

(iii) Colours

Colours are masculine when they function as nouns:

il rosa pink *l'arancione* orange

3

Colours made up from a colour adjective + a feminine noun remain masculine:

il verde (m.) + *la mela* (f.) = *il verde mela* apple green

(iv) Cardinal points

il nord, il settentrione the north
il sud, il meridione, il mezzogiorno the south
l'est, l'oriente the east
l'ovest, l'occidente the west

(v) Metals, minerals and chemical elements

l'oro gold   *il carbone* coal
il petrolio oil   *l'ossigeno* oxygen

(vi) Most trees

il melo apple tree   *il pino* pine-tree
(EXCEPTIONS: *la palma* palm-tree, *la quercia* oak, *la vite* vine)

(vii) Seas and lakes

il mare del Nord the North Sea   *il lago di Garda* Lake Garda

(viii) English nouns used in Italian

il week-end   *lo sport*   *il trading*

EXCEPTIONS:

- *la rockstar*, which refers to a man or a woman
- nouns referring to women:
  la baby-sitter, la hostess air hostess, *la top model* top model
  Miss Mondo Miss World, *la nurse* wet nurse
- *la gang, la holding* the holding company

(ix) Latin words

C'è stato un qui pro quo. There has been a misunderstanding.
(Note the difference from English use of *quid pro quo*.)

Non hanno dato l'imprimatur. They did not sanction it.

(x) Verbs and adjectives acting as nouns

Lo starnazzare delle oche salvò Roma.
The squawking of the geese saved Rome.

Non ha il senso del bello. He has no sense of beauty.

(xi) With combined nouns it is the gender of the first noun which governs the gender of the other parts of the sentence which must agree with the noun (e.g. article, adjectives, pronouns and past participle):

> *Sono state date molte multe record.*
> Many record fines were given.
>
> *La Borsa Valori di Tokio è importante come quella di New York.*
> The Tokyo Stock Exchange is as important as the one in New York.

(b) Feminine nouns

(i) Scientific, social and literary disciplines

la sociologia sociology   *l'informatica* computer science
(EXCEPTIONS: *il marketing, il trading*)

(ii) Abstract notions

l'amicizia friendship   *la religione* religion   *la paura* fear
(EXCEPTIONS: *l'amore* love, *il male* evil, *il bene* good, *l'odio* hatred)

(iii) Most fruit

una pesca peach   *una banana* banana

EXCEPTIONS:

l'ananas (m. and f.) pineapple	*il kiwi* kiwi
l'arancio (m.) *l'arancia* (f.) orange	*il lampone* raspberry
i datteri dates	*il limone* lemon
i fichi figs	*il pompelmo* grapefruit

(iv) Continents, states, towns, islands

EXCEPTIONS:

il Belgio Belgium	*l'Egitto* Egypt	*il Portogallo* Portugal
il Brasile Brazil	*l'Equador* Ecuador	*gli Stati Uniti*
il Canada Canada	*il Paraguai* Paraguay	the United States
il Cile Chile	*il Perù* Peru	*il Venezuela* Venezuela

2 Gender according to noun ending

(a) Masculine endings

Nouns ending in *-o* are masculine:

l'orologio watch, clock   *il governo* the government

EXCEPTIONS:

l'auto car	*la mano* hand
la dinamo dynamo	*la radio* radio
l'eco echo (m., in the pl. *gli echi*)	*la virago* virago
la foto photo	

(b) Feminine endings

(i) Many nouns ending in *-a* are feminine:

la cinepresa cine-camera   *la rosa* rose

EXCEPTIONS:

- Words ending in *-ma* (deriving mostly from Greek):

il cinema cinema   *il problema* problem
il clima climate   *il sistema* system
il diploma diploma   *il telegramma* telegram
il dramma drama   *il tema* theme, essay
il panorama view   *il teorema* theorem
il poema poem

- Other words:
il nulla nothingness
il pigiama pyjamas
il vaglia money order

- Nouns of professions, which can be masculine and feminine:
il giornalista male journalist   *la giornalista* woman journalist

(ii) Nouns ending in *-i*:

la bici bike   *l'oasi* oasis
la crisi crisis   *la sintesi* synthesis
la lavapiatti washing machine   *la tesi* thesis
(EXCEPTION: *il brindisi* toast)

(iii) Nouns ending in *-tà* and *-tù*:

la gioventù youth   *la capacità* ability

(iv) Nouns ending in *-ione*:

la lezione lesson   *la televisione* television

3 Masculine and feminine forms

(a) Different nouns for each sex

Sometimes the two sexes are described by two different words:

il padre father   *la madre* mother
il toro bull   *la vacca* cow
l'uomo man   *la donna* woman

(b) Same noun for both sexes

Some nouns refer to both sexes, in which case it is left to the article or an adjective to indicate whether the reference is to a male or a female. There are two types of nouns belonging to this group.

(i) Nouns ending in *-e*, usually indicating either a personal relationship or a profession:

l'assistente assistant	*l'ospite* guest
l'amante lover	*il / la cantante* singer
il / la consorte husband / wife	*il / la custode* caretaker
il / la nipote nephew / niece / grandchild	*l'agente* agent
il / la parente relative	*l'interprete* interpreter
il giudice judge	

Il cantante italiano Vasco Rossi si sta affermando in tutta Europa.
The Italian (male) singer Vasco Rossi is becoming popular all over Europe.

La mia cantante preferita rimane Edith Piaf.
My favourite singer (female) is still Edith Piaf.

Note that the plural ending *-i* does not differentiate the two sexes and may require the addition of extra words:

Ci sono più cantanti uomini che cantanti donne.
There are more male singers than female singers.

(ii) Nouns ending in *-a*, usually referring to a profession:

l'atleta athlete	*il / la giornalista* journalist
l'artista artist	*il / la musicista* musician
l'automobilista driver	*il / la pediatra* pediatrician
l'astronauta astronaut	*il / la pianista* pianist
il / la collega colleague	*il / la pilota* pilot
il / la farmacista chemist	*il / la regista* film director
il / la finalista finalist (in a competition)	

N.B. *l'omicida* murderer and *il / la suicida* suicide are both masculine and feminine.

With words ending in *-a* the plural ending differentiates the two sexes. It is *-i* for the masculine and *-e* for the feminine:

Alla televisione italiana lavora l'80 per cento di giornalisti e il 20 per cento di giornaliste.
Of the journalists working for Italian TV, 80 per cent are men and 20 per cent are women.

At present the masculine form is used to indicate both sexes:

> *I registi italiani hanno lasciato una profonda impronta negli anni cinquanta.*
> Italian film directors (men and women) left a deep impression on the fifties.

(c) Change of ending to denote gender

(i) With the following nouns the masculine ending *-e* is changed to *-a* to refer to the female sex:

il cameriere waiter	*la cameriera* waitress
l'infermiere male nurse	*l'infermiera* female nurse
il parrucchiere male hairdresser	*la parrucchiera* hairdresser
il signore Mr, sir	*la signora* Mrs, lady, madam

(ii) Most masculine nouns ending in *-o* change it to *-a* for the feminine form:

il bambino	*la bambina*	child
il bibliotecario	*la bibliotecaria*	librarian
il cuoco	*la cuoca*	cook
il figlio	*la figlia*	son, daughter
l'impiegato	*l'impiegata*	employee, clerk
l'operaio	*l'operaia*	manual worker
lo sposo	*la sposa*	spouse
lo zio	*la zia*	uncle, aunt
l'asino	*l'asina*	donkey
il cavallo	*la cavalla*	horse, mare
il gatto	*la gatta*	cat
il lupo	*la lupa*	wolf

(iii) Some nouns change the masculine ending to *-essa*:

il conte earl	*la contessa* countess
il diavolo devil	*la diavolessa* she-devil
il dottore doctor	*la dottoressa* woman doctor
il duca duke	*la duchessa* duchess
il leone lion	*la leonessa* lioness
il poeta poet	*la poetessa* poetess
il presidente president	*la presidentessa* woman president
il principe prince	*la principessa* princess
il professore teacher, professor	*la professoressa* woman teacher, professor
lo studente student	*la studentessa* woman student

(iv) Most masculine nouns ending in **-tore** change to **-trice** for the feminine form:

l'arredatore	l'arredatrice	designer
l'attore	l'attrice	actor, actress
l'autore	l'autrice	author
il direttore	la direttrice	director
l'imperatore	l'imperatrice	emperor, empress
l'ispettore	l'ispettrice	inspector
il pittore	la pittrice	painter
il presentatore	la presentatrice	presenter
lo scrittore	la scrittrice	writer
lo scultore	la scultrice	sculptor, sculptress
il senatore	la senatrice	senator
lo spettatore	la spettatrice	spectator
lo sponsorizzatore	la sponsorizzatrice	sponsor
il telespettatore	la telespettatrice	(TV) viewer

(EXCEPTION: *il dottore, la dottoressa* doctor)

(d) Names of animals and insects

Nouns for animals and insects usually have one word for both sexes. The sex is indicated by adding *maschio* for male or *femmina* for female:

È un bell'esemplare di leopardo femmina.
It's a beautiful specimen of the female leopard.

Hanno filmato l'aquila maschio. They have filmed the male eagle.

(EXCEPTIONS: *il maiale* pig, *la scrofa* sow, *il toro* bull, *la mucca / vacca* cow, *il gallo* cock, *la gallina* hen)

4 Different meanings according to gender

(a) Identical nouns with a different meaning according to the gender:

il boa boa	la boa buoy
il capitale financial capital	la capitale capital of a nation
il caso case	la casa house
il fine aim	la fine end
il fonte font	la fonte source
il fronte front	la fronte forehead
il radio radium	la radio radio

(b) Nouns with a different ending and meaning depending on the gender:

il baleno flash	*la balena* whale
il buco hole	*la buca* pit
il briciolo bit, tiny morsel	*la briciola* crumb
il cero candle	*la cera* wax
il foglio sheet	*la foglia* leaf
il limo slime, mud	*la lima* file
il mostro monster	*la mostra* exhibition
il modo manner	*la moda* fashion
il panno cloth	*la panna* cream
il parco park	*la Parca* fate
il pezzo piece	*la pezza* patch
il pianto cry	*la pianta* plant
il porto harbour	*la porta* door
il regolo ruler	*la regola* rule, regulation

For nouns that change gender and meaning in the plural see section 6f.

5 Gender of women's professions

There are not yet any rigid rules for the feminine forms of traditionally male-dominated professions. The initial tendency was to apply standard grammar rules:

● -*o* into -*a*:

l'architetto / l'architetta architect
lo psicologo / la psicologa psychologist

● -*o* into -*essa*:

il sindaco / la sindachessa mayor, mayoress

But these forms are now considered derogatory and the solution seems to be to use the masculine ending, even for women, and to indicate the sex in various other ways:

● by adding the Christian name:

l'inviato speciale Liliana Grubi
the special correspondent Liliana Grubi

Laura Franchi manager presso la FIAT Laura Franchi, FIAT manager

- by putting the feminine definite article in front of the noun:

    la Presidente della Camera dei Deputati
    the President of the Chamber of Deputies (lower house of Italian Parliament)

- by adding *donna* woman or *ragazza* girl before or after the noun:

    Vi è ancora chi non si fida di un amministratore donna.
    There are still people who do not trust a woman administrator.

    Le donne giudici sono ormai numerose nei tribunali italiani.
    There are many women judges in the Italian courts now.

    Abbiamo assunto due tecnici. Sono ragazze.
    We have appointed two engineers. They are girls.

However, *il soprano, il mezzosoprano, il contralto* are masculine even if they refer to a woman. Therefore the articles and adjectives referring to them are masculine too:

    un celebre soprano a famous soprano

6 Plural of masculine and feminine nouns

(a) Invariable nouns

Certain nouns do not change in the plural.

(i) Nouns ending with an accent:

    il tabù, i tabù taboo, taboos
    la città, le città town, towns
    un caffè, due caffè one coffee, two coffees
    un lunedì, tutti i lunedì
    one Monday, every Monday (literally: all the Mondays)

(ii) Nouns ending in a consonant (usually of foreign origin):

    il foulard, i foulard headscarf, headscarves
    il computer, i computer computer, computers
    il bar, i bar bar, bars
    il film, i film film, films

(b) Plural forms

Most nouns change their endings in the following way to form the plural:

	SINGULAR	PLURAL
feminine nouns ending in *-a*		*-e*
masculine nouns ending in *-a*		
masculine and feminine nouns ending in *-o*		*-i*
masculine and feminine nouns ending in *-e*		

la strada	*le strade*	road
il problema	*i problemi*	problem
il giardino	*i giardini*	garden
la mano	*le mani*	hand
l'autore	*gli autori*	author
la classe	*le classi*	class

(c) Nouns ending in *-a, -ca, -ga, -cia, -gia, -scia*

(i) Masculine nouns form the plural by changing the singular ending *-a* to *-i*:

il problema problem   *i problemi* problems

(EXCEPTION: *il cinema* does not change)

(ii) Feminine nouns form the plural by changing the singular ending *-a* to *-e*:

la luce light   *le luci* lights

(EXCEPTIONS: *l'ala, le ali* wing; *l'arma, le armi* weapon)

(iii) Nouns ending in *-ca* and *-ga* preserve the hard sound of the singular by adding an 'h'. They thus end in *-chi* and *-ghi* if masculine and *-che* and *-ghe* if feminine. There are very few masculine nouns in this group (all listed below) but many feminine ones:

il duca	*i duchi*	duke
il monarca	*i monarchi*	monarch
lo stratega	*gli strateghi*	strategist
il collega	*i colleghi*	colleague

(EXCEPTION: *il belga* the Belgian, *i belgi* the Belgians)

l'albicocca	*le albicocche*	apricot
l'amica	*le amiche*	friend (woman)
la banca	*le banche*	bank
la baracca	*le baracche*	hut

la barca	le barche	boat
la bottega	le botteghe	local shop
la paga	le paghe	wages
la zucca	le zucche	pumpkin

(iv) Nouns in **-cia** and **-gia** form the plural according to the following rules:

- when the accent falls on the 'i', the plural ends in **-cie** and **-gie**:

l'allergia	le allergie	allergy
la bugia	le bugie	lie
la farmacia	le farmacie	chemist shop

- when **-cia** and **-gia** are preceded by a vowel, the plural ends in **-cie** and **-gie**:

la camicia	le camicie	shirt
la ciliegia	le ciliegie (also ciliège)	cherry
la valigia	le valigie (also valige)	suitcase

- when **-cia** and **-gia** are preceded by a consonant, the plural ends in **-ce** and **-ge**:

la freccia	le frecce	arrow
la goccia	le gocce	drop
la mancia	le mance	tip
la pioggia	le piogge	rain

- The few nouns ending in **-scia** form the plural in **-sce**:

| la fascia | le fasce | band |
| la striscia | le strisce | strip |

But *scia* track preserves the 'i' in the plural: *scie*.

(v) Nouns ending in **-ea** form the plural regularly in **-ee**:

| l'area | le aree | area |

(d) Nouns ending in -o, -co, -go, -io

(i) Nouns ending in **-o** form the plural by changing it to **-i**:

| il soldato | i soldati | soldier |

(EXCEPTIONS:		
l'uomo	gli uomini	man
il logo	i logo	logo
l'eco (f.)	gli echi (m.)	echo)

13

Feminine nouns ending in -*o* do not change the ending.

(EXCEPTION: *la mano, le mani* hand)

(ii) Nouns ending in -*co* and -*go* preceded by a consonant change the ending to -*chi* and -*ghi*:

l'albergo	gli alberghi	hotel
il bosco	i boschi	wood
il chiosco	i chioschi	kiosk
il fungo	i funghi	mushroom
il mucchio	i mucchi	heap
il parco	i parchi	park

(EXCEPTIONS: These include: *il porco, i porci* pig)

(iii) Nouns ending in -*co* and -*go* preceded by a vowel form the plural in two ways:

- the following nouns form their plurals with the endings -*chi* and -*ghi*:

il baco	i bachi	silkworm
il carico	i carichi	load
il catalogo	i cataloghi	catalogue
il chirurgo	i chirurghi	surgeon
il cuoco	i cuochi	cook
il dialogo	i dialoghi	dialogue
l'epilogo	gli epiloghi	epilogue
l'incarico	gli incarichi	task
l'obbligo	gli obblighi	duty
il prologo	i prologhi	prologue
il profugo	i profughi	refugee
lo strascico	gli strascichi	aftermath
il valico	i valichi	mountain pass

- nouns which are related to professions form their plurals with the endings -*ci* and -*gi*:

il medico	i medici	doctor
il sociologo	i sociologi	sociologist
lo psicologo	gli psicologi	psychologist

Spoken Italian frequently uses the plural ending -*ghi* for nouns ending in -*ologo*: *i sociologhi*.

(iv) Nouns ending in -*io* form the plural with one 'i' only:

l'armadio	gli armadi	wardrobe
il bacio	i baci	kiss
il figlio	i figli	son

EXCEPTIONS: nouns with the stress on the 'i' of -*io* keep both:

il mormorio	*i mormorii*	murmur
il pendio	*i pendii*	slope
il rinvio	*i rinvii*	adjournment
lo zio	*gli zii*	uncle

(e) Nouns ending in -*e*

(i) If a noun ends in -*e* in the singular, the plural form ends in -*i*:

il sapone	*i saponi*	soap
il motore	*i motori*	engine
la canzone	*le canzoni*	song
la legge	*le leggi*	law

(ii) Nouns ending in -*ie* drop the 'e' in the plural:

la moglie	*le mogli*	wife
la superficie	*le superfici*	surface
l'effigie	*le effigi*	effigy

(EXCEPTION: *la serie, le serie* series)

(f) Irregular plurals

(i) The following nouns have irregular plural forms:

il dio	*gli dei*	god
il tempio	*i templi*	temple
il bue	*i buoi*	ox
il re	*i re*	king
la gru	*le gru*	crane

(ii) Nouns with a different meaning in the plural form:

la gente people	*le genti* peoples
il resto the rest, change	*i resti* ruins

(iii) Some nouns have two plurals, one masculine, one feminine, with different meanings:

il braccio arm, *i bracci* arms of a cross (of equipment), *le braccia* arms of a human being

il budello narrow tube, *i budelli* narrow tubes, narrow streets, *le budella* bowels

il ciglio edge, *i cigli* edges, *le ciglia* eyelashes

il corno horn, *i corni* (musical instruments), *le corna* horns (of animals) *il filo* thread, *i fili* strings, cables, *le fila* used figuratively, e.g. threads of a plot

il fondamento (hardly used in the sg.), *i fondamenti* basis, grounding, *le fondamenta* foundations of a building

il gesto gesture, *i gesti* gestures, *le gesta* deeds

il membro, i membri members, *le membra* limbs

il muro wall, *i muri* walls of a house, *le mura* walls of a town

l'osso bone, *gli ossi* bones of animals, *le ossa* bones of human beings

l'urlo cry, *gli urli* cries of animals, *le urla* shouts of human beings

(iv) Nouns with two plurals, one masculine, one feminine, without any difference in meaning:

il dito finger, pl. mostly used *le dita*

il ginocchio knee, *i ginocchi, le ginocchia*

il grido shout, cry, pl. mostly used *le grida*

il labbro lip, pl. mostly used *le labbra*

il lenzuolo sheet, *i lenzuoli, le lenzuola*

(v) The following nouns have double forms without a significant difference in meaning:

l'orecchio, l'orecchia   ear   *gli orecchi, le orecchie*

il frutto a piece of fruit

la frutta (collective noun for fruit off the tree, on the table, e.g. *Mi piace la frutta.* I like fruit.)

i frutti (fruit on the tree, or in a figurative sense, e.g. the fruits of science)

(vi) The following compound nouns remain invariable:

l'accendisigari	*gli accendisigari*	cigarette lighter
il cavatappi	*i cavatappi*	corkscrew
il portaombrelli	*i portaombrelli*	umbrella stand
l'aspirapolvere	*gli aspirapolvere*	vacuum cleaner
il cacciavite	*i cacciavite*	screwdriver
il portacenere	*i portacenere*	ashtray
il salvagente	*i salvagente*	life-jacket

N.B. *i senzatetto* the homeless occurs only as a plural.

ARTICLES

 Definite and indefinite articles

Italian has three types of article:
- the definite article (the)
- the indefinite article (a, an)
- the partitive article (some, any)

The form of the article is determined by whether the noun it refers to is masculine or feminine, singular or plural, and by the initial letter of the word which immediately follows the article: *un'amica simpatica* but *una simpatica amica*.

	DEFINITE		INDEFINITE	
	MASCULINE	FEMININE	MASCULINE	FEMININE
SINGULAR	*il / lo / l'*	*la / l'*	*un / uno*	*una / un'*
PLURAL	*i / gli / gl'*	*le*		

(a) The definite article

il before masculine singular words beginning with a consonant. This is the most frequent masculine form:

> *il treno* train   *il dizionario* dictionary

l' before masculine singular words beginning with a vowel or *h*:

> *l'assegno* cheque   *l'hotel* hotel

lo before masculine singular nouns beginning with *s* + consonant, *gn, pn, ps, x, y* and *z*:

> *lo sconto* discount   *lo zucchero* sugar
> *lo yogurt* yoghurt   *lo psicologo* psychologist

i before masculine plural words beginning with a consonant:

> *i giornali* newspapers   *i sindacati* trade unions

gli before masculine plural words beginning with a vowel, *s* + consonant, or *pn, ps, x, y,* or *z*:

> *gli alberghi* hotels   *gli spaghetti* spaghetti
> *gli zingari* gypsies

Gli may be written as *gl'* in front of words starting with *i*:

> *gl'italiani* the Italians

la before all feminine singular words:

> *la benzina* petrol

La is written *l'* in front of words beginning with a vowel:

> *l'automobile* car   *l'autostrada* motorway

le before all feminine plural words:

> *le riviste* magazines

(EXCEPTIONS: *gli dei* the gods, *per lo più* mostly, *per lo meno* at least)

(b) The indefinite article

un before a masculine singular word:

> *un gelato* an ice-cream   *un amico* a friend

uno before a masculine singular word beginning with *s* + consonant, *gn, pn, ps, x, y* or *z*:

> *uno sbaglio* a mistake   *uno zaino* a rucksack
> *uno pseudonimo* a pseudonym

una before a feminine singular word:

> *una ragazza* a girl

un' before a feminine singular word beginning with a vowel:

> *un' arancia* an orange

N.B. Note the importance of the apostrophe in distinguishing gender:

> *un assistente* a male assistant
> *un' assistente* a female assistant
> *un amante* a male lover
> *un'amante* a female lover

8 Uses of the definite article

(a) Same use in English and Italian

(i) English and Italian usually coincide in the use of the definite article when it refers to a noun which is clearly defined.

- The noun may be explicitly defined in the spoken or written text:

    Come sarà il mercato immobiliare del 1993?
    What will the construction market be like in 1993?

    I club italiani interessati hanno protestato.
    The Italian clubs which are involved have protested. (i.e. only those which are involved)

- It may be implicitly defined by circumstances or information shared by the speakers:

    Hai caricato le fatture nel computer?
    Have you entered the invoices on the computer? (in an office)

    Le compagnie aeree sono ancora in sciopero?
    Are the airlines still on strike? (i.e. those airlines we are interested in)

(ii) When the noun to which the article refers is used in a general sense, Italian and English usage coincide in the case of:

- Nouns indicating nationality:

    Gli inglesi amano restare in silenzio. Gli italiani preferiscono chiacchierare.
    The English love silence. The Italians prefer to chat.

- Singular or plural adjectives acting as nouns:

    Ah! La furba! Oh! The clever girl!

    i Ricchi e i Poveri (Italian pop group) The Rich and the Poor

(b) Differences between English and Italian

Apart from the above cases, when the noun to which the article refers is uncountable (i.e. it cannot be preceded by one, two, three) and is used in a general sense, Italian and English differ substantially.

Italian requires the definite article in the following cases:

(i) With plural nouns indicating a class or a category:

    Solo gli imbecilli non cambiano mai opinione.
    Only fools never change their minds.

    Le carote fanno bene alla vista. Carrots are good for one's sight.

    I temporali ti fanno paura? Do storms scare you?

(ii) With names of sports, hobbies, meals, illnesses, parts of the body, seasons, food, substances or matter:

    Il ferro è contenuto negli spinaci.
    Iron is present in spinach.

L'Aids è diffuso dappertutto oggi, non è vero?
Aids has spread everywhere today, hasn't it?

L'inverno si avvicina. Winter is approaching.

(iii) With abstract nouns:

La disoccupazione scendeva.
Unemployment was falling.

Gli sforzi della CEE hanno portato alla pace.
The efforts of the EC resulted in peace.

But the definite article is omitted when abstract nouns follow the verb:

C'è sospetto nelle sue parole.
There is suspicion in his words.

Questo significa problemi, amarezza, insonnia.
This means problems, bitterness, insomnia.

La mia materia preferita è economia.
My favourite subject is economics.

(iv) With names of languages:

Leggo l'arabo. I read Arabic.

È tradotto dal francese. It is translated from French.

But the article is optional with *parlare*:

Parla (il) tedesco? Do you speak German?

(v) With names of colours:

Quest'anno è di moda il rosa.
Pink is fashionable this year.

(vi) Before verbs or adverbs acting as nouns:

Ci fu l'esplodere della guerra fredda.
There was the outbreak of the cold war.

Vorrei sapere il perché.
I would like to know why.

(vii) In certain frequently used expressions:

alla TV / alla televisione on TV
farsi la barba to shave
fare il bagno to take a bath
dare il permesso to give (one's) permission

(viii) The definite article is also used to indicate the time, and before dates, seasons, festivals, ages, sizes, percentages:

all'alba at dawn

alle otto at eight

il treno delle otto the eight o'clock train

Sono le otto. It's eight o'clock.

il 20 ottobre del 1992 on 20 October 1992

il cinquecento / il millecinquecento / il sedicesimo secolo
the sixteenth century

l'estate del 1993 (denoting calendar time and seasonal climate)
the summer of 1993 / summer 1993

È alto. Supera il metro e ottanta. He is tall. He is over six foot.

Quel negozio fa il 25 per cento di sconto.
That shop gives a 25 per cent discount.

But as in English:

a primavera / di primavera in spring

(c) The definite article with possessives

The definite article is required before possessive adjectives and pronouns (see section 40a):

La sua voce è sexy. His / Her voice is sexy.

(d) The definite article with superlatives (see section 27a):

Il torneo di Wimbledon è il più importante della stagione.
Wimbledon is the most important tournament of the season.

(e) The definite article with relative pronouns
(see section 38d–f):

L'agenzia alla quale mi sono rivolta si è rivelata un disastro.
The agency to which I went has turned out a disaster.

Le tasse sono aumentate il che significa che aumenteranno anche i prezzi.
Income taxes have increased, which means that prices will go up too.

(f) The definite article with *tutto / tutti*

Tutti all, *entrambi* both and *tutti e due* both must be followed by the definite article (see section 42a):

> *tutti i sindacati* all trade unions
> *entrambi i / tutti e due i genitori* both parents

9   The definite article with proper nouns

Unlike in English, the definite article is required in the following cases:

(i) Before *signor, signora, signorina*, titles and professional qualifications followed by the surname, even when preceded by an adjective:

> *il signor Miglio* Mr Miglio
> *il dottore Lucini* Dr Lucini
> *la bella principessa Diana* beautiful Princess Diana
> *la cara signora Oddi* dear Mrs Oddi

But it is omitted when addressing someone directly, and before *Don* (the title given to priests) and foreign titles:

> *Signorina, ha dimenticato il biglietto.*
> Excuse me, miss, you've forgotten your ticket.

> *Don Gissani non è venuto.*
> Father Gissani didn't come.

> *Si chiamava 'Lady Di' prima di sposarsi.*
> She was known as 'Lady Di' before she got married.

(ii) Before a woman's surname and, in some regions, before both feminine and masculine names and family names:

> *la casa della Guidi* Mrs Guidi's house

> *È la bici della Carla e del Roberto.* (Northern Italian)
> It's Carla's and Robert's bike.

> *Ho visto i Gadda.* I saw the Gaddas.

(iii) Before the names of institutions:

> *La Fiat, la Ferrari, l'Alfa Romeo sono le principali case automobilistiche italiane.*
> Fiat, Ferrari, and Alfa Romeo are the main Italian car companies.

(iv) Before names of shares, which require the definite feminine plural article:

> *Le Pirelli sono salite.* Pirelli shares have gone up.

(v) Before names of football and other sports clubs:

> *Sei un tifoso del Milan o della Roma?*
> Are you a fan of Milan or Rome football club?

(vi) Before the names of some famous poets, novelists and painters:

> *il Petrarca, il Boccaccio, il Manzoni, il Verga, il Caravaggio*

(vii) With continents, countries, counties, lakes, rivers, seas, mountains, large islands and other geographical names formed by a proper noun + a common noun:

> *l'Africa, l'Italia, la Lombardia, il lago Michigan, la Senna, la Sicilia*
> (Capri, Cuba and other small islands do not take the article),
> *la stazione di Euston, l'aeroporto Kennedy, l'università di Warwick*

The definite article is used with towns and cities only when the town name is qualified:

> *la Barcellona delle Olimpiadi* the Barcelona of the Olympic Games

(viii) With cardinal points:

> *il nord, il sud, l'est, l'ovest* north, south, east, west

But: *Nord chiama sud. Ma il sud del paese non risponde.* < telegraphic language >

(ix) There is also a tendency to place the definite article before masculine names of daily newspapers and magazines:

> *Di solito legge il Corriere della sera tra i quotidiani.*
> Usually he reads the *Corriere della sera* of the dailies.

10 Omission of the definite article

(i) When nouns are part of a sequence the definite article may be omitted:

> *Dive, signore di moda, giornaliste hanno festeggiato il celebre stilista.*
> Stars, fashionable women, women journalists have celebrated the famous stylist.

> *Cioccolato, panna, crema, sì mi piacciono tutti.*
> Chocolate, cream, custard, yes, I like them all.

(ii) English and Italian also coincide in omitting the definite article in the following cases:

● When the noun follows the verb and a partitive article (*del* some, any) could be inserted before the noun:

> *Cambia lire in dollari?* Do you want to change lire into dollars?
>
> *Ci sono (dei) dati su questo argomento?* Are there (any) data on this subject?

● Verb + *di* + noun, used generically:

> *Discutevo di donne.* I was talking about women.

● Noun + *di* or noun + *in* (meaning 'regarding, dealing with, in relation to'):

> *Ecco il libro di storia e quello di fiori da giardino.*
> Here is the history book and the one on garden flowers.
>
> *un programma di vita* a programme for life
> *È esperto in arti magiche.* He is an expert in magic.

● With verb + *di* + noun:

> *Si diletta di musica.* He takes pleasure in music.
> *Si veste di cotone.* He wears cotton.

(iii) With nouns preceded by verbs or adjectives + *di*, e.g.:

avere bisogno / necessità to need	*pieno* full
carico loaded	*riempire* to fill
colmo full to the brim	*scoppiare* to burst
colmare to fill up to the brim	*completo* full up

and others with similar meanings:

> *Lo scompartimento era pieno di fumo.*
> The compartment was full of smoke.
>
> *Mi aveva riempito la testa di chiacchiere.*
> She had filled my head with chatter.

But if the noun is qualified the article is inserted:

> *con la testa piena delle chiacchiere di Luigi*
> with my head full of Luigi's chatter

Sometimes the adjective is omitted:

> *un bicchiere (pieno) di vino* a glass of wine
> *un piatto di minestra* a bowl of soup

(iv) With nouns + *di* indicating substance or matter of which
something is made or formed; *fatto* made or *costituito* formed may
be expressed or implied:

> *Ho comprato un cappello di paglia.*
> I bought a straw hat.

> *Quel grattacielo è fatto tutto di vetro.*
> That skyscraper is made entirely of glass.

(v) When abstract and unquantifiable nouns are preceded by *con* or
senza indicating manner, style:

> *Ha parlato con / senza ironia.* She spoke with / without irony.

But the definite article is used if the noun is qualified:

> *È entrata con l'eleganza di chi ha una grande tradizione familiare.*
> She made her entry with the elegance of a woman who has a
> great family tradition.

(vi) When the noun is preceded by *tra* or *fra* the definite article is
optional:

> *Tra scioperi e assenze ha lavorato due giorni.*
> Between strikes and absences he worked two days.

(vii) With words like *capace*, capable, *incapace* incapable, *incapacità*
incapacity, *abilità* ability:

> *È incapace di atti umanitari.*
> He is incapable of humanitarian gestures.

> *Dimostra incapacità di reazione.*
> He shows himself incapable of reacting. (literally: inability of
> reaction)

(viii) With verbs followed by *a*:

> *Giochi a ping pong / a carte / a dama?*
> Do you want to play table tennis / cards / draughts?
> EXCEPTION:
> *La ragazzina giocava alle bambole.*
> The little girl was playing with her dolls.

(ix) Unlike in English, the definite article is omitted in the following
everyday expressions:

> *a destra* on the right   *a teatro* at the theatre
> *a sinistra* on the left

(x) As in English, it is frequently omitted in headlines:

> *Slovenia in fiamme* Slovenia in flames
>
> *Azionisti prudenti* Cautious shareholders

(xi) In legal formulas:

> *Il paziente può uscire previa autorizzazione del primario.*
> The patient can leave when he / she has obtained authorization
> from the senior doctor.
>
> *Salvo parere positivo dell' architetto i lavori non possono cominciare.*
> Unless the architect gives the go-ahead work cannot start.

(xii) In apposition:

> *La frutta, alimento fondamentale nella dieta mediterranea, fa bene a tutti.*
> Fruit, the fundamental part of the Mediterranean diet, is good for everybody.
>
> *Sono parole pesanti, quelle del presidente.*
> They are weighty words, those used by the President.

11 Uses of the indefinite article

The indefinite article may precede a concrete or an abstract noun, a number, an adjective or a verb. It may be used to generalize as well as to be specific.

(a) To indicate a whole category

As in English the indefinite article may be used before a noun to indicate a whole category:

> *Un volo charter costa sempre meno di un volo di linea.*
> A charter flight always costs less than a scheduled flight.

In the following cases differences may exist between English and Italian usage:

(i) The indefinite article can be used with the following words in Italian but not always in English, e.g. in English you cannot talk about 'a research' or 'an information':

un affare a business transaction
un consiglio a piece of advice
un'informazione a piece of information
un parere a piece of advice
una ricerca a research project
una ricerca scientifica a scientific research project

(ii) The indefinite article can precede both a concrete and an abstract unquantifiable noun when this is qualified by an adjective or a specification:

È un miele molto dolce.
It's a very sweet type of honey.

Giorgia è di una bellezza straordinaria.
Giorgia is extraordinarily beautiful.

Otherwise, as in English, between the indefinite article and the unquantifiable noun there must be a word indicating a quantity or a type:

un pezzo / pezzetto di carta a piece / bit of paper
un filo d'erba a blade of grass
una goccia d'acqua a drop of water
una fetta di carne a slice of meat
un capo di abbigliamento an article of clothing

(iii) The indefinite article may precede the name of a town or a nation when qualified:

Una Venezia così scanzonata non l'avevo mai vista.
I had never seen such a carefree Venice.

(iv) The indefinite article precedes names of languages when these are preceded by a qualifying adjective:

Parla un buon tedesco. He speaks good German.

(v) The indefinite article indicates approximation with distances, costs, age or time:

Dista un cento metri. It's about a hundred metres from here.

Ha un trent'anni. He is about thirty years old.

Costa un ottanta mila lire. It costs approximately eighty thousand lire.

(vi) The indefinite article is used to compare someone with a famous person:

> *Non è certo un Einstein.* He's no Einstein.

(vii) The indefinite article indicates someone not specifically identified. If it is used with a surname, it is followed by *certo*:

> *C'era una Rossana tra gli studenti.*
> There was someone called Rossana among the students.
>
> *C'è uno che chiede di te.* There is someone asking for you.
>
> *una certa Clerici* a (certain) Miss Clerici

(viii) The indefinite article expresses vagueness in relation to time, place, etc.:

> *C'era una volta . . .* Once upon a time . . .
>
> *È successo un lunedì.* It happened on a Monday.
>
> *Un giorno gli scriverò.* One day I'll write to him.

(b) For emphasis

In the following cases the indefinite article is used for emphasis:

(i) The feminine form *una* may describe a notable event or accident:

> *Ne ha combinata una.* He has got into a fix.
> (literally: He has made a [mess].)
>
> *Te ne racconto una.* I'll tell you a good one.
> (literally: I'll tell you an [anecdote].)

Note that *uno* or *una* used on their own require the additional pronoun *ne* before the verb (see section 35a).

(ii) It is used to give emphasis with *tale, così, simile* such:

> *Un viaggio così non me lo dimentico.*
> I won't forget such a journey / a journey like that.
>
> *Una simile dichiarazione gli costerà cara.*
> Such a declaration will cost him dear.

(iii) In some cases the emphasis is indicated by the intonation falling on the indefinite article. It is therefore used more in speaking than in writing.

Lucia va con un ragazzo!
Lucy is going out with <u>such</u> an amazing guy!

Ho preso uno spavento! I had <u>such</u> a fright!

Bergerac aveva un naso! Bergerac had <u>such</u> a nose!

(iv) The intonation falling on the article also stresses a comparison:

Non cerco una banca ma quella vicino al parcheggio.
I'm not looking for <u>any</u> old bank but for <u>the one</u> near the car park.

(c) Before possessives

The indefinite article is used before possessive adjectives:

Vorrei una sua opinione. I would like your opinion.

un mio collega a colleague of mine

(d) With an adjective

It may be used with an adjective if the noun is implied:

solo uno / una grande just a large one

(e) Before an infinitive

The indefinite article can be placed before the infinitive of a verb in order to give it the meaning of a noun:

Oggi è stato tutto un rincorrersi di notizie sulla guerra.
Today there has been a rapid succession of news items on the war.

(f) Meaning 'one'

In some cases the indefinite article is used with the meaning of 'one':

- When *un* is contrasted with *un altro*:

  A lui piaceva un tipo di arredamento, a lei un altro.
  He liked one type of interior design, she liked another.

- When it is contrasted with another number:

  A lui basta un'ora di sonno, a lei ne occorrono due.
  He needs one hour of sleep, she needs two.

- As a number:

  Ti ho dato una sterlina o un dollaro?
  Have I given you one pound or one dollar?

• When a noun is implied but not stated or repeated:

> *Un tavolo per il pubblico e uno per i VIP.*
> One table for the public and one for the VIPs.

12 Omission of the indefinite article

In contrast with English the indefinite article is omitted:

(i) With exclamations introduced by *che*:

> *Che bel vestito!* What a nice dress!
> *Che musica assordante!* What a deafening piece of music!

(ii) When describing professions and jobs:

> *Sta studiando da infermiera.* She is training as a nurse.
> *Parlerà del suo lavoro da disc jockey.*
> He will talk of his work as a disc jockey.

However, the article is inserted when the occupation is more specific:

> *Sono un impiegato di banca.* I am a bank clerk.

(iii) When describing illnesses:

> *Ho mal di stomaco.* I have a stomach-ache.
> *Hai mal di testa?* Have you got a headache?

> EXCEPTIONS:
> *Ho un brutto raffreddore.* I have a bad cold.
> *Hai la febbre?* Have you got a temperature?

(iv) In forms of comparisons:

> *È sufficientemente stupido da non capire il trucco.*
> He is enough of a fool not to understand the trick.
> *È troppo bambina per essere presa sul serio.*
> She is too much of a child to be taken seriously.
> *È più meccanico che tecnico.*
> He is more of a mechanic than a technician.

(v) When a noun is qualified by another noun:

un tesoro di donna
a wonderful woman (literally: a treasure of a woman)

(vi) With appositions:

Ludovico Visconti, grande regista italiano, ha girato Il Gattopardo.
Ludovico Visconti, a great Italian film director, directed *The Leopard*.

13 The partitive article

To express the idea of an unspecified amount, Italian uses the contracted forms of *di* + definite article (see section 16), which agree in gender and number with the noun they refer to:

del before masculine singular words starting with a consonant:
del lavoro some / any work

dell' before masculine singular words beginning with a vowel:
dell'amore some / any love

dello before masculine singular words starting with *s* + consonant, or *gn, pn, ps, x, y, z*:
dello sporco some / any dirt   *dello zucchero* some / any sugar

dei before masculine plural words beginning with a consonant:
dei programmi some / any programmes

degli before masculine plural words beginning with a vowel or *s* + consonant, or *gn, pn, ps, x, y, z*:
degli esempi some / any examples.

Degli may be written *degl'* in front of words starting with *i*:
degl' inglesi some / any English

della before any feminine singular word:
della tristezza some / any sadness

dell' before feminine words beginning with a vowel:
dell'uva some / any grapes

delle before any feminine plural word:
delle lire some lire / any lire

14 Uses of the partitive article

As in English the use of the partitive article is optional. It is more frequently inserted in conversations and literary descriptions than in newspaper articles and technical or professional reports. It may be used in the following cases:

(i) With questions:

> *Ci sono dei risultati?* Are there any results?
>
> *Non c'è del vino?* Isn't there any wine?

(ii) With requests:

> *Dell'acqua minerale, per piacere.* Some mineral water, please.

(iii) With plural nouns:

> *Prendiamo delle salsicce?* Shall we have some sausages?

In Italian the following nouns are used with the definite article and so may take the partitive article:

degli affari business	*delle notizie* news
dei consigli advice	*dei pareri* opinions
delle informazioni information	*dei soldi* money
dei mobili furniture	

But when the noun is the subject and starts the sentence the partitive article tends to be omitted:

> *Voci lontane arrivavano in paese.* < literary >
> Some distant voices reached the village.
>
> *Pagamenti in ritardo non sono accettati.* < administrative >
> Delayed payments are not accepted.

(iv) With unquantifiable nouns:

> *Mi occorre del riso.* I need some rice.

One may use the plural form if the unquantifiable noun indicates portions:

> *Sì, dei caffè, per favore.* Yes, some coffees, please.

(v) With abstract unquantifiable nouns:

> *Ha dell' umorismo.* He has some sense of humour.

(vi) With abstract quantifiable nouns:

Ha delle qualità. She has some good qualities.

(vii) It is used before the word *altro* when it indicates quantity:

dell'altra carta some more paper

(viii) The partitive article is always necessary when it is used to contrast something undefined with something specific:

Non voglio dei fiori, voglio i fiori che ho visto ieri.
I don't want <u>any</u> old flowers, I want the flowers I saw yesterday.

15 Omission of the partitive article

(i) It is usually omitted in negative sentences:

Non ha tempo. He has no time.

Non c'è vino. There isn't any wine.

With quantifiable nouns there are three possibilities:

Non c'erano delle ragazze. ⎫
Non c'erano ragazze.   ⎬ There weren't any girls. /
Non c'era nessuna ragazza. ⎭ There were no girls.

(ii) With a plural noun it may be replaced by *alcuni* (m.pl.) or *alcune* (f.pl.):

~~X Ricordava le attività di delle giovani donne. X~~
Ricordava le attività di giovani donne. (more vague)
Ricordava le attività di alcune giovani donne. (more specific)
He recalled the activities of some young women.

(iii) It is also usually left out if there are other prepositions in the sentence:

Sono azioni della mamma.
They are my mother's shares.

But colloquially it is inserted:

L'ho fatto con delle uova. I have made it with eggs.

PREPOSITIONS

16 Basic and contracted prepositions

The basic prepositions are *a, con, da, di, fra, in, per, su* and *tra*.
Prepositions are used before nouns (*con il sapone* with the soap),
pronouns (*con me* with me) and infinitives (*con il presentare* by
presenting) but not with the gerund (~~X con presentando X~~).

No sentence or clause ends with a preposition:

> ~~X Il treno cui sono arrivata con era in ritardo. X~~
> *Il treno con cui sono arrivata era in ritardo.*
> The train I arrived on was late. (literally: the train with which I
> arrived)

Certain prepositions (*a, da, di, in, su*) contract and combine with the
definite article to form a single word as shown in the chart below,
e.g. *a + il = al*: *al ristorante* to the restaurant.

DEFINITE ARTICLE		*il*	*lo (l')*	*i*	*gli*	*la / l'*	*le*
PREPOSITION	*a*	*al*	*allo / (all')*	*ai*	*agli*	*alla / (all')*	*alle*
	da	*dal*	*dallo / (dall')*	*dai*	*dagli*	*dalla / (dall')*	*dalle*
	di	*del*	*dello / (dell')*	*dei*	*degli*	*della / (dell')*	*delle*
	in	*nel*	*nello / (nell')*	*nei*	*negli*	*nella / (nell')*	*nelle*
	su	*sul*	*sullo / (sull')*	*sui*	*sugli*	*sulla / (sull')*	*sulle*

In conversations as well as in literary texts *con* and *per* are
occasionally contracted: *col, coi,* etc., *pel, pei,* etc.

17 Functions of prepositions

a at / to / by

(i) Indirect object:

> *Scrivo a Piero.* I am writing to Peter.

(ii) Distance:

> *a quattro miglia da qui* four miles from here

(iii) Age:

> *a otto anni* (when he was) eight years old

(iv) Places, including towns and cardinal points:

> *a scuola* at school   *a casa* at home
> *alla stazione* at the station   *all'estero* abroad
> *a teatro* at the theatre   *all'aria aperta* in the open air
> *a Firenze* in Florence   *a sud* in the south

(v) Time, months, celebrations:

> *alle due* at two o'clock
> *a giugno* in June
> *a Natale* at Christmas

(vi) Prices and measurements:

> *a £7.000 al chilo* at 7000 lire a kilo

(vii) Instruments:

> *a mano* by hand
> *a macchina* machine-made
> *battuto a macchina* typed

(viii) Means of communication:

> *alla TV / radio / al telefono* on TV / the radio / the phone

(ix) Style:

> *all'ultima moda* in the latest style
> *a fiori* with a floral pattern

(x) Content of food:

> *dolce alla panna* a cream cake

(xi) At the beginning of a sentence *a* + infinitive has a conditional function:

> *A pensarci bene, non mi sembra caro.* = *Se ci penso, non mi sembra caro.*
> If I think about it, it doesn't seem expensive to me.

da at / by / from / to

(i) To be at or go to someone's home or public place (cf. French *chez*):

> *da Enrico* at Enrico's   *da lui* at his place

(ii) The agent in passive forms:

> *detto da uno straniero* said by a foreigner

(iii) Something which needs to be done:

> *carote da pelare* carrots to be peeled (See section 63b(ii).)

(iv) Cause:

> *colpito dal raffreddore* down with a cold

(v) Point of departure:

> *Ha decollato dagli Stati Uniti.* It took off from the USA.

(vi) Cost:

> *una pelliccia da sei milioni* a six-thousand-lira fur

(vii) Description:

> *una ballerina dai capelli corti* a short-haired dancer

(viii) Status:

> *da grande* as an adult   *da attore* as an actor

(ix) To translate 'for' with the present and past continuous tenses:

> *Non rispondeva da due giorni.*
> He had not been answering for two days.

(See sections 46d, 50b.)

di of

(i) *Di* + definite article forms the partitive article *del*, etc. (see section 13).

(ii) Specification:

> *una traduzione di inglese* an English translation
> *il professore di storia* the history professor
> *una casa di campagna* a country house

It is often preferable to use an adjective rather than a noun to qualify another noun:

> *uno studente universitario* a university student
> *l'assistenza ospedaliera* (the) hospital care

(iii) Ownership:

> *la barca del ministro* the minister's boat
> *la scultura del 500* sixteenth-century sculpture

Note how the Italian phrase may require the article with the preposition according to the rules governing the use of the definite article (see section 7).

(iv) Origin:

> *È di Parigi.* She is from Paris.
> *È di famiglia nobile.* He comes from a noble family.

(v) Substance:

> *vasi di terracotta* terracotta vases

(vi) Size:

> *una città di 10·000 abitanti* a town with a population of 10,000

(vii) For the use of *di* in comparisons see section 24b.

(viii) Age:

> *una bambina di sei anni* a six-year-old child

(ix) Time:

> *un viaggio di un'ora* an hour's journey
> *di notte / giorno / sera / mattina* by night / during the day / in the evening / morning

(x) Topic:

> *un articolo di politica* an article about politics

fra, tra between / among / amidst

> *fra amici* among friends   *parlare tra sè* to talk to oneself

Tra and *fra* also indicate time:

> *tra otto ore* in eight hours

in in / into

Note that in Italian the verb *entrare* is followed by *in*:

> *Entrò in cucina.* He entered / went into the kitchen.

In also indicates the end of a period of time in the future.

> *Guarirà in trenta giorni.* He will recover in thirty days.

per for

Per also expresses:

(i) Duration

The verb may be present, perfect or past participle.

> *un figlio voluto per dieci anni*
> a child who has been wanted for ten years

(See section 52b.)

(ii) Indication of future activity with *stare* + *per* + infinitive:

> *Stanno per arrivare.* They are going to arrive.

(iii) Scope or aim when followed by the infinitive:

> *Vorrei un vaso per nascondere quest'angolo.*
> I would like a vase (in order) to hide this corner.

su on / upon / about

> *È un articolo su un problema ecologico.*
> It's an article about an ecological problem.

Other prepositions

(i) Physical or figurative place:

a fianco di beside	*dopo di* after
al di là beyond	*fuori* outside
attraverso through	*insieme a* together
davanti a before, in front	*invece di* instead of
dentro inside	*oltre a* beyond
di qua da this side of	*lontano da* far away from
di là da beyond	*lungo* along
dietro a behind	

per mezzo di by means of   *sotto* below
prima di before   *verso* towards
sopra above   *vicino a* near

(ii) Time:

dopo di after   *fin da* since
durante during   *prima di* before
entro within

(iii) Limitation:

eccetto, fuorchè, tranne except   *senza* without

(iv) Others:

a causa di because of   *malgrado* despite
a confronto di compared to   *in quanto a* as far as
circa approximately   *nonostante* despite
contro against   *per conto di* on account of, by means of
in base a on the basis of   *in mezzo a* in the middle of
incontro towards   *secondo, a seconda di* according to

18 Prepositions with verbs, adjectives and nouns

Certain verbs, adjectives or nouns are always followed by a preposition. The most important constructions are given below.

(a) Verbs + *a* + noun

abituarsi a to get used to   *fare attenzione a* to pay attention to
assistere a to attend   *partecipare a* to participate in
badare a to pay attention to   *pensare a* to think about
credere a to believe in   *tenere a* to value
darsi a to take to

> *Fa attenzione alle strisce pedonali!*
> Pay attention to the zebra crossing!

Some verbs change their meaning according to the preposition which follows (see section 155), e.g.:

cominciare a to start to do something
cominciare con to start by doing something
decidersi a to make up one's mind to do something
decidere di to decide to do something

(b) Verbs + *a* + infinitive

★ In Italian, prepositions are never followed by the gerund. A preposition is always followed by the infinitive form.

abituarsi a	to get used to
affrettarsi a	to hurry / hasten to
aiutare a	to help someone to
andare a	to go to / end by
cominciare a (incominciare)	to begin to
condannare a	to condemn (someone) to
continuare a	to continue to
contribuire a	to contribute to
convincere a	to convince (someone) to
correre a	to run to (do something / and do something)
costringere a	to compel (someone) to
decidersi a	to make up one's mind to
divertirsi a	to have a good time (doing something)
esitare a	to hesitate (to do)
esortare a	to encourage (someone) to
fare bene / male a	to do the right / wrong thing (to someone)
fare meglio a	to be better off (doing)
fare presto a	to be quick / hurry up (to do something)
fermarsi a	to stop (doing something)
imparare a	to learn to
incoraggiare a	to encourage (someone) to
indurre a	to induce / to lead / to persuade (someone) to
iniziare a	to start to
insegnare a	to teach to
invitare a	to invite (someone) to
limitarsi a	to limit oneself to
mandare a	to send (someone) to
mettersi a	to start to
mirare a	to aim to
obbligare a	to oblige (someone) to
passare a	to stop (doing)
pensare a	to think of
persuadere a	to convince / persuade to
prepararsi	to prepare for (doing)
provare a	to try to
rassegnarsi a	to resign oneself to (doing)
ricominciare a	to start again to (do)
rinunciare a	to give up (doing)
riprendere a	to start again / to resume (doing)
riuscire a	to succeed in (doing)

sbagliare a	to make a mistake (in doing)
sbrigarsi a	to hurry to (do)
seguitare a	to continue (doing) / keep on (doing)
servire a	to be good for (doing)
sfidare a	to challenge / dare / defy (to do)
stare a	to stay (doing)
tendere a	to tend to
tornare a	to repeat (doing)
venire a	to come (and do something)
volerci a	to take, require (e.g. time to do something)

(c) Adjectives which are usually followed by *a*

adatto a suitable for / to	*incline a* prone to
affine a similar to	*indifferente a* indifferent to
analogo a analogous to	*inferiore a* inferior to
attento a careful of	*necessario a* necessary to / for
conforme a modelled upon	*nocivo a* harmful to
contrario a unfavourable to / contrary to	*noto a* well-known to
dannoso a detrimental to	*presente a* present
diretto a directed to	*pronto a* ready to / for
disposto a ready, disposed to	*propenso a* inclined to
essenziale a essential to / for	*sconosciuto a* unknown to
estraneo a alien to	*sensibile a* sensitive to
favorevole a favourable to	*simile a* similar to
fedele a faithful to	*sordo a* deaf to
gradito a appreciated by / pleasing to	*superiore a* superior to
grato a grateful to	*uguale a* equal to / like
idoneo a fit / suitable for	*utile a* useful for
	vicino a near to

Facile easy, *difficile* difficult, *buono* good and *ottimo* excellent require the following constructions:

a + infinitive of reflexive verb:

> *facile a dirsi / farsi* easy to say / do

da + infinitive with a passive meaning:

> *facile da fabbricarsi* easy to make / to be made

(d) Verbs + *di* + noun

accontentarsi di	to content oneself with
accorgersi di	to notice
dubitare di	to doubt (about)

essere informato di	to be informed about
fidarsi di	to trust in
infischiarsi di	not to care about
intendersi di	to be knowledgeable about
interessarsi di	to be interested in
lamentarsi di	to complain about
meravigliarsi di	to be surprised at / about
non poterne più di	not to be able to take any more of
nutrirsi di	to feed on, nourish with
occuparsi di	to take care of, attend to
pentirsi di	to be sorry about
preoccuparsi di / per	to worry about
rendersi conto di	to realize
ricordarsi di	to remember
ridere di	to laugh at
ringraziare di / per	to thank for
soffrire di	to suffer from
sporcare di	to dirty with
stupirsi di	to be astonished at
trattare di	to be about
vergognarsi di	to be ashamed about / of
vestirsi di	to dress in

Between the verb and the preposition there may be an adverb:
  Mi interesso solo di farfalle. I'm interested only in butterflies.

(e) Verbs + *di* + infinitive

accettare di	to accept / agree to (do)
accontentarsi di	to be content with
accorgersi di	to notice
accusare di	to accuse (someone) of
affermare di	to state / claim that
ammettere di	to admit to (being)
apprendere di	to learn from
aspettare di	to wait for
aspettarsi di	to expect to (do)
assicurare di	to assure of
augurare di	to wish for
augurarsi di	to wish that
avere bisogno di	to need to
avere fretta di	to be in a hurry to
avere il diritto di	to have the right to
avere intenzione di	to intend to
avere l'impressione di	to have the feeling / sensation that
avere paura di	to be afraid of
avere vergogna di	to be ashamed of

avere voglia di	to feel that (doing) / to want to (do)
avvertire di	to warn (someone) about / against
calcolare di	to reckon on
capitare di	to happen to
cercare di	to try to
cessare di	to stop (doing)
chiedere di	to ask to
comandare di	to order to
comunicare di	to communicate
concedere di	to allow to
confermare di	to confirm that
confessare di	to confess that
consentire di	to allow to
consigliare di	to advise to
contare di	to count on
credere di	to believe
decidere di	to decide to
dichiarare di	to declare that
dimenticare di	to forget to
dimostrare di	to demonstrate
dire di	to say / tell to
disperare di	to despair of
domandare di	to ask to
dubitare di	to distrust
evitare di	to avoid (doing)
fantasticare di	to imagine that
fare a meno di	to do without
fingere di	to pretend to
finire di	to finish (doing)
garantire di	to guarantee
giurare di	to swear to
immaginare di	to imagine
impedire di	to prevent from
imporre di	to order to
incaricare di	to ask to / entrust a task to
infischiarsi di	not to care about
lamentarsi di	to complain about
meditare di	to contemplate (doing)
meravigliarsi di	to be surprised about
meritare di	to deserve (to be)
minacciare di	to threaten with
negare di	to deny
offrire di	to offer to
ordinare di	to order to
ottenere di	to obtain, to get to (do something)
parere di	to seem to
pensare di	to plan to

Verbs + *di* + **infinitive** continued

pentirsi di	to repent to
permettere di	to permit to / allow to
precisare di	to specify
pregare di	to beg to
preoccuparsi di	to worry about
pretendere di	to demand to
prevedere di	to foresee
proibire di	to prohibit
promettere di	to promise to
proporre di	to propose to (do)
raccomandare di	to recommend
raccontare di	to tell
rendersi conto di	to realize
richiedere di	to ask to
ricordarsi di	to remember to
riferire di	to tell to
rifiutare di	to refuse to
ringraziare di	to thank (someone) for
rischiare di	to risk
ritenere di	to reckon to
rivelare di	to reveal
sapere di	to know
scegliere di	to choose to
scoprire di	to discover
sembrare di	to seem to
sentirsela di	to feel up to
sforzarsi di	to endeavour to
smettere di	to stop (doing)
sognare di	to dream about
sopportare di	to tolerate
sostenere di	to claim to
sperare di	to hope to
stabilire di	to agree to
stancarsi di	to get tired of
stupirsi di	to be astonished about / at
suggerire di	to suggest
supporre di	to suppose
temere di	to fear (doing)
tentare di	to attempt to
trascurare di	to neglect to
vantarsi di	to boast about
vergognarsi di	to be ashamed about
vietare di	to forbid to

44

(f) Adjectives + *di* + noun or verb

abbondante di	abundant in / rich in
avido di	greedy for
bisognoso di	in need of
capace di	capable of
certo di	certain of
colpevole di	guilty of
completo di	complete with
contento di	happy with
debole di	weak in
degno di	worthwhile
desideroso di	eager for / to
entusiasta di	enthusiastic about
esperto di	expert in
felice di	happy about
geloso di	jealous of
goloso di	greedy for
grato a qualcuno di qualcosa	grateful to someone for something
invidioso di	envious of
lieto di	happy to
maggiore di	larger, older than
malato di	ill with
meglio di	better than
migliore di	better than
minore di	smaller, younger than
pazzo di	mad with
peggiore di	worse than
pieno di	full of
povero di	poor in / lacking
privo di	without / deprived of
responsabile di	responsible for
ricco di	rich in
sano di	healthy of / in
sicuro di	sure of
sporco di	dirty with / stained with
stanco di	tired of
tipico di	typical of
vuoto di	empty, devoid of

(g) The construction noun + *di* + infinitive

This is usually equivalent to the English noun + -ing:

> *È il suo modo di vedere le cose.* It's his way of seeing things.

> *Non mi piace l'idea di uscire con questo tempo.*
> I don't like the idea of going out in this weather.

DESCRIPTIVE ADJECTIVES

19 Feminine and plural forms of the adjective

Adjectives are listed in dictionaries in the masculine singular form.
There are three groups of adjectives and they form the feminine and
the plural by keeping or changing the last vowel as indicated:

| | SINGULAR | | PLURAL | |
	MASCULINE	FEMININE	MASCULINE	FEMININE
Group A	*splendido*	*splendida*	*splendidi*	*splendide*
Group B	*grande*	*grande*	*grandi*	*grandi*
Group C	*ottimista*	*ottimista*	*ottimisti*	*ottimiste*

As a reminder, here is a chart of all noun and adjective endings:

MASCULINE NOUNS AND ADJECTIVES		FEMININE NOUNS AND ADJECTIVES	
SINGULAR	PLURAL	SINGULAR	PLURAL
-o	-i	-a	-e
-e	-i	-e	-i
-a	-i		

20 Irregular forms of adjectives

(a) Invariable adjectives

(i) Some colour adjectives are invariable: *blu* blue, *rosa* pink,
viola violet, *beige* beige, *pervinca* periwinkle, *arancione* orange, and
colours indicated by an object, e.g. *color mattone* brick colour. But
marrone brown can vary or remain unchanged:

> *Ho due camicette rosa e due marroni / e.*
> I have two pink and two brown shirts.

(ii) *Lontano* distant and *vicino* near are variable when they function
as adjectives (usually accompanying a form of *essere* to be); they
are invariable when they accompany other verbs or adverbs (e.g.
qui).

> *La stazione non è lontana.*
> The station is not far away.

Camilla abita lontano non vicino.
Camilla lives far away not nearby.

(iii) *Dabbene* < literary > respected, *dappoco* < literary > worthless and *perbene* respectable do not change:

È un uomo dabbene. He is a respected man.
È una persona perbene. He is a respected person.

(iv) Adjectives starting with *anti-* do not change:

luci antinebbia fog lamps
mina anticarro antitank mines
sistema antifurto antitheft device

(v) *Pari* equal, like, same, even and *dispari* odd, different, unequal do not change:

un numero pari an even number
Siamo pari. We are even.

(b) *Buono, grande, santo* and *bello*

Buono, grande and *santo* may adopt the following forms before singular nouns which do not start with *s* + consonant: *buon, gran, san.*

For example:

una gran commedia a great play
un gran pubblico a large audience

Grande before a vowel can take an apostrophe:

grand' attore great actor

Bello is irregular when used before a noun and it is regular when placed after it. Its irregular forms follow the same pattern as *dello*:

bel + masculine singular nouns starting with a consonant
bello + masculine singular nouns starting with *s* + consonant
bell' + masculine singular nouns starting with a vowel
bei + masculine plural nouns starting with a consonant
begli + masculine plural nouns starting with *s* + consonant or starting with a vowel

un bello studio a nice study
un bel giardino a nice garden
un giardino veramente bello a really nice garden

47

(c) The plural of adjectives ending in *-co, -go, -ca, -ga, -cia, -gia, -io*

(i) Adjectives ending in *-co* and *-go, -ca* and *-ga* insert 'h' to form the plural to preserve the hard sound. Thus their plurals end in *-chi, -ghi, -che* and *-ghe* (see section 6c(iii) and d(iii)).

bianca > bianche
> *un gruppo di case bianche* a group of white houses

lungo > lunghi
> *i capelli lunghi* long hair

(EXCEPTIONS: *greco > greci*, and some adjectives where the accent falls on the third syllable from the end such as *selvatico > selvatici* wild. But *carico > carichi* loaded.)

(ii) Adjectives ending in *-cio* and *-gio* end in *-ci* and *-gi* in the plural, if they are masculine. If they are feminine they end in *-cie* and *-gie* if the ending is preceded by a vowel; otherwise they also end in *-ci* and *-gi*:

grigio > grigi, grigie
> *Ho due gatti grigi e due cagnette grigie.*
> I have two grey cats and two small grey bitches / female dogs.

liscio > lisci, lisce
> *Queste sono lisce e morbide.* These are smooth and soft.

(iii) Adjectives ending in *-io* form the plural with only one *-i* :

ampio > ampi
> *viali ampi* large avenues

21 Agreement of adjectives with nouns

Italian adjectives can precede or follow a noun. They can also be separated from it by a verb. Whatever its position, the adjective takes the number and gender of the noun it refers to:

> *Questo articolo è di <u>un giornalista</u> arabo.*
> This article is by an Arab journalist.

> *Da qui si vedono enormi <u>cartelli</u> gialli.*
> From here we can see enormous yellow posters.

Le pareti erano riflesse immobili nel mare.
The walls were reflected motionless in the sea.

Tutto si è svolto in modo regolare.
Everything developed in a regular way.

★ As the examples show, the adjective takes the same gender and number as the noun it describes. But its final vowel may differ from that of the noun, depending on the group of the adjective (see section 19).

(a) One adjective qualifying two nouns

(i) The adjective is masculine plural when it qualifies one masculine and one feminine noun, whether singular or plural:

l'hotel e la piscina circondati da un parco
the hotel and the swimming pool surrounded by a park

Ho comprato due gonne e un maglione neri.
I bought two black skirts and a black jumper.

(ii) The adjective is feminine plural when it qualifies two singular feminine nouns:

> *Mi ha dato una rosa e una margherita molto profumate.*
> He gave me a rose and a daisy, both highly scented.

> EXCEPTION:
> *un corso di lingua e letteratura italiana*
> a course in Italian language and literature

(iii) In case of ambiguity one may be more specific by using expressions such as *anche questo* this too, *tutti e due* both, *tutti e tre* all three:

> *una villa e uno yacht ereditati = una villa e uno yacht, anche questo ereditato*
> a mansion and a yacht, which was also inherited

> *Ha due cani e una gatta adorabili = tutti e tre adorabili.*
> He has two dogs and a female cat, all three of them adorable.

(b) Adjectives referring to a verb

Occasionally an adjective qualifies a verb. In this case the adjective is masculine singular since it implies *in . . . modo* in a . . . way:

> *Va veloce.* It goes fast.
> *Parla chiaro.* She speaks clearly.
> *Mangiano sano.* They eat a healthy diet.

This combination of verb + adjective is frequent in advertising slogans:

> *Sciacqua morbido.* It gives a soft rinse.
> *Lava pulito.* It washes clean.

(c) Adjectives + *qualcosa* or *niente*

After *qualcosa* or *niente* use *di* + the masculine singular form of the adjective:

> *Hai visto qualcosa di bello?* Have you seen something nice?
> *No, non ho visto niente di bello.* No, I haven't seen anything nice.

(d) Adjectives qualifying the impersonal pronoun *si*

With the following impersonal forms the verb is used in the third person singular, but the adjective must be masculine plural (see section 36).

(i) With the impersonal pronoun *si* (one, people):

> *In Italia non si è abituati a fare la coda.*
> In Italy people are not used to queueing.

(ii) Equally, when an infinitive is used impersonally, the following adjective must be masculine plural:

> *Per restare giovani fate molta ginnastica.*
> To stay young take plenty of exercise.

> *Bisogna stare attenti ai pedoni qui.*
> One needs to look out for pedestrians here.

22 Adjectives functioning as nouns

There are cases where the noun is omitted and the adjective stands for a singular / plural / feminine / masculine noun. These adjectives will be referred to as noun-adjectives.

(i) The noun-adjective may be used with or without the article (unlike in English, where the article is required). It qualifies a group or a class as a whole:

> *una casa per anziani* a home for the elderly
> *È il mondo dei privilegiati.* It's the world of the privileged.

(ii) The noun-adjective is used to describe an abstract concept:

> *L'incredibile si è verificato.* The unbelievable has happened.

(iii) Unlike in English the noun-adjective is used to imply *uomo* man, *donna* woman, *tipo* chap, *gente* people. It may be preceded by an indefinite article, a partitive article or a number:

> *È un (uomo) orgoglioso.* He is a proud man.
> *Sono delle ambiziose.* They are ambitious women.
> *Mi sembrano due ignoranti.* They seem to me to be two ignorant people.

Occasionally the noun implied may refer to an object:

> *La Divina Commedia è un (poema) classico.*
> The Divine Comedy is a classic (work).

(iv) The Italian noun-adjective may be preceded by *questo / a / i / e* ('this ... one', these ... ones'), by *quello / a / i / e /* ('those ... ones, the / a ... one'), or by *uno / a* (see section 41):

> *Che cravatta metti? Questa vecchia?*
> Which tie will you wear? This old one?

> *Di quale ragazzo parli? Di quello alto?*
> Which guy are you talking about? The tall one?

> *Vendo questo registratore e ne compro uno nuovo.*
> I will sell this cassette recorder and buy a new one.

> *È il duro della compagnia.*
> He is the tough one of the group.

★ Note that, as in this last example, the equivalent of 'one' may be omitted in Italian.

(v) The noun-adjective can be qualified by another adjective, a prefix or a suffix. Note that the adjective precedes the noun-adjective.

> *È una bella bionda.* She is a good-looking blonde.
> *È uno stupidone!* He is a silly boy!

23 Position of adjectives

(a) Two or more adjectives

A noun can be preceded or followed by one or more adjectives:

> *le romantiche primavere italiane*
> the romantic Italian springs

> *il peso politico ed economico degli USA*
> the political and economic weight of the USA

> *il lento decisivo progresso di quel paese*
> the slow decisive progress of that country

(b) Descriptive and restrictive adjectives

Any adjective before the noun usually has a **descriptive**, subjective or evocative function. This construction tends to be found in a literary style. In the following example, *vecchi*, before the noun, evokes feelings, emotions and introduces colour:

Oggi la città divora i suoi vecchi quartieri.
Today the town is eating up its old quarters.

An adjective positioned after the noun, however, has a **restrictive** function. Its aim is either to lay emphasis on objective information or to differentiate, specify and circumscribe. This construction is often found in articles and reports dealing with scientific and economic information. Compare the previous example with the following:

Oggi la città distrugge i quartieri vecchi.
Today the town is destroying the old districts.

Vecchi in this position differentiates some districts from others: 'the districts which are old'. The tone conveyed is more matter-of-fact than in the previous sentence.

The correct position is not always immediately and instinctively perceptible to the non-native speaker. Since there are no rigid rules and the positioning of adjectives is frequently used to create stylistic effects, when in doubt it is advisable to place the adjective after the noun. Sections (c) and (d) below list a few cases where there is some consistency in the adjective position.

(c) Short adjectives

(i) The following adjectives and other frequently used ones are placed before the noun:

bello nice	*caro* dear	*cattivo* ugly
bravo good	*ottimo* excellent	
brutto ugly	*piccolo* small	

Sono cari ragazzi tutti e due.
They are dear boys, both of them.

Grazie. È stata un'ottima cena.
Thank you. It was a lovely dinner.

They may, however, follow the noun to give extra emphasis, which is often expressed by the tone of voice underlining them: *È stata una cena ottima.*

(ii) Short adjectives usually go before long nouns:

C'è un'alta natalità. There is a high birthrate.

(d) Adjectives that follow the noun

Adjectives follow the noun when they are:

(i) Adjectives preceded by an adverb such as *molto, tanto, assai* < literary > very, *troppo* too, *poco* hardly, *abbastanza* rather, *davvero* really, or ending in *-mente*:

> *Indagava su un omicidio veramente insolubile.*
> He was working on a really insoluble murder.

> *È stato un incidente molto serio.* It was a very serious accident.

Great emphasis is given by using the sequence *ben / assai* + adjective + noun:

> *un ben serio problema* a really serious problem

(ii) Used with *non:*

> *un incontro non piacevole* an unpleasant encounter
> *un tavolo non troppo grande* not too large a table

(iii) Adjectives longer than the noun:

> *una via stretta* a narrow road
> *un ruolo affascinante* a glamorous role

(iv) Adjectives of nationality:

> *Insegno a un gruppo multietnico.* I teach a multi-ethnic group.

But for an emotional effect the adjective can precede the noun:

> *l'italiana Trieste* the Italian Trieste

(v) Adjectives derived from nouns:

> *un corso universitario* a university course
> *la politica aziendale* the firm's policy

(vi) Adjectives describing physical, social or ideological conditions:

> *i suoi capelli tinti* his / her dyed hair
> *i paesi industrializzati* the industrialized countries
> *la sua formazione religiosa* his / her religious training

(vii) Adjectives indicating shape or colour:

> *una bici giallo banana* a banana-yellow bike

C'è stata una tavola rotonda sull'agricoltura.
There has been a round table on agriculture.

(viii) Present participles (endings *-ante*, *-ente*) and past participles (endings *-ato*, *-uto*, *-ito*) used as adjectives:

È un edificio cadente. It's a run-down building.

Abbracciò il fratello emigrato.
He embraced his brother who had emigrated.

(ix) An adjective governing a phrase:

un fotografo famoso negli anni sessanta
a photographer famous in the sixties

(x) Two adjectives in opposition:

Preferisco i mobili antichi ai moderni.
I prefer antique to modern furniture.

(e) The position of two or more adjectives

In all the following rules there is considerable flexibility in positioning two or more adjectives around a noun.

(i) Short adjectives precede long ones *or* the short one precedes the noun and the long one follows it:

una breve avventurosa vacanza / *una breve vacanza avventurosa*
a short adventurous holiday

(ii) *Bello, bravo, cattivo* and other common adjectives tend to occur in the sequence: *bello* + noun + other adjective:

Che bei capelli lunghi! What beautiful long hair!

But in a description one might say:

due belle tipiche strade di montagna
two typically pretty mountain streets

(iii) Adjectives which must follow the noun, as previously indicated, keep this position. The other adjective can precede the noun or follow the first adjective:

i paesi islamici bisognosi the needy Islamic countries
i ricchi paesi islamici the rich Islamic countries
la recente gara ciclistica / *la gara ciclistica recente*
the recent bicycle race

(iv) Adjectives with a 'descriptive' function precede the noun, those with a 'restrictive' function follow it (see section 23b above):

> *i piccoli < descriptive > produttori agricoli*
> the small agricultural producers
>
> *i produttori agricoli piccoli < restrictive >*
> those agricultural producers who are small

(v) Overall, Italian adjectives tend to follow the same sequence as those in English, but placed one before and one after the noun:

> *certi animali rari* certain rare animals
> *lo stesso codice segreto* the same secret code

(vi) Two adjectives may be linked by the sequence *tra . . . e*:

> *un volto tra sereno e preoccupato*
> a face half calm half thoughtful

(f) Adjectives with noun + complement

With a noun governing a phrase (a complement) one adjective may precede the noun and one may follow it:

> *la particolare natura pubblica del prodotto*
> the particular public nature of the product

But if one of the adjectives governs the phrase it must follow the noun:

> *Sto leggendo un romanzo inglese celebre per il suo stile.*
> I am reading an English novel well known for its style.

(g) Adjectives whose meaning changes according to the position

(i) The meaning of the following adjectives varies according to their position:

Abitano famiglie numerose.	*Abitano numerose famiglie.*
Large families live there.	Several families live there.
Aspetto dati certi.	*Aspetto certi dati.*
I am waiting for irrefutable data.	I am waiting for some data.
Conosco casi diversi.	*Conosco diversi casi.*
I know different cases.	I know several cases.

Cerco delle decorazioni semplici.	*Cerco delle semplici decorazioni.*
I am looking for simple decorations.	I am only looking for decorations.
È il presidente stesso.	*È lo stesso presidente.*
It's the president himself.	It's the same president.
È un programma unico.	*È un unico programma.*
It's an exceptional programme.	It's a single programme.
È un vero amico.	*È una storia vera.*
He's a true / real friend.	It's a true story.

(ii) These adjectives change meaning according to the position with some nouns only:

> *un alto ufficiale* a high-ranking officer
> *un ufficiale alto* a tall officer
> *un grand' uomo* a real man
> *un uomo grande* a big man
> *un pover uomo* a man of no significance
> *un uomo povero* a man with no money

(iii) Some combinations of noun + adjective have an idiomatic meaning:

> *un libro giallo* a thriller
> But *un libro con la copertina gialla* a yellow book (i.e. with a yellow cover / jacket)
> *la camera oscura* darkroom
> *la luna nuova* the new moon
> *merci di largo consumo* popular consumer goods

DEGREES OF COMPARISON

24 The comparative

(a) Forms of comparison

Comparisons may be made with an adjective, an adverb or a pronoun, between nouns, verbs or adverbs, following the pattern below:

più . . . di / che	more / -er . . . than
meno . . . di / che	less . . . than / not so . . . as
più / meno . . . di quanto + verb	more / less . . . than + verb
di quello che + verb	
(così) . . . come	} as . . . as
(tanto) . . . quanto	

(b) *di, che*

(i) Comparisons may be simple (without 'than'):

Chi è più forte? Who is stronger?

Può ripetere più lentamente per favore?
Could you repeat that more slowly please?

(ii) Complex comparisons express 'more . . . than'. In this case the second element of the comparison is introduced by *di* or *che*.

- *Di* in the sense of 'than' combines with the definite article in the usual way: *dello, del*, etc. (see section 16).

  Questa è una relazione meno dettagliata della prima.
  This is a less detailed report than the first.

  È una riunione più importante della precedente.
  It's a more important meeting than the previous one.

- When the comparison is between two words of the same grammatical category, i.e two adjectives, two nouns, two verbs or two adverbs, *che* replaces *di*:

  Secondo me fa più freddo che caldo.
  To my way of thinking it's more cold than warm.

Si fa più presto a dire che a fare.
It's quicker to say than to do.

This rule applies even if one element of the comparison is implied or the word order is different:

È meno rischioso (avere) un infarto che viaggiare in autostrada.
It's less risky to have a heart attack than to travel on the motorway.

Ha organizzato una festa più che un funerale. = Più che un funerale ha organizzato una festa.
He has organized a party rather than a funeral.

● *Che* instead of *di* is also used before *mai*:

più forte che mai stronger than ever

(c) Comparisons with a verb

When a comparison is made with a verb, 'than' is translated by *di quanto, di quanto non* or *di quello che non*. In this usage *non* is not a real negative and so may be omitted. *Di quanto* is followed by the subjunctive (see section 59f). If the verb is a compound tense the auxiliary is frequently dropped and only *di* is used:

È più alta di quanto sembri / di quanto non sembri. = È più alta di quello che sembra.
She is taller than she appears.

È stato un incontro più difficile di quanto avessimo (subj.) *previsto. = È stato un incontro più difficile del previsto.*
It was a more difficult meeting than had been foreseen.

(d) *Così . . . come* and *tanto . . . quanto*

(i) *Così* and *tanto* are usually omitted in the first part of the comparison:

~~I prezzi a Milano sono così alti come in altre capitali.~~
I prezzi a Milano sono alti come in altre capitali.
Prices in Milan are as high as in other capitals.

Era bianco come un lenzuolo.
He was as white as a sheet.

(ii) *Tanto* and *quanto* are often used together to emphasize a comparison between two adjectives:

Hanno preso misure tanto imponenti quanto inconcludenti.
They have taken measures which are as impressive as they are ineffectual.

(iii) This comparison may be reinforced even further with *tanto più / meno . . . quanto più / meno*:

> *Quanto meno complesso è un esempio tanto più facile capirlo.*
> The less complex an example is, the easier it is to follow it.

(e) *come*

Come conveys the idea of 'as', 'like', in the sense of 'as well as', before a noun, a pronoun or a verb:

> *arte intesa come commercio* art perceived as commerce
>
> *Sai giocare bene a tennis come lei?*
> Can you play tennis as well as she does?
>
> *Racconterò la storia come la racconterebbe un attore.*
> I'll tell you the story as an actor would do.

(f) Comparisons with pronouns

If the second part of the comparison includes a pronoun, the stressed form *di me*, *di te*, *di lui*, etc. is required (see section 34):

> *Mio marito è più ordinato di me.*
> My husband is tidier than I am.

(g) Comparisons with an indefinite article

Comparisons can also be made with an indefinite article:

> *L'industria richiede un più ampio intervento della CEE.*
> Industry requires a stronger intervention by the EC.

(h) Adding emphasis

Adjectives in a comparison can be reinforced with words such as *molto, assai* much:

> *Sarà molto / assai più utile sfruttare il petrolio che cercare ancora carbone.*
> It will be much more useful to exploit oil than to look for more coal.

(i) *più*

Più on its own forms a comparison in the following cases:

(i) *Sempre più, sempre di più* more and more

The first is placed before an adjective or adverb, the second after a verb:

> *sempre più spesso* more and more often
> *È sempre più scontento.* He is more and more unhappy.
> *Lavora sempre di più.* He works more and more.

(ii) *Non . . . più* no longer

> *Non è più aggiornato sulla politica italiana.*
> He is no longer up to date with Italian politics.
>
> *Non è più un potere repressivo.*
> It's no longer a repressive power.

(iii) *Più o meno, più . . . meno* more or less

> *Più o meno è la stessa cifra.*
> It's more or less the same figure.
>
> *Parola più parola meno, sono 5000 parole.*
> There are more or less 5000 words.

(iv) *Quanto più possibile* as much / as many as possible

Quanto agrees with the noun it refers to:

> *È tutta propaganda per ottenere quanti più voti possibili.*
> It's all propaganda to get as many votes as possible.

(v) *Più . . . più . . .* the more . . . the more, *più . . . meglio* the more . . . the better

> *Più lo mandi giù più ti tira su.* (A famous Italian commercial for coffee)
> The more you drink it the more it perks you up.
>
> *Più se ne parla meglio è.*
> The more one talks about it the better.
>
> EQUALLY: *Meno ci penso meglio è.*
> The less I think about it the better.

(j) Comparisons in an apposition

Unlike in English, comparisons in an apposition need not be introduced by means of a relative clause:

> *Il cliente, più attento oggi ai prezzi, sceglie tra diverse marche.*
> The customer, who today is more careful about prices, chooses between different makes.

(k) Idiomatic expressions

Comparisons of similarity such as the following ones are frequently used:

dormire come un ghiro	to sleep like a log / a top (literally: a dormouse)
lavorare come uno schiavo	to work like a slave
lento come una lumaca	as slow as a snail
sano come un pesce	as fit as a fiddle (literally: a fish)
sordo come una campana	as deaf as a post (literally: a bell)
svelta come una lepre	as quick as a hare
contenta come una Pasqua	as happy as a sand-boy (literally: Easter)

25 Comparisons with quantities

(a) Comparison of cost

costare	to cost		*di più di*	more than
guadagnare	to earn		*di meno di*	less than
spendere	to spend		*lo stesso di / uguale a*	as much as
pagare	to pay		*come / quanto*	as much as
valere	to be worth			

Costa di più 10'000. It costs more than 10,000 lire.
qualche migliaio di più / in più a few thousand more

(b) Comparison of speed

andare	*a più / meno di*	
correre	*a più / meno di*	to do more / less than
fare	*più / meno di*	

Quell'auto va a più di 200 km all'ora.
That car does more than 200 km an hour.

(c) *molto / a / i / e* much, many

These may be used to intensify a comparison:

Ragazzini? Ce ne sono molti di più di ieri.
Little boys? There are many more than yesterday.

(d) *tanto / a / i / e ... quanto / a / i / e* as much . . . as,
as many . . . as

Quantity may be expressed with these forms, which are also used in
negative sentences for 'so much' and 'so many':

> *C'è tanto detersivo quanto ne occorre.*
> There is as much washing powder as is needed.
>
> *Non sono stati fatti tanti sforzi quanti sarebbero stati necessari.*
> Not as much effort has been made as was necessary. (literally: Not
> so many efforts have been made as would have been necessary.)

26 The absolute superlative

(a) *Molto, tanto, assai*

The absolute superlative of adjectives and adverbs is used to
reinforce their meaning. It is usually formed either by placing a
word before the adjective (e.g. *molto* very) or by adding a suffix to
the adjective (e.g. *bello* nice, *bellissimo* very nice).

(i) *Molto, tanto* and *assai* very are invariable before the adjective or
adverb. *Molto* is by far the most frequent of the three:

> *È un ritratto molto originale.*
> It's a very original portrait.
>
> X ~~Abitano in una casa molta lussuosa.~~ X
> *Abitano in una casa molto lussuosa.*
> They live in a very luxurious house.
>
> *Abbiamo trovato una ragazza alla pari tanto brava.*
> We have found a very good au pair girl.
>
> *Sono entrati molto tardi.* They went in very late.

Note that the absolute superlative follows the noun:

> X ~~C'è una molto forte luce.~~ X
> *C'è una luce molto forte.*
> It's a very strong / powerful light.

(ii) Prefixes that add a superlative quality to the adjective are **super-,
arci-, ultra-, extra-, stra-, iper-, multi-** (see also section 162a):

> *Quel vaso è stracolmo, attenta.*
> That vase is full to the brim, be careful.
>
> *È un aneddoto arcinoto.* It's a very well-known anecdote.
>
> *Va bene per le pelli ultrasensibili.* It's good for very sensitive skins.

(iii) The superlative can also be formed by repeating the same adjective twice:

> *L'agnellino stava buono buono vicino alla pecora.*
> The little lamb was lying <u>very</u> quietly near the sheep.
> *Il cavallo stava fermo fermo.*
> The horse stood <u>very</u> still.

(iv) Another adjective may be added to denote a superlative:

> *fermo immobile* very still
> *innamorato cotto* deeply in love
> *pieno zeppo* completely full
> *ricco sfondato* rolling in money
> *stanco morto* dead tired

(v) *Tutto* (invariable) + certain adjectives is a synonym for *totalmente* entirely:

> *La commessa era tutta soddisfatta.*
> The shop assistant was completely satisfied.

(b) *-issimo* very

As frequent as *molto* is the absolute superlative formed with the suffix *-issimo/a/i/e* added to the masculine plural form of the adjective (without the final vowel). This form of superlative agrees in gender and number with the noun it refers to:

> | *vecchio* | > *vecchi* | *vecchissimo* |
> | *attento* | > *attenti* | *attentissimo* |
> | *lento* | > *lenti* | *lentissimo* |

It is placed after the noun or on its own:

> *È un palazzo altissimo.* It's a very high building.
> *È altissimo per la sua età.* He is very tall for his age.

The suffix *-issimo* may also be added:

(i) To some short adverbs

The final vowel of the adverb is dropped before the suffix is attached:

> | *presto* | *prestissimo* | very early |
> | *tardi* | *tardissimo* | very late |

-issimamente may also be added to the original adjective form of adverbs ending in *-mente*:

> *sicuro* certain
> *sicuramente* certainly
> *sicurissimamente* absolutely certainly
>
> *Sicurissimamente non te l'ho detto io.*
> I'm absolutely positive I haven't told you.

(ii) To some nouns, after dropping the masculine ending:

> *amico > amic amicissimo*
>
> *Sono amicissime.*
> They are very close friends.
>
> *È padronissimo di non venire.*
> He can do whatever he likes. (literally: He is his very own master not to come.)

(iii) To adjectives functioning as nouns, after dropping the last vowel:

> *l'entusiasmo dei giovanissimi* the enthusiasm of the very young
> *le ultimissime della sera* the latest evening news

This device is chiefly employed in advertisements and newspaper headlines. Here are some examples:

> *affaronissimo* a super bargain
> *augurissimi* very best wishes
> *campionissimo* a super champion
> *Canzonissima* (the name of a TV show) from *canzone*, song
> *fedelissimo* a long-standing supporter
> *primissima qualità* very first choice
> *ultimissimo grido* the very lastest in fashion
> *organizzazione svizzerissima* a super Swiss organization
> *veglionissimo* super New Year's Eve
> *affarissimo* excellent bargain

(c) A noun qualifying another noun

The absolute superlative idea is also conveyed by a noun qualifying another noun:

> *È un gioiello di ragazzo.* He is an outstanding young man.
> *Che amore di bambino!* What a wonderful child!

(d) Irregular forms

Buono and *cattivo* also have two irregular absolute superlative forms: *ottimo* excellent, very good and *pessimo* very bad:

> *Ottimo consiglio, grazie.* An excellent piece of advice, thank you.

> *È una pessima soluzione.* It is a very bad solution.

27 The relative superlative

(a) Structures

The relative superlative has two patterns because the adjective can be placed after the noun or before it.

(i) The adjective after the noun:

> *il / la / i / le* + noun + *più* + adjective + *di* . . .
> the most / the -est . . . of / in . . .

> *il / la / i / le* + noun + *meno* + adjective + *di* . . .
> the least . . . of . . .

> *È la giornata più / meno calda.*
> It's the warmest / least warm day.

> *È uno dei paesaggi più / meno pittoreschi.*
> It's one of the most / least picturesque landscapes.

(ii) Alternatively *il / la / i / le più / meno* can be placed before the noun. But this construction is acceptable only if the second element of the comparison – introduced with *di* – is expressed:

> *È la più calda giornata dell'anno.*
> It's the hottest day in the year.

> *È uno dei più pittoreschi paesaggi del mondo.*
> It's one of the most picturesque landscapes in the world.

N.B. In either structure, the article is not repeated:

> X ~~Vengono dalle più povere le zone d'Italia.~~ X
> *Vengono dalle più povere zone d'Italia.*
> They come from the poorest regions of Italy.

> X ~~È la macchina da scrivere la più economica.~~ X
> *È la macchina da scrivere più economica.*
> It's the cheapest typewriter.

(b) The second element of the comparison

This is usually introduced by *di*, sometimes by *fra*, *tra*, or a verb in the subjunctive mood (see section 59f):

> *È il francobollo più prezioso della raccolta.*
> It is the most valuable stamp in the collection.

> *È tra le regioni più povere.*
> It's among the poorest regions.

> *È il temporale più violento che io ricordi.* (subj.)
> It's the most violent storm that I can remember.

> *È il modo più semplice che si conosca.*
> It's the simplest way one knows.

(c) *di gran lunga* by far

Another way of expressing the relative superlative is with *di gran lunga*:

> *È di gran lunga la strada più signorile della città.*
> It is by far the most elegant street of the town.

(d) Superlatives in headlines

Headlines often omit the verb:

> *La sfida Roma Inter la più vista dell'anno.*
> The Roma–Inter Milan match has the largest audience of the year.
> (literally: The Roma–Inter Milan match the most seen of the year)

28 Irregular comparative and superlative forms

(a) *Migliore, peggiore, maggiore* and *minore*

These comparatives regularly form the plural in *-i*. They generally indicate abstract qualities and the English equivalent varies according to the context. They drop the last vowel before masculine singular nouns.

(i) They can be used as comparatives:

> *Il secondo candidato era migliore / peggiore del primo.*
> The second candidate was better / worse than the first.

Nel nuovo lavoro ha maggiori / minori responsabilità.
In his new job he has greater / fewer responsibilities.

(ii) Or as relative superlatives:

È il terzo miglior tempo.
It is the third best time.

È stata la migliore rappresentazione.
It has been the best performance.

Il maggior problema di oggi è la disoccupazione.
Today our greatest problem is unemployment.

(iii) *peggiori* and *migliori* can be used as nouns:

Hanno vinto i peggiori.   The worst have won.
Le migliori sono state le russe.   The best were the Russian women.

Note that *il più buono* instead of *il migliore* is still considered unacceptable in formal texts.

(iv) *maggiore* and *minore* indicate age:

È maggiore / minore di lui.
He is older / younger than him / he is.

È la maggiore / la minore delle cugine.
She is the oldest / youngest cousin.

(b) *meglio* and *peggio*

(i) These adverbs usually qualify a verb, which may be implied:

Stai meglio?   Do you feel better?
Peggio di così, non so.   I have never known anything worse than this.

È meglio un uovo oggi che una gallina domani.
A bird in the hand is worth two in the bush.
(Literally: It's better an egg today than a chicken tomorrow.)

(ii) They are sometimes used instead of *il migliore* and *il peggiore* and can also act as nouns:

La mia ricetta è meglio / migliore della tua.
My recipe is better than yours.

Questo giornale è peggio / peggiore di una comare.
This newspaper is worse than a scandalmonger.

il meglio e il peggio della vita   the best and the worst of life

(c) *il massimo* and *il minimo*

These superlatives convey several meanings:

È il massimo che possa (subj.) *fare.*	It's the most / best I can do.
con la massima cura	with the greatest care
il massimo della velocità	top speed
il massimo dei voti	full marks
la tariffa minima	the lowest charge
il minimo sforzo	the least effort
la minima idea	the slightest idea
il minimo che si possa fare	the least one can do

ADVERBS

29 Forms and types of adverb

(a) Adverbs

Adverbs may qualify the meaning of adjectives, other adverbs, verbs, nouns, complements or a clause. They are invariable:

> *innanzi tutto con grazia*
> above all with grace

> *occhiate così furiose che facevano quasi un rumore*
> looks that could kill
> (literally: glances so furious that they almost spoke)

> *È molto affidabile.*
> He is very trustworthy.

> *Ti sta proprio bene.*
> It really suits you.

> *Ho la quasi certezza.*
> I am almost certain.

(b) Types of adverb

(i) Adverbs of manner

● They are formed by adding *-mente* to the feminine form of adjectives ending in *-o*:

> *rapido > rapida > rapidamente* quickly

or to adjectives ending in *-e*:

> *cortese > cortesemente* kindly

But some adjectives ending in *-lo, -to, -ro* drop the vowel before adding *-mente: legger (o) mente* slightly.

● Basic adverbs not derived from adjectives include *bene* well, *male* badly, *adagio* slowly, *così* so, thus, *peggio* worse, *meglio* better, *volentieri* with pleasure.

● Some adjectives can qualify a verb in the masculine singular:

> *Una vecchia cameriera che serviva umile.*
> An old waitress who served with humility.

(ii) Adverbs of place

qui / qua here	*lontano* far away
lì / là there	*vicino* near
giù down	*dietro* behind
su above	*davanti* in front
dove where	*fuori* outside

(iii) Adverbs of time

adesso / ora now	*sempre* always
ancora again	*poi* after
mai never	*ogni tanto / qualche volta* sometimes
spesso / sovente often	

(iv) Adverbs of quantity

molto / tanto / tutto very	*quasi* almost
poco not very	*almeno* at least
abbastanza rather	

(v) Expressions of assertion, denial, doubt

sì yes	*forse* perhaps
no no	*probabilmente* probably

(vi) For interrogative and negative adverbs see sections 39 and 44.

(c) Position

(i) Adverbs of quantity precede the adjective:

> *Mi sento molto legata a mia sorella.*
> I feel very close to my sister.

(ii) Adverbs of manner can be placed between the verb and the object, or after the object, or before the verb:

> *Accarezzava affettuosamente il cavallo.*
> *Accarezzava il cavallo affettuosamente.*
> *Affettuosamente accarezzava il cavallo.*
> He was gently stroking / gently stroked the horse.

They can be placed between the auxiliary and the past participle:

È un'auto che si è raramente rotta / che raramente si è rotta / che si è rotta raramente.
It's a car which has rarely broken down.

They can be placed between the verb and the complement:

Il suo nemico non era necessariamente il mio nemico.
His enemy wasn't necessarily my enemy.

(iii) For adverbs of time and place, the word order is very flexible, being used to create stylistic effects. If an adverb of time and an adverb of place occur in the same clause their positions are optional. The stress falls on the more significant adverb.

Arriva spesso tardi. / Arriva tardi spesso. / Spesso arriva tardi.
He often arrives late.

(iv) For comparative and superlative forms see sections 24, 25, 26 and 27.

(v) Adverbial phrases may replace adverbs of manner. The prepositions *a, con, da, di, per* followed by a noun can paraphrase an adverb:

Il servizio postale funzionava a stento. = Il servizio postale funzionava stentatamente.
The postal service was hardly working.

Glielo diceva con dolcezza. = Glielo diceva dolcemente.
He told her gently.

Si comportò da vile. = Si comportò vilmente.
He behaved like a coward.

L'ho detto per scherzo! = L'ho detto scherzosamente.
I said it jokingly.

PRONOUNS AND ADJECTIVES

30 Personal subject pronouns

(a) Forms

SINGULAR		PLURAL	
io	I	*noi*	we
tu	you sg. (informal)	*voi*	you pl. (informal)
lei	you sg. (formal)	*loro*	you pl. (formal)
lei / ella	she		
lui / egli	he	*loro*	they (m. and f.; only for people)
esso / essa	it (m. and f.)	*essi / esse*	they (m. and f.; for both people and objects)

(b) Forms of address

● *Tu* is used for relatives, friends, children, colleagues and, generally, for people with whom one is on first-name terms. It is followed by verbs in the second person singular. *Tu* is more and more common among young people and colleagues. However, if in doubt, it is better to use *lei* and wait for the other person to offer the invitation '*diamoci del tu*' or '*dammi pure del tu*' ('please use *tu* to me'). It is up to the older or more senior person to make the invitation.

● *Lei* is used with strangers, elderly or senior people, distant acquaintances, and those you are dealing with in an official capacity. It is followed by the verb in the third person singular. Hence the verb ending coincides with that of 'she' and 'he'. It sounds like the English form of address to bishops: 'How is your grace?' (see also section 69). The custom of writing *Lei* (with a capital L) when addressing somebody in formal letters or documents is dying out.

> *Scusa sei tu Lucia?*
> Excuse me, are you Lucia?
>
> *Dottoressa, è stanca?* (to a woman) *Dottore, è stanco?* (to a man)
> Doctor, are you tired?

● **Voi** is used to address two or more people formally or informally. It is followed by the second person plural of the verb:

> *Luisa, Franco, venite anche voi?*
> Luisa and Franco, are you coming too?
>
> *Signori, accomodatevi.*
> Gentlemen, please take a seat.

● **Loro** is now hardly ever used to mean 'you' (pl.), even in official speeches.

● **Ella** and **egli** are falling into disuse. Nowadays, except in literary language, *esso, essa, essi* and *esse* essentially refer to animals and objects.

(c) Uses

(i) Unlike in English, subject pronouns are normally omitted:

- when the verb is expressed and the subject is clear from the context
- when the verb is impersonal
- when the verb refers to weather conditions

> *Ritorno tra poco.* I'll be back soon.
> *Non sono ancora ritornati.* They haven't come back yet.
> *Bisogna cambiare posto.*
> We must change seats. (literally: It is necessary to change seat.)
> *Lampeggia.* There is lightning.

(ii) Subject pronouns are inserted when there is a need to emphasize the subject or to create a contrast:

> *Sì. Lui è spagnolo, lei è portoghese.*
> Yes. He is Spanish, she is Portuguese.
>
> *Io sono convinta, invece loro non sono affatto convinti.*
> I am convinced whereas they are not at all.
>
> *E lui, serio e intelligente, ha salutato come se niente fosse* (subj.).
> And he, a serious and intelligent man, offered his greeting as if nothing had happened.

(d) Position

Subject pronouns are placed after the verb in the following cases:

(i) For emphasis:

il confronto fatelo voi!!!

> *Non la penso così, io.* That's not what I think.
> *Se lo dici tu.* If you think so.
> *È Maria? – Sì. È lei.* Is it Maria? – Yes, it's her.
> *Quelli siamo noi.* That's us there. (literally: Those are we.)
> *Eri tu?* Was that you?

N.B. Notice that with the verb *essere* to be these subject pronouns translate both the English formal and informal forms, 'I' and 'me':

> *Chi lo sa? – Io.*
> Who knows? – I do / Me.

(ii) To reply to phone calls:

> *Pronto? Il dottor Bianchi, per favore. – Sono io.*
> Hallo? Can I speak to Dr Bianchi, please? – Speaking.

(iii) After a past participle:

> *Partiti voi, ci siamo sentiti molto soli.*
> After you left, we felt very lonely.

(iv) With the emphatic pronoun *stesso*:

> *L'ha visto lui stesso.* He saw it himself.

(e) Pronouns without a verb

Sometimes pronouns are used on their own.

(i) With words such as:

solo, solamente, soltanto only	*tranne, eccetto* except
anche also	*anziché, invece* instead of
perfino, pure even	*no* no
neanche, nemmeno, neppure not even	*almeno* at least
sì yes	

Almeno lui! Him at least!   *Tu sì. Lui no.* You yes. Not him.
Anche noi? Us as well?   *Tranne loro quattro c'erano tutte.*
Solo loro? Only them?   Except for those four they were all there.

(ii) They are also used after the comparative form *come* as, like; see section 24e:

Sa l'italiano come loro. He knows Italian as they do.

(iii) For emphasis:

E io? And what about me?

E voi, chi siete? And you, who are you?

Non sembri più tu. You don't look your old self any longer.

★ When two pronouns are coordinated by *e / ed*, their order is free: *io e lui, lui ed io*, but it is more common to say *io e te* than *io e tu*.

(iv) In exclamations and some expressions such as:

contento tu if you are happy

a tu per tu face to face

dare del tu to address someone with the informal *tu* form

Beati voi! Lucky you!

Povero me! Poor me!

31 Direct object pronouns

(a) Forms

Direct object pronouns agree in gender and number with the noun they replace.

SINGULAR			PLURAL	
mi		me	*ci*	us
ti		you < informal >		
la	*l'*	you < formal >	*vi*	you (pl.)
lo	*l'*	him, it (m.)	*li*	them (m.)
la	*l'*	her, it (f.)	*le*	them (f.)

(b) Use

(i) *La* is used when referring to either a man or a woman formally (i.e. someone you address as *lei*). Adjectives related to it accordingly take the masculine or the feminine form. But past participles related to *la* take the feminine form:

> *La vedo calmo.*
> I see you look calm (to a man).
>
> *La vedo contenta.*
> I see you look happy (to a woman).
>
> *L'ho trovata bene signor Rompi.*
> I'm glad to see you well, Mr Rompi. (literally: I found you well)

Note that before a verb starting with a vowel or 'h', *lo* and *la* are written with the apostrophe *l'*:

> *L'avrei fatto.* I would have done it.

(ii) Lo is used as an invariable pronoun with two groups of verbs:

- *essere* to be, *diventare* to become, *sembrare* to seem
- *chiedere* to ask, *credere* to believe, *dire* to say / tell, *sapere* to know, *sperare* to hope

It may replace an adjective, a noun or an entire phrase. In English it is conveyed by 'it', 'so', 'one' or sometimes it is not translated.

> *Sì. Lo so.* Yes, I know.
>
> *Te lo dicevo.* I told you (so).
>
> *È pulito? – Certo che lo è.* Is it clean? – Yes, of course it is.
>
> *Lo spero bene.* I hope so.
>
> *Sembra intelligente, ma non lo è.*
> He seems intelligent, but he isn't.

Note that *lo* refers to the whole sentence and is therefore used even when the subject of the main verb is feminine:

> *Sono un'ammiratrice di . . . e continuerò sempre a esserlo.*
> I am an admirer (female) of . . . and will always be one.

★ Unlike their English equivalents these common verbs are followed by a direct object pronoun:

ascoltare	*li ascolto*	I listen to them
aspettare	*li aspetto*	I wait for them
cercare	*li cerco*	I look for them
guardare	*li guardo*	I look at them
pagare	*li pago*	I pay for them

(c) Position

(i) Italian object pronouns generally precede the verb:

Luca l'ha fermato ieri. Luke stopped him yesterday.
Sì. L'avrei fatto. Yes. I would have done it.
Perchè non li mangia? Why doesn't he eat them?

(ii) In a negative sentence *non* precedes the pronoun:

Mamma mia! Non li ho ringraziati.
Good Heavens! I haven't thanked them.

(iii) Direct object pronouns follow and form one word with the imperative, the infinitive, the past participle and the gerund (see section 60d).

● The imperative:

Portali qui. Bring them here.
Non portarlo. Don't bring it here.

Some verbs in the imperative double the consonant before pronouns (see section 60d).

● The infinitive drops the final vowel before the pronoun is added:

Venite a aiutarmi. Come and help me.

★ If the infinitive is preceded by *dovere* must, *potere* can, *volere* to want, or some other verbs like *sapere* to know how to, or *cominciare a* to start to, *provare a* to try to, the pronoun may either be attached to the infinitive after dropping the last vowel or precede the entire verbal phrase:

Lo devo contattare / Devo contattarlo.
I must contact him.

La comincio a scrivere / Comincio a scriverla.
I am starting to write it.

● The past participle:

Depennatolo . . . Once ticked off . . .

For agreement of the past participle with the direct object, see section 64d.

● The gerund:

Dandolo a sua suocera . . . Giving it to his mother-in-law . . .

(iv) Object pronouns also form one word with *ecco*:

Eccomi! Here I am!   *Eccoci!* Here we are!
Eccoti! Here you are!   *Eccovi!* Here you are! (pl.)
Eccolo! Here he / it is!   *Eccoli!* Here they are! (m.)
Eccola! Here she / it is!   *Eccole!* Here they are! (f.)

(d) Emphatic position

In both the spoken and written language, the direct pronoun is sometimes used together with the noun it should replace to emphasize the noun. It may be placed between the noun and the verb or before the verb (see section 138b):

La televisione, la guardo spesso.
TV – I often watch it.

La guardo volentieri la televisione.
I love watching TV. / I do love watching TV.

(e) Stressed direct object pronouns

The following pronouns are used after the verb either to stress the object or to make a comparison:

SINGULAR		PLURAL	
me	me	*noi*	us
te	you (informal)	*voi*	you (pl.)
lei	you (formal)	*loro*	them
lei	her		
lui	him		

Cercavo proprio te. I was looking precisely for you.

Sostituisce me o lei? Is she replacing me or her?

Ho riconosciuto sia lei che lui. I recognized both of them.

32 Indirect object pronouns

(a) Forms

Indirect object pronouns are used with verbs when the action is directed to or done for someone. Compare:

DIRECT	INDIRECT
Leggo un libro. I read a book.	*Scrivo a Carla.* I write to Carla.
Lo leggo. I read it.	*Le scrivo.* I write to her.

Gli spedisco il libro. I am sending the book for him / on his behalf.

Their forms are the same as those of the direct pronouns in the first and second persons singular and plural:

SINGULAR		PLURAL	
mi	to me	*ci*	to us
ti	to you < informal >	*vi*	to you (pl.)
le	to you < formal >	*gli*	to them (m. and f.)
gli	to him	*loro*	to them < literary >
le	to her	*a loro*	to them

Gli is starting to replace *a loro*, in both the written and spoken language.

(b) Position

(i) Indirect objects precede the verb, except for *a loro* and *loro* which follow it.

> *Gli telefoniamo? = Telefoniamo a loro?*
> Shall we ring them up?

> *Le chiese scusa.*
> She apologized to her.

(ii) Like direct object pronouns, indirect object pronouns follow the infinitive, the imperative, the past participle and the gerund, forming one word with them:

> *senza scrivergli* without writing to him / them

> *Si è rifiutato di parlarmi.* He refused to speak to me.

> *Mandami una cartolina.* Send me a card.

(iii) With *dovere* must, *potere* can, to be able, or *volere* to want, the position of the indirect object pronouns is optional. They can precede the first verb or be attached to the end of the infinitive after its last vowel is dropped:

> *Le vorrei fare una domanda. = Vorrei farle una domanda.*
> I would like to put a question to you.

> *Vi devo far fare un fax? = Devo farvi fare un fax?*
> Do I have to send you a fax?

(c) The following Italian verbs take an indirect object:

dare	*gli hai dato*	you gave him
dire	*gli hai detto*	you told him
chiedere	*gli hai chiesto*	you asked him

domandare	gli hai domandato	you asked him
far male	gli hai fatto male	you hurt him
insegnare	gli hai insegnato	you taught him
piacere	gli è piaciuto	he liked him
rispondere	gli ha risposto	he answered him
somigliare	gli somiglia	he looks like him
telefonare	gli ha telefonato	he rang him up
voler bene	gli vuole bene	she loves him

The indirect object is also required by impersonal verbs (see section 67a):

Gli occorrono tre giorni. He needs three days.

33 Direct and indirect object pronouns together

(a) Combined forms

When direct and indirect object pronouns are used in the same sentence, they combine in the following way:

INDIRECT OBJECT PRONOUN	DIRECT OBJECT PRONOUN				
	lo	*la*	*li*	*le*	*ne*
mi	me lo	me la	me li	me le	me ne
ti	te lo	te la	te li	te le	te ne
le < formal >	glielo	gliela	glieli	gliele	gliene
gli and *le*	glielo	gliela	glieli	gliele	gliene
ci	ce lo	ce la	ce li	ce le	ce ne
vi	ve lo	ve la	ve li	ve le	ve ne
gli (to them)	glielo	gliela	glieli	gliele	gliene
a loro	lo (verb) loro	la . . . loro	li . . . loro	le . . . loro	ne . . . loro

È vero. Te lo giuro. It's true. I swear it (to you).

Glielo so dire domani.
I'll be able to tell you < formal > / him / her tomorrow.

Ce li danno stasera. They'll give them to us tonight.
Me lo presti? Will you lend it to me?

Note that *gli* combines with the other pronoun and forms a single word. Before a vowel or 'h' *glielo* and *gliela* drop the last vowel and take an apostrophe:

Gliel'avete detto? Have you told her / him?

(b) Position

Combined pronouns take the same position in a sentence as single direct or indirect pronouns. They regularly precede the verb. But they follow and form one word with the imperative, past participle, gerund and the infinitive (with the last vowel dropped). With *dovere* must, *potere* can, and *volere* to want, they can precede the first verb or be attached to the end of the infinitive:

> *Quei soldi? Teneteveli!*
> That money? You can keep it!

> *La televisione? Accendetela pure!*
> The TV? Do switch it on!

> *Ho chiesto di portarceli.*
> I asked for them to be brought to us.

> *Devo raccontarglielo. = Glielo devo raccontare.*
> I must tell it to him / her / them.

> *Possiamo telefonarglielo. = Glielo possiamo telefonare.*
> We can phone him / her / them about it.

The past participle, if preceded by this combination of pronouns, agrees in gender and number with the direct object:

> *Quella fotografia, gliel'hai fatta?*
> That photograph of him, did you take it?

34 Pronouns after a preposition

(a) Forms and use

The following are called stressed or disjunctive pronouns and are used after prepositions (for a list of prepositions see section 16):

PREPOSITION	PRONOUN	
a	*me*	to me / at me
di	*te*	of you
da	*lei*	from you < formal >
con	*lui*	with him
secondo	*lei*	according to her
per	*sè*	for oneself
fra / tra	*noi*	among us
su	*voi*	on / about you
in	*loro*	
	essi (m. pl.)	in them
	esse (f. pl.)	

Sono i direttori delle filiali che ad essa (la società principale) fanno capo.
They are the directors of the subsidiaries on which they depend.

L'ho preso da lei. I took it from her.

(b) *Sè*

Sè is used after a preposition when it refers to the subject (third person). It corresponds in English to 'oneself, him(self), her(self), itself, them(selves)':

Giovanni ha portato suo figlio con sè.
John has brought his son with him.

Grazia ha fatto tutto da sè.
Grace has done everything by herself.

But if the pronoun does not refer to the subject, the word to use is *lui* or *lei*:

Con chi è andato il bambino? Con lui o con lei?
(With whom did the child go? With him or with her?)
Who did the child go with? Him or her?

(c) Prepositions which require *di* or *da* before the pronoun:

contro di me against me	*prima di noi* before us
dentro di noi within ourselves	*senza di loro* without them
dietro di voi behind you	*sopra di lui* above him
dopo di loro after them	*sotto di lei* under her
fuori di sè beside himself	*su di sè* upon oneself
presso di te at your home	*verso di me* towards me

35 *Ne, ci* and *vi*

(a) *Ne*

(i) *Ne* has a variety of meanings though there is no single equivalent English word (cf. French *en*). It has the same position as object pronouns. Note that it never means 'no' or 'not'.

It is compulsory in the following cases:

● When it replaces a noun which expresses an undefined quantity ('some / any of it / of them'):

Del pane? – Grazie, non ne voglio.
Some bread? – No, thank you, I don't want any.

Determinazione? Ne ho certamente.
Determination? I have certainly got (plenty of) it.

But the idea of 'all of it', 'all of them' is conveyed with *tutto / a / i / e / :*

Non l'ho letto tutto. Ne ho lette alcune pagine.
I haven't read it all. I have read a few pages (of it).

- When there is a number and the noun is implied:

  Ne tolgo tre. I am removing three (of them).

- To convey the idea of 'about it / her / him / them':

  Tutti i rotocalchi ne parlano. All the tabloids are talking about it.

- When it replaces a noun or a clause governed by a verb requiring *di*, such as *avere bisogno di* to need, *avere voglia di* to feel like, *avere paura di* to fear, *accorgersi di* to realize.

  Avrebbero bisogno di studiare. Lo so che ne avrebbero bisogno.
  They need to study. I know they need to do so.

  Hai voglia di venire a spasso? – No. Non ne ho voglia.
  Do you feel like going for a walk? – No. I don't feel like it.

- When it indicates the idea of 'from it', implying a physical or a figurative place:

  Come sono usciti da quella storia? Ne sono usciti bene?
  How did they come out of that affair? Did they come out well?

  Ne torno ora. I've come / I'm coming back from it now.

- When it indicates a cause, a situation (i.e. by something):

  Sono irritato da questo approccio. – Ne sono irritato anch'io.
  I have been irritated by this approach. – I have been irritated by it too.

- Sometimes *ne* is an integral part of a verb:

	andarsene	to go away
	aversene a male	to be offended
!!	*fregarsene* < vulgar >	not to care
	farne delle sue	to be up to one's own usual tricks
	non poterne più	to be unable to stand something any longer
	starsene	to be, to stay

Se ne vanno già?
Are they going away already?

La micia se ne stava in poltrona.
The pussycat was in the armchair.

● *Ne* may be used even when the noun is expressed. It's a device to reinforce the meaning. In this case the noun is preceded by *di* :

Ho fatto tanti viaggi. / Ne ho fatti tanti di viaggi. / Di viaggi ne ho fatti tanti.
I went on many journeys. / I went on many of them. / I travelled a lot.

Io di esperienza ne ho. / Io ne ho di esperienza.
Experience, I have got plenty of that.

Il consumismo, dello sviluppo capitalistico ne è l'essenza.
The consumer society is the very essence of capitalism.

(ii) Position of *ne*

● *Ne* takes the same position as the indirect object pronouns (see section 32b):

Ne cerco? Shall I look for some?

Ne posso cercare. = Posso cercarne. I can look for some.

Sì. Cercane. Yes. Look for some.

● When used with another pronoun it is placed between the pronoun and the verb:

Me ne dai una? Can you please give me one?

Me ne sono accorto subito. I immediately became aware of it.

● For *ne* with irregular imperatives, see section 60d:

(b) *Ci* and *vi*

(i) *Ci* and *vi* (less frequent), meaning 'there', take the same position as object pronouns:

Ci / vi siamo andati ieri.
We went there yesterday.

Posso andarci / andarvi in macchina. = Ci posso andare in macchina.
I can go by car.

(ii) With reflexive verbs, *ci* and *vi* are placed between the reflexive pronoun and the verb:

raccapezzarcisi to make out

Non mi ci raccapezzo. I can't make anything out.

Mi ci sono lavata le mani (in quell'acqua). I washed my hands in it
(in that water).

(iii) *Ci* and *vi* are found with verbs followed by the prepositions *a, in*
and *su* (see section 18):

Ci abbiamo pensato noi. (= Abbiamo pensato a comprare i fiori.)
We thought about it (buying flowers).

Sì. Ci conto. (= Conto su qualcosa.)
Yes. I'll count on it. / I'm counting on it (something).

Non ci credo. (= Non credo nell'oroscopo.)
I don't believe in it (horoscopes).

(iv) *Ci* can also be added to the verb *avere* in conversations:

Avete il portafoglio? Sì. Ce l'abbiamo.
Have you got the wallet? Yes. We've got it.

(v) *Ci* is an integral part of the following verbs and the phrase:

C'era una volta . . . Once upon a time . . .

entrarci	*Non c'entro con loro.*	I have nothing to do with them.
correrci	*Ci corre una bella differenza.*	There is a remarkable difference.
farci caso	*Non ci ho fatto caso.*	I didn't pay any attention to it.
metterci	*Ci ho messo un'ora.*	It took me an hour.
rimanerci	*Ci sono rimasto male.*	I felt disappointed / embarrassed.
sentirci	*Ci senti?*	Can you hear (it)?
starci	*Ci sono stato la notte*	I stayed the night.
vederci	*Non ci vedo bene.*	I can't see properly.
volerci	*Ci vuole pazienza.*	It requires patience.

(c) *Ce n'è, ce ne sono*

Ci followed by *ne* becomes *ce*:

C'è del latte? Sì. Ce n'è. Is there some milk? Yes. There is (some).

Occasionally it may refer to a plural noun as a global entity:

I fotografi, e ce n'è moltissimi, chiamano il divo da tutte le parti.
Photographers, and there are many of them, call the star from all sides.

Ce ne sono parecchie di margherite in questa zona.
There are a lot of daisies just here / around here.

36 Use of the pronoun *si*

The pronoun *si* (no accent) has various roles. It is similar to *on* in French.

(a) The impersonal *si*

(i) The impersonal *si* functions as the subject of intransitive verbs and of verbs of knowledge and opinion:

Si dice che sia una donna ricca.
People say / It is said / One says that she is a rich woman.

Non si sa mai.
One never knows.

Si vociferava che un fantasma s'aggirasse nel castello.
Rumour had it that a ghost haunted the castle.

If the verb is used in a compound tense, the auxiliary is *essere* in the third person singular. The past participle is masculine singular if the main verb usually takes *avere* as auxiliary:

Ho creduto che fosse (subj.) *un UFO.*
I believed it was an UFO.

Si è creduto che fosse un UFO.
It was thought it was an UFO.

N.B. But if the main verb usually requires *essere* as auxiliary in compound tenses, the past participle is masculine plural even though the verb is still in the third person singular (for a list of these verbs see section 64d):

È partito. He has left.

Si è partiti in ritardo. We have left late. / We left late.

If the reference is only to women, one may say:

Si è partite in ritardo. / Siamo partite in ritardo.

(ii) The impersonal *si* is also used to depersonalize remarks or tone down forms of direct address or reproaches:

Si deve accellerare il ritmo per far fronte alla data di scadenza.
One needs to work more quickly (to accelerate the rhythm) to meet the deadline.

(iii) In the construction *si è* + adjective, the adjective is always masculine plural; see also section 21d(i):

> *Quando si è giovani si è più spensierati.*
> When one is young one is more carefree.

(b) The passive *si*

(i) The passive *si* is very frequently used. The verb may or may not be followed by a noun. If there is a noun, the verb is in the third person singular or the third person plural, depending on whether the noun is singular or plural. The construction is thus the following:

si + sg. verb + sg. noun   or   *si* + pl. verb + pl. noun

> *Si costruisce troppo in questa città.*
> Too many houses are being built in this town.
>
> *Si apre una mostra di pittori moderni oggi a Torino.*
> An exhibition of modern painters is opening today in Turin.
>
> *Perchè non si vedono le montagne?*
> Why can't we see the mountains?

(ii) The same rule applies even if the verb is in the infinitive preceded by a form of *dovere* must, *potere* can, *volere* to want:

> *Si può bere quest'acqua?* Can one drink this water?
>
> *Si devono pelare queste patate?*
> Do we have to peel these potatoes? / Do these potatoes have to be peeled?

(iii) In compound tenses the auxiliary is *essere* and the past participle is masculine singular if there is no noun after the verb. If there is a noun after the verb, the past participle agrees in gender and number with it:

> *Si è bevuto troppo oggi.*
> There was too much drinking today. / People drank too much today.
>
> *Si sono bevuti troppi bicchieri di vino ieri.*
> Too many glasses of wine were drunk yesterday.

(c) Reflexive and reciprocal pronoun *si* (see section 36)

> *Si sono fatti male?* Did they hurt themselves?

(d) Expressing decisions

Si is used to express categorical decisions:

> *Allora, si va tutti al cinema stasera.*
> So, we are all going to the cinema tonight.

(e) With other pronouns

(i) If the impersonal *si* and the reflexive *si* are needed in the same sentence, the first *si* is replaced by *ci*:

> X *Si si è divertiti vero?* X
> *Ci si è divertiti vero?*
> We had a good time, didn't we?

(ii) *Si* follows direct and indirect objects:

> *Perchè mi si dice questo?*
> Why is someone telling me this? / Why am I being told this?
>
> *La si è cercata dappertutto.*
> She has been looked for everywhere. / People have looked everywhere for her.

(iii) Before *ne*, *si* becomes *se*:

> *Se ne ricordava.* He remembered about it.
>
> *Se ne dicono tante.* There are a lot of rumours about it.
> (literally: People say many things about it.)

(f) In commercial Italian

(i) *Si* is frequently used in advertisements. Note that *si* is placed at the end of the verb in the third person. Whether the verb is singular or plural depends on whether the noun which follows is singular or plural. In the plural form the verb drops the last vowel before adding *si*. The singular form is frequently used with plural nouns.

NON-COMMERCIAL FORMS	COMMERCIAL FORMS	
Si vende auto usata.	*Vendesi auto usata.*	Second-hand car for sale.
Si affittano due negozi.	{ *Affittansi due negozi.* { *Affittasi due negozi.*	Two shops to let.
Si cerca commessa.	*Cercasi commessa.*	Shop assistant wanted.

(ii) It is used in business letters:

NON-COMMERCIAL FORMS	COMMERCIAL FORMS	
Si veda la fattura n.10.	*Vedasi la fattura n.10.*	See invoice no.10.

37   Reflexive pronouns and verbs

(a) Reflexive pronouns

Reflexive pronouns always accompany reflexive verbs. These are recognizable by the ending of the infinitive forms: *-arsi, -ersi, -irsi*.

vantarsi	to pride oneself
mi vanto	I pride myself
ti vanti	you pride yourself < informal >
si vanta	he / she prides himself / herself
	you pride yourself < formal >
ci vantiamo	we pride ourselves
vi vantate	you pride yourselves
si vantano	they pride themselves

(i) Reflexive pronouns usually precede the verb:

Mi sento bene. I feel well.

Dodici governi si sono impegnati a fondare l'Unione Europea.
Twelve governments have committed themselves to founding a united Europe.

(ii) They follow the imperative (second person singular and first and second person plural), the infinitive, the gerund and the past participle:

Mettiti un po' di rossetto. Put on some lipstick.

Non sentendosi bene andò a casa.
Since she did not feel well she went home.

(iii) When *dovere* must, *potere* can, *volere* to want and a few other verbs like *cominciare* to start, *sapere* to know accompany the main verb, the pronoun may precede or follow both verbs:

Comincio ad annoiarmi = Mi comincio ad annoiare.
I am starting to get bored.

Voglio proprio divertirmi = Mi voglio proprio divertire.
I really want to enjoy myself.

(iv) The reflexive pronoun *si* becomes *ci* before the impersonal pronoun *si*. In a compound tense the past participle is masculine plural:

X *Si si é fermati fuori dalla stazione.* **X**
Ci si è fermati fuori dalla stazione.
We stopped outside the station.

(b) Reflexive verbs

There are many reflexive verbs in Italian. Here are some key ones:

accorgersi	to realize
addormentarsi	to fall asleep
adeguarsi	to adapt
affermarsi	to make oneself known
alzarsi	to get up
ammalarsi	to fall ill
annoiarsi	to get bored
appropriarsi	to take possession of
assumersi	to take upon oneself
astenersi	to abstain
avvicinarsi	to approach
comportarsi	to behave (oneself)
disinteressarsi	to take no interest in
divertirsi	to enjoy oneself
farsi la barba	to shave
farsi male	to hurt oneself
fermarsi	to stop (oneself)
fidanzarsi	to get engaged
impegnarsi	to commit oneself
inchinarsi	to bow
innamorarsi	to fall in love
inserirsi	to become part of
lamentarsi	to complain
lavarsi	to wash (oneself)
limitarsi	to limit (oneself)
mettersi d'accordo	to agree
pentirsi	to regret
pettinarsi	to comb one's hair
profumarsi	to spray on perfume
rendersi conto	to realize, to become aware
rifugiarsi	to take refuge
sdraiarsi	to lie down
sedersi	to sit down
sentirsi	to feel
soffermarsi	to linger (on)
sposarsi	to get married
svegliarsi	to wake up
svilupparsi	to develop

svolgersi	to take place, to develop
trasferirsi	to move
voltarsi	to turn round

(i) Some of these verbs are not reflexive if they take a direct object:

> *Ha sviluppato quel tema con intelligenza.*
> He has developed that theme intelligently.

> *Quella ditta si è sviluppata velocemente.*
> That company has developed rapidly.

(ii) Often English expresses the sense of the reflexive by a possessive adjective rather than a reflexive verb. In Italian the possessive adjective is not usually necessary with reflexive verbs:

> X *Mi lavo le mie mani.* X
> *Mi lavo le mani.* I wash my hands.

(iii) In compound tenses the auxiliary of reflexive verbs is *essere*, with the past participle agreeing in gender and number with the subject (see section 64b):

> *Si è annoiata?* Did you get bored? / Were you bored?

(iv) Because most Italian reflexive pronouns do not differ from personal pronouns, to understand whether a verb has a reflexive meaning or not one must look either at the verb ending or at the auxiliary. Compare:

> *Mi sono divertito.* I enjoyed myself.   *Mi diverto.* I enjoy myself.
> *Mi ha divertito.* He has amused me.   *Mi diverte.* He amuses me.

(c) False reflexives

Sometimes reflexive pronouns are placed before non-reflexive verbs to underline the personal or emotional involvement of the subject. These are also called false reflexives. Compare:

> *Ho comprato un vestito nuovo.*
> I bought a new dress.

> *Mi sono comprata un vestito nuovo.*
> I bought myself a new dress.

> *Si sono fatti un bel viaggio.*
> They organized a nice trip for themselves.

(d) Reciprocal pronouns

Reflexive pronouns can also act as reciprocal pronouns. Sometimes the reciprocal action is stressed by an extra expression such as *reciprocamente, a vicenda, l'un l'altro, fra l'altro, fra loro, gli uni con gli altri*.

> *Si sono aiutati (gli uni con gli altri).*
> They helped each other.

(e) Emphatic forms

There is also an emphatic form for reflexive pronouns:

Penso a me stesso / a.	I think of myself.
Pensi a te stesso / a.	You think of yourself. < informal >
Pensa a se stesso / a.	He / she thinks of himself / herself.
	You think of yourself. < formal >
Pensiamo a noi stessi / e.	We think of ourselves.
Pensate a voi stessi / e.	You think of yourselves.
Pensano a se stessi / e.	They think of themselves.

Note that *sè* followed by *stesso / a / i / e* has no accent.

The reflexives *si* and *se stesso* can also refer to an impersonal subject, in which case the past participle must be masculine plural:

> *È bello sentirsi amati.*
> It's nice to feel that one is loved. (literally: to feel oneselves loved)

> *Bisogna pensare anche a se stessi, no?*
> One needs to think of oneself too, don't you think?

(f) *di sè* self

(i) It can be used with adjectives:

sicuro di sè	self-confident
pieno di sè	full of himself / herself / oneself
soddisfatto di sè	self-satisfied

(ii) It can be used with nouns:

il controllo di sè	self-control
la padronanza di sè	self-control
il rispetto di sè	self-respect

(iii) It can be used with verbs to form idiomatic expressions:

in sè / di per sè / in sè e per sè (non è un problema)	in itself (it is not a problem)
uscire di sè	to lose one's mind
non essere più in sè	to be off one's head
va da sè che	it goes without saying that

38 Relative pronouns

(a) Forms and uses

The following are the Italian relative pronouns:

che / chi / cui	that / which
il quale / la quale / i quali / le quali	who / whom
il cui / la cui / i cui / le cui	whose

(i) *che*

Che is by far the most frequently used relative pronoun. It is invariable and refers to people or things, masculine, feminine, singular or plural:

la merce che è arrivata the goods which have arrived
l'aereo che ho preso the plane I took

C'è della gente che ha bisogno di affermarsi.
There are people who need to assert themselves / make themselves known.

(ii) *Che* can be subject or object. In either case it cannot be omitted in Italian:

l'aumento che ci hanno dato the increase they gave us

X ~~Gli inglesi amano molto un piatto rustico si chiama jacket potato.~~ X

Gli inglesi amano molto un piatto rustico che si chiama jacket potato.
Gli inglesi amano molto un piatto rustico. Si chiama jacket potato.
The English love a country dish called 'jacket potato'.

(iii) *Che* with the meaning of 'when' is used only colloquially:

quella sera che ci siamo conosciuti < coll. >
quella sera quando ci siamo conosciuti < formal >
the evening (when) we met

(iv) The past participle related to *che* may agree in gender and number with the noun *che* refers to:

> *La ricetta che ho preparato / preparata è italiana.*
> The recipe I prepared is Italian.

(v) *Il che* is invariable and replaces a whole sentence. It is usually found in written Italian. The spoken language prefers *e ciò / questo* or *e*:

> *Hanno parlato a lungo, il che si è rivelato utile.* (= *e si è rivelato utile* < spoken >)
> They have spoken at length, which has turned out to be useful.

(c) *il quale / la quale / i quali / le quali*

These forms correspond to *che*. They take the gender and number of the noun implied and are used instead of *che* to add emphasis or to prevent misunderstanding:

> *Ha incontrato la ragazza di mio fratello il quale l'aveva lasciata per un'altra ragazza.*
> He met the girlfriend of my brother, who had left her for another girl.

(d) Relatives with prepositions

After prepositions one may use:

(i) *il / la quale, i / le quali*

> *il viaggio dal quale non c'è ritorno*
> the journey from which there is no return

> *la causa per la quale combatteremo*
> the cause for which we shall fight

> *nel qual caso bisogna rinunciare*
> in which case we have to give up

(ii) *cui*

Cui is invariable and is used after prepositions:

> *a cui* to which, to whom
> *con cui* with whom
> *davanti a cui* before / in front of whom
> *di cui* whose, of whom
> *dopo di cui* after whom
> *per cui* for whom

prima di cui before whom
secondo cui according to whom

il tipo di occhiali di cui ti dicevo
the type of glasses I spoke to you about

il libro secondo cui Shakespeare era italiano
the book according to which Shakespeare was Italian

È quel pittore di cui ho il quadro.
It's the painter whose picture I have.

Note the expression *ragion per cui* (consequently).

(e) *il cui / la cui / i cui / le cui*

(i) Preceded by the definite article, *cui* means 'whose' or 'of which'.
The article agrees with the noun following *cui*:

l'agente il cui permesso è essenziale
the agent whose permission is essential

questa fase i cui primi passi sono così difficili
this phase, the first steps of which are so difficult

(ii) It is often replaced by other less formal expressions. Compare:

Ti presento la signora Rossi il cui marito è il direttore della banca.
May I introduce to you Mrs Rossi, whose husband is the director of the
bank.

Ti presento la signora Rossi. Suo marito è il direttore della banca.
May I introduce you to Mrs Rossi. Her husband is the director of the
bank.

la città in cui c'è stato il summit = la città dove c'è stato il summit
the town where the summit was held

lo stile in cui è scritto = lo stile come è scritto < coll. >
the style in which it is written

(iii) *A cui* may be reduced to *cui*, which is equally formal:

l'avvocato a cui mi rivolsi = l'avvocato cui mi rivolsi
the lawyer to whom I turned

(iv) *Per cui* links two sentences. It corresponds to the English
'therefore', 'so', 'thus', 'hence':

Non c'era più una maggioranza, per cui si è ricorsi alle elezioni.
There was no longer a majority, therefore elections were called.

(f) *colui che* (m.sg.), *colei che* (f.sg.), *coloro che* (m. and f.pl.)
he / she who, those who, the one(s)

These relative pronouns are confined to literary Italian. They correspond to *chi*:

> *Coloro che non hanno trovato lavoro devono lasciare il paese.*
> < literary >
> *Chi non ha trovato lavoro deve lasciare il paese* < written and spoken >
> Those who haven't found a job must leave the country.

(g) *chi*

Chi may be subject or object. It is always singular and requires the third person singular of the verb. It is used:

(i) In generalizations and proverbs:

> *C'è chi perde la testa per i computer.*
> There are those / some who go crazy over computers.
>
> *Chi rompe paga.* Breakages must be paid for.

(ii) It may be followed by a personal pronoun:

> *Chi di loro ha più di sessant'anni paga metà prezzo.*
> Those of them who are over sixty pay half price.

(iii) It may be preceded by a preposition:

> *A chi compra questo modello, viene dato un omaggio.*
> All those who buy this model will be given a gift.

(iv) In correlation: 'some . . . others . . .'

> *C'era chi cantava, chi ballava, chi chiacchierava.*
> Some sang, some danced and others talked.

(h) *quello che, ciò che, quanto* that which, what

(i) These forms are invariable. They are synonyms and refer to things or a whole concept, forming a single unit of sense even if they are made up of two words. They can be subject or object:

> *Quello che dice è giusto.*
> *Ciò che dice è giusto.*   What he says is right.
> *Quanto dice è giusto.* < more formal >
>
> *Ecco il catalogo. È quello che cercavi?*
> Here is the catalogue. Is it what you were looking for?

(ii) They can be intensified by adding *tutto*:

> *È entusiasta di tutto quello / tutto ciò che / tutto quanto fa sua moglie.*
> He is enthusiastic about everything his wife does.

(iii) *quello/a/i/e che, tutti/e quelli/e, tutti/e quanti/e* the one, all those, everybody

> *Hai preso il libro? – Ho preso quella che era sul tavolo.*
> Have you taken the book? – I took the one which was on the table.

> *Tutti quelli che conoscevo erano inglesi.*
> All those I knew were English.

> *Conoscevo tutti quanti alla festa.*
> I knew everybody at the party.

39 Pronouns and adjectives with questions and exclamations

(a) Questions

Questions are generally formed either by using an interrogative adverb or adjective or by adding a question mark at the end of a sentence or by raising the pitch of the voice at the end.

The word order is usually the same as in a statement (see also section 138a):

Alessandra ritorna domani.	*Alessandra ritorna domani?*
Alexandra is coming back tomorrow.	Is Alexandra coming back tomorrow?

A more rhetorical structure is:

> *Forse che De Chirico non è un grande pittore?*
> How could we say that De Chirico is not a great painter?

(i) Interrogative adverbs

> *come?* how?
> *come mai?* why? how come?
> *dove?* where?
> *perchè?* why? what ... for?
> *quando?* when?

● When a sentence begins with one of the above words, the subject is placed after the verb or, for emphasis, before the interrogative adverb:

> *Dove lavora tuo marito?*
> Where does your husband work?
>
> *Tuo marito, dove lavora?*
> Your husband works where?

● With *perché?* and *come mai?* the subject may be placed before the verb:

> *Perché / come mai il gatto non ha mangiato?*
> Why hasn't the cat eaten?
>
> *Perché Claudia ha spento la TV?*
> Why has Claudia switched the TV off?

● *Dove? come?* and *quando?* take an apostrophe when followed by *è:*

> *Dov'è?*   Where is it?
> *Com'è?*   What is it like?
> *Quand'è?* When is it?

● Interrogative adverbs (except *come mai?*) can be treated as nouns by placing the definite article before them:

> *Cerca il perché, il dove, il come e il quando.*
> Look for the why, the where, the how and the when.

● They can also be followed by an infinitive:

> *Perché andare al cinema?* Why go to the cinema?
>
> *Dove andare a quell'ora?* Where could we go at that time?

(ii) Interrogative adjectives

quanto / a / i / e . . . ?	how much, how many? + noun
quale, quali . . . ?	which, what? + noun
che . . . ?	what, what kind of, which? + noun

They all agree in gender and number with the noun they refer to, except *che?* which is invariable. *Che?* and *quale?* are interchangeable:

> *Quanti figli hai?* How many sons (children) do you have?
>
> *Quale pizza ordiniamo? = Che pizza ordiniamo?*
> What pizza / which pizza shall we order?

(iii) Interrogative pronouns

chi?	who? whom?
che? che cosa? cosa?	what?
quanto / a / i / e?	how much? how many?
quale / i?	which one? which ones?

● They can all be subject or object of the verb. *Cosa?* is the most frequent in conversations. *Chi?* can refer to one or more people, male or female:

> *Che cosa / Cosa ti metti?* What are you wearing?
>
> *Chi ascolti?* Whom are you listening to?
>
> *Chi sono e perchè uccidono?*
> Who are they and why are they killing?

● Adjectives referring to *che?* are masculine singular:

> *Che racconti di bello?* How's life treating you? (literally: What of nice are you telling?)

● *Quanto?* and *quale?* take the gender and number of the noun to which they refer. If *quanto* refers to an undefined quantity, its ending is -*o* (masculine singular). The word order is the following: *quanto / quale* + verb + subject:

> *Che begli aranci! Quanti ne vuoi?*
> What lovely oranges! How many do you want?
>
> *Piselli? Quali compro?*
> Peas? Which ones shall I buy?

● They can be followed by an infinitive:

> *Quale leggere?* Which one should we read?
>
> *Quanto tagliarne?* How much shall I cut?

● *Che cos'è?* is used to ask for an explanation. *Qual è?* (notice there is no apostrophe) is used to find out the identity, the quality.

> *Che cos'è l'informatica?* What is computer science?
>
> *Qual è il problema?* Which / What is the problem?

(iv) Prepositions + *chi?* (*a chi? per chi? di chi?* etc.)

● *di, a, con* always precede *chi?*:

> *A chi spedisci il fax?*
> Who(m) are you sending the fax to?
>
> *Con chi sei andata al cinema?*
> Who(m) did you go to the cinema with?

- *Di chi?* may mean 'about / of / by whom' or 'whose'. The word order is the following: *di chi?* + verb + subject.

> *Di chi è quel quadro?*
> Whose painting is it? / Who is this painting by?

(v) Indirect questions

All interrogative adverbs, adjectives and pronouns may be used in indirect questions. They may be introduced by verbs such as *mi chiedo* I wonder, *non so* I don't know, *vorrei sapere* I would like to know.

> *Non so perchè non sia / è venuto.*
> I don't know why he hasn't come.

> *Mi domando chi verrà / venga.*
> I wonder who will come.

(vi) In conversations, questions can end with tags such as *vero? non è vero? no?*

> *Preferisci la verdura cruda, vero / non è vero?*
> You prefer raw vegetables, don't you?

> *Chiamiamo un taxi, no?*
> We'll call a taxi, shall we?

(b) Exclamations

Interrogative adjectives and pronouns can be used to form an exclamation. While the voice rises on the last word in a question, in an exclamation it falls.

(i) *Che!* ('how . . .! what . . .! what a . . .!') may be used before a noun or an adjective. It is invariable:

> *Che bella ragazza!* What a good-looking girl!

> *Che ragazza!* What a girl!

> *Che difficile!* How difficult!

> *Che buio!* How dark it is!

But it may be omitted:

> *(Che) Belli questi fiori!* How lovely these flowers are!

(ii) *Come . . . ! quanto . . . !* ('how . . . !') are also used with verbs. They are invariable.

> *Come sei abbronzata!* How suntanned you are!
>
> *Quant'è scritto bene!* How well written it is!

Note that the verb immediately follows *come* and *quanto*.

(iii) *Quale . . . !* ('what . . . !') is fairly rare and is used with unquantifiable nouns:

> *Quale sorpresa! (= Che sorpresa!)* What a surprise!

40 Possessive adjectives and pronouns

(a) Forms

Possessive adjectives and pronouns share the same forms. They are almost always preceded by the definite article.

	SINGULAR		PLURAL	
	MASCULINE	FEMININE	MASCULINE	FEMININE
my / mine	il mio	la mia	i miei	le mie
your / yours < informal >	il tuo	la tua	i tuoi	le tue
your / yours < formal >	il suo	la sua	i suoi	le sue
his / her / its	il suo	la sua	i suoi	le sue
our / ours	il nostro	la nostra	i nostri	le nostre
your / yours	il vostro	la vostra	i vostri	le vostre
their	il loro	la loro	i loro	le loro

Notice that *loro* is invariable.

There are some important differences between Italian and English.

(i) *Il suo, la sua, i suoi, le sue* have two meanings. They are used to refer to a third party ('his, her') and to address someone formally ('your'):

> *Sono i suoi appunti signora?* Are they your notes (madam)?
>
> *Sono i suoi appunti?* Are they his / her notes?

(ii) Italian possessives are usually preceded by the definite article:

> *il suo rapporto privilegiato con l'Occidente*
> his privileged relationship with the West
>
> *Dove sono le tue chiavi?* Where are your keys?
>
> *Qui ci sono le mie.* Here are mine.

(iii) But in the following cases possessive adjectives are used without the definite article:

● when they precede a singular noun denoting a family relationship:

> *Come sta tuo marito?* How is your husband?

But notice that *loro* keeps the article:

> *La loro mamma era un'insegnante.*
> Their mother was a teacher.

The article is also kept when the noun is modified by a suffix or an adjective:

> *la mia nonnina* my sweet grandmother
> *il nonno materno* my maternal grandfather

● when addressing a person directly:

> *mio caro amico* my dear friend
> *mia gentile collega* my kind colleague

These could be letter openings.

(iv) Possessives agree in gender and number with the noun they
precede or refer to:

> *Maria è uscita con il suo ragazzo.*
> Mary went out with her boyfriend.
>
> *Franco è uscito con la sua ragazza.*
> Franco went out with his girlfriend.

Since *ragazzo* is masculine singular, the possessive form is
masculine singular, whereas *ragazza* is feminine singular and so the
possessive form is feminine singular. In cases where *il suo / le sue*
could mean both 'his' or 'her', *di lui* or *di lei* are used in formal texts.
But in most cases Italians find an alternative solution to avoid
ambiguity:

> *È la sua auto. Di Debora intendo.*
> It is her car. Deborah's I mean.
>
> *Michela parlava con Roberto mentre rubavano la sua auto.*
> < ambiguous >
> Michela was talking to Roberto while his / her car was stolen.
> *Michela parlava con Roberto. Nel frattempo l'auto della ragazza*
> *veniva rubata.* < unambiguous >
> Michela was talking to Roberto. Meanwhile the girl's car was
> stolen.

(b) Position

Possessive adjectives usually precede the noun. They follow it in
some cases where the definite article is no longer required:

(i) In some set phrases:

> *affari miei*   my own business
> *a casa mia*   at my place / at my home
> *in camera vostra*   in your room
> *è colpa nostra*   it's our fault
> *da parte loro*   as far as they are concerned
> *per conto mio*   in my opinion

> *a suo tempo*   at that time / at the proper time
> *in un mondo tutto suo*   in a world of his own

(ii) In expressions frequently used in commercial letters:

> *l'assegno emesso a vostro favore*
> the cheque issued in your name
>
> *È nostra convinzione / opinione . . .*
> It is our belief . . .
>
> *Rimango a vostra disposizione.*
> I'll be happy to be of help in the future.

(iii) With the verb *essere* + possessive pronoun when the article is optional:

> *È il suo / È suo?* Is it yours? < formal > / Is it his / hers?

(iv) With exclamations:

> *Dio mio!* Good Heavens!
> *Mamma mia!* My goodness!

(v) In expressions of affection:

> *Amore mio . . .* My love . . .
> *L'abbiamo trattato come nostro ospite / amico.*
> We have treated him as if he were our guest / friend.

Compare:

> *Questa è casa mia.* This is my home. < affectionate >
> *Questa è la mia casa.* This is my house. < objective >

(vi) As a regional variant in some parts of Central Italy.

> *È figlio mio.* He is my son.

(c) Possessives in relief

These two sequences, which bring the possessive into relief, can be adopted in informal and formal style (see section 138a):

> *Il suo è un atteggiamento incredibile.* < normal >
> *È un atteggiamento incredibile, il suo.*
> He has adopted an incredible attitude.
>
> *È una presenza, la sua, che dà coraggio.*
> His presence gives us courage.

(d) Idiomatic uses

Possessive adjectives are also often used to create emotional effects:

> *Penso alla mia bella città.*
> I am thinking of my beautiful town.
>
> *Non volle abbandonare alla sua sorte il paese.*
> He didn't want to abandon the country to its fate.
>
> *La storia ha dato torto ai nostri avversari.*
> History has proved our adversaries wrong.

(e) Omissions

As in English, possessives express legal ownership or moral and sentimental bonds. But in Italian they are sometimes replaced by the article alone.

(i) Referring to parts of the body:

> *Mi sono fatto male al ginocchio.*
> I hurt my knee.

Certain phrases omit the article as well: *in faccia* on his face, *in fronte* on her forehead, *in testa* on my head.

(ii) Possessives also tend to be omitted if the link between the item and its owner is obvious. Compare:

> *Non trovo gli appunti.* I can't find the / my notes.
>
> *Non trovo i vostri appunti.* I can't find your notes.
>
> *Dove ho lasciato la macchina?* Where did I leave my car?

(f) Possessives acting as nouns

Possessives can function as nouns:

(i) In some idiomatic phrases:

> *Mi aspettano i miei.* My parents are waiting for me.
>
> *Ci ho rimesso del mio.* I have lost money.
>
> *C'è poco di suo in questo tema.*
> Not much of this essay is his own. (literally: There is little of his own in this essay.)
>
> *Dirò anch'io la mia.* I will give my opinion too.

Sta dalla tua. He is on your side.

È dei nostri. He is one of ours.

il Nostro our man (Rather archaic; today it is used with irony or ironic affection to indicate the protagonist of a past or present event.)

(ii) In commercial letters:

In risposta alla vostra del 12 ottobre ...
In reply to your letter dated October 12th ...

Mi creda, il suo ... Yours sincerely ...

(g) Other words indicating possession

(i) *un mio, questo mio* of mine

Italian possessives can be directly preceded by an indefinite article, a number or *questo* ('this') and *quello* ('that'):

un vostro studente a student of yours

C'erano voci di una sua caduta dal potere.
There were rumours of his fall from power.

tre loro filiali three of their subsidiaries

questa nostra chiacchierata this conversation of ours

(ii) *il proprio, la propria, i propri, la proprie* one's own

These forms are used instead of 'his / her / their' when the subject is an indefinite pronoun, or the verb is impersonal:

Ognuno deve assumersi le proprie responsabilità.
Everybody must assume his own responsibilities.

(iii) *altrui, d'altri* of someone else

The two words have the same meaning but the first is more formal.

Non mi piace che s'impicci degli affari altrui. < formal >
I don't like his interfering in other people's business.

Pensa un po'. Arrivare dopo mezzanotte in casa d'altri.
Just think. To arrive after midnight at somebody else's home.

41 Demonstrative adjectives and pronouns

(a) Forms

The demonstratives may be adjectives (followed immediately by a noun) or pronouns (occurring on their own). They take the gender and number of the noun(s) they precede or refer to.

(i) *Questo* has the following forms both as adjective and as pronoun:

questa (m. sg.)	this	*questi* (m. pl.)	these
questa (f. sg.)	this one	*queste* (f. pl.)	these ones
	the . . . one		the . . . ones

Quest' (m. and f. sg.) is used before words starting with a vowel.

(ii) *Quello* has the following forms as a pronoun:

quello (m. sg.)	that one	*quelli* (m. pl.)	those ones
quella (f. pl.)	the . . . one	*quelle* (f. pl.)	the ones

Quell' (m. and f. sg.) is used before words starting with a vowel.

(iii) *Quello* as an adjective follows this irregular pattern:

quel (m. sg.)
quello (m. sg.) before words starting with *s* + consonant, *z*, *gn*, *y*
quell' (m. and f.) before words starting with a vowel
quella (f. sg.)
quei (m. pl.)
quegli (m. pl.) before words starting with *s* + consonant, *z*, *gn*, *y*, and a vowel
quelle (f. pl.)

Buoni questi pomodori! These tomatoes are delicious!

Quest'albicocca non è buona. This apricot is not nice / no good.

Mi dai quei fogli? Can you give me those sheets?

Questi sono i cardini dell'accordo.
These are the cornerstones (literally: the hinges) of the agreement.

N.B. Note the shortened forms:

stasera this evening
stanotte tonight
stamattina this morning

(b) Uses

(i) The demonstratives are sometimes reinforced with *qui* ('here') or *là* ('there') in conversation, while in the written language emphasis is obtained by separating them from the noun or placing them after it (see section 138c):

> *Ti piace quella giacca là?* Do you like that jacket over there?
>
> *È una voce, quella di Modugno, che riesce ad offrire impareggiabili emozioni.*
> Modugno's voice can stir incomparable feelings.
>
> *Preferisco questa qui bianca.* I prefer this white one.
>
> *È una guerra di distruzione questa.*
> It's a war of destruction this one. / This is a war of destruction.

(ii) Emphasis is also obtained by adding *uno / una di* before the demonstratives and stressing them in speech:

> *Ha ricevuto uno di quegli aumenti!*
> He has received such an increase!

(iii) When used on their own or with an adjective, demonstratives may correspond to the English 'this ... one', 'that ... one', 'the one', 'the ones':

> *È questo?* Is it this one?
>
> *Scegliete queste bianche?* Are you choosing these white ones?
>
> *I due trattati, quello sulla politica e quello sull'economia ...*
> The two treaties, the one on politics and the one on economics ...
>
> *Il problema della casa è urgente come quello dell'occupazione.*
> The housing problem is as urgent as that of employment.

(iv) When followed by *di* demonstratives may indicate possession and may be expressed in English with an apostrophe 's':

> *È quello di Francesca?* Is it Francesca's?

(v) The demonstratives can be used with quantifiers and possessives:

> *Abbiamo mangiato quel poco che era rimasto.*
> We ate the little that had been left.
>
> *quel suo bizzarro professore*
> *quel bizzarro del suo professore*
> his bizarre lecturer (literally: that bizarre of his lecturer)

(vi) *Quello* and *questo* may imply 'man', 'person':

> *Chi è? È quello dei giornali?*
> Who is he? Is he the newsagent's man?
>
> *Sono quelli di prima, sono quelli di sempre.*
> They are the same as before, they are their old selves.
>
> *E questo, che vuole?* < slightly rude >
> What does *he* want?

(vii) *Quello* and *questo* may be used in juxtaposition, meaning 'the former ... the latter':

> *Quello è morto, questo ha novant'anni.*
> The former is dead, the latter is ninety years old.

In prose *questi* or *quest'ultimo* are used to refer to the last person mentioned:

> *Quest'ultimo scrittore tende a essere conciso.*
> This last writer tends to be concise.
>
> *Questi è stato ambasciatore a Mosca.*
> The latter has been ambassador to Moscow.

(viii) In some cases, which are difficult to classify, the use of the determiners does not have an English equivalent:

> *Ma questo è assurdo.* But that's absurd.
>
> *In questo momento tutto va bene.*
> At present everything is going well.
>
> *Questo veramente non me l'aspettavo da lui.*
> I really didn't expect him to do something like this.
>
> *Ne dice di quelle.* He says all sorts of things.
>
> *Ehi! Sentite questa.* Hey! Listen to this.

(c) Other demonstrative pronouns

(i) *Costui* (m. sg.), *costei* (f. sg.), *costoro* (m. and f. pl.) ('this, these')
refer only to people and nowadays are often used in a derogatory
context:

> *Costoro non mi piacciono.*
> I don't like this lot / these people.

(ii) *Codesto / a / i / e*, referring to the object next to the listener, is
nowadays used only in Tuscany. The equivalent standard Italian is
quello / a / i / e.

(iii) For *quello / a / i / e che* as a relative pronoun see section 38h.

(iv) *Ciò* ('this, that') refers to a whole idea. It is invariable and any
adjectives or past participle related to it are masculine singular:

> *Tutto ciò è piuttosto strano.* All this is rather strange.

● When *ciò* replaces an indirect object (usually after a verb
followed by the preposition *a*) it may be replaced by the less
emphatic *ci*:

> *Rinuncio a ciò. = Ci rinuncio.*
> I give / I am giving this up.

● When the verb is governed by *di, ciò* may be replaced by *ne*:

> *Quando vuoi discutere di ciò? = Quando ne vuoi discutere?*
> When do you want to discuss this?

● Note the expression:

> *E con ciò?* So what?

(v) *Lo stesso, il medesimo* the same

● *Lo stesso* and *il medesimo* are interchangeable but *stesso* occurs
more frequently. They agree in gender and number with the noun
they accompany or refer to:

> *gli stessi errori* the same mistakes
> *le stesse parole* the same words

● If positioned after the noun they intensify the meaning:

> *È venuta la segretaria stessa a portarlo.*
> The secretary herself came to bring it.

- *Stesso* may have a general indefinite sense, e.g.:

  Vuoi tè, caffè? — È lo stesso.
  Would you like tea or coffee? — I don't mind.

- *Stesso* can also mean 'exactly' and be conveyed by 'very'.

  in quello stesso istante at that very moment

42 Quantifiers

The following adjectives and pronouns describing a quantity agree in gender and number with the noun they accompany. If they indicate a general quantity the ending is masculine singular.

(a) *tutto*

tutto il / tutta la	the whole
tutti i / tutte le	all, all the, every
tutti e due	both the . . .
tutto / a / i / e	all of it / all of them / them all
tutto	all

(i) *Tutto / tutta / tutti / tutte* are always followed by a definite or indefinite article:

  tutta la sera the whole evening
  tutta una vita a whole life
  Ho lezione tutti i giorni. I have a class every day.

They may be reinforced by *quanto*:

  tutte quante le opere all the works

(ii) *Tutto* may describe quantity:

  Mi piace tutto. I like everything.

  Il formaggio? L'ho mangiato tutto.
  The cheese? I have eaten it all.

(iii) *Tutto* describes length of time and space:

  in tutto il mondo all over the world
  tutto il giorno throughout the day

(iv) *Tutto* precedes or follows the subject pronoun:

  Noi tutti / tutti noi siamo d'accordo. We all agree.

(v) *Tutto* may be followed by *questo* or *quello* this, that:

> *Dove metto tutta questa roba?* Where do I put all this stuff?

(vi) With numbers the article is omitted and *e* (and) is added between *tutto* and the number.

> *tutti e quattro* all four

(vii) *Tutti e due* and *entrambi* (both) are synonymous. They can be placed before or, for emphasis, after the noun:

> *Sono tutti e due cari ragazzi.*
> *Sono cari ragazzi tutti e due.*
> *Sono cari ragazzi entrambi.* < literary >
> Both are dear boys.

(viii) For *tutto* + adjective (e.g. *tutta contenta*) see the absolute superlative, section 26a.

(ix) For the use of *tutto* to form new words, see section 166 on neologisms.

(b) *Molto / a / i / e* much, many, a lot, a great deal, plenty

(i) *Molto* is frequently used in affirmative, negative and interrogative sentences:

> *C'è molta gente.*
> There are a lot of people.

> *Ha viaggiato per molte ore?*
> Has she travelled for many hours?

> *Molti non possono permetterselo.*
> Not many people can afford it.

(ii) *Molto* also indicates time:

> *Ha aspettato molto tempo.*
> He has waited a long time.

> *Ti occorre molto prima di finire?*
> Will it be long before you finish?

(iii) The superlative form is *moltissimo / a / i / e* very many, a great deal:

> *Ero con moltissimi altri turisti.*
> I was with many other tourists.

(iv) For the invariable adverb *molto* very, see section 26a.

(c) *Tanto / a / i / e* much, many, so much, so many

It has a slightly stronger meaning than *molto*:

> *Ha avuto tanti amori.* He had so many love affairs.

(i) *Tanto* may be preceded by *così* to introduce a consequence:

> *Ha studiato così tanto che gli è venuto un esaurimento nervoso.*
> He studied so much that he had a nervous breakdown.

(ii) *Tanto* is used in comparisons with *quanto*:

> *Ho letto tanto quanto ho potuto.* I read as much as I could.

(iii) The superlative form is *tantissimo / a / i / e.*

> *Ho mangiato tantissimo.*
> I have eaten a lot.

(d) *Troppo / a / i / e* too much, too many

È stato messo troppo sale.
There is too much salt in it.

Ha inserito troppi colori.
He has introduced too many colours.

(i) *Troppo* may follow a verb:

È costato troppo. It cost too much.

(ii) *Troppo* may refer to time:

Ha guidato troppo. He drove for too long.

(e) *Parecchio / parecchi / parecchia / parecchie* several

Parecchio is more frequent in written than in spoken Italian, where it is replaced by *molto*.

Parecchie leggende lo confermano.
Several legends confirm it.

Sono stato via parecchi giorni.
I have been away several days.

(f) *Qualche* some, any

(i) *Qualche* is invariable and can only be followed by a singular noun and a singular verb:

Mi è rimasta qualche sterlina.
I have a few pounds left.

Vedi qualche differenza?
Do you see any difference?

(ii) In negative sentences *qualche* is replaced by *nessuno / -a*:

Mi dispiace. Non ho nessun fermaglio.
I'm sorry. I don't have any clips.

But:

Non lo vedo da qualche tempo.
I haven't seen him for some time.

(iii) *Qualche* may indicate something vague:

Lo leggerò qualche giorno. I'll read it one day.

115

(g) *Alcuni / e* some, any, a few

> *Ho preso a prestito alcuni libri.* I have borrowed a few books.

The singular form (*alcun / alcuno / alcuna*) is usually adopted with unquantifiable nouns and in negative sentences. It follows the pattern of the indefinite article *un / uno / un'*:

> *Non vedo alcuna differenza.* I don't see any difference.
>
> *Non esiste alcun problema.* There isn't any problem.

(h) *Poco / poca / pochi / poche / un poco di* a few, few, little, a little, a bit

> *C'è poca luce.* There is little light.
>
> *Pochi lo ignorano.* Few ignore him.
>
> *Me ne dai un poco?* Will you give me a bit of it?
>
> *Vuoi un po' di torta?* Would you like a piece of cake?

Un po' is a shortened form of *un poco*. The superlative form is *pochissimo / a / i / e*.

> *Ne abbiamo incontrati pochissimi.* We have met very few of them.

(i) The quantifiers as subjects

Molti / e, tanti / e, troppi / e, parecchi / parecchie, pochi / poche may act as subjects in two ways, preceding the verb or following it. In the latter case the quantifier is preceded by *in*:

> *Molti lo sanno. = Lo sanno in molti.*
> Many people know it.

(j) Images indicating quantity

un mucchio di soldi	a load of money
una montagna di debiti	a mountain of debts
un mare di guai	a sea of troubles
un pozzo di scienza	a font of learning (literally: a well)
una caterva di libri	stacks of books
un sacco di bugie	a pack of lies (literally: a sack)
una barca di problemi	no end of problems (literally: a boat)
una strage di errori	endless mistakes (literally: a massacre
un casino di automobili	no end of cars
< vulgar >	(literally: a brothel)

43 Indefinite adjectives and pronouns

Indefinite adjectives precede the noun and agree with it in gender and number.

ADJECTIVES		PRONOUNS	
l'altro / a + sg. noun	the other	*l'altro / a*	the other one
gli altri / le altre + pl. noun	the others	*gli altri / le altre*	the others / the other ones
un altro / un' altra + sg. noun	another	*l'uno / a e l'altro / a*	both / each other
		un altro / un'altra	another one
		qualcosa	something
		qualcuno	someone
ogni	every, each	*ognuno*	each one
		ciascuno	everyone
qualunque	any		
qualsiasi	any, whatever	*chiunque*	anybody, whoever, whichever
un certo / una certa	a certain	*certi / certe*	some

(a) *altro / a / i / e* other

It agrees in gender and number with the noun it defines:

> *Vuoi un'altra mela?*
> Do you want another apple?

> *Qualcuno ha altre proposte?*
> Has someone got other proposals?

> *Dove sono gli altri?*
> Where are the others?

If *altro* indicates an undefined quantity, it corresponds to the English 'anything else', 'what else':

> *Se non c'è altro / dell'altro chiudo l'incontro.*
> If there isn't anything else I'll close the meeting.

> *Mi chiedo cos'altro ho dimenticato.*
> I wonder what else I forgot.

> *Non c'è nient'altro.*
> There is nothing else.

Notice the meaning of *l'uno e l'altro* ('both') and *o l'uno o l'altro* ('either'):

> *Ho preso l'uno e l'altro.* I took both.
>
> *O l'una o l'altra è sbagliata.* Either one or the other is wrong.

L'un l'altro may have a reciprocal meaning:

> *Si sono influenzati l'un l'altro.* They influenced each other.

(b) *ogni* every, each

It is invariable and only precedes singular nouns:

> *Ho messo lo zucchero in ogni tazza.*
> I put the sugar in every cup.

(c) *ognuno* and *ciascuno* everyone

Ognuno is more frequent than *ciascuno*. *Ciascuno* is preferred in the expression *uno / una per ciascuno* (one each).

> *Ognuno dice la sua.* Everyone has his own opinion.

(d) *qualcosa* something

> *Ti posso offrire qualcosa?* Can I offer you something?
>
> *Non avete qualcos' altro oltre a questo?*
> Haven't you got anything else apart from this?
>
> *Hai qualcosa da fare?* Have you got something to do?

In negative sentences *niente* is used (see section 44c (ii)):

> *Non ho niente da fare.* I have nothing to do.

(e) *qualcuno / a* somebody

> *qualcuna di voi* some of you
>
> *C'era qualcuno che conoscevi?* Was there anyone you knew?

Qualcuno may indicate unspecified identity:

> *Qualcuno lo aggiusterà lunedì.*
> Someone will repair it on Monday.

(f) *qualunque* and *qualsiasi* any, whatever, whichever

These two words have the same meaning.

(i) They can precede or follow the noun:

> *a qualsiasi costo* at any cost / at all costs
>
> *una famiglia qualunque* any family
>
> *Passami un giornale qualunque.* Pass me any newspaper you like.

(ii) They may be used with the following construction: *qualunque /
qualsiasi* + verb + noun with the verb in the subjunctive form (see
section 59g):

> *Qualunque / qualsiasi sia il prezzo, lo compriamo.*
> Whatever the price, we'll buy it.

(iii) They may be used as a subject pronoun with *uno*:

> *Uno qualunque / qualsiasi di noi* anyone of us

(g) *chiunque* whoever, anyone (who / whom), anybody

(i) When *chiunque* corresponds to 'whoever', 'no matter who', it is
followed by the subjunctive (see section 59g):

> *Chiunque telefoni, non ci sono.*
> Whoever rings up, I am not here.

Di must be inserted between *chiunque* and a personal pronoun:

> *Chiunque di voi lo senta, glielo dica.*
> Whichever of you hears from him, should tell him.

Chiunque may be preceded by a preposition:

> *A chiunque appartenga questa bicicletta, di certo non è mia.*
> Whoever this bicycle belongs to, it is certainly not mine.

(ii) When the meaning is 'anybody', the verb which follows is the
indicative:

> *Chiunque è in grado di farlo.*
> Anyone can do it.

Chiunque may be placed after the verb for emphasis:

> *L'avrebbe visto chiunque in quella posizione.*
> Everybody would have seen him in that position.

(h) *certo/a/i/e* certain

(i) *Certo* may be an adjective:

> *È necessaria una certa flessibilità.* A certain flexibility is necessary.

(ii) The plural form, *certi*, may act as a pronoun:

> *Certi pensano che la recessione sia finita.*
> Some people think that the recession has finished.

44 Negatives

(a) *no*

No is the most straightforward form of denial. *Non mica* is a frequent colloquial form typical of Northern Italy:

> *La risposta non può essere che no.* The answer can only be no.
>
> *Non la voglio mica.* < coll. > I don't want it.

(b) *non*

(i) The most common form of the negative sentence in Italian uses *non* before the verb (or before the auxiliary for compound tenses), or before the object pronouns +verb:

> *Purtroppo non ho pazienza.*
> Unfortunately I have no patience.
>
> *Il referendum contro la caccia non è stato ancora approvato.*
> The referendum against hunting has not been approved yet.
>
> *Non lo vorrei disturbare.*
> I wouldn't like to disturb him.

(ii) In Italian negative sentences, *non* is used together with negative pronouns, adjectives and adverbs:

> *Non c'era nessuno.* (literally: There was not nobody.)
> There was no one there.
>
> *Non ho visto neanche una stella.*
> I haven't even seen a star. (literally: I haven't seen not even a star.)
>
> *Nessuna squadra di equitazione aveva mai avuto tanto successo.*
> No (horse) riding team had ever had such a success.
> (literally: No horse-riding team had never had such a success.)

(c) Negative words

NEGATIVE ADJECTIVES

nessuno / a + noun   no . . .
non . . . alcuno   no . . ., not . . . any

NEGATIVE PRONOUNS

nessuno / a   no one, none
niente   nothing

NEGATIVE ADVERBS AND CONJUNCTIONS

mai	never	*nemmeno*	⎫	
non . . . più	no . . . more	*neppure*	⎬ not even	
non . . . affatto	not at all	*neanche*	⎭	
niente	nothing			
non . . . per niente	nothing at all	*nè . . . nè*	neither . . . nor	
non . . . mica	not . . .			

(i) *nessun, nessuno* (m. sg.) *nessuna* (f. sg.)

● *Nessun* is much more frequent than *non . . . alcuno / a*. Grammatically, it only qualifies singular nouns, although it may imply a plural one. *Nessun* is used before masculine nouns starting with a consonant or a vowel:

> *Non aveva fatto nessun errore.*
> He had made no mistakes.
> He had not made any mistakes.

Nessuno is used before masculine nouns starting with *s* + consonant, *gn, x, y, z*.

If no noun follows, the form is *nessuno / a*.

> *Non lo accetto in nessun modo.*   I don't accept it in any way.
>
> *Non è arrivata nessuna lettera.*   No letter has arrived.

● The verb used with *nessun* is always singular. If *nessun* is placed at the beginning of the sentence, *non* is omitted:

> *Non è stato dato nessun annuncio.*
> *Nessun annuncio è stato dato.*
> No announcements have been made.

● For the negative form of the partitive article see section 14.

● *Nessun* may be preceded by a preposition:

> *Non c'è per nessuno.*
> He isn't there for anyone.
>
> *Con chi sei stato? Con nessuno?*
> Who have you been with? No one?

● As a pronoun with a general meaning *nessun* is always masculine singular. If it refers to a specific noun by means of *ne*, it may be masculine or feminine:

> *C'erano le ragazze? No. Non ce n'era nessuna.*
> Were the girls there? No. None of them was there.

(ii) *niente, nulla* < literary > nothing, not . . . anything

● *Niente* and *nulla* are interchangeable, but *niente* is the more frequently used. They require *non* before the verb:

> *Non credo a niente.* I don't believe in anything.

● If *niente* or *nulla* is used as the subject, the verb is singular. Any adjective or past participle related to them is masculine singular:

> *Non è cambiato nulla / niente.* Nothing has changed.

● If *niente* or *nulla* starts the sentence, *non* is not used:

> *Niente è più brutto dell'invidia.* Nothing is uglier than envy.
> *Se niente è utile . . . = Se non è utile niente . . .* If nothing is useful . . .

● *Di* is required between *niente* or *nulla* and an adjective. *Da* is required between one of them and a verb:

> *Non c'era niente di divertente in discoteca.*
> The discotheque was no fun.
> (literally: There was nothing entertaining in the discotheque.)
> *Non c'è niente da fare.* There was nothing to do / to be done.

● *Niente* acquires a positive meaning in interrogative sentences:

> *Hai bisogno di niente? / qualcosa?* Do you need anything?

● *Niente* may be used as an adjective before a singular or a plural noun but it remains invariable:

> *Niente zucchero, grazie.* No sugar, thank you.

● Both *niente* and *nulla* can act as nouns if the definite article is used before them:

> *È sparito nel nulla.*
> He has disappeared into thin air. (literally: nothingness)
> *Si è fatto dal nulla.* He is a self-made man.
> *È fatto di niente.* It's nothing.
> *È una cosa da nulla.* It's nothing important.

(iii) *nè . . . nè* neither . . . nor

Both can be used, but you may choose to use only one:

> *Non sono più di moda (nè) le gonne lunghe nè gli stivali.*
> Neither long skirts nor boots are fashionable any more.

(iv) *neanche, neppure, nemmeno* not even
These words are interchangeable:

> *Mi dispiace. Non abbiamo neanche caffè.*
> I'm sorry. We don't even have coffee.

VERBS

All verbs require different endings to indicate the subject (person) and the time of the action (tense): to add these various endings to the stem of the verb is to conjugate the verb.

> *Lo so. Paola parla raramente, io parlo sempre.*
> I know. Paula doesn't talk much, I'm always talking.
>
> *Peccato! Ci portava sempre il latte fresco. Ora non lo porta più.*
> What a shame! He always used to bring us fresh milk. Now he doesn't bring it any more.

Italian verbs are divided into three groups (conjugations) according to their ending in the infinitive, which is the form given in dictionaries:

1ST CONJUGATION:	*ritorn – are* to return	*arriv – are* to arrive
2ND CONJUGATION:	*perd – ere* to lose	*spegn – ere* to switch off
3RD CONJUGATION:	*sent – ire* to hear	*sal –ire* to go up

To form the various tenses the infinitive ending is dropped and the appropriate ending is added according to subject and tense.

45 Present indicative

(a) *essere* and *avere*

(i) *Essere* and *avere* are irregular verbs. They are conjugated as follows in the present tense:

	essere		**avere**	
io	sono	I am	ho	I have
tu < informal >	sei	you are	hai	you have
lui / lei		he / she is		he / she has
esso / essa	è	it is	ha	it has
lei < formal >		you are		you have
noi	siamo	we are	abbiamo	we have
voi (pl.)	siete	you are	avete	you have
loro / essi / esse	sono	they are	hanno	they have

These two verbs are also called 'auxiliary verbs' (from the Latin *auxilium*, aid) because they help other verbs to form their past tenses. For the use of *essere* and *avere* as auxiliary verbs see section 64d.

(ii) Notice the frequently used phrases *c'è* ('there is') and *ci sono* ('there are'):

> *C'è posto?* Is there a seat?
> *Ci sono due posti?* Are there two seats?

● In negative sentences *non* precedes *ci* and *c'*:

> *No. Non ci sono posti.* No. There are no seats.

● When followed by the pronoun *ne* the word *ci* becomes *ce* and the word order is *ce ne* (see section 35):

> *Ce n'è uno solo.* There is only one.
> *Sì. Ce ne sono due.* Yes. There are two.

(b) The conjugations

The present tense of the three regular conjugations is formed as follows:

		1st	**2nd**	**3rd**
		arriv<u>are</u>	*perd<u>ere</u>*	*sent<u>ire</u>*
		to arrive	to lose	to hear
I	*io*	*arriv<u>o</u>*	*perd<u>o</u>*	*sent<u>o</u>*
you < informal >	*tu*	*arriv<u>i</u>*	*perd<u>i</u>*	*sent<u>i</u>*
he / she	*lui / lei*	*arriv<u>a</u>*	*perd<u>e</u>*	*sent<u>e</u>*
it	*esso / essa*	*arriv<u>a</u>*	*perd<u>e</u>*	*sent<u>e</u>*
you < formal >	*lei*	*arriv<u>a</u>*	*perd<u>e</u>*	*sent<u>e</u>*
we	*noi*	*arriv<u>iamo</u>*	*perd<u>iamo</u>*	*sent<u>iamo</u>*
you (pl.)	*voi*	*arriv<u>ate</u>*	*perd<u>ete</u>*	*sent<u>ite</u>*
they	*loro / essi /*	*arriv<u>ano</u>*	*perd<u>ono</u>*	*sent<u>ono</u>*
	esse			

For the passive form of the present indicative, see section 66.

(c) Notes on endings

(i) Some verbs of the third conjugation take different endings:

	preferire to prefer
io	*prefer<u>isco</u>*
tu	*prefer<u>isci</u>*
lui / lei / esso / essa / lei < formal >	*prefer<u>isce</u>*
noi	*prefer<u>iamo</u>*
voi	*prefer<u>ite</u>*
loro / essi / esse	*prefer<u>iscono</u>*

- This second group includes:

agire to act	*fornire* to provide
ambire to aspire	*guarire* to recover
ammonire to admonish	*impedire* to prevent
ardire to venture	*inserire* to insert
capire to understand	*patire* to suffer
chiarire to clarify	*percepire* to become aware of
costruire to build	*punire* to punish
demolire to demolish	*rapire* to kidnap
favorire to favour	*scolpire* to sculpt
ferire to hurt	*subire* to suffer
finire to finish	*tradire* to betray
fiorire to flourish	*unire* to join

- The following verbs can use both types of conjugation:

aborrire to abhor	*mentire* to lie
applaudire to applaud	*nutrire* to nourish
assorbire to absorb	*tossire* to cough
inghiottire to swallow	

(ii) First-conjugation verbs ending in *-care* and *-gare* take the following endings with *tu* and *noi* in order to retain the hard sound of the infinitive:

dimenticare to forget
tu dimentichi, noi dimentichiamo

investigare to investigate
tu investighi, noi investighiamo

(iii) First-conjugation verbs ending in *-iare* drop the 'i' of the stem with *tu* and *noi* in order to avoid a repetition:

studiare to study
tu studi (not *studii*)
noi studiamo (not *studiiamo*)

But if the 'i' is stressed, it may be preserved:

sciare to ski   *tu scii, noi sciiamo*

Similarly:

avviare to start off   *spiare* to spy
inviare to send

(iv) *Cucire* to sew adds an 'i' to the first-person singular and plural endings to preserve the soft sound of 'c' in the infinitive: *io cucio, noi cuciamo*.

(d) Irregular verbs in the present tense

Many common verbs are irregularly conjugated in the present tense (see Appendix 1).

(e) Omission of subject pronouns

Personal pronouns are usually omitted when the verb is expressed (see section 30). They are inserted when:

(i) One wants to contrast the two subjects:

> *Vorrei sapere perchè lui è venuto e lei no.*
> I would like to know why he came and she didn't.

(ii) There is a specific need to stress the subject, in which case the subject pronoun usually goes after the verb:

> *Perchè non sei venuto tu?* Why didn't you come?

(iii) One is checking someone's identity:

> *Sei tu Michela?* Is that you, Michela?
> *Sì. Sono io.* Yes. It's me.

Note that *sono io, siamo noi*, etc. are the equivalent of the impersonal construction in English 'it is me, us' (see section 30d).

46 Uses of the present indicative

The Italian present tense may convey the sense of the simple, emphatic or continuous present, and in some circumstances the future and the past.

(a) Simple present

Specifically the present tense indicates:

(i) A current situation:

> *Le soap opera attraggono un grosso pubblico anche in Italia?*
> Do soap operas attract a large audience in Italy too?

The emphatic form can be expressed with words such as *eccome*:

> *L'attraggono, eccome!* They do!

(ii) A timeless situation:

> *L'ansia colpisce anche i bambini.*
> Stress hits children too. / Children too are hit by stress.

(iii) It is also used on radio and TV sports commentaries:

> *Schillaci dribbla Robinson, gol!*
> Schillaci dribbles to Robinson, goal!

(b) The continuous present

The present can also be used:

(i) When there is a recurrent action or state:

> *Incontri ancora Paolo?*
> Do you still meet Paolo? / Are you still meeting Paolo?
> *Sì. Lo incontro tutti i giorni.*
> Yes. I meet him every day. / I'm meeting him every day.

(ii) When the action is in progress:

> *Trasmettono un bel film.* They are showing a good film.

(c) *stare* + gerund

A more emphatic form of the continuous present is:

stare (irregular) + the gerund (verb ending in *-ando*, 1st conjugation, or *-endo*, 2nd and 3rd conjugation; see section 65):

> *La tele sta trasmettendo che stanno facendo un colpo di stato in Russia.*
> The TV is announcing that a *coup d'état* is taking place now in Russia.

This construction is also used to contrast an habitual situation with a continuous one:

> *Di solito li legge qui ma adesso il sta leggendo in camera sua.*
> Usually he reads them here but right now he is reading them in his room.

Alternatively, Italians opt for repeating the simple present in each clause:

> *Di solito abita in Inghilterra, però attualmente vive in Italia.*
> Usually he lives in England, but he is currently living in Italy.

(d) To denote an action or state starting in the past and carrying on in the present

There are three types of sentence that convey this meaning.

(i) present + *da* + a phrase of time:

> *Non piove da alcuni giorni.*
> It hasn't rained for a few days.
> *Combattono da luglio.*
> They have been fighting since July.

(ii) *è da* + phrase of time + *che* + present tense:

> *È da lunedì che non telefona.*
> He has not rung up since Monday.

(iii) *È* + singular word of time + *che* + present
  Sono + plural word of time + *che* + present

> *È un anno che ci minacciano con le elezioni politiche.*
> They have been threatening us with a general election for a year.

> *Sono due notti che non dormo.*
> I haven't slept for two nights.

Note the expressions:

> *Da quanto tempo conosci Anna?*
> How long have you known Anna?
>
> *Da quando studi italiano?*
> How long have you been studying Italian? (literally: since when)
>
> *Fino a quando resti in Inghilterra?*
> How long are you staying in England? (literally: until when)
>
> *È tanto che aspetta?*
> Have you been waiting for long?

(e) Present tense + *per*

The present tense + *per* acts as continuous present when the action or state has recently ceased. This usage is typical of news headlines (see sections 17 and 53b).

> *Alpinista sopravvive in un crepaccio per diciotto giorni.*
> Climber survives / has survived in a crevasse for eighteen days.

(f) Present tense describing future action

The Italian present tense is also used to describe an action in the future. It may be:

(i) An imminent action:

> *Comincio tra un momento.* I'll start in a moment.

(ii) An action which is considered certain:

> *Prendo il treno delle 10.*
> I'm taking the 10 o'clock train / I will / shall take the 10 o'clock train.
>
> *Il 12 settembre i Ministri degli Esteri della CEE si incontrano a Bruxelles.*
> On September 12th EC foreign ministers will meet / are meeting in Brussels.

(iii) A progressive future:

> *Quando ritornate dalla Spagna?*
> When will you be coming back from Spain?

(iv) Determination or the intention to do something in the future:

> *Quando compri un' auto nuova?*
> When are you going to buy a new car?

(v) An invitation for a future event:

> *Vieni al cinema con noi stasera?*
> Are you coming / will you come to the cinema with us tonight?

(vi) The present may replace the future after the following conjunctions, in both written and spoken style: *appena, non appena* as soon as, *fino a che, fino a quando* till, until, *se* if:

> *Se non nevica (nevicherà) quest' inverno, sarà un disastro per l'agricoltura.*
> If it doesn't snow this winter, it will be a disaster for agriculture.

(g) Describing a past action

The present tense may replace a past tense to confer the immediacy and liveliness of the present on a state or action in the past. This use of the 'historical present' is typical of:

(i) Newspaper headlines:

> *Auto si schianta contro corriera: nove morti.*
> Car crashes into coach: nine dead.

(ii) Oral story-telling and written narrative:

> *Una settimana fa incontro Irene . . .*
> A week ago I bump into Irene . . .

> *'Che bocca grande che hai!', esclamò Cappuccetto Rosso. Il lupo l'ascolta, finge di sorridere, apre la bocca e . . .*
> 'What a large mouth you have!', said Little Red Riding Hood. The wolf listens, pretends to smile, opens its mouth and . . .

(iii) Works of history or history of art:

> *La cupola diventa l'elemento dominante di quasi tutte le chiese rinascimentali.*
> The dome became the dominant element of almost all Renaissance churches.

47 Future and future perfect

(a) *essere* and *avere*

	essere	*avere*
io	sarò I shall / will be	avrò I shall/will have
tu	sarai	avrai
lui / lei esso / essa }	sarà	avrà
lei	sarà	avrà
noi	saremo	avremo
voi	sarete	avrete
loro essi / esse }	saranno	avranno

(b) The conjugations

The future is formed by removing the infinitive ending and adding the following ones:

	1st *ritornare* to return	2nd *ridere* to laugh	3rd *inserire* to insert
io	ritornerò	riderò	inserirò
tu	ritornerai	riderai	inserirai
lui / lei esso / essa }	ritornerà	riderà	inserirà
lei	ritornerà	riderà	inserirà
noi	ritorneremo	rideremo	inseriremo
voi	ritornerete	riderete	inserirete
loro essi / esse }	ritorneranno	rideranno	inseriranno

(c) Irregular future conjugations

For common verbs which have an irregular future form, see Appendix 1.

(d) Verbs ending in *-care*, *-gare*, *-sciare*

(i) Verbs ending in *-care* and *-gare* insert an 'h' before the endings of the future to maintain the hard sound of the infinitive throughout the conjugation:

criticare to criticize	*legare* to tie up
criticherò I shall criticize	*legherò* I shall tie up
criticherai you will criticize, etc.	*legherai* you will tie up, etc.

(ii) Verbs ending in *-ciare*, *-giare* and *-sciare* drop the 'i' of the stem throughout the conjugation:

schiacciare to crush	*lasciare* to leave
schiaccerò I shall crush, etc.	*lascerò* I shall leave, etc.
assaggiare to taste	
assaggerò I shall taste, etc.	

(e) The future passive

For the passive form of the future see section 66.

8 Uses of the future

(a) Describing future actions

As seen in section 46f the present tense forms are frequently used to express the future. The future tense itself is used:

(i) To stress a sense of the future:

È un investimento che renderà tra un anno.
It is an investment which will pay off in a year's time.

Secondo un'antica profezia il mondo finirà nel 2050.
According to an old prediction the world will end in 2050.

Note that in this context the future is also used after *appena, non appena* as soon as, *finchè, finché non* until, *quando* when, *se* if:

Se non archivierai con cura non troverai mai niente.
If you don't file accurately you'll never find anything.

(ii) It is also used to give the idea of a continuous future. In this case the future may be expressed with the present or with the future form of *stare* + verb gerund: *-ando* (1st conjugation), *-endo* (2nd and 3rd conjugations).

A quest' ora staranno / stanno volando sopra Londra.
By now they will be flying over London.

(iii) It conveys certainty about future events:

Quella ditta fallirà senz'altro. That company is bound to fail.

(iv) Occasionally it conveys a command:

Tu non mi lascerai! You will not leave me!

(b) Other meanings of the future tense

The Italian future tense not infrequently denotes:

(i) Possibility:

Che uccelli saranno? Cinciallegre o cinciarelle?
What birds can they be? Great tits or blue tits?

(ii) Approximation:

Saranno sei o sette anni che non vado a Parigi.
I haven't been to Paris for six or seven years.
It must be six or seven years since I went to Paris.

(iii) Concession:

Sarà un vinto, sarà uno sconfitto, ma io lo trovo simpatico.
He may be a loser, he may be a defeated man, but I like him.

(iv) Incredulity:

Non sospetterai che l'abbia fatto apposta!
You can't imagine that I have done it on purpose!
Surely, you don't imagine I have done it on purpose!

(v) Scepticism:

Sarà. Ma le sue spiegazioni non mi convincono.
It may be so. But her explanations don't convince me.

(c) Historical future

Biographers sometimes use the future to narrate actions of the past which are subsequent to the events already told. The change of tense adds liveliness to the narration.

Tornato a Milano nel 1901, lo scultore Eugenio Pellini continuerà a lavorare fino al 1929.
Having returned to Milan in 1901, the sculptor Eugenio Pellini carried on working until 1929.

(d) The future perfect

The future perfect is formed with the future tense of *avere* or *essere* (see section 47a) followed by the past participle (see section 64b).

> *Tra un'ora avrò finito questo lavoro.*
> In an hour I will have finished this job.

Like the simple future, the future perfect is also used after *appena*, *non appena* as soon as, *finchè* until, *quando* when, *se* if:

> *Non appena avranno approvato il bilancio potremo pianificare il futuro.*
> As soon as they have approved the budget we shall be able to plan for the future.

(e) Other constructions expressing the future

Other constructions expressing the future are:

- *stare* + *per* + infinitive (the most common of these constructions):

  > *Sta per uscire il nuovo romanzo di Gesualdo Buffalino.*
  > The new novel by Gesualdo Buffalino is about to come out.

- *essere sul punto di* + infinitive   to be on the point of (doing)
- *essere in procinto di* + infinitive < rather formal >   to be going to (do), be on the point of (doing)
- *essere sull' orlo di* + infinitive   to be on the brink / verge of (doing)

  > *Che peccato! Era proprio sul punto di vincere la gara.*
  > What a pity! He was really on the point of winning the competition.

  > *Erano in procinto di imbarcarsi.* < rather formal >
  > They were about to board the ship.

  > *Sono sull' orlo di una guerra civile?*
  > Are they on the verge of a civil war?

- *dovere* + infinitive:

  > *Deve arrivare alle 7.* It is due to arrive at 7 o'clock.

- *stare* + *a* + infinitive:

  > *Ma! Staremo a vedere.* Well! We shall see.

49 Imperfect indicative

(a) *Essere* and *avere*

(i)

	essere		*avere*	
io	ero	I was	avevo	I had
tu	eri	you were	avevi	
lui / lei	era		aveva	
esso / essa	era		aveva	
lei	era		aveva	
noi	eravamo		avevamo	
voi	eravate		avevate	
loro	erano		avevano	
essi / esse	erano		avevano	

(ii) Notice the phrases *c'era* there was, and *c'erano* there were:

Non c'era altro da fare. There was nothing else to do.

C'erano tutti? Were they all there?

C'era una volta . . . (Once upon a time . . .) is the traditional way for fairy tales to begin.

(b) The conjugations

The imperfect is formed by removing the ending of the infinitive and adding the following ones:

	1st *pensare* to think	2nd *credere* to believe	3rd *sentire* to hear
io	pensavo	credevo	sentivo
tu	pensavi	credevi	sentivi
lui / lei	pensava	credeva	sentiva
esso / essa	pensava	credeva	sentiva
lei	pensava	credeva	sentiva
noi	pensavamo	credevamo	sentivamo
voi	pensavate	credevate	sentivate
loro	pensavano	credevano	sentivano
essi / esse	pensavano	credevano	sentivano

(c) Irregular verbs

Very few verbs are irregular in the imperfect tense; *dire* to say, to tell, *fare* to make, to do, *tradurre* to translate add the appropriate endings to these stems: *dic–, fac–, traduc–*.

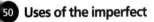 ## 50 Uses of the imperfect

The name *imperfetto*, derived from the Latin verb *imperficere*, means 'not entirely finished, not completed, not perfected'. As its name indicates, this tense describes states or actions whose progress or duration has been interrupted. In other words, it places the emphasis on the continuity of past states and actions and not on their completion. For this second purpose Italian uses the perfect or the past historic tenses. Compare:

> *Ricordava il silenzio solenne che c'era sul set cinematografico.*
> He recalled (his thoughts were lingering on) the solemn silence on the film set.

> *Ricordò il silenzio solenne che c'era sul set cinematografico.*
> He recalled (for a limited time) the solemn silence on the film set.

More specific uses of the imperfect are described below:

(a) Repetitive actions

The imperfect is used for an habitual situation or action, sometimes conveyed in English with 'used to' or the iterative 'would':

> *Erano i fiori che lei amava.*
> They were the flowers she loved / used to love.

> *Fiero dei suoi segreti li custodiva con orgoglio.*
> Proud of his secrets, he would keep / kept them with pride.

(b) Continuous states or actions in the past

(i) An action in progress, often expressed in English by the past continuous ('was / were –ing'):

> *Una voce interna lo ammoniva.*
> An inner voice was warning him.

> *Che cosa fai? Niente. Guardavo il mare.*
> What are you doing? Nothing. I was just looking at the sea. /
> I am looking at the sea.

(ii) A continuous action in the past can also be expressed either

- with the imperfect of **stare** + the gerund -*ando* (1st conjugation), -*endo* (2nd and 3rd conjugation) or
- with the imperfect of **andare** + the gerund (see section 65):

> *Stava lavando i piatti.*
> He was washing up.

> *Andava raccogliendo tutto ciò che riguardava la Prima Guerra Mondiale.*
> He was collecting everything that concerned the First World War.

(iii) To indicate 'since when' or 'for how long' an action <u>which was still continuing</u> had been in progress, the imperfect is accompanied by *da*:

> *Quel problema lo tormentava da tempo.*
> That problem had been worrying him for quite a while (and had not ceased tormenting him).

The same meaning is conveyed by these other phrases:

- **era da** + phrase or word of time indicating when the situation had started + **che** + imperfect

> *Era da un secolo che flirtava con lui.*
> She had been flirting with him for ages (and was still flirting).

> *Era dalle 4 che non dormiva.*
> She had not slept since 4 o'clock (and was still not sleeping).

- **era** + singular word indicating the length of time + **che** + imperfect

> *Era un anno che non parlava francese.*
> He hadn't spoken French for a year (and was still not speaking it).

- **erano** + plural word indicating the length of time + **che** + imperfect

> *Erano mesi che scriveva quel racconto.*
> He had been writing that short story for months (and was still writing it).

But, if the situation or action has stopped at the time of the narration, this is indicated by the past historic or perfect tense + *per* (see sections 53 and 54). Compare:

> *Temeva di non riuscire a ottenerlo.*
> She was afraid he could not obtain it (she was still afraid).

Per un momento temette / ha temuto di non riuscire a ottenerlo.
For a moment he feared he could not obtain it (but then managed to).

(c) Other uses

(i) The imperfect is used to indicate the past in most sentences where the verb is either 'to be' or 'to have':

Era stanco, non aveva tempo e non aveva voglia di lavorare.
He was tired, he had neither the time nor the desire to work.

Avevano molti soldi ma non erano simpatici.
They had a lot of money but they were not pleasant people.

(ii) It also describes physical, mental, emotional, social, professional and religious states:

Il volto somigliava a un'antica moneta.
His face resembled an ancient coin.

Mostrava un'astuzia naturale.
He showed a natural cunning.

Non aveva alcuna considerazione per il denaro.
He had no consideration for money.

Era contemporaneamente nobile e plebeo, ateo e religioso.
At the same time he was noble and plebian, atheist and religious.

(iii) It describes landscapes, interiors, atmospheres:

Due fari mettevano in risalto le linee pure della chiesa.
Two spotlights threw the pure lines of the cathedral into relief.

Tappeti poveri coprivano i pavimenti.
Threadbare carpets covered the floors.

(iv) Age, time:

Era vicino ai sessanta. He was almost sixty.
Erano le otto passate. It was past eight o'clock.

Note the different use of *è nato* and *era nato*. The first is used if the account is given in the present, the second if the account is in the past:

Sai, Marco è nato un mese prima.
You know, Mark was born a month earlier.

Il protagonista apparteneva alla borghesia del posto. Era nato nel 1870.
The protagonist belonged to the local middle class. He was born in 1870.

(v) Weather conditions, if the emphasis is on their duration and not as a completed fact; otherwise the past historic or perfect tense is used. Compare:

> *Pioveva a dirotto.* It was pouring with rain.
> *Piovve a dirotto quella notte.* It poured with rain that night.

(vi) Verbs such as *sapere* to know, *conoscere* to know, to be informed about, *credere* to believe, *pensare* to think, *valere la pena* to be worthwhile, *volere* to want most commonly occur in the imperfect, unless they describe an action or a situation lasting for a short time and on a defined occasion:

> *Ci voleva pazienza.* One needed patience.
>
> *Ci volle tutta la sua pazienza in quel momento.*
> He needed all his patience at that time.
>
> *Valeva la pena sprecare la vita così?*
> Was it worthwhile wasting one's life like this?
>
> *Pensavo d'andarci domani.*
> I thought I could go tomorrow.
>
> *Non sapevo che tu parlassi cinese.*
> I did not know you could speak Chinese.
>
> *L'ho saputo solo ieri.* I learnt of it only yesterday.

(d) The imperfect in conversational Italian

(i) It often replaces the conditional:

> *Volevo intervenire ma . . .* < more casual >
> I wanted to intervene but . . .
>
> *Avrei voluto intervenire.* < more formal >
> I would have liked to intervene.

(ii) It may replace the subjunctive:

> *Se correvo di più prendevo il treno.* < more casual >
> *Se avessi corso di più avrei preso il treno.* < grammatically more accurate >
> If I had run faster I would have caught the train.

(iii) It is used to soften a request in both informal and formal situations (i.e. shops, professional encounters):

> *Volevo un chilo di mele.* One kilo of apples, please.

Volevo chiederle un' informazione.
Could I ask you for some information?

(e) The imperfect used instead of the past historic

In historical narrations or in newspaper reports, the imperfect replaces the past historic to prolong the emotional impact of events. Compare:

Nel 1990 crollava il muro di Berlino e finiva la guerra fredda.
In 1990 there was the fall of the Berlin Wall and the end of the cold war.

Nel 1990 crollò il muro di Berlino e finì la guerra fredda.
In 1990 the Berlin Wall fell and the cold war ended.

(f) The imperfect in subordinate clauses

When the main clause is in the past, the imperfect is used in the following types of subordinate clause:

(i) To report a simultaneous action

I suoi nemici dicevano che imbrogliava.
His enemies used to say he cheated.

(ii) Indirect questions

The imperfect may be used in place of the subjunctive in indirect questions (the verb in the main sentence could be *mi domandavo*, 'I wondered' or *non sapevo se*, 'I did not know if'). The subjunctive used to be compulsory in such cases. Nowadays it is used less and less, even in literary prose and newspaper articles. Compare:

Voleva sapere che cosa suo figlio faceva quella sera.
Voleva sapere che cosa suo figlio facesse (subj.) *quella sera.*
< grammatically more accurate >
He wanted to know what his son was doing that evening.

(iii) Relative clauses

The imperfect is used in relative clauses after verbs of perception (e.g. *guardare* to look at), where the English equivalent is an -ing form (i.e. continuous).

Guardava la donna che camminava alla sua destra.
He was looking at the woman walking on his right.

51 Pluperfect indicative

The pluperfect indicative is formed with the imperfect of the auxiliary *avere* or *essere* followed by the past participle of the main verb (see section 64b).

> *Lo aveva incontrato una volta sola.*
> He had met him only once.

> *Quando era arrivato la cena era pronta.*
> When he (had) arrived, dinner was ready.

52 Perfect indicative

The perfect – *il passato prossimo* in Italian – is another compound tense. It is formed with the appropriate form of the present tense of one of the two auxiliary verbs *avere* or *essere*, followed by the past participle of the main verb (see section 64b).

(a) *essere* and *avere*

	essere		*avere*
io	*sono stato / a*	I have been / I was	*ho avuto* I have had / I had
tu	*sei stato / a*		*hai avuto*
lui / lei	*è stato / a*		*ha avuto*
esso / essa	*è stato / a*		*ha avuto*
lei	*è stato / a*		*ha avuto*
noi	*siamo stati / e*		*abbiamo avuto*
voi	*siete stati / e*		*avete avuto*
loro / essi / esse	*sono stati / e*		*hanno avuto*

Note that the past participle of *essere* – **stato** – agrees in gender and number with the subject:

> *La signora Motta non è stata affatto contenta dei risultati.*
> Mrs Motta hasn't been at all happy with the results.

(b) The past participle

The past participle of the three conjugations is formed by removing the ending of the infinitive and adding the endings of the past participle:

	INFINITIVE		PAST PARTICIPLE	
1st	*salut – are*	to greet	*salut – ato*	greeted
2nd	*sap – ere*	to know	*sap – uto*	known
3rd	*cap – ire*	to understand	*cap – ito*	understood

I	*io*	*ho*	
you < informal >	*tu*	*hai*	
he / she	*lui / lei*	*ha*	
it	*esso / essa*	*ha*	+ { *salutato*
you < formal >	*lei*	*ha*	*saputo*
we	*noi*	*abbiamo*	*capito*
you (pl.)	*voi*	*avete*	
they	*loro / essi / esse*	*hanno*	

(c) Irregular endings

Verbs ending in *-cere* and *-scere* have a past participle ending in *-iuto*:

> *tacere* to keep silent, *taciuto*
> *riconoscere*, to recognize, *riconosciuto*

For other irregular past participles see Appendix 1.

(d) The perfect tense in a negative sentence

With a compound tense, *non* precedes both parts of the verb as well as object pronouns:

> *Non ho capito molto.* I haven't understood a great deal.
> *Non gli ho chiesto nulla.* I haven't asked him anything.

53 Uses of the perfect

The use of the *passato prossimo*, the perfect tense, needs to be considered in relation to the *imperfetto*, the imperfect tense, and the *passato remoto*, the past historic (see sections 50–55).

(a) Use of the perfect rather than the imperfect

(i) The perfect tense is used to record a state or an activity which has been completed rather than an event in the past interrupted while in progress, for which the imperfect would be used. Compare:

> *Gli ho parlato di quella faccenda.* (perfect)
> I spoke / I have spoken to him about that business.

> *Mentre gli parlavo di quella faccenda . . .* (imperfect)
> While I was speaking / I spoke to him about that business . . .

> *L'ho incontrato a Milano.*
> I met him in Milan.

> *Hai colpito nel segno.*
> You have hit the nail on the head. (literally: You have hit on the mark.)

> *Quel marchingegno non ha funzionato.*
> That gadget hasn't worked / did not work.

(ii) To refer to a state or an activity which has lasted for a specified period and has stopped by the time it is reported. The word used to define the period is *per*.

> *Ieri ho letto per un'ora.*
> Yesterday I read for an hour.

Compare:

> *La battaglia è infuriata per un mese.* (perfect)
> The battle has raged for a month.

> *La battaglia infuriava da giorni.*
> The battle has been raging for days.

(iii) To talk of an action which occurred when another one was in progress:

> *Pensavo proprio a voi quando mi avete telefonato.*
> I was just thinking / I had been thinking of you when you rang me up.

(b) Use of the perfect rather than the past historic

(i) When the action is relatively recent and the effects are still felt:

Ho letto questo libro per la prima volta cinque anni fa.
I read this book for the first time five years ago.

(ii) When the emphasis is on the event rather than on the time it happened:

Nel 1945 è finita la Seconda Guerra Mondiale.
In 1945 the Second World War ended.

Fu nel 1945 che finì la Seconda Guerra Mondiale.
It was in 1945 that the Second World War ended.

(iii) In radio, newspapers and TV reports:

Si è aperta ieri la Conferenza di Parigi.
The Paris Conference opened yesterday.

Il capo del Cremlino e il capo della Casa Bianca si sono incontrati mercoledì.
The occupants of the Kremlin and the White House met on Wednesday.

(iv) In financial reports:

Nell'anno trascorso abbiamo aperto 10 nuove filiali.
In the past year we have opened ten subsidiaries.

(c) The perfect tense in subordinate clauses

(i) The perfect tense is used if the main clause is in the present:

Pensa che sono venuta in Italia per la prima volta vent'anni fa.
Just think, I came to Italy for the first time twenty years ago.

(ii) It is also used instead of the perfect subjunctive in informal speech.

Mi chiedo come ha fatto a ottenere quel contratto. /
Mi chiedo come abbia fatto a ottenere quel contratto. < more formal >
I wonder how he has managed to get that contract.

(d) Regional use

The use of the perfect tense also varies according to region. In Northern Italy people use the perfect tense, whether the time of the action is recent or remote, to describe a specific past state or action which is seen as completed. This does not apply to formal written narrative. In Southern Italy preference is given to the past historic. Central Italy prefers the perfect tense if the action is recent or still related to the present and the past historic if the action is in the distant past.

54 Past historic and past anterior

(a) *essere* and *avere*

	essere		*avere*	
io	fui	I was	ebbi	I had
tu	fosti	you were	avesti	you had
lui / lei	fu	he / she was	ebbe	he / she had
esso / essa	fu	it was	ebbe	it had
lei	fu	you were	ebbe	you had
noi	fummo	we were	avemmo	we had
voi	foste	you were	aveste	you had
loro	furono	they were	ebbero	they had

Note the phrases *ci fu* (there was) and *ci furono* (there were). They report an event which took place in the past. Their use in place of *c'era* stresses a sense of something happening in contrast to a sense of something being; it emphasizes the event and the suddenness and immediacy of its happening. Its use in place of *c'è stato* emphasizes the sense of historical perspective:

> *Ci furono dieci morti in quell'incidente aereo.*
> There were ten fatalities in that aeroplane crash.

> *C'erano dieci passeggeri su quel treno.*
> There were ten passengers on that train.

> *Ci sono stati dieci morti sull'autostrada questa settimana.*
> Ten people have died on the motorway this week.

(b) The conjugations

To form the past historic the following endings are added after dropping the infinitive endings:

	1st	**2nd**	**3rd**
	viaggiare	*cedere*	*intuire*
	to travel	to yield	to guess
io	*viaggiai*	*cedei* or *-etti*	*intuii*
tu	*viaggiasti*	*cedesti*	*intuisti*
lui / lei	*viaggiò*	*cedè* or *-ette*	*intuì*
lei	*viaggiò*	*cedè* or *-ette*	*intuì*
noi	*viaggiammo*	*cedemmo*	*intuimmo*
voi	*viaggiaste*	*cedeste*	*intuiste*
loro	*viaggiarono*	*cederono* or *-ettero*	*intuirono*

For the passive forms of the past historic see section 66:

> *Fu licenziato.* He was sacked.

55 Uses of the past historic

The past historic has to be seen in relation to the imperfect and the perfect. Unlike the imperfect, it refers to a state or an action in the past seen as completed rather than continuous, habitual or in progress. Unlike the perfect tense, it is used in the following ways in formal language in Northern and Central Italy, and in conversations in the South.

(a) To emphasize the historical context

It is therefore the past tense of biographies and historical works:

> *i cento giorni che cambiarono il mondo*
> the hundred days that changed the world

> *Ei fu.* He was.
> Alessandro Manzoni, *Cinque maggio*.
> [The opening line of a famous poem to announce Napoleon's death. *Ei* was the poetic word for 'he'.]

(b) To convey a sense of detachment from the moment of the narration

In literary narrative it is preferred to the *passato prossimo* which is used to record informal conversations:

> *Si innamorò per sempre di quella donna, concluse Ludovico.*
> He fell in love for ever with that woman, Ludovico concluded.

(c) To stress the definitiveness of a past action

Non se ne parlò più. We didn't speak about it again.

(d) To emphasize that the state or event lasted for a precise period of time

Often in the sentence the phrase *per sempre* or just *sempre* is spelled out or implied.

Fu sempre un uomo di grande energia.
Throughout his life he was a man of great energy.

Ebbe un successo incredibile.
He had incredible success (on that occasion).

But

Aveva (imperfect) *un successo incredibile con le ragazze.*
He used to have incredible success with girls.

(f) The past anterior

This tense is limited almost entirely to formal prose. It is formed by the past historic of the auxiliary *essere* or *avere* plus the past participle of the main verb. It is used in subordinate clauses after expressions of time like *come* as, as if, *dopo che* after, *finchè non* until, *non appena che* no sooner:

Non si addormentò finchè non ebbe smesso di piovere.
She didn't fall asleep until it stopped raining.

56 Present and past conditional

(a) *essere* and *avere*

	essere	*avere*
io	*sarei* I should / would be	*avrei* I should / would have
tu	*saresti*	*avresti*
lui / lei	*sarebbe*	*avrebbe*
esso / essa	*sarebbe*	*avrebbe*
lei	*sarebbe*	*avrebbe*
noi	*saremmo*	*avremmo*
voi	*sareste*	*avreste*
loro	*sarebbero*	*avrebbero*
essi / esse	*sarebbero*	*avrebbero*

(b) The conjugations

The conditional is formed by adding the following endings to the infinitive stem:

	1st	2nd	3rd
	desiderare	scrivere	suggerire
	to wish	to write	to suggest
io	desidererei	scriverei	suggerirei
tu	desidereresti	scriveresti	suggeriresti
lui / lei	desidererebbe	scriverebbe	suggerirebbe
esso / essa	desidererebbe	scriverebbe	suggerirebbe
lei	desidererebbe	scriverebbe	suggerirebbe
noi	desidereremmo	scriveremmo	suggeriremmo
voi	desiderereste	scrivereste	suggerireste
loro	desidererebbero	scriverebbero	suggerirebbero

(c) Verbs ending in -care, -gare, -ciare, -giare, -sciare

(i) As with the future, verbs ending in -care and -gare insert 'h' between the stem and the ending to preserve the hard sound of the infinitive:

pagherei, pagheresti, etc.

(ii) Verbs ending in -ciare, -giare and -sciare drop the 'i' of the stem before adding the conditional ending:

cominciare: cominc(-)erei, cominc(-)eresti, etc.

(d) Irregular verbs

Verbs which are irregular in the future are irregular in the conditional too. See Appendix 1.

(e) The past conditional

The past conditional is formed from the present conditional forms of the auxiliary, essere or avere, followed by the past participle of the main verb:

Lo avrei amato tanto se solo fosse nato.
I would have loved him so much if only he had been born.

Maria non sarebbe andata. Mary would not have gone.

57 Uses of the conditional

(a) Same uses in English and Italian

(i) To express a wish:

> *Mi piacerebbe passare tre settimane in Italia.*
> I should / would like to spend three weeks in Italy.

To convey the forcefulness of 'should', one may add *proprio*, *veramente*, *quanto*. Compare:

> *Quanto mi piacerebbe passare tre settimane in Italia.*
> I should like to spend three weeks in Italy.

> *Mi sarebbe veramente piaciuto imparare le lingue.*
> I should have liked to learn languages.

> *Vorrei smettere di fumare.*
> I would like to stop smoking.

> *Avrei voluto salutarli.*
> I would have liked to say hello to them.

(ii) To tone down a suggestion, an opinion:

> *Sarebbe folle arrabbiarsi per uno scherzo.*
> It would be foolish to get angry over a joke.

> *Mi sembrerebbe poco opportuno.*
> It would seem hardly appropriate to me.

> *Con un'auto nuova sarebbe stato tutto più bello.*
> With a new car everything would have been better.

(iii) To soften a request. In this case the conditional often replaces *per piacere*, *per favore* and is the equivalent of the English 'could' (see section 84d).

> *Mi passeresti un'altra mela?*
> Could you pass me another apple, please?

> *Sarebbe stato opportuno che la commissione avesse deciso diversamente.*
> It would have been appropriate if the committee had decided differently.

(iv) To indicate an expectation:

> *È lo stile che ci si aspetterebbe da una parigina.*
> It's the style one would expect from a girl from Paris.

(v) To express surprise when confronted by a hypothesis:

'E così i grandi attori sarebbero la rovina del teatro?' pensava il vecchio attore.
'So great actors would be the ruin of the theatre?' the old actor thought.

(vi) To enquire about a possibility:

Andresti / saresti andata al lavoro coi mezzi di trasporto pubblici?
Would you go / would you have gone to work by public transport?

(b) Further uses in Italian

(i) To express irritation:

E dove andresti? < annoyance, sarcasm >
And where do you think you are going?

Come sarebbe a dire?
What is this supposed to mean?

E questo cosa sarebbe?
And what is this supposed to be?

(ii) To give an unconfirmed piece of information or news that needs to be presented as not yet officially confirmed. It is a common feature of news media. A sentence such as *si dice che* is implied:

Quel sonnifero sarebbe nocivo.
That sleeping pill is harmful according to unconfirmed reports.

Il questionario lo avrebbe confermato.
The questionnaire confirmed it, they say.

Il presidente sarebbe stato un agente segreto.
There are rumours that the president was a secret agent.

(c) The continuous conditional formed with *stare*

It is expressed by the conditional of *stare* followed by the gerund form: *-ando* (1st conjugation) and *-endo* (2nd and 3rd conjugations) (see section 65).

Se avesse anche solo un po' di buon senso non starebbe scherzando.
If he had any sense he wouldn't be joking.

(d) Conditional of *dovere*

The conditional form of *dovere* translates 'should' (see section 62c):

> *Dovrei passare alcuni giorni in Italia così conoscerei meglio i clienti.*
> I should spend a few days in Italy so I could get to know my customers better.

> *Penso che avrebbe dovuto restare a letto. Non si sente bene.*
> I think he should have stayed in bed. He doesn't feel well.

(e) Further uses of the past conditional

(i) The past conditional conveys supposition:

> *Non si sarebbe fermato in tempo.*
> Very likely he did not stop in time.

(ii) Surprise or disbelief at unexpected information:

> *Così, sarebbe andato a Edinburgo!*
> So, he's supposed to have gone to Edinburgh! (but I know better)

> *Gianni non l'avrebbe mai fatto deliberatamente!*
> John would never have done it on purpose!

(f) The conditional in hypothetical sentences

(i) The present conditional also expresses the hypothetical consequence in a clause introduced by *se* if:

> *Arriveremmo prima se andassimo in auto.*
> We would arrive sooner if we went by car.

The conditional may be used even when the 'if' clause is only implied:

> *C'è chi non attraverserebbe quella strada neppure sotto scorta.*
> Some wouldn't cross that road even (even if they were) escorted.

(ii) The conditional is also used when the condition is not expressed, but is implied by the sense of the preceding text.

The sense of the paragraph preceding the following example is: If one considered the high fees of surgeons and lawyers then . . . .

> *Nessun impresario obietterebbe sul compenso versato a un grande artista.*
> No agent would object to the remuneration given to a great artist.

(iii) In conditional sentences, the past conditional describes an event which would have taken place if a specific condition had occurred. The specific condition may be introduced by *se* if, *solo se* only if, *a condizione che* on condition that, *altrimenti* otherwise, *anche se* even if, though + the subjunctive:

> *Avrei accettato l'incarico solo se mi avessero aumentato lo stipendio.*
> I would have accepted the appointment / assignment only if they had increased my salary.

> *Avrei divorziato solo a condizione che mi avessero* (subj.) *lasciato i bambini.*
> I would have divorced only on condition that they left me the children.

> *Anche se la barca fosse stata / era ferma, nessuno avrebbe sentito la sua voce.*
> Even if the boat had been / were still, no one would have heard his voice.

> *Ma quale senso avrebbe avuto il mio impegno politico se lasciassi che la mia città andasse alla deriva?*
> But what would have been the point of my political commitment if I allowed my town to go under?

(g) The conditional in subordinate clauses

(i) With verbs of knowledge, opinion, information and indirect questions, when the verb in the main clause is in the *present*, the *present conditional* is used in the subordinate clause to indicate a probable or possible event:

> *È ovvio che non firmerebbe il contratto a quelle condizioni.*
> It's obvious she would not sign the contract under those conditions.

> *Non so a chi servirebbe.* I don't know who would use it.

(ii) When the main verb is in the present, the past conditional may be adopted to refer to a possibility before the time referred to in the main sentence:

> *Temo che un'errata decisione avrebbe causato problemi di traffico.*
> I fear that a wrong decision would have caused traffic problems.

Sometimes the main verb may be implied:

> *Chissà dove saremmo finiti!*
> Who knows where we would have ended up!

(iii) In the following cases Italian uses the past conditional to convey two different meanings:

● If the verb of opinion, information or indirect question in the main clause is in the past, the conditional in the subordinate clause is always in the past, whether it expresses an action which has or has not taken place. The meaning is indicated by the context or the situation:

> *Disse che nuove prove sarebbero state rese pubbliche nei prossimi giorni.*
> He said that new evidence would be made public in the next few days.
> He said that new evidence would have been made public in the next few days.

> *Credevo che Paolo sarebbe venuto.*
> I thought Paul would come. / I thought Paul would have come.

> *Di una cosa era certa: mai lo avrebbe voluto come amico.*
> Of one thing she was certain, she would never want / have wanted him as a friend.

● But in reported speech the present conditional is used even if there is a past tense in the main clause:

> *Hanno detto che preferirebbero prosciutto.*
> They said they would prefer ham.

> *Ha detto che abolirebbe l'ordine dei giornalisti.*
> He said he would abolish the journalists' association.

Note that the full sentences should be: They said that if it were left to them they would prefer ham. / He said that if it were left to him he would abolish the journalists' association.

(iv) When referring to the future in narrative, one uses the past conditional:

> *(I lettori sapevano che . . .) un giorno l'avrebbe sposata.*
> (The readers knew that . . .) he would marry her one day.

(v) When the main clause has a verb in the past tense indicating hope, forecast, fear, promise or opinion, the past conditional can replace the imperfect subjunctive in the subordinate clause. This stresses that the foreseen event refers to a moment subsequent to the statement in the main clause:

Ero convinta che Clara si fidanzasse con Giorgio. (imperfect
subjunctive – simultaneous action)
I was convinced that Clara was getting engaged to Giorgio.

Ero convinta che Clara si sarebbe fidanzata con Giorgio. (past
conditional – subsequent action)
I was convinced that Clara would get engaged to Giorgio.

(vi) The same rule applies in these other cases:

● If the verb in the main clause is a past conditional:

Avrebbe giurato che piovesse. (simultaneous actions)
I could have sworn it was raining.

*Si sarebbero potute fare riforme che avrebbero alzato il tenore di
vita.* (subsequent action)
They could have made reforms which would have raised the
standard of living.

● Or a future:

*Quelle finalità saranno perseguite con quella determinazione che
mio padre avrebbe desiderato.*
Those objectives will be pursued with the determination my father
would have wished.

Note that the conditional may be replaced by the imperfect where
the idea of a subsequent action is less strong:

Sarà fatto come voleva.
It will be done as he wished.

Sarà fatto come avrebbe voluto.
It will be done as he would have wished.

(vii) The past conditional is also used in subordinate clauses
anticipating a purpose:

*Avevano acceso due micce cosicchè all'esplosione sarebbe
fatalmente seguito l'incendio.*
They had lit the fuse so that the explosion would inevitably have
been followed by a fire.

(viii) Finally, the past conditional may also indicate destiny:

Non sarebbe stato così. It was not to be.

58 The subjunctive mood

All the tenses that have been described in sections 45–57 belong to the indicative mood. The following tenses belong to the subjunctive mood. The subjunctive mood can best be described as a manner of speaking and writing which either gives a more gentle tone to opinions, suggestions, indirect questions and statements or adds a touch of formal elegance to a sentence.

Sometimes it is optional, sometimes it is compulsory. There are four tenses in the subjunctive mood. The present, imperfect, perfect and pluperfect subjunctive correspond to the present, imperfect, perfect and pluperfect indicative. The choice between indicative or subjunctive in a subordinate clause depends on the verb or other elements in the main clause. See also complex sentences (section 140).

(a) *essere* and *avere*

essere

	PRESENT SUBJUNCTIVE	PERFECT SUBJUNCTIVE
io	sia I am / may be	sia stato / a I have been / may have been
tu	sia	sia stato
lui / lei	sia	sia stato
esso / essa	sia	sia stato
lei	sia	sia stato
noi	siamo	siamo stati / e
voi	siate	siate stati
loro	siano	siano stati

	IMPERFECT SUBJUNCTIVE	PLUPERFECT SUBJUNCTIVE
io	*fossi* I were / might be	*fossi stato / a* I had been / might have been
tu	*fossi*	*fossi stato / a*
lui / lei	*fosse*	*fosse stato*
esso / essa	*fosse*	*fosse stato*
lei	*fosse*	*fosse stato*
noi	*fossimo*	*fossimo stati / e*
voi	*foste*	*foste stati*
loro	*fossero*	*fossero stati*

avere

	PRESENT SUBJUNCTIVE	PERFECT SUBJUNCTIVE
io	*abbia* I have / may have	*abbia avuto* I have had / may have had
tu	*abbia*	*abbia avuto*
lui / lei	*abbia*	*abbia avuto*
esso / essa	*abbia*	*abbia avuto*
lei	*abbia*	*abbia avuto*
noi	*abbiamo*	*abbiamo avuto*
voi	*abbiate*	*abbiate avuto*
loro	*abbiano*	*abbiano avuto*

	IMPERFECT SUBJUNCTIVE	PLUPERFECT SUBJUNCTIVE
io	*avessi* I had / might have	*avessi avuto* I had had / might have had
tu	*avessi*	*avessi avuto*
lui / lei	*avesse*	*avesse avuto*
esso / essa	*avesse*	*avesse avuto*
lei	*avesse*	*avesse avuto*
noi	*avessimo*	*avessimo avuto*
voi	*aveste*	*aveste avuto*
loro	*avessero*	*avessero avuto*

(b) The conjugations

(i) The present subjunctive of regular verbs

	guidare to drive	*scrivere* to write
io	*guidi* I drive / may drive	*scriva* I write / may write
tu	*guidi*	*scriva*
lui / lei *esso / essa* }	*guidi*	*scriva*
lei	*guidi*	*scriva*
noi	*guidiamo*	*scriviamo*
voi	*guidiate*	*scriviate*
loro	*guidino*	*scrivano*

	dormire to sleep	*guarire* to recover
io	*dorma* I sleep / may sleep	*guarisca* I recover / may recover
tu	*dorma*	*guarisca*
lui / lei *esso / essa* }	*dorma*	*guarisca*
lei	*dorma*	*guarisca*
noi	*dormiamo*	*guariamo*
voi	*dormiate*	*guariate*
loro	*dormano*	*guariscano*

For a list of some of the verbs taking the same ending as *guarire* see section 45c.

(ii) The present subjunctive of verbs ending in *-care*, *-gare*, *-iare*

● Verbs ending in *-care* and *-gare* in the infinitive insert an 'h' before adding the present subjunctive endings to preserve the hard sound of the infinitive:

> *pescare* to fish *tu peschi*
>
> *legare* to bind *voi leghiate*

● Verbs ending in *-iare*, *-ciare*, *-giare*, *-sciare*, *-gliare* drop the 'i' before adding the present endings to avoid a double 'i':

> *cianciare* to chatter *cianci*
>
> *sfoggiare* to show off *sfoggi*
>
> *scrosciare* to pelt down *scrosci*
>
> *sbagliare* to make a mistake *sbagli*

● Verbs whose accent falls on the 'i' of *-iare* can keep 'ii':

> *studiare* to study *studino* or *studiino*

(iii) The perfect subjunctive

The perfect subjunctive is formed from the present subjunctive form of *essere* or *avere* plus the past participle:

> . . . *che abbia mangiato* . . . that she has eaten / may have eaten
>
> . . . *che siano venuti* . . . that they may have come

(iv) The imperfect subjunctive

	1st	2nd	3rd
	guidare	*scrivere*	*dormire*
	to drive	to write	to sleep
io	*guidassi*	*scrivessi*	*dormissi*
	I drove / might drive	I wrote / might write	I slept / might sleep
tu	*guidassi*	*scrivessi*	*dormissi*
lui / lei *esso / essa* }	*guidasse*	*scrivesse*	*dormisse*
lei	*guidasse*	*scrivesse*	*dormisse*
noi	*guidassimo*	*scrivessimo*	*dormissimo*
voi	*guidaste*	*scriveste*	*dormiste*
loro	*guidassero*	*scrivessero*	*dormissero*

(v) The pluperfect subjunctive

The pluperfect subjunctive is formed from the imperfect subjunctive of *avere* or *essere* plus the past participle.

59 Uses of the subjunctive

(a) The subjunctive in main clauses

(i) It expresses a formal oral or written invitation (see section 84):

> *Si esaminino le cause della rivoluzione francese.*
> I suggest we examine the causes of the French Revolution.

> *Basti osservare il grafico.* < formal >
> We may look at the graphic. (literally: It may be enough . . .)

> *Basta osservare il grafico.* < informal >
> Let's look at the graphic. (literally: It's enough . . .)

(ii) It is used in sentences governed by an unexpressed *se* (if) or an unexpressed verb requiring the subjunctive:

> *Che mi lascino in pace! (Voglio che mi lascino in pace.)*
> I wish they would leave me in peace! (literally: that they leave me in peace!)

> *Avessi vent' anni in meno! (Se avessi vent'anni in meno . . . .)*
> If only I were twenty years younger!

> *Che abbiano perso il treno? (Mi chiedo se abbiano perso il treno).*
> It may be that they have missed the train.

> *Dove sono le zone che offrano grandiosi scenari? (Ci si deve interrogare su . . .)*
> We need to ask ourselves which regions offer beautiful scenery.

(b) The subjunctive in subordinate clauses

Today the subjunctive is often seen as a stylistic device rather than a grammatical necessity. The subjunctive used to be required in the following cases but now sometimes the indicative is accepted as well.

(i) When the subordinate clause is a question introduced by these verbs or expressions:

> *capire, comprendere* to understand
> *domandare, chiedere* to ask
> *informarsi* to get information about
> *cercare di sapere* to try to find out
> *porsi domande* to ask oneself, etc.

The question may also be introduced by:

> *perché* why   *quanto / i* how much, how many
> *quale / i* which   *che cosa* what
> *come* how   *se* if
> *dove* where   *come mai* how it came to be that, etc.
> *quando* when

> *Non capisco dove stia / sta la ragione o il torto.*
> I don't understand who is right and who is wrong. (literally: . . . where the right or the wrong lies.)

> *Resta sospesa la questione su chi abbia / ha ucciso quell' uomo.*
> The question remains who has killed that man.

> *Ma non mi spieghi perché tu non l'abbia / hai fatto.*
> But you are not explaining why you haven't done it.

> *Ma dove sta scritto che un parlamentare non possa criticare il parlamento?*
> But where is it written that an MP cannot criticize Parliament?

The question may be governed by the previous clause:

> *È sempre più difficile dire chi siano gli eserciti. E chi dia loro gli ordini.*
> It is more and more difficult to say who the armies are. And who gives them their orders.

(ii) When the main sentence expresses opinion, doubt, preference or suggestion with verbs or phrases such as:

> *credere* to believe
> *pensare, ritenere* to think
> *immaginare* to imagine
> *mi sembra che, mi pare che* it seems to me that
> *avere l'impressione che* to be under the impression that
> *essere sicuri* to be sure
> *essere incerti* to be uncertain
> *essere convinti* to be convinced

presumere to assume	*piacere* to like
sospettare to suspect	*dispiacere* to be sorry
negare to deny	*suggerire* to suggest
dubitare to doubt	*consigliare* to advise
supporre to suppose	*essere d'accordo* to agree
preferire to prefer	

Non credo che le sanzioni bastino.
I don't think that sanctions are sufficient.

Non mi pareva che ci fossero toni polemici nel suo discorso.
I didn't think that there were polemical overtones in his speech.

Ci comunicò il suo sospetto: che qualcuno avesse voluto derubarlo.
He informed us of his suspicion: that someone had wanted to rob him.

(iii) With verbs describing feelings (fear, worry, joy, hope) such as:

mi interessa I am interested in
rallegrarsi to be glad about
mi fa piacere to be pleased
mi entusiasma it makes me enthusiastic
preoccuparsi to worry
vivere con la preoccupazione che to live with the worry that
mi rattrista it makes me sad
temere to fear
sperare to hope
avere paura, avere timore to fear, to be afraid

Ci rallegra che si sia / è laureata.
We are happy that she has received her degree.

Mi interessava che studiassero.
I was keen that they should study.

(iv) With verbs of expectation:

augurarsi to wish
non vedere l'ora to be looking forward
aspettarsi to expect
illudersi to delude oneself
prevedere to foresee
sperare to hope

Mi aspettavo che mi desse delle risposte chiare.
I was expecting to be given clear answers. (literally: I was expecting that he gave me clear answers.)

Non c'è previsione che non sia stata / è stata smentita dalla storia.
There isn't a prediction that has not been contradicted by history.

(v) Surprise:

sorprendersi to be surprised
dichiararsi sorpreso, stupefatto / meravigliarsi to declare oneself
surprised, amazed, astonished
essere stupefacente che it is surprising that

Non mi meraviglia che non l'abbia / ha più sposato.
It doesn't surprise me that she hasn't married him.

(vi) The subjunctive is also used when the main clause has a verb of command, volition, wish, request:

ordinare to order	*chiedere, domandare* to ask
comandare to command	*implorare* to implore
volere to want	*decretare* to decree
desiderare to wish	*insistere* to insist
supplicarre to implore	*intendere* to intend
richiedere to request	*pregare* to pray
pretendere to demand	*proporre* to propose
esigere, domandare to require	*decretare* to rule
contestare to question	*stipulare* to stipulate
impedire to prevent	*interessare* to generate interest

Voleva che Enrico le telefonasse.
She wanted Henry to ring her up. (literally: she wanted that Henry rang her up.)

Esigeva sempre che il servizio fosse perfetto.
She always required the service to be perfect.

Gli studenti contestavano che l'istruzione non fosse gratuita.
The students questioned why education was not free.

A noi interessa che la produzione non perda terreno.
Our common interest is that production doesn't decline. (literally: lose ground)

(vii) The subjunctive is used when the verb of the main clause is a statement or denial. For instance, *dire* to say, tell, *spiegare* to explain, *significare* to mean:

> *Si dice che oggi l'immagine conti / conta più della parola.*
> It is said that today image counts more than words.

> *Spiegò come fosse un grande filosofo.*
> He explained that he was a great philosopher.

> *Questo non significa che fosse / era ottuso.*
> This does not mean he / she was thick.

But if the main verb denotes certainty the subordinate clause requires the indicative. Compare:

> *Dico che non è vero.*
> I say it isn't true.

> *Sono sicura che non è vero.*
> I'm sure it is not true.

> *Non sono sicura che non sia vero.*
> I'm not sure that it isn't true.

(viii) Verbs giving or refusing permission or giving advice such as:

> *permettere* to permit
> *dare il permesso* to give permission
> *lasciare* to allow
> *raccomandare* to recommend
> *consentire* to consent
> *trovarsi d'accordo* to agree
> *suggerire* to suggest
> *proporre* to propose
> *impedire* to prevent
> *proibire* to forbid

> *La legge non permette che le discoteche restino aperte dopo le tre.*
> The law does not allow discotheques to stay open after three a.m.

(ix) Some of the above verbs requiring the subjunctive in the subordinate clause may alternatively be followed by an infinitive construction:

> *Raccomanda a Giuseppe che vada adagio.*
> *Raccomanda a Giuseppe di andare adagio.*
> Advise / warn Giuseppe to go slowly.

(c) Impersonal expressions requiring the subjunctive

(i) *È* + adjective (masculine singular) is followed by the subjunctive unless the adjective indicates certainty: *è necessario, opportuno, possibile, probabile, importante, bello* it is necessary, suitable, possible, probable, important, good or *non è vero, non è sicuro, non è certo* it is not true, not certain. Compare:

> *Non è vero che il nostro debito nazionale sia così alto.*
> It isn't true that our national debt is as high as that.

> *È vero che il nostro debito nazionale è così alto.*
> It is true that our national debt is as high as that.

N.B. Note that the subjunctive is required even if the *è* + adjectival clause is postponed:

> *Che venga o che non venga – è lo stesso.*
> Whether she comes or whether she doesn't – it is all the same.

and also with expressions which are equivalent in meaning to *è* + adjective:

> *In base all'assurda idea che l'istruzione non debba / deve essere per tutti . . . =*
> *È assurdo che l'istruzione non debba essere per tutti.*
> On the basis of the absurd idea that education must not be for everybody . . .

(ii) Impersonal phrases such as:

> *bastare* it is enough
> *bisognare* it is necessary
> *occorre* one needs
> *è bene, è peccato* it's a pity
> *è una vergogna* it's a shame
> *non importa* it doesn't matter
> *può darsi* it may be

or equivalent expressions, require the subjunctive:

> *A lui bastava che i treni arrivassero in orario.*
> It was sufficient for him that the trains arrived on time.

> *È d'accordo con la necessità che si vada alle urne.*
> He agrees with the need to go to the polls. (literally: the poll booths)

> *Bisogna ricordare quale fosse / era il dolore della famiglia.*
> One has to remember what the family's grief was like.

(d) Conjunctions requiring the subjunctive

The following conjunctions, when followed by a verb, require the subjunctive mood:

(i) *prima che* before + verb and *senza che* without + verb:

> *Voglio finire prima che i nostri ospiti arrivino.*
> I want to finish before our guests arrive.

> *Tornò a casa senza che lo sentissi.*
> He returned home but I didn't hear him / without my hearing him.

N.B. This construction is used only when the subject of the main clause is different from that of the subordinate clause. If the subjects of the two clauses are the same, *prima* and *senza* are followed by the infinitive (see section 63b):

> *Voglio finire prima di ricevere gli ospiti.*
> I want to finish before I receive my guests.

> *Tornai a casa senza disturbare nessuno.*
> I returned home without disturbing anybody.

(ii) *Finchè, finchè non* (the *non* is optional) may take the subjunctive if the action refers to a future time:

> *Lo tormenterà finché cederà.*
> She will torment him until he gives in.

(iii) Conjunctions of concession:

> *benchè, sebbene* though, although
> *anche se, quand'anche, seppure* even if
> *quantunque* notwithstanding
> *malgrado che* despite the fact
> *per quanto* no matter how

> *Lo amo benchè abbia un pessimo carattere.*
> I love him even though he has an awful temperament.

> *Anche se non venisse, non cadrebbe il mondo.*
> Even if he didn't come, it wouldn't be the end of the world.

(iv) Conjunctions of purpose and result:

> *affinchè* so that
> *perchè* so that
> *in modo che* in order that
> *onde, acciocchè* < formal literary > so that

Stanno facendo tutto il possibile affinchè la gente smetta di fumare.
They are doing everything possible to make people stop smoking.
(literally: so that people stop smoking.)

(v) Conjunctions of condition:
purchè provided that
a patto che so long as
a condizione che on condition that

Gli ho regalato questo cucciolo a condizione che lo chiamasse Fuffi.
I gave him this puppy as a present on condition that he called him Fuffi.

(vi) Conjunctions indicating a limit:
a meno che unless
non . . . che only
eccetto che, salvo che barring the fact that

Ce la farò a meno che non ci sia un ingorgo.
I'll make it unless there is a traffic jam.

(vii) Conjunctions indicating comparisons:
come se as if
quasi as if

Agisce come se nulla fosse.
He is behaving as if nothing were happening.

Portava le minigonne quasi fosse tornata una ragazzina.
She was wearing miniskirts as if she were a little girl again.

(e) The subjunctive with superlatives and comparatives

(i) The superlative structure *il più, il meno* the most, the least + adjective + verb, or adjectives such as *il migliore* the best, *il peggiore* the worst, *il primo* the first, *l'ultimo* the last, *il solo, l'unico* the only one, require the subjunctive:

È stata la più bella vacanza che abbia mai fatto.
It's the best holiday I have ever had.

Per me è l'unico che sappia interpretare Shakespeare.
For me he is the only one who knows how to act in Shakespeare.

(ii) The subjunctive is also necessary in constructions involving a comparative form + verb, *più di* ('more than') + verb, *meno di* ('less than') + verb:

> *È meno utile di quanto si creda.*
> It's less useful than one thinks.

(f) The subjunctive with indefinites

(i) The subjunctive is used in subordinate clauses introduced by indefinite adjectives or pronouns:

> *chiunque* whoever
> *qualunque* whatever
> *qualunque cosa* whatever
> *comunque, in qualunque modo* however, no matter how
> *per quanto* no matter how
> *per quanti / e* no matter how many
> *per* + adjective + *che* no matter how
> *dovunque* wherever

> *Chiunque calunni / calunnia è un vigliacco.*
> Anyone who slanders is a coward.

> *Qualunque fosse la sua posizione è stato maleducato.*
> Whatever his position, he has been rude.

> *Per caro che sia va a ruba.*
> No matter how expensive it is, it sells very well.

(ii) Indefinite articles, *un, uno, una* a, an, and pronouns *qualcuno* someone, *qualcosa* something are also followed by the subjunctive:

> *Cerco qualcosa che vada bene con questo cappotto.*
> I'm looking for something that goes with this coat.

> *Vorrei comprare un ombrello che stia in questa valigia.*
> I would like to buy an umbrella which would fit into this suitcase.

(g) The subjunctive with the hypothetical 'if'

(i) *Se* (if), *quando, qualora* and *dove* when they mean 'in case' are followed by the imperfect or pluperfect subjunctive when the main clause has, respectively, a present conditional or a past conditional verb (see also section 140k):

Che cosa faresti se avessi dieci miliardi?
What would you do if you had ten billion?

Che cosa avresti fatto se avessi avuto dieci miliardi?
What would you have done if you had had ten billion?

N.B. The conditional in the main sentence may be implied:

Se solo sapessi dove l'ho messo! (implied: *farei . . .*)
If only I knew where I put it! (I would do . . .)

(Sarebbero) Guai se fosse veramente così.
There would be problems if it were really like this.

(ii) But *se* is followed by the indicative and not by the subjunctive if it emphasizes the time more than the hypothesis:

Se fa bello andiamo in spiaggia = quando fa bello andiamo in spiaggia.
If it is nice we go to the beach.

Se fa / farà bello andremo in spiaggia.
If it is nice we'll go to the beach.

(iii) The use of the imperfect after *se* is characteristic of colloquial Italian, though not infrequent.

Se era in ritardo telefonava. <coll.>
If she was late she would phone.

The more correct sequence of tenses would be:

Se fosse stata in ritardo avrebbe telefonato.
Has she been late she would have rung.

60 The imperative

(a)

The forms of the imperative are the following:

	avere to have	*essere* to be
(tu)	abbi	sii
(lei)	abbia	sia
(noi)	abbiamo	siamo
(voi)	abbiate	siate
(loro)	abbiano	siano

	lavorare to work	*prendere* to take	*sentire* to listen	*finir*
(tu)	lavora	prendi	senti	finis
(lei)	lavori	prenda	senta	finis
(noi)	lavoriamo	prendiamo	sentiamo	finia
(voi)	lavorate	prendete	sentite	finit
(loro)	lavorino	prendano	sentano	finis

- The *noi* imperative form is the equivalent of the English 'let us' + verb.
- The *lei / loro* forms are borrowed from the subjunctive to convey formal invitations and requests (see section 58a).

> *Sia gentile signora, mi lasci passare.*
> Would you be so kind as to let me through, please.

(b) The negative imperative

Prohibitions are formulated by placing *non* before the imperative forms except with *tu*. In this case prohibition is conveyed with *non* + the infinitive:

Non essere così impaziente, Luisa. Don't be so impatient, Louise.

(c) Imperative with subject pronouns

The subject pronoun is introduced either to emphasize the command to a specific person or to clarify who has to carry out the request:

Loredana, porta tu questa borsa.
Loredana, can <u>you</u> take this handbag, please.

Rispondi tu, per favore. Can <u>you</u> answer, please.

(d) Imperative with object pronouns

(i) Direct and indirect object pronouns (single or in combination) and *ci* and *ne* are added to the end of the imperative to form one word. The position of the stress does not change (see sections 31–33 and 35):

Descrivimelo. Describe it to me.
Parlacene. Talk to us about it / them.

But for the *lei* form direct and indirect object pronouns go before the imperative:

Signora Lucchini, gli ritelefoni. Mrs Lucchini, ring him up again.

(ii) When a pronoun is added to the imperative *tu* forms of *andare* to go, *dare* to give, *dire* to say, *fare* to make, and *stare* to stay, you must double the initial letter of the pronoun, except for *gli*:

Và / vacci domani. Go there tomorrow.
Dammi un bacio. Give me a kiss.
Dammene uno anche a me. Give one to me too.
Di' / dille di no. Say no to her.
Fa / facci un buon caffè. Make us a good coffee.
Sta / stalle vicino. Be close to her.

But

Digli di sì. Tell him yes.

(iii) With the negative imperative, the pronoun may be positioned either before or after the verb:

> *Non trattenerla troppo a lungo.*
> *Non la trattenere troppo a lungo.*
> Don't keep her for too long.
>
> *Non la firmi, per cortisia.* Would you please not sign it?

With the *lei* and *loro* forms the pronouns always precede the verb:

> *Non lo prenoti così presto. Dr Franchi.*
> Don't book it so early, Dr Franchi.

(iv) Reflexive pronouns follow the same rules as other object pronouns:

> *Servitevi.* Help yourselves.
> *Non stancarti troppo.* Don't get too tired.

61 Uses of the imperative

(a) In speech

(i) Exhortation:

> *Prendi un caffè.* Do have a coffee.   *Proviamo.* Let's try.

(ii) Invitation:

> *Si accomodi.* Please take a seat.
> *Guarda che bello!* Look how nice it is!

The tone of command may be softened with the addition of *pure* after the verb:

> *Entri pure, signora.* Madam, please come in.

(iii) Requests, orders, commands

In these contexts the imperative is addressed to children and to people with whom one has very close links. The tone of direct command can be softened by words such as *per favore, per piacere* (on how to make requests see section 86):

> *Sii gentile con lui, per piacere.* Be kind to him, please.
>
> *Abbia la cortesia di farmi passare, per favore.*
> Let me go through, please.

Ci porti l'olio per favore.
Can you bring us the oil, please? (in a restaurant)

(iv) It is found in the course of animated discussions:

Lascia perdere. Forget about it.   *Calmati.* Calm down.

(b) In writing

The imperative is used in the following ways in written Italian.

(i) In standard expressions in commercial correspondence:

Vogliate spedire . . . Please send . . .
Voglia gradire i nostri più cordiali saluti Yours sincerely / faithfully.

(ii) In advertisements and political slogans:

Sorridi alla vita con il rossetto Alfa. Smile at life with Alfa lipstick.
Votate per il Partito della Felicità. Vote for the Happiness Party.

(iii) In newspapers and magazines to address readers in an informal
way or to address one reader who has asked advice:

Cari lettori . . . non fatevi ingannare dalle promesse di questo governo.
Dear readers . . . don't be deceived by the promises of this
government.

Gentile lettrice, metta dei geranei sul balcone . . . .
Dear Mrs . . ., why don't you put some geraniums on the balcony . . . .

(iv) In handbooks and recipe books. This style can also be used
figuratively, for instance, in literary criticism:

*Si prendano due grandi paradigmi culturali, come quello del gioco
e quello del viaggio. Si accostino in un titolo. Poi si ponga
quest'ultimo . . . (Loredana Polezzi, Introduzione a Lady Bell,
Piccolo manuale di giochi per viaggiatori, Sellerio, Palermo, 1990)*
I invite you to / Let's take two major cultural paradigms, playing
and travelling. Let's place them side by side in the title of a book.
Then let's put the title . . .

(v) The imperative is also used in essays and reports to introduce
examples or evidence:

Si prenda il caso di . . . Let's take the case of . . .
Si consideri . . . Let's consider . . .

62 The modals: *dovere*, *potere* and *volere*

Dovere, potere and *volere* have a variety of meanings:

> *dovere* must, has to, should, ought to
> *potere* can, could, to be able to
> *volere* to want, to wish, would like

All three are irregular (see Appendix 1). They function on their own or govern another verb:

> *Non vado perchè non posso.* I'm not going because I can't.
> *Dovrebbe partire tra un'ora.* She should leave in an hour.

(a) Modal verbs in compound tenses

(i) If used on their own they usually form compound tenses with *avere*.

(ii) If followed by a verb, modals require the auxiliary of that verb. If it is *essere*, *dovuto*, *potuto* and *voluto* agree in gender and number with the subject. If it is *avere* they don't change unless there is a direct object pronoun preceding the verb, in which case they agree with it (see section 64d).

> *Ha dovuto comprare un'auto di seconda mano.*
> He has had to buy a second-hand car.
>
> *Non è potuta partire prima.*
> She could not leave before.
>
> *L'ho dovuta comprare a rate.*
> I had to purchase it by instalments.

(iii) Note that when the modal is followed by *essere*, the auxiliary required is *avere*:

> *Non ho potuto essere d'accordo.* I could not agree.

(iv) With reflexive verbs two constructions are possible. Either the reflexive pronoun precedes the modal and the past participle changes accordingly, or the pronoun is attached to the end of the infinitive and the past participle does not change:

> *Maria si è dovuta alzare. / Maria ha dovuto alzarsi.*
> Maria had to get up.

(b) Modals with the infinitive

Object and reflexive pronouns may precede the modal verb or be attached to the infinitive following it. Note that in the second case the infinitive drops the last vowel:

> *L'avrei voluta aprire. (= Avrei voluto aprirla.)*
> I would have liked to open it.

(c) *dovere*

Dovere has several meanings which are conveyed by 'must', 'have to', 'had to', 'should', 'ought to', 'to be to', 'to be supposed to', 'to be bound to', 'to need', 'to be due'. For 'should' as part of the conditional tense, see sections 56 and 57a.

(i) Essentially *dovere* is used to indicate:

● A sense of necessity, which may be objective or subjective, or an official requirement (the present or future of *dovere*):

> *Devo / dovrei tornare a casa perchè è tardi.*
> I must / should go back home because it's late.

> *Dovevo / Avrei dovuto riposare, secondo il dottore.*
> I had to / should have rested, according to the doctor.

> *Secondo la legge dovrò andare in pensione tra due anni.*
> By law I will have to retire in three years' time.

● Moral obligation (the present or conditional of *dovere*):

> *La società deve / dovrebbe provvedere anche al benessere dei meno privilegiati.*
> Society must / ought also to take care of the less well off.

● Probability, possibility (the conditional or subjunctive of *dovere* in subordinate clauses):

> *Mi sembra che debba piovere.* I think it's going to rain.

> *I giornali scrivono che dovrebbe essere assolto.*
> Newspapers write that he should / is likely to be acquitted.

● An opinion strongly felt (the conditional of *dovere*)

> *I due partiti dovrebbero sedersi a un tavolo e discutere.*
> The two political parties should / ought to sit round a table and talk.

- Likelihood (the conditional of *dovere*)

    Dovrebbero trovare un accordo questa settimana.
    They should reach an agreement this week.

- An objective forecast (the present or past indicative of *dovere*):

    Questa recessione deve / doveva essere seguita da una ripresa economica.
    This recession has to be / must be / was to be followed by an economic recovery.

- Expectations about the future and the past (conditional of *dovere*)

    L'esperimento dovrebbe avere successo.
    The experiment ought to be successful.

    L'esperimento avrebbe dovuto avere successo.
    The experiment ought to / should have been successful.

- It indicates that something which was anticipated or expected did not happen (the past conditional of *dovere*):

    Avrebbero dovuto finire il lavoro.
    They should / ought to have finished the work.

- That something is morally, ethically or professionally wrong (the past conditional of *dovere*):

    Non doveva / avrebbe dovuto imbrogliare.
    He should / ought not have cheated.

(ii) In conversations

It is frequently used in conversations to express:

- An intuition which is more or less certain (the present or conditional of *dovere*):

    Ma devi essere la ragazza di Matteo!
    But you must be Matthew's girlfriend!

    Dovrebbe mancare un'ora a Milano.
    It should take one hour to Milan.

- The unavoidability of an action (the present or past indicative of *dovere*):

    Devo risponderle oggi. I must / I have to reply to her today.

    Doveva risponderle lunedì. He had to reply on Monday.

● It is also used to urge someone to do something, to make heart-felt suggestions to a listener with whom one is on close terms (the present or conditional of *dovere*):

> *Devi affittare quell'appartamento. È un affare.*
> You must rent that flat. It's a bargain.
>
> *Dovresti prendere un sonnifero.*
> You should take a sleeping pill.

● To state with firmness that something is the case (the present or past indicative of *dovere*):

> *Deve essere così. / Non può essere che così.* It has to be like that.
>
> *Doveva essere così.* It had to be like that.

● To check that something is appropriate (the present indicative or conditional of *dovere*):

> *Devo / Dovrei invitarla?* Should I invite her?

● That something is due or is bound to happen (the present indicative or conditional of *dovere*):

> *L'aereo da Berlino non deve / dovrebbe atterrare alle 8 precise?*
> Isn't the plane from Berlin due to arrive at exactly 8 o'clock?
>
> *Deve per forza passare di qui se viene in auto.*
> He is bound to pass this way if he comes by car.

● To offer help (the present of *dovere*):

> *Devo chiudere la porta? / Chiudo la porta?* < less emphatic >
> Shall I close the door?

(iii) In reported speech

With verbs such as *dire* to say, *sapere* to know, *credere* to think, *confermare* to confirm, *dovere* is in the perfect indicative if the tone is informal, in the conditional if the tone is more formal:

> *Il Ministro degli Esteri ha confermato che doveva / avrebbe dovuto ritornare in Israele.*
> The Foreign Minister has confirmed that he had to go back to Israel.

However, in reported speech that depends on verbs of suggestion, advice or recommendation, the subjunctive is sufficient to convey the idea of obligation. No form of *dovere* should be added:

> *Ha chiesto che l'incontro finisca entro domani.*
> He asked that the meeting should finish by tomorrow.

> *L'insegnante consigliò che si ritirasse.*
> The teacher advised that he should withdraw.

(iv) In conditional clauses

In conditional clauses, the use of the subjunctive often suffices to convey 'should'. However, *dovere* may be used to emphasize the potentiality of the hypothesis:

> *Se dichiarassero uno sciopero generale, il governo si dimetterebbe.*
> Should they declare a general strike, the government would resign.

> *Se dovessero dichiarare uno sciopero, il governo si dimetterebbe.*
> If they were to declare a strike, the government would resign.

(v) Further cases where the idea of 'should' or 'must' is not expressed explicitly in Italian:

● When something is certain to happen, the expression *non può che* is preferred:

> *L'introduzione della benzina senza piombo non può che portare a un minore inquinamento.*
> The introduction of lead-free petrol must lead to less pollution.

● When one wants to add a persuasive tone to an invitation, *mi fa / farebbe molto piacere se* is used:

> *Mi fa piacere se accetti questa pianta / mi farebbe molto piacere se accettassi.*
> Please (you must) accept this plant from me.

● When introducing one's own opinion or apology tactfully, one may start with *vorrei* or a conditional form or convey the idea of likelihood in the subordinate clause:

> *Vorrei scusarmi.* I must apologize.

> *Inizierei con il sottolineare che . . .*
> I ought to start by stressing that . . .

> *Penserei / direi che dovrebbe durare a lungo.*
> I should think that it would last quite a while.

(vi) In other phrases expressing necessity or requirements

andare + past participle

● To inform of legal regulations:

> *I moduli vanno ritirati in banca.*
> The forms must be collected from the bank.

● To indicate what one thinks are necessary solutions:

> *Per accellerare l'unificazione europea vanno sviluppati la qualità e la quantità degli scambi.*
> To accelerate European unification the quality and quantity of the exchanges need to be improved.

● To give indications or warnings about using appliances. The impersonal verb *bisognare* is also used:

> *La stampante del computer non va mai lasciata accesa.*
> The computer printer must never be left switched on.

> *Prima di tutto bisogna accertarsi che le batterie siano cariche.*
> First of all you need to make sure the batteries are charged.

● In a speech or an essay to introduce a point:

> *Va ricordato . . .*   It must be remembered
> *Va notato . . . che*   Notice that
> *Va tenuto presente . . .*   Bear in mind that

avere da + infinitive

> *Hanno da fare il bilancio.*
> They must prepare the budget.

c'è da / ci sono da + infinitive

> *C'è da osservare la capacità di reazione dei titoli.*
> One ought to pay attention to how shares will react.

venire da + infinitive

> *Viene da chiedersi come funziona il mercato delle aste.*
> One must wonder / wonders how the auction market works.

(d) *potere*

Potere corresponds to 'may, can, could, might, to be able to, to be allowed, to be possible, to manage to, to succeed'.

(i) Generally *potere* expresses:

- Moral, practical or legal power or the possibility of doing something:

    Sua madre può risposarsi se vuole.
    His mother can remarry if she wants to.

    Alla gara non possono partecipare i minorenni.
    Teenagers cannot take part in the competition.

    Se volessero, potrebbero comprare una casa nuova.
    If they wished they could buy a new house.

- The physical or intellectual ability to achieve something:

    Potrebbe scalare quella montagna, se volesse.
    She could climb that mountain, if she wished.

- To stress the possibility of being able to have or do something:

    In una giornata senza nuvole si possono vedere persino le Alpi.
    In a cloudless day even the Alps can be seen.

But if one does not wish to emphasize the possibility, *potere* is usually left out.

    Da qui si vedono le Alpi. One can see the Alps from here.

- An opportunity to do something:

    In Italia si possono mandare i bambini all'asilo a tre anni.
    In Italy children can go to nursery school when they are three years old.

- Probability, which can also be expressed by *può darsi* or *forse*:

    L'anno prossimo potreste avere / può darsi che abbiate lo stesso professore.
    You could / might have the same teacher next year.

- In comparisons:

    L'organizzazione non avrebbe potuto essere migliore.
    The organization could not have been better.

- Possibility in the future:

    Quel trattato potrebbe rivelarsi decisivo.
    That treaty could be decisive.

- Uncertainty about the past:

    Quel terrorista avrebbe potuto causare una carneficina.
    That terrorist could have caused total carnage.

(ii) In reported speech, it expresses ability, possibility, permission:

    Ritengono che la carestia avrebbe potuto essere evitata.
    They reckon that famine could have been avoided.

    Ha detto che per oggi potresti fare a meno del registratore.
    He said you could do without the tape-recorder for today.

    Hanno riferito che ci potrebbero essere ulteriori tagli.
    They reported that there could be further cuts.

(iii) In speech, forms of *potere* are found in expressions of courtesy:

- To offer assistance:

    Posso aiutarti ad apparecchiare? / Ti aiuto ad apparecchiare?
    Can / May I help you to lay the table?

- To ask for assistance:

    Carla, mi puoi aiutare / mi aiuti?
    Carla, can you help me please?

Note that in expressions of courtesy the insertion of *potere* frequently is redundant and that it is better to omit it.

- To comment on what people could / should do:

    Potrebbero tenere meglio il giardino.
    They could keep the garden tidier.

- To ask a question with irony:

    Si può sapere dove vai?
    And where are you going? / Might one ask where you are going?

- To express incredulity:

    Ma non possono bombardare una delle più belle città del mondo!
    I can't believe they will bomb one of the most beautiful towns in the world!

    Non può avere scritto questo! He can't have written this!

- To ask for and grant permission:

    Potete pagare con la carta di credito.
    You can / may pay by credit card.

    Potrei usare il bagno? Could / May I use the bathroom?

- To check whether something is harmful:

  Si può bere quest'acqua? Can one drink this water?

- In understatements or when one wishes to play down one's opinions, although Italians prefer to be more straightforward and tend to use *potere* rarely. They choose instead *forse*, the future or the present of the main verb:

  Come va? How are you?

  Non mi lamento. / Non mi posso lamentare. I can't complain.

  Potrebbe avere quarant'anni. / Avrà quarant'anni.
  She may be forty.

  Va aggiunto che . . . It may be added that . . .

  Forse ha agito con troppa impulsività.
  You might say she acted too impulsively.

  Hai perfettamente ragione. / Sono d'accordissimo con te.
  You couldn't be more right. / I couldn't agree with you more.

  Potrebbe essere una buona idea andare / Buona idea andare là per il week-end.
  It might be a good idea to go there for the week-end.

  Sarebbe meglio portare un'altra bottiglia di vino, no?
  Might it be wise to bring another bottle of wine?

- Note the difference between *potere, sapere* and *riuscire*:

  Oggi non posso nuotare perchè non ho il bikini.
  Today I can't swim because I haven't got my bikini (<u>lack of opportunity</u>).

  Sai nuotare? Io sì.
  Can you swim? I can. (<u>skill</u>)

  Non riesco a pronunciare questa parola.
  I can't pronounce this word. (<u>inability to succeed</u>)

- *tanto vale . . .* translates 'one may as well':

  Tanto vale che lo mangi tutto.
  You may as well eat it all.

(e) *volere*

(i) *Volere* corresponds to the English 'to want', 'to wish', 'would like', 'to have the intention':

> *Vorrebbero trovare un lavoro.*
> They would like to find a job.

> *Non so che cosa volevano fare.*
> I don't know what they intended to do.

> *Voleva iniziare una raccolta di libri d'arte.*
> She wanted to start an art book collection.

> *Avrebbe voluto curarsi con l'agopuntura.*
> She would have liked to be treated with acupuncture.

> *Voleva che andassimo da loro la domenica.*
> She wanted us to go there on Sunday.

> *Augusto volle che Cleopatra fosse trattata come una regina.*
> Augustus wanted Cleopatra to be treated like a queen.

(ii) As the above examples show, *volere*, like other verbs of volition, desire and suggestion, has two constructions:

- *volere* + *che* + **subjunctive** is required when the main and the subordinate clauses have two different subjects.

- *volere* + **infinitive** is used when they have the same subject.

(iii) *Vorrei* ('I would like') takes the same constructions as *volere* above:

> *Vorrei che fosse sempre bel tempo.*
> I would like the weather to be good all the time.

> *Avrei voluto nascere più ottimista.*
> I would have liked to be born more optimistic.

(iv) volere translating 'would':

● When 'would not' describes unwillingness to do something or refusal to do it:

> *Non volevano accettare la realtà.*
> They would not accept reality.

> *Non voleva accettare l'assegno dopo il litigio.*
> She would not accept the cheque after the quarrel.

★ Note that 'would', when used to describe a regular event in the past, is translated by the imperfect tense (section 50a) and in reported speech its meaning is conveyed with the conditional (section 57).

● The following are cases of understatement or tactful approach where 'would' is <u>not</u> conveyed with a form of *volere*:

> *Penso che sia d'accordo con me che la politica internazionale è influenzata da problemi etnici.*
> I think you would agree that international politics are influenced by ethnic relations.

> *Immagino che non lo conosci.*
> You wouldn't know him, would you?

> *Sandra, portami quei fascicoli per favore.*
> Sandra, I would like you to get me those files.

(v) Some expressions with *volere*:

> *voler dire* to mean:
> *Che cosa vuol dire?* What does it mean?

> *voler bene* to be fond of, to love:
> *Ti voglio bene.* I love you.

> *volerci* to be required:
> *Ci vuole pazienza con i bambini.*
> One needs patience with children.

63 The infinitive

(a) Forms

(i) Verbs are given in dictionaries in the **present infinitive form**, which has three endings: **-are** indicating verbs of the first conjugation, **-ere** of the second and **-ire** of the third, e.g. *recitare* to play on the stage, *scegliere* to choose, *influire* to influence.

(ii) **The perfect infinitive** is formed with the infinitive of *essere* or *avere* (auxiliary) + the past participle: *essere fermato* to have stopped, *avere ottenuto* to have obtained. The perfect infinitive is required every time the action it describes has taken place before the action of the main sentence:

> *Mi ricordo di aver passato la luna di miele qui.*
> I remember having spent / spending the honeymoon here.

(iii) Object pronouns follow the infinitive and form a single word with it after the last *-e* of the infinitive is dropped:

> *Vorrei dirglielo.* I would like to tell him that.

(iv) With perfect infinitives of reflexive and reciprocal verbs, the reflexive pronoun is attached to *essere* and the past participle agrees in gender and number with the subject:

> *Sono uscita senza essermi truccata, stamattina.*
> I went out without any make-up this morning.

(b) Uses

Both the present and perfect infinitive can be used in main and subordinate clauses, and as nouns.

(i) The infinitive in main clauses

● The infinitive is used in public notices, recipe books, manuals, to give official directions, regulations or commercial instructions:

> *Prendere una pillola dopo i pasti.*
> Take one pill after meals.
>
> *Lasciare cuocere il riso dieci minuti.*
> Let the rice cook for ten minutes.
>
> *Non sporgersi dal finestrino.*
> Do not lean out of the window.

● To express a negative order or recommendation, the infinitive provides the *tu* form of the imperative (see section 60b):

> *Non ritornare tardi.* Don't be late back.

● When giving examples, *per non parlare di . . .* not to mention / let alone . . . is used:

> *Non mi piace la musica rock, per non parlare poi di quella pop.*
> I don't like rock music, let alone pop.

● In narrative / rhetorical style it is used after *ecco*:

> *D'un tratto ecco ricomparire il delfino.*
> All of a sudden here was the dolphin again.

Or with questions or exclamations expressing anger, doubt or hypothesis:

> *Che fare? Dipendere da loro? Mai.*
> What was I to do? Depend on them? Never.

> *Pensare che mi avrebbero trattata così.*
> To think they would treat me like that!

(ii) In a subordinate clause

● It is used after *è* + adjective when the subject of the verb in the subordinate clause is undefined. If the subject is specified the infinitive is replaced by *che* + subjunctive (see section 59b). Compare:

> *È piacevole passeggiare oggi.*
> It is a pleasant day to go for a walk.

> *Non sarebbe più logico che venissero qua loro?*
> Wouldn't it make more sense if they came here?

● After *che* + adjective in exclamations:

> *Che bello stare a prendere il sole!* How nice to lie out in the sunshine!

● After modals, impersonal verbs, verbs of perception, verbs of desire, wish, preference and promise, and *fare*:

> *Mi piace ascoltare la musica la sera.* I like to listen to music in the evenings.

N.B. But the infinitive can only be used if its implied subject is the same as that of the main clause. Alternatively the construction is: main clause + *che* + subjunctive (see section 59b):

> *Speriamo di vincere qualcosa.* Let's hope we win something.

Speriamo che vincano qualcosa. Let's hope they win something.

● In sentences introducing an aim or a purpose: *per* + infinitive:

Ho trenta giorni per decidere. I have thirty days to decide.

Mi mancano tre esami per laurearmi.
I still need to take three exams to get my degree.

● The infinitive is preceded by *da* when it indicates that something can be done or ought to be done:

Che cosa c'è da vedere in questo paesino?
What is there to see / to be seen / worth seeing in this village?

È una strada da evitare.
It's a road to avoid / to be avoided / that should be avoided.

● Or in result clauses with *così / abbastanza / tanto . . . da* + infinitive or *troppo . . . per*:

Faceva così caldo da non riuscire a stare fuori.
It was so hot that it was impossible to stay outside.

Sono troppo stanco per andare a cena fuori.
I am too tired to go out to dinner.

In indirect questions introduced by *come, chi, che cosa*:

Non ho fatto scelte su come comportarmi.
I did not make any choice about how to behave.

Non so che cosa mettere.
I don't know what to wear.

(iii) Prepositions + infinitive

These prepositions are followed by the infinitive if the subject of their clause is the same as that of the main clause:

dopo after	*piuttosto di* rather than
invece di instead of	*senza* without
oltre a apart from	
prima di before	

È morto prima di vedere il suo paese in una guerra civile.
He (has) died before seeing his country involved in civil war.

Non riesco a vedere senza mettermi gli occhiali.
I can't see without putting on my glasses.

Dopo always requires the perfect infinitive:

Dopo aver bevuto questo buon boccale di birra mi sento meglio.
After drinking a good glass of beer I feel better.

(iv) Verbs, adjectives, nouns + a / di + infinitive (see section 18)

Some verbs require *a* before the infinitive, other verbs require *di*:

Ha solo cercato di essere se stesso. He has only tried to be himself.

In quella battuta è riuscito a concentrare tutta la sua ironia.
He has managed to concentrate all his irony in that joke.

(v) Infinitives as nouns

Verbs in the present or perfect infinitive form can act as nouns:

● In this role the infinitive may be preceded by an article, a possessive or an adjective. The gender of the infinitive-noun is always masculine:

Lo stadio era un allegro sventolare di bandiere.
The stadium was a cheerful sea (literally: waving) of flags.

L'essere fotografato vicino a quel delinquente non ha aiutato la sua carriera politica.
Being photographed next to that criminal has not helped his political career.

Il suo crescere la turbava.
The fact that he was growing up was upsetting her.

● The present infinitive can be used as subject of the clause or as a complement:

Fu svegliato dal gridare dei bambini.
He was woken up by the children shouting.

Nel ritornare a casa sono caduta.
I fell over on my way home.

64 Present and past participles and compound tenses

(a) The present participle

To form the present participle the following endings are added to the stem of the verb: *-ante* for the first conjugation, *-ente* for the second and third conjugations.

It is a form of the verb not frequently used. It replaces a relative clause:

Era una voce fremente di rabbia = Era una voce che fremeva di rabbia.
It was a voice trembling with rage.

Nowadays in most cases the present participle acts as an adjective:

> *una donna attraente* an attractive woman
> *una voce tonante* a thundering voice
> *un'esperienza interessante e divertente* an interesting and
>   entertaining experience
> *occhi sorridenti* smiling eyes
> *un pubblico pagante* a fee-paying audience
> *un albero morente* a dying tree
> *un attimo fuggente* a fleeting moment

Sometimes it acts as a noun:

> *gli aspiranti* the candidates
> *il flottante* floating funds < financial >

(b) The past participle and compound tenses

(i) The past participle is formed by dropping the ending of the infinitive, *-are, -ere, -ire,* and adding respectively *-ato* (first conjugation), *-uto* (second conjugation) and *-ito* (third conjugation). For irregular forms see Appendix 1.

(ii) It is used to form all compound tenses with the auxiliary verbs *avere* or *essere*:

> *Ho avuto un incidente d'auto.* I have had a car accident.
> *Siamo stati via un mese.* We have been away for a month.
> *Ho mangiato troppo oggi.* I have eaten too much today.
> *È riuscito?* Has he succeeded?

Compound tenses are the following:

- the perfect or *passato prossimo: ho finito* I have finished
- the pluperfect or *imperfetto passato: avevo finito quando . . .*
  I had finished when . . .
- the past anterior: *quando ebbi finito* when I had finished . . .
- the future perfect: *quando avrò finito* when I('ll) have finished
- the conditional perfect: *avrei finito se . . .* I would have finished if . . .
- the perfect subjunctive: *pensa che io abbia finito* he thinks I have
  finished
- the pluperfect subjunctive: *pensava che io avessi finito* he thought
  I had finished
- the perfect infinitive: *che bello avere finito* how nice to have inished
- the past gerund: *avendo finito* having finished

(c) Pronouns with compound tenses

Object and reflexive pronouns generally precede compound tenses. With modals they can precede them or follow the infinitive:

> *Ho dovuto leggerlo velocemente = L'ho dovuto leggere velocemente.*
> I had to read it quickly.

With the past infinitive and past gerund the pronoun is attached to the end of the auxiliary, after dropping the final 'e' of the infinitive:

> *L'averlo saputo mi ha riempito di gioia.*
> Hearing it has filled me with joy. (literally: Having heard it . . .)
>
> *Avendoli persi devo comprare un altro paio di guanti.*
> I must buy another pair of gloves, having lost the others.

(d) The auxiliary verbs *essere* and *avere*

(i) Most verbs form compound tenses with the auxiliary *avere*.

(ii) If the auxiliary is *avere*, the past participle is invariable unless a direct object pronoun – *lo, la, l', li, le* and *ne* – precedes the verb.

> *Hai avuto molti regali?*
> Did you have a lot of presents?
>
> *Ne ho avuti pochi ma di valore.*
> I have had only a few but those I've had are valuable.
>
> *Ho bevuto una birra davvero buona.*
> I have drunk a really good beer.
>
> *Anch'io l'ho bevuta con piacere.*
> I too drank it with pleasure.
>
> *I tuoi amici li ho visti cinque minuti fa.*
> I saw your friends five minutes ago.

The past participle may agree with the object if the verb is preceded by a relative pronoun:

> *Come si chiama la signora che abbiamo incontrato / a?*
> What's the name of the woman we met?

Note that only the pronouns *lo* and *la* are contracted to *l'* before all the forms of *avere*.

(iii) The following verbs form their compound tenses with *essere* as auxiliary, and the past participle agrees in gender and number with the subject it refers to:

- *essere:*

  Scusa se sono stato noioso. I am sorry if I have been boring.

- Verbs in the passive form:

  La riunione è stata rimandata a domani.
  The meeting has been moved to tomorrow.

- Reflexive and reciprocal verbs (see section 37):

  Quando si è innamorati non si hanno problemi.
  When one is in love one has no problems.

  In questi ultimi anni la nostra atletica si è impoverita.
  In the last few years the quality of our athletics has declined.

  Si sono salutati con freddezza.
  They greeted each other coldly.

- Verbs accompanied by a reflexive pronoun to add emphasis (see section 37c). Compare:

  Ho comprato un piccolo gioiello.
  I have bought a small gem / piece of jewellery.

  Mi sono comprata un piccolo gioiello per il mio compleanno.
  I bought myself a small gem for my birthday.

- Certain verbs which often describe a physical or figurative movement and are not followed by a direct object:

  L'incendio è cominciato lì.
  The fire has started / started there.

  La gara è iniziata ieri.
  The competition started yesterday.

  Ne sono accadute di tutti i colori.
  All sorts of things have happened / happened.

- Impersonal verbs such as *capitare* to happen, *accadere* to occur, *bastare* to be sufficient, or verbs with the impersonal subject *si* one, people:

  È bastata la cipolla?
  Was there enough onion?

  Allora, di che cosa si è discusso?
  So, what has been discussed?

- Common verbs requiring *essere* when they are not followed by direct objects:

accadere to happen	*intervenire* to intervene
affogare to drown	*invecchiare* to grow old
ammontare to amount	*mancare* to be lacking
andare to go	*maturare* to ripen
andarsene to go away	*migliorare* to improve
apparire to appear	*morire* to die
appassire to wither	*nascere* to be born
arrivare to arrive	*parere* to seem
atterrare to land	*partire* to leave
aumentare to increase	*passare* to pass by
avanzare to advance	*peggiorare* to get worse
avvenire to happen	*penetrare* to penetrate
bastare to be enough	*piacere* to like
cadere to fall	*planare* to glide
capitare to befall	*prevalere* to prevail
cessare to cease	*restare* to stay
continuare to continue	*rientrare* to go back in
convenire to suit	*ringiovanire* to grow younger
correre to run	*risultare* to result
costare to cost	*riuscire* to succeed
crescere to grow	*salire* to go up
decollare to take off	*saltare* to jump
diminuire to decrease	*scappare* to run away
dipendere to depend	*scendere* to come down
dispiacere to be sorry	*scomparire* to disappear
divenire to become, grow (gradually)	*scoppiare* to explode
	seguire to follow
diventare to become, turn (suddenly)	*sembrare* to seem
	servire to serve
durare to last	*sfilare* to parade
emergere to emerge	*sfuggire* to escape
entrare to enter	*sorgere* to rise
esplodere to explode	*sparire* to disappear
essere to be	*stare* to stay
finire to finish	*subentrare* to take over
fiorire to flourish	*succedere* to happen
fuggire to run away	*sussistere* to exist
giacere to lie down	*svanire* to vanish
giungere to arrive	*svenire* to faint
guarire to recover	*terminare* to end
impazzire to go mad	*uscire* to go out
ingrassare to put on weight	*venire* to come
iniziare to start	*vivere* to live

(iv) The following categories of verbs can take either *essere* or *avere* as auxiliary:

● Verbs related to weather conditions:

> *Ha nevicato da voi? / È nevicato da voi?*
> Has it snowed where you live?

But expressions with *fare* require *avere*:

> *Che tempo ha fatto?* What has the weather been like?

● *dovere, potere, volere*, when followed by a verb in the infinitive, form the perfect tense with *essere* if this is the auxiliary which the verb usually requires:

> *È dimagrita parecchio!* She has slimmed down a lot!
> *Per forza! È dovuta dimagrire.* Of course! She had to.

However, *avere* is becoming equally acceptable and is widespread in both the written and spoken language:

> *Per forza! Ha dovuto dimagrire.*
> Of course! He had to slim.

● *dovere, potere, volere* always require *avere* when they are not followed by an infinitive:

> *Non ha voluto il té? No. Non l'ha voluto.*
> Didn't he want any tea? No. He didn't want any.

> *Non sei potuta andare a Londra? Mi dispiace. Non ho potuto.*
> Didn't you go to London? I'm sorry. I haven't been able to. /
> I couldn't.

● With *dovere, potere, volere* accompanying a reflexive verb there are two options (see section 62a):

> *Ha dovuto vestirsi di nero.*
> *Si è dovuta vestire di nero.*
> She had to dress in black.

As the examples show, with the auxiliary *avere* the reflexive pronoun must be attached to the end of the infinitive. With the auxiliary *essere* the reflexive pronoun must be placed before the auxiliary.

(v) Some verbs have two different meanings depending on whether they are used intransitively (no direct object follows) in which case they require *essere*, or transitively (a direct object follows) in which case they require *avere*:

> *Il suo lavoro è molto migliorato.* His work has improved a lot.
> *Ha molto migliorato il suo lavoro.* She has improved his work a lot.

(vi) The following intransitive verbs are nowadays used equally with *essere* or *avere*:

appartenere to belong	*è / ha appartenuto ai nonni* it belonged to the grandparents	
atterrare to land	*è / ha atterrato* it has landed	
avanzare to advance	*è / ha avanzato lentamente* he has advanced slowly	
brillare to twinkle	*è / ha brillato tutta la notte* it twinkled the whole night	
decollare to take off	*è / ha decollato* it has taken off	
durare to last	*è / ha durato anni* it has lasted for years	
echeggiare to echo	*è / ha echeggiato di applausi* it echoed with applause	
infuriare to rage	*il temporale è / ha infuriato* the storm raged	
planare to glide	*è / ha planato* it glided	
prevalere to prevail	*è / ha prevalso su tutti* he has prevailed on everybody	
ricorrere to appeal	*è / ha ricorso in Cassazione* he has appealed to the Supreme Court	
trasalire to be startled	*è / ha trasalito* he was startled	
vivere to live	*è / ha vissuto tre anni* he lived three years	

(vii) Some verbs of movement take *essere* when they refer to place and *avere* when they refer to time:

correre to run	*Siamo corsi alla stazione.* We ran to the station.	
	Abbiamo corso per un'ora. We ran for an hour.	
saltare to jump	*È saltato dall'albero.* It jumped from the tree.	
	Ha saltato su e giù per tutta l'ora. She jumped up and down for the whole hour.	
volare to fly	*È volato nel cielo.* It flew in the sky.	*Ha volato poco.* He has not flown a lot.

(viii) A few verbs change their meaning according to the auxiliary:

convenire to suit	*Gli è convenuto.* It suited him.	*Ha convenuto che . . .* He has agreed that . . .

procedere to proceed	*È proceduto bene.*
	It has gone well.
	Ha proceduto come d'accordo.
	She has behaved as agreed.
mancare to be missing	*È mancata l'acqua.*
	There was no water.
	Ha mancato di parola.
	He broke his word.

(e) The past participle used on its own

It is frequently used:

(i) In newspaper reports or in narrative as a more concise and elegant form instead of the past gerund or *dopo* + past infinitive:

> *Finita l'epoca del neorealismo cominciò quella degli spaghetti western = Dopo che fu finita . . . or Essendo finita . . .*
> After the neo-realist era was over, we had the spaghetti western.

(ii) To shorten a compound tense:

> *Rintanato nel suo studio, dipinse gli ultimi capolavori.*
> Confined in his study, he painted his last masterpieces.

It is frequently used in news headlines:

> *Distrutta dallo scandalo la campionessa? = È stata distrutta . . . ?*
> Has the champion (woman) been destroyed by the scandal?

(iii) To shorten relative sentences and create a more striking effect:

> *Innamorato del mare. È lui l'uomo protagonista =*
> *È lui che è innamorato del mare. È lui l'uomo protagonista.*
> In love with the sea. He is the hero.

> *A sessantanove anni, portati benissimo, è ancora popolarissimo.*
> At sixty-nine, not looking his age, he is still extremely popular.

(iv) As an adjective:

> *Ha pianto per la morte dell'amato-odiato rivale.*
> He has cried over the death of the rival whom he loved and hated.

(v) When the past participle is used on its own, reflexive and object pronouns are attached to the end of the past participle:

> *Rimessosi dallo shock ha ricominciato la campagna anti -nucleare.*
> After he recovered from the shock he started his anti-nuclear campaign again.

Baciatala, le diede il messaggio.
After kissing her, he gave her the message.

★ Note the unusual agreement. If the verb takes *avere* as its auxiliary, the past participle agrees in gender and number with the object:

Accettata la mela, Eva la offerse anche ad Adamo.
Having accepted the apple, Eve offered it to Adam as well.

But if the past participle takes *essere* as its auxiliary, it agrees with the subject:

Arrivati sulla spiaggia i due francesi decisero di fare una nuotata.
Once they arrived on the beach, the two French men decided to take a swim.

The past participle precedes its subject if this is different from that of the main sentence (i.e. an absolute clause):

Finita la cena, cominciarono a discutere di calcio.
Once dinner was over, they started to discuss football.

(vi) The past participle may be preceded by *appena*:

Appena ricevuto il fax, spedì la merce.
As soon as he had received the fax he sent off the goods.

65 The gerund

(a) Forms

The Italian gerund is formed by replacing the infinitive endings *-are*, *-ere*, *-ire* with **-ando** for the verbs of the first conjugation and **-endo** for the second and third conjugations. These endings are invariable.

sincronizzare sincronizzando synchronizing
esprimere esprimendo expressing
comparire comparendo appearing

(i) The present gerund expresses an action occurring at the same time as the action of the main clause. It may also describe an action which precedes a future action in the main clause:

Gli partì il colpo pulendo il fucile.
He fired a shot while cleaning his gun.

Non adoperando gli occhiali ti rovinerai la vista.
If you don't use glasses you'll ruin your eyes.

(ii) The **past gerund** is made up of *avendo* having or *essendo* being + the past participle. With *essendo*, the past participle agrees in gender and number with the subject:

> *Avendo finito il lavoro si addormentò.*
> Having finished work he fell asleep.

> *Essendo risultati sospetti i quadri non furono più venduti.*
> Being of dubious origin the paintings were no longer sold.

(iii) The **passive gerund** is made up of *essendo stato / a / i / e* plus the past participle agreeing in gender and number with the subject it refers to:

> *Essendo stata trasferita decise di cominciare una nuova vita.*
> Having been transferred she decided to start a new life.

(iv) Object, reflexive and reciprocal pronouns are attached to the end of the present gerund to form one word:

> *Esaminandola bene, trovo la situazione sempre più assurda.*
> Having examined it thoroughly, I find the situation more and more absurd.

> *Incontrandoci dopo tanti anni, ci siamo commossi.*
> Having met after many years, we were moved.

> *Sentendosi troppo sola, decise di rivolgersi ad un'agenzia matrimoniale.*
> Feeling very lonely, she decided to go to a dating agency.

(b) Uses

★ **(i)** The gerund in Italian can only refer to the subject:

> *Sfogliando il giornale ho visto l'annuncio della mostra su Mantegna.*
> Going through the newspaper I saw the announcement of the Mantegna exhibition. (While I was going through . . . I saw . . .)

> *La ragazza che vedevo tornando da scuola . . .*
> The girl I saw when I was walking back from school . . .
> ~~X The girl I saw when she was walking back from school. X~~

197

(ii) The above rule is sometimes broken in the following cases:

● When the gerund clause is linked to the main clause by a relationship of cause:

Avendo la mamma l'influenza, la bimba andò a stare dai nonni.
Since her mother had flu, the child went to stay with her grandparents.

● When the gerund refers to the subject of the relative sentence to which it is linked:

Il rumore spaventò la nonna che chiamò aiuto temendo i ladri.
The noise frightened Grannie, who fearing burglars called for help.

● When the subject of the gerund is impersonal:

Avendo nevicato molto la partita venne annullata.
As it had snowed a lot the match was cancelled.

La situazione era comica considerando chi erano i protagonisti della lite.
The situation was comic if one considers who was involved in the quarrel.

● With set phrases:

stando così le cose given the situation

il bilancio / il tempo permettendo
the budget / weather conditions permitting

strada facendo along the road.

● In colloquialisms, although (as in English) it is not considered grammatically correct:

Parlando con Sergio mi ha detto che sua figlia era stata promossa.
Talking to Sergio he told me his daughter had passed the exams.

(iii) It is never preceded by *mentre* while, *quando* when, or other prepositions such as *con, in,* etc. Their meaning is already expressed by the gerund:

Leggendo il giornale mi sono accorta dell'errore.
X̶ ̶M̶e̶n̶t̶r̶e̶ ̶l̶e̶g̶g̶e̶n̶d̶o̶ ̶.̶.̶.̶ ̶X̶
Reading the paper I realized the mistake.

L'opposizione è stata criticata per non aver mosso obbiezioni.
X̶ ̶L̶'̶o̶p̶p̶o̶s̶i̶z̶i̶o̶n̶e̶ ̶è̶ ̶s̶t̶a̶t̶a̶ ̶c̶r̶i̶t̶i̶c̶a̶t̶a̶ ̶p̶e̶r̶ ̶n̶o̶n̶ ̶a̶v̶e̶n̶d̶o̶ ̶m̶o̶s̶s̶o̶ ̶obbiezioni.̶ ̶X̶
The opposition was criticized for not objecting.

Alternative solutions are: *mentre*, etc. + a present, past or future tense:

Mentre leggevo il giornale . . . Whilst I was reading the paper . . .

(iv) It is never used as a word depending on a noun or an adjective:

~~X È un ottimo modo di investendo azioni. X~~
È un ottimo modo di investire le azioni.
It's an excellent way of investing shares.

(v) It is used with *pur* although. Note that the gerund should not be omitted:

Pur essendo fra i saldi è cara.
Though on sale it is expensive.

(c) Meanings

The gerund can express cause, a relative clause, condition, means, time. Note how the position of the gerund is extremely variable.

Un giovane della valle non trovando lavoro emigrò.
A young man from the valley emigrated, since he could not find a job.

Le foglie secche cadendo avevano ricoperto il prato.
The dry leaves which had fallen had covered the field.

Un'astronave correva per il cielo lasciandosi dietro una scia di stelle.
A space ship was running across the sky leaving behind a stream of stars.

Diventando ricco il pescatore diventò avaro.
As he grew rich the fisherman became mean.

Valutando i pro e i contro ho concluso che non è giusto.
Weighing up the pros and the cons, I have reached the conclusion that it is not right.

(d) The gerund in continuous tenses

(i) *Stare* + **the gerund** describes an action in progress in the present, past, future or conditional (see sections 46c, 48b, 50a, 57c):

Il design italiano sta attraversando un momento favorevole.
Italian design is going through a good phase.

Dicono che l'Italia si stia americanizzando.
People say that Italy is acquiring an American lifestyle / becoming Americanized.

- *Stare* is irregular (see Appendix 1).

- Pronouns can precede *stare* or follow the gerund:

    Lo stavano ammirando.
    Stavano ammirandolo.
    They were admiring it.

(ii) *Andare* + **the gerund** describes the repetition of the action in progress. It is less frequent than *stare*:

> *È una parola il cui uso si va diffondendo tra i giovani.*
> It's a word which is used more and more by young people.

> *Mi vado chiedendo da mezz'ora dove ho messo quel vestito.*
> I have spent half an hour wondering where I put that dress.

- This construction cannot be used with verbs of movement:

    ~~X *Andava ritornando a riva quando ha visto lo squalo.* X~~
    Stava ritornando a riva quando ha visto lo squalo.
    He was returning towards the shore when he saw the shark.

(iii) *Venire* + **gerund** is rather rare. It underlines the development of the action:

> *Veniva formandosi un movimento d'opinione.*
> A groundswell of opinion / pressure group was forming.

★ (iv) The gerund never forms a continuous tense with *essere* or *andare*:

    ~~X *Ero camminando.* X~~ (I was walking: *Camminavo.*)
    ~~X *Vado leggendo.* X~~ (I am going to read: *Leggerò.*)

66 The passive voice

The examples below illustrate the difference between the active and passive voices:

	SUBJECT	VERB	OBJECT OR AGENT
ACTIVE	*I terroristi*	*hanno liberato*	*gli ostaggi.*
	The terrorists	have set free	the hostages.
PASSIVE	*Gli ostaggi*	*sono stati liberati*	*dai terroristi.*
	The hostages	have been set free	by the terrorists.

(a) Forms

(i) The passive is formed by *essere* in the appropriate tense + the past participle. The past participle agrees in gender and number with the object. The agent is introduced by *da* (by).

> *È un'attrice amata e ammirata da tutti.*
> She is an actress loved and admired by everybody.

> *Il nuovo libro di Sergio Atzeni sarà pubblicato a fine mese.*
> The new book by Sergio Atzeni will be published by the end of the month.

> *Durante la guerra il pane e il burro erano razionati.*
> During the war bread and butter were rationed.

> *Le riforme furono varate troppo tardi.*
> Reforms were approved too late.

> *Se la corsa non fosse stata fermata avrebbe vinto lui.*
> If the race hadn't been stopped he would have won.

(ii) The passive is also formed with **venire + past participle.** Its meaning is the same as *essere* + past participle but it cannot be used in compound tenses:

> *Quanti libri vengono tradotti dall'italiano all'inglese?*
> How many books are translated from Italian into English?

> *Questa versione venne smentita dalle autorità.*
> This version was denied by the authorities.

> *Il film verrà girato vicino a Trieste.*
> The film will be shot near Trieste.

(iii) *Andare* + **past participle** conveys the idea of obligation or suggestion. It is used instead of *dover essere*:

> *L'argomento va presentato in modo convincente = L'argomento deve essere presentato.*
> The subject needs / ought to be presented in a convincing way.

(iv) *Da* + **infinitive** has an implicit passive meaning.

> *Penso che la TV sia tutta da reinventare.*
> I think TV should be totally reinvented.

★ (b) Verbs not to be used in the passive voice

In Italian (unlike in English) the following verbs cannot be made passive because they are intransitive, i.e. they cannot take a direct object:

> *domandare, chiedere a una persona* to ask a person
> *dare a una persona* to give to a person
> *dire* to tell, to say
> *insegnare* to teach
> *mostrare* to show
> *offrire* to offer
> *promettere* to promise
> *proibire* to forbid

> X ~~Gli studenti sono stati insegnati.~~ X
> *Ho insegnato italiano a studenti di tutte le nazioni.*
> I have taught Italian to students of all nationalities.
> Students of all nationalities have been taught by me.

> X ~~Lui è stato detto la verità.~~ X
> *Gli ho detto la verità.*
> He was told the truth (by me).

67 Impersonal verbs and *piacere*

(a) Impersonal verbs

Impersonal verbs are only used in the third person singular and can be grouped as follows:

(i) Verbs related to the weather: *piovviggina* it's drizzling, *è sereno* it's sunny, etc. For other weather expressions see section 172. However, if these verbs are used in a figurative sense they can have a personal subject:

> *Sul palcoscenico piovevano pomodori.*
> Tomatoes were pouring on the stage.

(ii) Verbs describing necessity, events, appearance:

> *accade, avviene, capita* it happens
> *bisogna, occorre, è necessario* one needs
> *basta* it's enough
> *conviene, è meglio* it's best

mancare to be missing, to lack
non importa it doesn't matter
può darsi it may be
trattarsi di to be about
volerci, metterci to require (referring to time)

Bisogna andare in farmacia.
We need to go to the chemist's.

Che cosa occorre comprare?
What do we need to buy?

Si tratta di soldi non di amore.
It's a question of money not of love.

Mancava la carne per fare le lasagne.
I didn't have the meat to make lasagne. (literally: The meat was missing.)

Ci ho messo tre ore. It took me three hours.

These verbs are usually followed by the infinitive unless a specific subject is introduced before the verb which follows the impersonal one:

Bisogna sperare sempre. One always needs to hope.

Bisogna che il mondo speri sempre. The world always needs to hope.

Note that verbs of happening may take a plural subject, usually placed after the verb or an indirect object pronoun, stressed or unstressed:

Accadono troppi incidenti stradali il sabato sera.
There are too many car accidents on Saturday evenings.

A mio figlio occorrono dei jeans, non gli occorrono dei pantaloni eleganti.
My son needs jeans, he doesn't need smart trousers. (literally: To my son / to him jeans are necessary . . .)

(iii) Adjective (m. sg.) + *essere*:

È stato faticoso? Has it been tiring?

(iv) Most verbs can acquire an impersonal meaning if they are preceded by the impersonal subject pronoun *si*. This is one of the most widely used constructions (see section 36).

Non si pensava che Colombo sarebbe riuscito nella sua impresa.
People didn't think that Columbus would succeed in his enterprise.

(b) *piacere*

(i) The construction with *piacere* is different from that of 'to like' and 'to enjoy'. In Italian you say 'something is pleasing to someone'. What 'pleases' is the subject, which may go before or after the verb. If it is something singular the verb is in the third person singular (*piace, piaceva,* etc.), if it is plural the verb is in the third person plural (*piacciono, piacevano*). The person 'it is pleasing to' may precede or follow the verb.

> *Agli inglesi piace il giardinaggio.* (literally: To the English is pleasing gardening.)
> *Il giardinaggio piace agli inglesi.* (literally: Gardening is pleasing to the English.)
> The English like gardening.
>
> *Agli inglesi piacciono gli spaghetti ben cotti.*
> The English like well-cooked spaghetti.
>
> *A mia nonna piaceva la musica di Verdi.*
> My grandmother liked Verdi's music.

(ii) If what is liked is expressed by a verb, *piacere* is in the third person singular, whether the next verb is followed by a singular or plural object.

N.B. Note that the verb is in the infinitive form:

> *Ai Romani piaceva ascoltare i poemi.*
> The Romans liked listening to poems.

To sum up:
piace + sg. noun
piace + verb (+ sg. or pl. noun)
piacciono + plural noun or two nouns

(iii) *Piacere* is irregular (see Appendix 1).

(iv) *Piacere* forms its compound tenses with *essere*, and the past participle agrees in gender and number with the subject, i.e. with what is liked.

> *Vi è piaciuta quella lezione?* Did you enjoy that lesson?
>
> *Non mi sono piaciuti gli esempi.* I didn't like the examples.

(v) *Piacere* is generally used with unstressed pronouns. The stressed pronouns are chosen to place more emphasis on likes and dislikes. Note that 'it' or 'them' do not need to be translated:

mi / a me	*piace*	I like it
	piacciono	I like them
ti / a te	*piace*	you like it
	piacciono	you like them < informal >
gli / a lui	*piace*	he likes it
	piacciono	he likes them
le / a lei	*piace*	she likes it / you like it < formal >
	piacciono	she likes them / you like them
ci / a noi	*piace*	we like it
	piacciono	we like them
vi / a voi	*piace*	you like it
	piacciono	you like them
gli / a loro	*piace*	they like it
	piacciono	they like them

A me non piace quella cucina ma a mio marito sì.
I don't care for that type of cooking but my husband does.

Le piace questa recita? A me non molto.
Do you like this performance? I am not very keen on it.

(vi) A subordinate clause following *piacere* may use two structures:

piacere che + subjunctive if the person who likes is not the subject of the subordinate clause

piacere + the infinitive if the person who likes is also the subject of the subordinate clause
Compare:

A mio padre non piace che mia sorella vada fuori con quel ragazzo.
My father doesn't like my sister going out with that young man.

A mia sorella piace andare fuori con quel ragazzo.
My sister likes going out with that young man.

(vii) The following are common expressions with *piacere*:

Mi piace di più. I prefer it.
Piace anche a me. I like it too.
Non piace neanche a me. I don't like it either.
Mi piace tanto. I like it a lot.
Faccio quello che mi pare e piace. I do as I please.
Non mi piace affatto. I don't like it at all.
Piaccia o non piaccia. Whether one likes it or not.
A chi piace? Who likes it?

(viii) *Non piacere* means 'to dislike' and follows the same construction as *piacere*:

> *Ai miei figli non piace lo sport.* My children don't like sport.
> *Non gli piace per niente.* He doesn't like it all.

As the examples show, the word order is noun + *non* + verb or *non* + pronoun + verb.

(ix) *Piacere* is occasionally used with a personal subject:

> *Mi piaci con i capelli corti.*
> I like you with short hair. (literally: You are pleasing to me with short hair.)
>
> *Io piaccio a pochi colleghi perchè ho un cattivo carattere.*
> Most colleagues don't like me because I have a difficult temperament. (literally: I am attractive to few colleagues because . . .)

68 Causative verbs and verbs of perception

(a) *fare* + infinitive

(i) This construction is used to give the idea of either causing something to happen, or of ordering, convincing, or allowing someone to do something. It corresponds to 'to have', 'to make', 'to get someone to do something'.

Unlike in English, the object follows the infinitive:

> *Dove fai lavare le tue coperte?*
> Where do you have your blankets washed?
> (literally: Where do you make to wash your blankets?)
>
> *Guarda, il sole ha fatto fiorire i primi crochi!*
> Look, the sun has brought the first crocuses into flower!

(ii) The action can be described in general terms with no explicit object expressed:

> *L'incontro aveva fatto sperare in una riconciliazione.*
> The meeting had given [the world] hope of a reconciliation.

(iii) When the person who is made to carry out the action is indicated by a pronoun, the word order is: pronoun + *fare* + infinitive. For example:

> *Mi hanno fatto spostare l'auto.*
> They have made me move the car.
> (To me they have made to move the car).

To give more emphasis, stressed pronouns are used:

> ***A me*** *hanno fatto spostare l'auto,* ***a te*** *no.*
> They have made only me move the car, not you.
>
> *Hanno fatto spostare l'auto solo a me.*
> They have asked only me to move the car.

(iv) Object pronouns follow and are attached to *fare* when this is in the infinitive, gerund, past participle or the imperative (see sections 31–33). If *fare* is preceded by *dovere, potere* or *volere*, the object pronoun can precede them or follow *fare* (see section 62b):

> *La fattura? Non ho potuto farla preparare prima = Non l'ho
> potuta fare preparare prima.*
> The invoice? I haven't been able to have it prepared before.
>
> *Falla entrare, per favore.* Show her in, please.

(v) If the verb following *fare* is reflexive, the reflexive pronoun is omitted:

> *rilassarsi: Quel viaggio mi ha fatto rilassare.*
> X *Quel viaggio mi ha fatto rilassarmi.* X
> That journey has relaxed me.

(vi) Here is a list of frequent combinations of *fare* + an infinitive:

far aspettare	to keep someone waiting
far cadere	to drop
far chiamare	to send for
far entrare	to let people in
far esercitare	to practise
far esplodere	to explode
far notare	to point out
far osservare	to call to someone's attention
far pagare	to charge
far partire un'auto	to start off a car
far proseguire	to forward
far risaltare	to enhance, bring out, emphasize
far sapere	to inform, let someone know

(b) *Fare* + *che* + subjunctive is a more emphatic form:

> *Fa che possiamo vederci.*
> Arrange things so that we can see each other.

> *Fa che non perdano la calma.*
> Make sure they do not lose their self control.

(c) *Farsi*

There is also the reflexive form *farsi*:

> *farsi annunciare* to get / have oneself announced
> *farsi mandare* to manage to be sent
> *farsi capire* to make oneself understood

(d) Compound tenses

Compound tenses require the auxiliary *essere* with the past participle agreeing in gender and number with the subject:

> *Elisabeth, dove ti sei fatta fare quel vestito?*
> Elisabeth, where did you have that dress made for you?

(e) *Lasciare* + infinitive

(i) *Lasciare* + infinitive + object corresponds to the English 'to let / allow someone do something':

> *Non lasci uscire il gatto?* Don't you let the cat out?

(ii) If the object is a pronoun, it precedes *lasciare*:

    La lasci passare? Can you let her pass?

But if *lasciare* is in the infinitive, gerund, past participle or the imperative form, the pronoun follows and is attached to it. The pronoun may precede *dovere, potere, volere* or follow the infinitive:

    Lasciami pensare un attimo.
    Let me think a while.

    Vorrei lasciarlo pensare. = Lo vorrei lasciar pensare.
    I would like to let him think.

(iii) With a reflexive verb the reflexive pronoun is usually omitted:

    riposarsi to rest oneself

    Ti lascio riposare e poi vengo.
    I'll let you rest and then I'll come.

(f) Verbs of perception

(i) The most common verbs of perception are *ascoltare* to listen, *guardare* to watch, *osservare* to observe, *sentire* and *udire* to hear, *vedere* to see. If they are followed by another verb, the possible word orders are:

verb of perception + infinitive + object / person
verb of perception + object / person + infinitive
verb of perception + *che* + verb

    Abbiamo visto uscire Lisetta. = Abbiamo visto Lisetta uscire. =
    Abbiamo visto Lisetta che usciva.
    We saw Lisetta go out / going out.

If the verb has a direct object the only construction is verb + object / person + infinitive:

    Abbiamo guardato Miriam cantare il suo nuovo disco.
    We watched Miriam sing her new record.

    X ~~Ti ho visto correndo al supermercato.~~ X
    (This would mean: I saw you yesterday while I was running to the supermarket.)
    Ti ho visto correre al supermercato.
    I saw you running to the supermarket.

(ii) If the object / person is expressed by a pronoun, this precedes the verb of perception:

Li abbiamo sentiti entrare. We heard them come in.

But if the verb is in the infinitive, gerund, past participle or imperative, the pronoun is attached to the end of the verb:

Ascoltalo cantare. Che voce!
Listen to him singing. What a voice!

(iii) If the verbs are used reflexively (*sentirsi* to hear **oneself**, *ascoltarsi* to listen to oneself), compound tenses are formed with the verb *essere* and the past participle agrees in gender and number with the subject:

Mi sono sentita chiamare. I heard myself being called.

PART 2

Contemporary functional language

MAKING COMMUNICATION EFFECTIVE

A correct use of grammar and vocabulary goes a long way in establishing good working relationships and a friendly rapport with the Italians. It is more friendly to say to someone *'suo marito e un cane'* (your husband and a dog) than *'suo marito è un cane'* (your husband is a dog). Equally, there is a difference between suggesting that *'la signora tal dei tali ha un amante'* (Mrs so and so has a male lover) and that *'la signora tal dei tali ha un' amante'* (Mrs so and so has a female lover)!

But grammatical competence is not enough. A breakdown in communication may be equally caused by the clumsy choice of an expression which is unsuitable to the situation or social context.

An indication of the importance attributed today to correct communication is evident in the studies carried out by two fairly recent disciplines, sociolinguistics and pragmatics, on the various registers and forms of communication among people of different ages, in professional situations, in correspondence and on the telephone.

In the following chapters Italian and English sentences do not match word for word. They are equivalent in register, style and suitability in the situation. It is important not to underestimate the importance of smiles, tone of voice, eye contact, and other facial movements in oral communication. They often say more than words do.

59 Forms of address

(a) *tu* or *lei?*

In Italy people may be addressed formally with the *lei* form, which grammatically corresponds to the third person singular of the verb, or informally with *tu*, which corresponds to the second person singular. This is called *darsi del lei* or *darsi del tu* (literally: to give each other *lei* or *tu*). See also section 30b.

There are no rigid rules about the use of the two forms because the choice depends on age, working and social contexts and, not least, fashion. However, since choosing the wrong form may cause offence, it is important to remember the following points.

Adult strangers are always addressed with *lei*:

> *Scusi, è tanto che aspetta l'autobus?*
> Excuse me, have you been waiting long for the bus?

Older and more senior people are addressed with *lei* until they ask to be called *tu*, usually saying: *Diamoci del tu, no?* or *Perchè non ci diamo del tu? Dammi pure del tu*. And this normally implies calling people by their first name.

In a professional context, colleagues of the same status call each other *tu* but with someone in a superior position the *lei* form is still expected. Moreover, even if *tu* is used, both men and women tend to call each other and refer to colleagues by surname:

> *Salvemini* (may be a man or a woman), *usi tu la fotocopiatrice?*
> Salvemini, are you going to use the photocopier?

It is still customary among people who are now over sixty to address each other with *lei* and signor / signora + the first name as a sign of a long-standing acquaintance or even friendship:

> *Signora Clara, ha bisogno di qualcosa?*
> Mrs Clara, is there anything you need?

The Amèrican fashion of calling people by their first name has spread through Italy too and nowadays people pass from the *lei* to the *tu* form very quickly. The young (until approximately the age of thirty) almost automatically call each other *tu*. But, if in doubt, it is worth making the effort to recall the verb ending of *lei* and use it rather than risk offending someone. The unexpected *tu* form has the same effect on an Italian as using a first name would have on an English person who did not wish to be on such terms with someone.

(b) Titles

If the *lei* form is used, people are addressed with *signore, signora, signorina* or the appropriate professional title: e.g. *Scusi, dottore* (Excuse me, doctor) / *ingegnere / architetto / avvocato / ragioniere / professore / professoressa*. These titles may be followed by the surname. In this case *signore, dottore, professore* drop the final 'e':

> *Signor Ceresa / Dottor Veronesi*

Introductions

Note that the difference between a formal and informal approach often simply depends either on the last vowel of the verb to distinguish between the *tu* and the *lei* form, or on a pronoun, e.g. the informal *ti* or the formal *la*, *le*. For these pronouns see section 31b.

Introductions among Italian people are always accompanied by handshaking.

(a) Introducing oneself *(presentarsi)*

(i) In a professional context, a meeting or a conference, introduce yourself with first name and surname, omitting any professional title:

- walking towards someone holding out a hand to shake:

    Guido Benigni. Piacere.
    My name is Guido Benigni. How do you do?

- or, sitting next to someone at a meeting:

    Permette, Gino Andreoli.
    May I introduce myself? / Excuse me, my name is Gino Andreoli.

- adding information about yourself:

    Buona sera. Sono Giulia Gallotta, dell'università di . . . Non credo ci siamo mai incontrate.
    Good evening. I'm Giulia Gallotta from the university of . . . I don't think we've met.

    Sono un amico / una collega di (name of a common acquaintance) *che anche lei conosce, immagino.*
    I am a friend / a colleague of . . . I expect you know him / her.

For how to say what your job is, see section 12a:

    Sono il direttore della sede centrale della Gables di Manchester.
    I am the director of Gables headquarters in Manchester.

(ii) People under thirty and people in the world of education tend to be less formal. The *tu* form is used even in first encounters. Straightforward forms such as the following are the most common:

    Salve! Paolo – Eleonora. (handshaking)
    Hallo! Hi! I'm Paolo – Eleonora.

Ho l'impressione che ci siamo già incontrati. Non sei Franca Ruspoli? Sono Michele Santori.
I think we have already met. Aren't you Franca Ruspoli? I am Michele Santori.

Mi sbaglio o ci siamo già visti? Sono . . .
I have a feeling we have met before. My name is . . .

(b) Introducing someone *(fare le presentazioni)*

(i) The most frequent and straightforward form is to introduce people by their name and surname. According to tradition men must be introduced to women and younger or less important to older or more senior people. Except among peers, where professional titles are taken for granted, or in informal gatherings, titles precede the surname. It is customary to get up when introduced, except for elderly people or women when introduced to men!

Antonello Sereni . . . Mariarosa Santoni . . . (handshaking)
L'ingegnere Dotti . . . la professoressa Caballi . . .

In planned encounters – gatherings, meetings, conferences, dinner parties – slightly more elaborate introductions may be used with both *lei* and *tu*:

A proposito Elena, conosci Roberta?
By the way Helen, do you know Roberta?

Signora Vezzola, vorrei presentarle l'assistente personale del direttore generale.
Mrs Vezzola, I would like to introduce you to the managing director's personal assistant.

Avrei piacere che conoscessi . . . Allow me to introduce you . . .
Vorrei farle conoscere . . . I would like you to meet . . .

If someone approaches your group or has just entered the room you may say:

Conoscete già il dottor . . . ?
Do you already know Dr . . . ?

Vi siete già incontrati? . . . La dottoressa Petrelli . . . Il dottor Ignazi . . .
Have you met before? . . . Dr Petrelli . . . Dr Ignazi . . .

Toh, guarda chi è arrivato! Vorrei presentarvi . . . < coll. >
Oh, look who's here! Let me introduce you to . . .

Vieni ti vorrei far conoscere Giovanna Quatermine.
Come and meet Giovanna Quatermine.

If you want to be introduced to someone you may ask:

> *Puoi presentarmi a . . . ?* Can you introduce me to . . . ?

Or someone may anticipate you and say:

> *So che avevi piacere di incontrare il professore Durazzi. Vieni che te lo presento.*
> I know you wanted to meet Professor Durazzi. Let me introduce you to him.

(ii) Teenagers prefer first names:

> *Chiara – Stefano – Ciao Ciao* (+ handshaking).

Or if one of the two people has been mentioned before, the name may be preceded by *questo / a*:

> *Questa è Chiara.* This is Chiara.

Or other informal ways:

> *Ciao a tutti! Sono l'amico di Valentina.*
> Hallo everybody! I'm Valentina's friend!

(iii) Official occasions may be opened with:

> *Gentili colleghi / Illustri colleghi, ho il piacere di presentarvi . . .*
> < informal >
> Colleagues, I am pleased to introduce to you . . .
>
> *Gentile pubblico, è con immenso piacere che vi presento l'avvocato . . .* < formal >
> Ladies and gentlemen, I have great pleasure in introducing Mr . . ., the distinguished lawyer . . .

(c) Responding to introductions

(i) Acknowledging the introduction:

The most common phrases are:

> *Piacere – Piacere* (+ handshaking) How do you do?
> *Molto lieto / a.* Nice to meet you. / Pleased to meet you.

Slightly more elaborate ways are:

> *È tanto che volevo incontrarla.* (to a man or a woman)
> *Desideravo incontrarla da parecchio.* (See section 31b.)
> I've been looking forward to meeting you.
>
> *È da tanto che desideravo incontrarla.*
> I have been wanting to meet you for some time.

(ii) Acknowledging (or not acknowledging) an earlier introduction:

> *Conosce / i . . . ?* Do you know . . . ?
>
> *No. Non ci siamo mai incontrati.*
> No. We have never met.
>
> *No. Non ho ancora avuto il piacere.* < formal >
> No. I don't believe we have met.
>
> *Sì. Ci ha presentati Carlotta.*
> Yes. We have been introduced by Carlotta.

(iii) Expressing appreciation to the person introduced:

> *Mi fa molto piacere incontrarla.*
> I'm delighted to make your acquaintance.
>
> *Ho sentito parlare molto di lei da Laura Loppi.*
> *Laura Loppi mi ha parlato molto del suo lavoro.*
> I've heard so much about you / your work from Laura Loppi.

(iv) Nowadays in informal situations and among young people *piacere* tends to be replaced by a simple *Salve!* Hi! or, with teenagers, *Ciao!* Hallo! with handshaking.

71 Greetings

It is not necessary to have been previously introduced before greeting strangers – a practice which applies to both sexes.

Strangers are greeted in lifts, when neighbours on the beach, on campsites, when sitting at a nearby table in hotels, in encounters during walks in the mountains.

Colleagues are greeted not only first time in the morning but every time they are met along corridors, perhaps only with a smile. Not acknowledging an encounter with them, even if it is the tenth time in a day, is rude.

Handshaking takes place only when people meet after they haven't seen each other for some time. One kiss on both cheeks and a hug is reserved for relatives, friends and close acquaintances. Two men tend to prefer a very warm handshake or placing a hand around the other man's shoulder. A new fashion is creeping in: one kiss on both cheeks between women or a man and a woman is now considered sophisticated, e.g. the fashionable hairdresser kissing his clients or the twenty-year-old son kissing his mother's female friends.

(a) Greetings

(i) When using the *lei* form the most common ways of greeting are:

Buongiorno.	Good morning. / Good morning, sir.
Buongiorno signora.	Good morning madam.
'Giorno.	Morning.
Buona sera.	Good evening. / Good afternoon.
	(Some people use it after dark, others soon after one o'clock. It is equivalent to 'Good afternoon' and 'Good evening'.)

Italian people do not automatically place the first name after greetings:

Buona sera.	Good evening, Mrs Taylor.
Sera!	G'd evening, Ted.

(ii) When using the *tu* form:

    Ciao! or *Salve!*   Hi! Hallo!

In both formal or informal situations the first name or the surname is added only for a special effect.

(iii) Variations on formal and informal greetings:

Salve! Come va la vita? < coll. >
Hallo! How's life?

È un pezzo che non ci si vede!
We haven't seen each other for a while!

Guarda chi si vede!
Hallo stranger! / Look who's here!

Chi non muore si rivede!
Fancy meeting you!

Pensavamo proprio a lei in questo momento.
Just the person we wanted to see. / We were just thinking about you.

Parlar del diavolo compar la pelle.
Talk of the devil . . .

(iv) Teenagers stick to *ciao*. A very recent trend has girls and boys kissing each other on both cheeks every time they meet, e.g. every day at school. Boys kissing boys is not fashionable.

(v) Opening a meeting. The tone may be formal or pleasantly humorous:

> *Signori e signore, buongiorno a tutti e benvenuti.*
> Ladies and gentlemen, hallo and welcome to all.

(vi) Welcoming someone who has arrived:

> *Buongiorno. Ha fatto buon viaggio? / Ciao. Tutto bene in viaggio?*
> Good morning. Did you have a nice journey? / Hallo! Good journey?

> *Siete stanchi / -che? Qualcosa da bere?*
> Are you tired? Would you like something to drink?

(b) Conversational remarks

> *Ah! Buongiorno. Come sta? / Come stai?*
> Hallo! Good morning. How are you? / How are you keeping?

The replies may be:

> *Bene. Grazie e lei? / tu?* Fine. Thank you. How are you?
> *Grazie. Non c'è male. E lei?* Thank you. Not too bad. And you?
> *Abbastanza bene. / Così così.* Quite well. / So so. Thank you.
> *Si tira avanti.* < coll. > Mustn't grumble. Thank you.

From the above examples note that *grazie* is not as automatic as the English 'thank you'.

The Italian question, *come sta?* is not a pure formality. It presupposes a reply with some personal information. It is often the beginning of a conversation about:

(i) The family and work:

> *Tutto bene? E i tuoi / i suoi?*
> Everything is all right? And how's your family?

> *Come va la vita?* How are things?

> *Come va col lavoro?* How are things at work?

> *Come vi trovate nella nuova casa?*
> How do you find your new house? / How do you like your new house?

(ii) Health:

> *Ho sentito che non è stata bene / è stata poco bene.*
> I heard you have not been well / you have not been too well.

> *Come va adesso?* How are you now?

(iii) Catching up with the latest news:

> *Cosa mi racconti di nuovo?* What's the latest?
> *Hai sentito di Fiorella?* Did you hear about Fiorella?

(iv) Commenting on clothes, looks:

> *La trovo bene. / Sei in forma eh?* < coll. >
> You look well. / Are you in good shape?
>
> *Sempre elegante. / Che bel vestito!*
> Smart as always. / Smart as ever.

(c) Saying goodbye

In most cases people part with a handshake. Friends, relatives and close acquaintances kiss each other on both cheeks (for men this varies regionally). Teenagers – boys with girls and girls with girls – currently kiss each other goodbye with one kiss on both cheeks.

(i) These are the most frequent forms of goodbye:

> *Ciao!* Cheerio! Cheers!
> *Arrivederci.* Goodbye. Bye-bye. I'll be seeing you.
> *Arrivederla signora.* < more formal >
>
> *Speriamo di rivederci presto. Ciao.*
> I look forward to seeing you again soon. Cheerio.
>
> *Dai un bacio ai tuoi bambini da parte mia.*
> Give your children a kiss for me.
>
> *Stammi bene, neh?* < coll. >
> Take care, won't you?
>
> *A tra poco allora.* See you soon.
> *A stasera.* See you tonight.
> *Ci vediamo.* I'll be seeing you!
> *Ci sentiamo.* I'll be seeing you! See you around!
>
> *Va be' ci vediamo da Nicola. Ciao.* < informal >
> See you at Nicola's.
>
> *Tante belle cose. Arrivederci. Buongiorno.* (A sequence of
> greetings is a sign of friendliness.)
> All the best. Goodbye.
>
> *Mi ha fatto molto piacere averla incontrata dopo così tanto tempo.*
> It has been lovely seeing you after so long.
>
> *Mi saluti tanto suo marito.*
> Give my regards to your husband.

Estenda i miei più fervidi saluti alla signora. < formal >
Give my kindest regards to your wife. / Please convey my very best
wishes to your wife.

(ii) Wishing people well on parting:

Buon divertimento / soggiorno / viaggio. Buone vacanze.
Have a good time / journey. / I hope you have a good holiday.

In bocca al lupo. (literally: in the mouth of the wolf) (for exams,
interviews)
I'll keep my fingers crossed.

Vi auguro che tutto vada per il meglio.
I hope everything goes well.

Le auguro ogni successo con il nuovo lavoro.
Every success in your new job.

Le porgo i nostri più sentiti auguri di buon proseguimento.
< formal, also used in letters >
Our best wishes for your future.

(d) Keeping in touch

(i) Suggesting you keep in touch:

Cerchiamo di incontrarci tra non molto.
We must meet again soon.

Dai! Dobbiamo vederci più spesso.
Yes! We must see each other more often.

Teniamoci in contatto. Let's keep in touch.

Fatti sentire, mi raccomando. I hope to hear from you.

Si tenga in contatto tramite la mia segretaria. < professional >
Do keep in contact through my office.

(ii) Suggesting you keep in touch by phone:

Ti do un colpo di telefono. I'll give you a ring.
Perché non mi telefoni? Why don't you ring me?
Perché non mi telefona? You are welcome to ring me.

Ci faresti veramente piacere se telefonassi. (subj.)
It would be nice if you could phone.

(iii) Making promises:

Senz'altro. Mi faccio sentire appena torno.
I'll certainly be in touch as soon as I'm back.

D'accordo. Ti telefono appena so il nuovo indirizzo.
OK. I'll ring you up as soon as I have the new address.

Ecco le do il mio biglietto (da visita). Can I give you my card?

(iv) Suggesting you prolong the encounter:

Cosa ne diresti di . . . un caffè? / Ti va l'idea di andare al cinema?
Have you time for . . . a coffee? What about going to the cinema?

Avete voglia di andare a fare due passi?
Why don't we go for a walk?

Le va di sedersi qui fuori con noi?
Would you like to join us for a drink outside here?

(e) Ending the encounter

(i) Declining:

Grazie ma ho premura. / Ho un precedente impegno.
Thank you but I'm in a hurry. / I have a previous engagement.

Mi dispiace proprio. Sono qui con un'amica.
I'm really sorry. I'm here with a friend.

Sarà per un'altra volta. It will have to be another time.

È molto gentile da parte sua ma devo essere a casa entro le sei.
< more formal >
It's very kind of you but I must be home by six.

(ii) Leaving:

Mi dispiace di dover andare ma c'è mio marito che mi aspetta.
I'm sorry to have to go but my husband is waiting for me.

Accipicchia devo volare. < coll. > Goodness me, I've got to dash.

Scusate ma devo proprio andare. Sorry, but I have to go.

Non posso trattenermi oltre. I can't stay any longer.

Sarà meglio che cominci a mettermi in moto. (literally: to set in motion or switch on the engine)
I'm afraid I shall have to leave soon.

72 Small talk

In Italy a casual encounter can easily continue with small talk. Equally a conversation may be sparked off by the most innocuous remark. The topics are often the same. In Italian it is important not to let silence fall. It is considered unsociable and, often, rude (see section 108). Here are some suggestions on how to carry on a conversation. It is not so much the content which is important as the positive image of one's self that a few sentences can project.

(a) Some prompts

(i) Comments of admiration or disapproval (see section 39):

Stupendo, vero? Musica stupenda!
Splendid, isn't it? Great music!

Che magnifico panorama! What a superb view!

Mamma mia, che orrore questo quadro!
Goodness me, this painting is dreadful!

Roba da matti! < coll. > *Il traffico in questa città! / Questi prezzi!*
It's sheer madness! The traffic in this town! / These prices!

(ii) Comments on the weather are not as infrequent as is sometimes claimed. Instead of the usual

Che caldo! Nice and warm, isn't it?

Che freddo! How cold it is!

Peccato che sia brutto oggi! What a shame it's not nice today!

one may ask questions about the local weather:

È sempre così bello qui?
Is the weather always as nice as this here?

Nevica spesso? Does it often snow?

C'è spesso nebbia di questa stagione? Is there often fog at this time of the year?

(iii) Paying a compliment to a baby, talking to / about a child or a pet:

Che bel bambino! What a pretty child!

Quanti anni hai? How old are you?
Vai già a scuola? Do you go to school?
Che classe fai? What year are you in?

Di che razza è? What breed is it?
Come si chiama? What's her / his name?

Note that generally Italians use the masculine gender for pets.

(iv) Remarking on local or international events:

Ha sentito di . . . / Ha letto quell' . . .?
Did you hear about . . . / Have you read that . . .?

Avete sentito il telegiornale? Have you heard the news?

(b) A couple of devices to let the others do the talking

If your Italian is still inadequate for a full conversation, it is advisable not to withdraw into what may look like a supercilious silence to an Italian, but to ask simple questions which show a genuine interest in what the other person has to say:

(i) The easiest way is to choose between:

> *Ah sì!? Dove?* Really! Where?   *Come mai?* How come?
> *Come?* How?   *Chi è?* Who is he?
> *Quando?* When?   *Con chi?* With whom?
> *Perché?* Why?

or to comment with stock phrases:

> *Davvero!* Really!
> *Però!* Indeed!
> *Caspita!* It's incredible!
> *Guarda un po'!* Amazing, isn't it?
> *Se ne sentono di tutti i colori!* You hear all sorts!
> *Accipicchia! Accidenti!* < coll. > Blast! Good gracious!
> *Ma va!* < coll. > Never!

!! In informal situations both teenagers and adults use without restriction stock phrases which are sexual metaphors or indirect blasphemous images. In a foreign language, although one needs to understand them, it is advisable not to use registers which one would not use in one's own mother tongue:

> *Cazzo! Porco Giuda! Porca Eva! Merda! Puttana! Troia! Balle! Che rottura! Ma che razza di . . .*

(ii) Other people's opinions, likes and dislikes, may be asked more elaborately:

> *Cosa gliene pare di questo albergo? / del programma?*
> What's your opinion of this hotel? / of the programme?
>
> *Cosa ne pensa? Le è piaciuto?*
> What do you think? Did you like it?
>
> *Secondo lei / te è stato utile questo incontro?*
> Do you think it has been a useful meeting?

225

(c) Breaking the ice

Hotels, campsites, beaches, organized trips, canteens, receptions and professional meetings provide situations where keeping to oneself is not appreciated behaviour in Italy. It may be considered downright rude. Here are some suggestions on how to break the silence and join the others:

> *Scusi, mi tolga una curiosità. Perché . . .?*
> I hope you don't mind if I ask you why . . .?
>
> *Scusi se la disturbo, che cosa significa . . .?*
> I'm sorry to disturb you but what does . . . mean?
>
> *Scusi, disturbo se apro la finestra?* (followed by a remark on the weather)
> Excuse me, do you mind if I open the window?
>
> *Scusi, mi fa dare un'occhiata al suo giornale?*
> Sorry to trouble you, but may I have a look at your newspaper?

followed by:

> *Non parlo molto bene l'italiano ma lo leggo.*
> I don't speak Italian a lot but I can read it.

or

> *Ci sono notizie su Wimbledon?*
> Is there any news about Wimbledon?
>
> *Mi può imprestare un attimo una biro? / una copia della relazione?*
> Excuse me, may I borrow your biro for a moment? / a copy of the report?
>
> *È libero questo posto? / Posso sedermi qui?*
> Is this seat free? / Can I sit here?

At an organized meeting, if a group is ready to go out, join it by saying:

> *Vi dispiace se mi unisco a voi? Sono . . .*
> Excuse me, may I join you? My name is . . .

If it is your turn to make people feel at home (e.g. replying to people who have asked if they can sit next to you or asked for a newspaper or an ashtray) some expressions are:

> *Prego!* (the most frequent and all-purpose) With pleasure!
> *Faccia pure.* Please do (open the window).
> *Si figuri. Si immagini* (e.g. replying to someone who has asked if a deckchair can be moved) You are welcome.
> *Certamente! Con piacere.* Certainly. With pleasure. By all means!

3 Invitations and offers

(a) Please

Words such as *per piacere*, *per favore*, *per cortesia* < the most formal of the three > are used less automatically in Italian than in English. A smile or a conditional form is a common substitute:

> *Mi spediresti questa lettera?*
> Can you post this letter for me please?

On the other hand, *prego* is automatically said after *grazie* thank you:

> *Ecco il caffé.* Here's the coffee.
> *Grazie.* Thank you.
> *Prego.* Don't mention it. / It's a pleasure.

(b) Invitation to one's own home

> *Vieni qualche volta.* Pop in sometime.
>
> *Senti, venite a trovarmi se passate dalle mie parti.*
> Listen, come and see us if you are passing.
>
> *Telefona che ci incontriamo una sera.*
> Do ring up so we can meet one evening.
>
> *Mi raccomando . . . vieni.* (literally: I recommend you)
> It would be nice if you came.
>
> *Fai un salto domani.* < coll. > Drop in tomorrow.
>
> *Venga a trovarmi appena ha un momento.*
> Come and see me when you have a spare moment.

(c) Invitation to do something together

(i) Informal invitations include:

> *Ti piacerebbe andare a vedere . . . / a sentire . . . ?*
> Fancy going to see . . . / to listen to . . . ?
>
> *Perché non . . . facciamo una corsa fino a . . . ?*
> Why don't we . . . go for a ride to . . . ?
>
> *Ti / vi va di andare in discoteca / in pizzeria?*
> Won't you come to a disco / to the pizzeria?
>
> *Cosa ne dite di . . . andare a mangiare un gelato? / fare una spaghettata a casa mia?*
> What about . . . going out for an ice cream? / having some spaghetti at my place?

Ti andrebbe di fare un giro in barca?
Do you feel like a boat trip?

Andiamo a vedere quel film, dai! < among friends >
Come on, let's go and see that film!

Ti gira di fare un giro in bici? < coll. >
Feel like going for a bike ride?

(ii) More formal phrases are:

Le farebbe piacere . . .
Would you care to . . .

Noi andiamo sulla Marmolada. Venga con noi.
We are going up to the Marmolada. Won't you join us?

Che cosa ne direbbe di raggiungerci più tardi al caffé Greco?
Would you like to join us at the Café Greco later on?

Ci farebbe immenso piacere se veniste a cena da noi. < also used in letters >
We should be delighted if you were able to come to dinner.

Saremmo lieti se poteste venire da noi per un aperitivo. < formal >
We should be very pleased if you could come for a drink.

(d) Offering a lift

Ti do un passaggio in macchina? Can I give you a lift home?

Sei a posto con la macchina? < coll. > Are you all right for transport?

Posso offrirle un passaggio? May I offer you a lift?

La porto a casa se crede. May I give you a lift?

(e) Inviting someone to dinner or other special occasions

Mi dovrebbe fare la cortesia di essere nostro ospite quando viene a Roma. < formal >
It would give us great pleasure if you would be our guest when you come to Rome.

Perché non venite da noi a cena uno di questi giorni? Vi telefono così ci mettiamo d'accordo.
Why don't you come to dinner soon? I'll ring you up so we can fix a day.

Do una festa per inaugurare il nuovo negozio. Sei libera?
I'm giving a 'shopwarming' party. Are you free?

Se trovo due biglietti per il concerto alla Scala, mi fai compagnia?
If I can get two tickets for the concert at La Scala, will you come with me?

Diamo un cocktail per festeggiare l'arrivo di Walter, volete essere nostri ospiti? < formal >
We are giving a drinks party to celebrate Walter's arrival. Can you come?

On a more formal level one could say:

Ci farebbe piacere se poteste venire anche voi a cena.
It would be nice if you too could come to dinner.

Flavio sarebbe felicissimo se veniste a passare il prossimo weekend da noi in montagna.
Flavio would be delighted if you could come to spend next weekend at our place in the mountains.

(f) Accepting an invitation

(i) If you have been invited to a private home, as you enter you may say:

Permesso? May I come in?

(ii) General forms of expressing interest in an invitation are:

Sì. Grazie. Accetto / Vengo volentieri.
Yes. Thank you. I'd like to very much.

Va bene. Grazie. Mi fa molto piacere.
Yes. I would, very much.

Sì. Sarebbe bello. Ottima idea.
That would be very nice. Great.

Mi andrebbe benissimo. D'accordo.
That's a very good idea. OK by me.

Ti prendo in parola. < informal > You're on.

Non me lo faccio dire due volte. < informal > I won't say no.

More formally one may say:

È molto gentile da parte vostra. Ci farebbe molto piacere.
It is very kind of you. We'd very much like to.

(g) Offering something

(i) To offer a seat, or to ask someone else to go ahead, or help himself, either formally or informally, the key word is:

> *Prego!* After you!
> *Prego!* Please do come in.
> *Prego, signora, si accomodi.*
> Please take a seat. / Do make yourself at home.
> *Da questa parte, prego.* This way, please.

(ii) Offering a drink. At home something to drink is not offered as soon as the person has arrived but only after the conversation has been in progress for a while.

> *Caffé o qualcosa di più forte?*
> Coffee or something stronger?

> *Un caffé? Un liquore? Un amaro? Dei cioccolatini? Cosa posso offrirti?*
> What would you like? A coffee or something alcoholic? Chocolates?

> *Sentite, prendete una fetta di torta?*
> Will you have a slice of cake?

Slightly more formally:

> *Signora Gianna, signora Casella, le posso offrire qualcosa? Un . . .*
> Mrs Gianna, Mrs Casella, can I offer you something? Would you like a . . .?

Usually one does not accept immediately. At first one declines and only after the offer is reiterated once or twice does one finally accept. The most frequent standard sequence of interactions is:

> *No. Grazie non disturbarti.* < *tu* form >
> *No. Grazie. Non si disturbi.* < *lei* form >
> (literally: No. Thank you. Don't disturb yourself.)

> *Ci metto un minuto. Lo faccio anche per me.*
> It will only take a minute. I'll make one for myself too.

> *Ma non prende veramente niente? Proprio no?* < slightly more formal >
> Are you sure you won't? Won't you really? / Really not?

Accepting, one may say:

> *Se non è di troppo disturbo.*
> If it is not too much trouble.

> *Va bene. Grazie. Prendo un caffé.*
> Thank you very much. I'll have a coffee.

Beh, sì grazie. Ai dolci / A un buon caffè non so dire di no.
OK. Thank you. I can never resist cakes / a good coffee.

Sì. Lo prendo volentieri. Grazie.
Yes. I'd love one. Thank you.

If you really want to decline you may say:

Grazie. È come se l'avessi accettato.
(the meaning is: I have appreciated your offer even if I have been unable to accept it.)

If you are longing for something, you may say to friends:

Posso chiederti di farmi un caffè? Sto morendo dalla voglia.
Can I ask you for a coffee? I'm dying for one.

(iii) Offering a snack or an informal meal:

Senti, ti fermi a cena? Why don't you stay for dinner?

Dai! Fermatevi a mangiare da noi. Cosa vi preparo?
Please. Have something to eat with us. What would you like?

Se vuol venire anche lei . . . poi la riaccompagno a casa. < *lei* form >
Would you like to come too? Then I can take you home.

(h) Declining invitations and offers

Something to drink:

No. Grazie. Io no. No. Thank you. Not for me.
Io non prendo niente. Grazie. I won't have anything. Thank you.
Una sigaretta? No. Meglio di no. A cigarette? No. Better not.

To go to somebody's place or join in some activity:

Grazie. Ma non posso. Devo . . .
Thank you for asking. But I can't this time. I must . . .

Che peccato. Mi sarebbe piaciuto moltissimo, ma . . .
What a shame! Much as I should have liked . . .

Per quanto mi attiri l'idea, mi dispiace ma . . .
Much as I would like to, I'm sorry but . . .

No. Grazie. Sarà per un'altra volta.
Thank you. I can't. Next time, perhaps.

Purtroppo non riesco a venire.
I am very sorry, but I don't think I can.

Veramente! Non posso proprio restare.
I really can't stay.

On a more formal level:

> *Per quanto abbia fatto il possibile per liberarmi del precedente impegno . . .* < also in letters >
> Although I have done my best to free myself from the previous engagement . . .

> *Se per lei va bene lo stesso, preferisco rimandare.*
> If it's all right with you, I'd rather come / do it another time.

> *È con rammarico che devo rifiutare.* < formal >
> Much to my regret I have to refuse.

> *Mi dispiace moltissimo ma non sono in grado di accettare il vostro invito.* < also in letters >
> I'm awfully sorry but I won't be able to accept your invitation.

74 Checking the language

(a) Asking someone to repeat something

> *Scusa? Che cosa? Come?* Excuse me? What did you say?
> *Prego?* Pardon? I beg your pardon?
> *Cosa?* < familiar > What?

To focus on one word:

> *Scusi / Scusa non ho capito / afferrato la prima parola / il cognome.*
> I'm sorry, I haven't understood / caught the first word / the surname.

> *Come ha detto, scusi? Le dispiace ripetere?*
> I'm sorry. Could you repeat it?

> *Scusi ha detto Milano o Merano?*
> Excuse me. Did you say Milano or Merano?

(b) Checking the meaning

> *Come si dice . . . ?* How do you say . . . ?
> *Che cosa vuol dire . . . ?*
> What does . . . mean?

> *Ma non significa . . . ?*
> But doesn't it mean . . . ?

> *Ah! Credevo che volesse dire . . .*
> Ah! I thought it meant . . .

> *Come si chiama . . . ?*
> What do you call . . . ?

Ha senso dire . . .?
Can you say . . .?

Aiutami a dire che . . .?
How can I say that . . .?

Mi puoi dare un altro esempio?
Can you give me another example?

In quale caso si usa con questo significato?
When do you use it with this meaning?

Si usa solo parlando?
Is it used only in speech?

Ma c'è un altro modo di dirlo?
But is there another way of saying it?

Come posso dirlo in modo meno formale?
How can I say it less formally?

(c) Asking if it is correct

È giusto o è sbagliato? Is it right or wrong?
È corretto o no? Is it correct or not?
Andrà bene questa parola? Is this word suitable?
Mi sa dire se è giusto, per favore? Can you tell me if it is right?
Allora come devo dire? So what should I say?
Che cosa non va con . . .? What's wrong with . . .?

(d) Telling people whether something is right or wrong in your mother tongue

Sì. Va bene. È giusto. Yes. It's fine. It's correct.
No. Mi sembra che non vada bene. No. I don't think it's right.
È senz'altro giusto. It's certainly right.
Perfetto. Giustissimo. You're dead right.
Questo termine va a puntino. Spot on.
Non sono sicuro neanch'io. I'm not really sure myself.

No. Neanche per sogno! < informal >
Never in a thousand years! (literally: not even in a dream!)

È il termine più adatto / più adeguato. < formal >
It's the most suitable term.

Si tratta di una frase chiara / ben formulata. < formal >
It's a well-phrased sentence.

(e) Correcting someone

No. Si dice . . . No. We say . . .

È giusta anche se . . . It's right even if . . .

Un'espressione più corretta mi sembrerebbe . . . < formal >
I think it would be more correct to say . . .

È meglio dire . . . It's better to say . . .

Le dispiace se le correggo questa parola . . .? < formal >
Do you mind if I correct this word . . .?

Scusa, ma non si dice proprio così.
Sorry, but it's not really how we say that.

(f) Finding out about pronunciation

Come si pronuncia? Così o così?
How do you pronounce it? Like this or like that?

Perchè si pronuncia così? Why do you pronounce it like that?
Si dice sempre così? Do you always say it like this?
Dove cade l'accento? Where does the accent fall?
L'intonazione è giusta? Is the intonation right?

Per favore se sbaglio mi correggi / corregge?
If I make a mistake, please can you correct me?

(g) Finding out about spelling

Come si scrive? How do you spell it?
Ci vuole l'accento? Does it have an accent?
Si scrive con la doppia? Is it spelt with a double letter?
È giusto scritto così? Is it right written like this?

Scusa, ti dispiace controllare se ho fatto degli errori di ortografia?
Sorry, excuse me, could you check whether I have made any
spelling mistakes?

SOCIAL FORMULAS

75 Paying compliments

(a) In relation to people's looks, clothes, food, standard forms are:

Che buono / carino! / Com'è buono! / Quanto è delicato!
That's nice / good / delicious!

Come sei elegante! You look smart!

Mai visto niente di così ben rifinito.
I never saw anything so well finished.

(b) More personal remarks are frequent and welcome:

Sei sempre all'ultima moda!
You are always fashionable!

Fai tipo! < youth slang > You look great!

Come ti dona quel colore / quel maglione.
I must say that colour / that jumper does suit you.

Mi piace da matti il tuo salotto.
I love your sitting-room.

Mi piacciono da morire i tuoi orecchini.
I adore your earrings.

(c) More formal expressions are:

Mi permetta di esprimerle la mia ammirazione per il gusto eccellente con cui sceglie i colori.
Allow me to express my admiration for the excellent taste you've shown in your colour scheme.

76 Offering congratulations

(a) Standard forms:

Congratulazioni! / Complimenti! / Felicitazioni!
Congratulations!

Complimenti vivissimi! My warmest congratulations!

Le nostre più sentite congratulazioni! < formal >
Our heartiest congratulations!

Complimenti sinceri per l'esito degli esami. < formal >
I'd like to congratulate you on your examination results.

Sei stata proprio brava. Well done.

Fantastico! It was great!

Vai di bella! < youth slang > (literally: Carry on like that!)

!! *Che figa che sei!* < youth slang > (admiration expressed directly to someone)

Che storia! = *Che belli!* < youth slang > (expressing admiration for people and objects)

!! *Che figo!* < youth slang > (expressing admiration for someone passing by)

See sections 164–5.

The following examples are more formal:

I nostri più fervidi rallegramenti e auguri!
Our heartiest congratulations and best wishes!

Mi permetta di felicitarmi per . . .
          di esprimere le nostre felicitazioni . . .
          di porgere le nostre congratulazioni a nome mio e della ditta.
Please accept my congratulations and those of the company.

(b) Replying to compliments and congratulations:

Grazie. Mi metti in imbarazzo. Thank you. I feel embarrassed.
Grazie. Che gentile. It's very nice of you.
Non è gran che. È meno di quanto sembri.
There is nothing to it actually.
La ringrazio per la telefonata.
It was very nice / good of you to ring up.

Apologies

In Italian, *scusa* and *scusi* are far from being as frequently used as 'sorry' in English. For instance, they are not used to apologize for a grammatical mistake, for a noise inadvertently made (a door slammed, a lid dropped, etc.). *Mi scusi* or *scusami* are stronger forms:

> *Mi scusi il ritardo.* I apologize for the delay.

The reply may be:

> *Prego. Non c'è di che.* It's all right. Don't worry.
>
> *Non fa nulla. / Non importa. / Ci mancherebbe altro.*
> It doesn't matter. / It's no problem. / That's quite all right.

or:

> *Mi scusi lei.* My fault.
> *No. È tutta colpa mia.* Don't. It's entirely my fault.

More heartfelt expressions are:

> *Sono spiacente.*
> *Sono veramente spiacente.*
> I am sorry. / I am really sorry. I beg your pardon.
>
> *Non sai quanto mi spiaccia.*
> I really feel awful about it.
>
> *Non trovo parole per scusarmi.* < formal >
> I can't tell you how sorry I am.
>
> *Mettiamoci una pietra sopra, va bene?* < informal >
> Let's forget about it, all right? / Let bygones be bygones.

Expressing understanding

With exclamations:

> *Che brutto! Poveretto!*
> That's awful! Poor soul! / Poor thing!
>
> *Che peccato! Che sfortuna! Che rabbia!*
> What a shame! Hard luck! How maddening!
>
> *Accidenti no!* < coll. > *Che scalogna!* < coll. >
> Hell! No! What a shame!

Expressing direct sympathy:

> *Se c'è qualcosa che posso fare . . .* If there is anything I can do . . .
> *Mi dispiace. Non lo sapevo.* I'm sorry. I didn't know.
> *Non sai quanto mi dispiace.* I am so upset.
> *Capisco!* I know how you feel! / I do sympathize.

Colloquially, people are encouraged with:

> *Lascia perdere!* Never mind!
> **!!** *Fregatene!* Don't give a damn!

Youth slang includes:

> *Sono tutti pallosi.* (referring to unbearable parents)
> They are all bores!
>
> *Non ce n'e più.*
> You can't carry on like this any longer. (e.g. with that girl /
> boyfriend)

To calm down and reassure someone some useful words are:

> *Su, dai, calmati.* < informal >
> Come on, calm down.
>
> *Non preoccuparti. Vedrai che è una cosa da niente.*
> Don't worry. You'll see there is no need to worry.
>
> *Vorrei rassicurarla che . . .*
> I would like to reassure you that . . .

Two proverbs may be useful:

> *Il diavolo non è brutto come lo si dipinge.*
> The devil is not as black as he is painted.
>
> *Cane che abbaia non morde.*
> His bark is worse than his bite.

79 Dealing with interruptions

In the course of a conversation or a discussion or even a public
debate, Italian people feel much more at ease in interrupting and
expressing their opinion than the English. Particularly in the course
of private conversations this is a sign of keen participation, not of
disregard for other people's words. It is often followed by the
expression:

> *Mi scusi se l'ho interrotta. / Scusami se ti ho interrotto.*
> I'm sorry to have interrupted you.

If you find this too difficult to accept, you can easily say:

> *Scusi, volevo finire di dire che è un verdetto scandaloso.*
> Sorry, can I just finish saying that it is a scandalous verdict.

> *Fammi finire il mio ragionamento / la storia.*
> Let me finish what I was saying / the story.

If you are with close friends and constant interruptions don't allow you to understand what is going on you can jokingly say:

> *Un gallo per volta, per favore!*
> One at a time, please! (literally: One cock at a time, please!)

Interruptions are also common in professional situations. If the phone interrupts a conversation in an office, these are very frequent ways of apologizing for the interruption:

> *Mi scusi, un attimo.*
> Excuse me for a moment.

> *La prego di scusarmi, sarò breve.* < formal >
> Please excuse me, I will be very quick.

If it is necessary to leave the office, an informal way of explaining and apologizing is:

> *Mi può aspettare cinque minuti? Torno subito.*
> Could you wait five minutes? I'll be very quick.

> *Sarò velocissima.*
> Back in a sec.

A more formal way is:

> *La prego di scusarmi. Devo assentarmi un attimo.*
> Would you please excuse me for a moment.

INFORMATION

 80 **Asking for information**

The most common way to ask for information is:

> *Per Venezia?* The road to Venice, please?
> *(Scusi) Il prefisso per Venezia (per piacere)?* (Excuse me), what is
> the code for Venice, please?

Alternatively you can use interrogative words (see section 39):

> *Quant'è quel cappello?* How much is that hat, please?
> *Dov'è l'ufficio informazioni?* Where is the tourist office?
> *Chi sono?* Who are they?
> *Che ora è?* What time is it please?

More complex forms are:

> *Vorrei delle informazioni sulla Mostra del libro.*
> I would like to have some information about the Book Fair.
>
> *Mi piacerebbe sapere se ci sono dei libri su Giotto.*
> I wonder if you could tell me whether there are any books on
> Giotto.
>
> *Mi sa dire dov'è / quant'è / che cosa sono / dove trovo . . .?*
> Could you tell me where is / how much is / what are / where can I
> find . . .?
>
> *Mi può indicare che cosa devo fare per iscrivermi all'ACI?*
> Would you be able to tell me what I have to do to become a
> member of the Italian Automobile Club?
>
> *Per cortesia mi dia l'indirizzo di quella ditta.*
> Could you please give me that company's address?

More informally:

> *C'è qualcuno che sa se la mensa è aperta giovedì?*
> Does anybody know whether the canteen is on Thursdays?
>
> *Sai qualcosa sul nuovo accordo?*
> Do you know anything about the new agreement?
>
> *Hai idea di quando arriveranno i nuovi apparecchi?*
> Any idea when the new equipment arrives?

More forcefully:

>*Mi scusi se la disturbo ma avrei bisogno di sapere a che ora chiudete.*
>I'm sorry to bother you but I need to know what time you close.

Informally to a group of friends:

>*Mi sapete dire quando arriva Franco Rossi?*
>Do you know when Franco Rossi is expected?

>*C'è nessuno che sappia / sa come far funzionare questo computer?*
>Does anybody know how to make this computer work?

Sharing information

Information can be given indirectly, by asking questions such as the following:

>*Sapevi che . . . / Sai che . . . ?*
>Did you know that . . . / Do you know that . . . ?

>*Hai sentito che . . . / Hai sentito dire che . . . ?*
>Did you hear that . . . ?

>*Hai sentito l'ultima sul caporeparto?*
>Did you hear the latest on the boss?

>*Sei stata informata del nuovo regolamento?*
>Have you been informed of the new rules?

Replies vary from the informal:

>*Sì. Grazie. Lo sapevo. / L'ho saputo proprio ora.*
>Yes. Thank you. I knew. / I have just been told.

>*No. Non ne sapevo niente.* No. I knew nothing about it.

>*Non ne ho idea.* I have no idea.

>*Non ne so molto. / Ne so poco o niente.*
>I don't know much about it.

>*No. Non me lo aveva detto nessuno.*
>No. No one had told me anything. / I haven't been told anything.

to more formal answers:

>*So da fonte certa che non è vero.*
>I have it on good authority that it is not true.

>*È mia convinzione che sia (subj.) vero.*
>It is my firm belief that it is true.

Sì. Ne sono al corrente. Yes. Thank you. I'm fully **aware**.

Non so nulla al riguardo, mi dispiace.
I'm sorry but I know nothing about it.

82 Acknowledging ignorance

(i) Admitting you don't know

Non lo so. Mi spiace. Sorry. I don't know.
Non lo so neanch'io. I don't know either.
Non glielo so dire. I can't help you.
Non ho idea. I have no idea.
Non ho la più pallida idea. I haven't the faintest idea. I'm sorry.

(ii) Saying you can't recall

Per quel che mi ricordo non è mai arrivato.
To the best of my recollection it never arrived.

Per quanto frughi nella memoria non ricordo.
No matter how much I search my memory, I don't recall it.

L'ho sulla punta della lingua. < informal >
It's on the tip of my tongue.

Non me lo ricordo (purtroppo).
I don't remember it (unfortunately). I'm sorry.

Mi spiace. Non riesco a ricordarlo.
I'm sorry. I can't think of it.

Ho un vuoto di memoria.
My mind has gone blank.

Non mi viene in mente.
I'm sorry. I can't recall it.

No. Non me ne ricordo proprio.
I have no recollection of it.

Buio pesto. < coll. > Search me.

Non ho la benché minima idea. < coll. >
I haven't got a clue.

In an office people may say:

Abbia pazienza un attimo. Devo cercare in questo catalogo.
Bear with me. I must look it up in this catalogue.

(iii) Saying you forgot

L'ho dimenticato. I forgot.

Ci devo pensare. / Devo pensarci su. < coll. >
I need to think about it.

Devo ammettere che mi sono dimenticata.
I have to admit I forgot.

Scusa, ma mi è sfuggito di mente.
Forgive me, but it quite slipped my mind.

83 Reminding people

- Friendly forms:

  Mi raccomando non dimenticarti che si cena alle 8.
  You will remember, won't you, that we dine at 8 o'clock?

  Ti ricordi vero che hai il motorino in strada?
  You remember, don't you, that you left the motorbike outside on
  the road?

  Ma non ti ricordi che alle otto si va al cinema?
  But don't you remember that we're going to the cinema at eight?

  Non ti sei dimenticata che l'appuntamento è lunedì vero?
  You haven't forgotten that the appointment is on Monday, have
  you?

- Formal and professional forms:

  Mi scusi se le faccio presente che la data è sbagliata.
  I hope you won't mind if I remind you that it is the wrong date.

  Mi scusi se mi permetto di rammentarle la data.
  May I remind you of the date?

  Ci premuriamo rammentarle che è scaduto il contratto.
  May we draw your attention to the fact that the contract has
  expired?

- Possible answers are:

  Sì. Certo. / Sì, sì, mi ricordo. / Sì, sì, va bene.
  Yes. Of course. / I remember. / Yes, fine, thank you.

  Ah! Ora che ci penso . . .
  Ah! Now that I think about it . . .

Grazie per avermelo ricordato.
Thanks for reminding me.

Come potrei dimenticarlo?
How could I forget?

Se la memoria non mi tradisce la lettera è arrivata lo scorso aprile.
If my memory doesn't let me down the letter arrived last April.

Mi scusi. Non so proprio come ho potuto dimenticarmi.
I *am* sorry. I don't know how I came to forget it.

- On a professional level the answers could be:

    Vi preghiamo di scusarci per il mancato pagamento. Stiamo cercando di chiarire questo punto con urgenza.
    Please accept our apologies for the delay in payment. We are seeking urgent clarification about it.

    Vi assicuriamo tutta la nostra attenzione affinché ciò non si verifichi più.
    Please rest assured we shall make sure it does not happen again.

REQUESTS AND THANKS

4 Help

(a) Offering help

Lasci, glielo faccio io. < *lei* form > Please let me do it for you.

Lascia, te lo faccio io. < *tu* form > Here, I'll do it for you.

Te la lavo? Shall I wash it for you?

Gliela batto a macchina? Should I type it (for you)?

Posso aiutarti? / aiutarla? Can I help (you)?

Posso fare qualcosa (per lei)? Would you like any help?

Posso darle / darti una mano? May I give you a hand?

T'aiuto? L'aiuto? Need some help?

Ha / Hai bisogno di qualcosa? Is there anything you need?

More formally:

Mi permette di aiutarla? May I be of assistance?

Se possiamo essere d'aiuto non esiti a chiedercelo.
If we can be of assistance, please don't hesitate to ask.

(b) Accepting help:

Note that *per piacere* or *per favore* are never used to accept an offer.

Grazie. Yes, please.

Grazie infinite. Many thanks.

Ne avevo veramente bisogno. I really needed help.

Grazie. Mi farebbe veramente un favore.
Thank you. You would really be doing me a favour. / It would be a great help.

Molto gentile. Non so come ringraziarla.
You are most kind. I can't thank you enough.

(c) Refusing help

No. Grazie. Non importa.
No. Thank you. It doesn't matter. / Never mind.

Grazie. Non disturbarti, veramente.
Thank you. Don't bother, really.

No. Non c'è bisogno. Faccio da sola.
No. There's no need. I can manage.

Grazie. Non si preoccupi. Non è un problema.
Thank you for offering. But it's no problem.

Formal and professional expressions are:

La ringrazio dell'offerta / del suo interessamento ma ho trovato un'altra soluzione.
I'm very grateful for your offer / for your concern but I have found a way out.

Vi siamo grati ma al momento attuale preferiamo declinare la vostra gentile offerta.
We regret to say that at present we have to decline your very kind offer.

(d) Asking for help

Aiutami un attimo, dai. Can you help me, please.

Mi faresti un piacere? Will you do me a favour, please?

Posso chiedere un favore? (to a group)
Could I ask someone to help?

More formal:

Saresti / Sarebbe così gentile da portare questo pacco?
Would you be kind enough to carry this parcel?

Ti / Le dispiacerebbe abbassare la TV?
Would you mind turning down the TV?

Avrei bisogno di una cortesia.
I would be grateful if you could do me a favour.

La pregherei di farmi un favore.
Do you think you could do me a favour?

Mi potrebbe fare un piacere / darmi una mano?
Could I ask you to help / lend me a hand?

5 Advice

(a) Asking for advice

Per te / lei . . . Secondo te / lei . . . In your opinion.

Dovrei . . . secondo te? Should I . . . in your opinion?

Pensi / Credi che dovrei . . .? Do you think I should . . .?

Mi darebbe un consiglio riguardo a questo problema? < formal >
Le sarei grata se mi desse un consiglio riguardo a questo problema.
< formal >
I would appreciate your advice about this problem.

Che cosa faresti / farebbe nella mia situazione?
What would you do if you were me?

Se fossi al mio posto / nei miei panni che cosa diresti? < informal >
If you were me / in my shoes what would you say?

Che linea di condotta mi suggeriresti?
What course of action would you recommend?

(b) Giving advice

Credo / Penso che dovresti venire. I think / I feel you should come.

Perché non mangi? Why don't you eat?

Se fossi in te porterei il bikini. If I were you, I would wear a bikini.

Potrebbe essere un'idea fare una gita insieme.
It might be an idea to take a trip together.

Per me / Secondo me non è prudente.
I don't think it's wise.

A more straightforward approach is conveyed by the use of the imperative tense (see section 61):

Non usare la lana. Don't use wool.

Non fare uscire il gatto con questo freddo.
Don't let the cat go out in this cold.

Signora, non lasci la borsa incustodita.
Don't leave / I shouldn't leave your handbag unattended.

Forcefully:

Per l'amor di Dio lascia stare.
For goodness sake, leave it alone.

La prego, non attraversi.
<u>Please</u> don't cross the road.

86 Requests

Grammatically the moods used to make a request are the **imperative** for people usually addressed as *tu*, the **subjunctive** for people usually addressed as *lei*. In both cases, a softer approach is the conditional. Alternatively the request may be made indirectly. *Per piacere / per favore* are not automatically used as in English; consequently when these words are used they have a more forceful meaning. Overall, Italians tend to be more direct in asking people to do something. Words equivalent to 'may', 'can', 'could', 'would', 'might', when expressing a request, are often omitted in Italian or, in formal cases, replaced by the subjunctive of the main verb. For this use of the subjunctive see also section 59a.

(i) Making a request

● In an office:

> *Spedisca il fax entro le dieci.*
> Can you send the fax by ten o'clock, please.
>
> *Mara, telefona al geometra Sapori.*
> Mara, ring up Mr Sapori (the surveyor).
>
> *Dia priorità a questa fattura.*
> Can you / Could you deal with this invoice first?
>
> *Non voglio essere disturbato.*
> Can you make sure I'm not interrupted, please?

● At home:

> *Eh . . . digli di richiamarmi.*
> Er . . ., tell him to call me later, please.
>
> *Metti il sale.*
> Add the salt, please.
>
> *Non interrompermi adesso.*
> Please don't interrupt me now.

● A softer approach may be conveyed by the conditional (see section 57a):

> *La pregherei di passare domani.*
> Would you mind coming back tomorrow?
>
> *Vorrei che andassimo in banca insieme.*
> Could we go to the bank together?
>
> *Le dispiacerebbe se entrassimo in questo negozio?*
> Would you mind if we went into this shop?

● An indirect request may be formulated as follows:

> *Le / Ti ho già chiesto di cercare l'indirizzo di ...?*
> Have I already asked you to find the address of ...?

> *Scusi, c'è la coda. / Guardi, siamo in coda.*
> Excuse me, there is a queue. (to ask people to wait their turn)

(ii) Replying to requests

> *Senz'altro. Lo faccio subito.* Fine. I'll do it now.
> *D'accordo. (Non si preoccupi.)* All right. (Don't worry.)
> *Sì. Va bene. Certo.* Yes. Fine. OK. Certainly. I'll do it now.
> *Agli ordini!* < jokingly > (literally: to your orders) As you say!
> *Più che volentieri.* I'll do it with pleasure.
> *Come no!* < coll. > I'd love to.
> *Con piacere.* I'll be glad to do it.
> *Va benissimo.* I'll be pleased to.
> *Non mi dispiace affatto.* I'm quite happy to do it.
> *Grazie di avermi avvertito.* < formal > Thank you for telling me.

Promises

> *Certamente, sì.* Certainly. Sure.
> *Ma sì.* Yes. Of course.
> *Lo farò senz'altro.* By all means. I'll do it.
> *Non ci sono problemi.* I see no problems.
> *Non preoccuparti.* Don't worry.

> *Ti prometto che / Me ne incarico io.*
> I promise / I'll make sure that I see to this matter.

> *Non si discute nemmeno!* < informal > Certainly!
> *Che amico sarei!* We're friends, aren't we?
> (implied: What sort of a friend would I be if I didn't help you?)

> *Come no! Sarà fatto.* Naturally! I'll take care of that.

More formally:

> *Sarò felice di essere vostro ospite.* I'll be happy to be your guest.
> *Lo faccio con piacere.* I'll be delighted to do it.
> *Sarà mia premura.* It will be my pleasure.

88 Permission and refusal

(i) Asking permission

Posso entrare? Can I / May I come in please?

Ci sono problemi se spedisco la lettera domani?
Is it all right if I send the letter tomorrow?

Le dispiace se chiudo la finestra? < formal >
Do you mind if I close the window?

Disturbo se accendo la radio?
Does it bother anyone if I switch on the radio?

Le / Vi dà fastidio se grattugio della cipolla?
Do you mind if I grate some onion?

Qualcuno ha qualcosa da dire se fumo? < informally to a group >
Any objection if I smoke?

Faccio una doccia, va bene?
Is it all right if I have a shower?

More formally:

Ho il suo assenso per inoltrare questa pratica?
Do I have your authorization / approval to present this document?

Vorrei che mi autorizzasse a procedere.
May I have your permission to procede?

(ii) Giving permission

The word *pure* can follow any verb to give consent with elegance and warmth:

Prego! Please do! Help yourself!
Fa pure! < *tu* form > Do go ahead.
Faccia pure. < *lei* form > You are welcome. By all means. Please!

Ci mancherebbe. / Ci mancherebbe altro.
Please do not hesitate! You are welcome.

Certo! Sa dov'è? / Sa come fare? Devo aiutarla?
Certainly! Do you know where it is? / Do you know how to do it?
Can I do anything to help you?

Ma vai! (literally: you go!) < youth slang > Go ahead!

More formal:

Mi sembra perfettamente appropriato.
That seems perfectly acceptable.

Non vedo niente in contrario. I can't see any objection.

Non vedo perché ci debbano essere obbiezioni.
I don't see why you shouldn't.

(iii) Refusing to do something

Non posso. Scusa. Mi dispiace.
I'm sorry. I can't.

Non so come fare.
I'm sorry, I don't know what to do.

Non saprei come fare.
I wouldn't know how to do it, sorry.

Mi spiace ma non capisco niente di auto.
I'm sorry but I don't understand anything about cars.

Non saprei da che parte cominciare, veramente.
I really wouldn't know where to start.

Cerca di capire. Non ce la faccio.
Try to understand. I can't help you.

Proprio non riesco. I just can't do it.

È aldilà delle mie possibilità. It's beyond me.

The following are extremely frequent phrases for refusing to do something. They are sexual metaphors with a vulgar connotation. The last one is only rude and equivalent to 'Go to hell!'

‼ *Non rompere (le scatole)!*
‼ *Ma vaffa . . . !*
‼ *Ma va via . . . !*
   Ma va a quel paese! (literally: But go to that country!)

In a formal or professional context one may say:

La prego di scusarmi ma mi trovo nell'impossibilità di accogliere la sua richiesta.
I would like to convey my apologies for not being able to accept your request.

(iv) Refusing to give permission

Mi dispiace, ma mi dà fastidio il fumo.
I'm sorry, but I can't stand smoke.

Se non ti dispiace, preferisco / preferirei di no.
If you don't mind, I'd rather not.

Scusa, ma non vedo perché.
Sorry, but I don't see why.

Firm denial:

Non se ne parla neanche. It's out of the question, I'm afraid.
È fuori discussione. It's not on.
Assolutamente no. No way.

Official denial:

Non posso dare il permesso.
I cannot give permission for this.

Non ho l'autorità per acconsentire.
I have no power to authorize it.

89 Thanking

(i) Offering thanks

La / Ti ringrazio sentitamente per la lettera di referenze. < formal >
Thank you so very much for the reference.

Grazie. / Grazie infinite. / Grazie mille. / Molte grazie.
Thank you. / Many thanks. / Thanks a million. / Thank you very
much.

Grazie di tutto. Thank you for everything.

Grazie per essere venuto. Thanks for coming.

Formal expressions are:

Le porgo i miei più sentiti ringraziamenti.
I'm really very grateful to you.

Non so come ringraziarla anche a nome di mia moglie.
Both my wife and I are very much obliged to you.

*È con i sensi della più viva riconoscenza che le invio questo piccolo
ricordo.*
I should like to express my gratitude / appreciation by sending you
this small token.

Non trovo parole per dirle quanto ci ha fatto piacere.
I can't thank you enough.

La ringrazio per tutto quello che ha fatto per noi.
Thank you for all you have done for us.

Thanking for a present or for a few days as a guest:

> *Il più affettuoso / cordiale grazie per i divertenti giorni a casa vostra.*
> My most heartfelt thanks for my enjoyable stay at your home.
>
> *È stata una bellissima serata.*
> Thanks for such a nice evening.
>
> *Grazie. È bellissimo. Lo desideravo da tanto.*
> Thank you. It's very nice. I have wanted to have one for a long time.

(ii) Acknowledging thanks

> *Prego. / Grazie a lei. / Non c'è di che.*
> My pleasure. / Thank <u>you</u>. / Not at all.
>
> *Ma figurati. / Ma immaginati.*   That's all right. / OK.
>
> *Non dirlo neanche.*   Don't even mention it.

To friends:

> *Non dire sciocchezze.*   Don't be silly.

More formally:

> *Dovere.* < old-fashioned >
> My duty.
>
> *È il minimo che potessi fare.*
> It was the least I could do.
>
> *È stato un piacere.*
> I am delighted I was able to help. / It was a pleasure.
>
> *Se posso essere d'aiuto un'altra volta.*
> If I can be of help any other time (don't hesitate to ask).

FEELINGS

 90 **Expressing one's own feelings and moods**

When Italian people ask questions such as *Come sta?, Come va?* they don't expect merely the conventional *Bene, grazie e lei / tu?* as a tag to everyday greetings. They have asked the question to show they are available for a short conversation and even have a genuine interest in you. The most immediate reply to the above conventional questions often describes one's own feelings and moods at that moment. It is perfectly acceptable and very common in Italian culture to talk about oneself, one's own joys and frustrations, one's own business and family. The verb in the first person singular is very frequent although, unlike English, the pronoun *io* is implied. The following are some of the simplest constructions to use in reply:

Sono + adjective

> *Oggi sono proprio contenta.*
> *Sono veramente felice.*
> *Sono felicissima.*
> I'm really happy today.
>
> *Non sono per niente contenta di Luigi.*
> I'm far from happy about Luigi.

Mi sento + adjective

> *Non mi sento troppo bene. Forse ho l'influenza.*
> I don't feel very well. Perhaps I've got flu.

Mi trovo + adverb

> *Sai, mi trovo bene con la nuova lavatrice.*
> You know, I'm quite satisfied with the new washing machine.

Mi pare / Mi sembra di + verb

> *Mi pare di impazzire qualche volta.*
> Sometimes I feel I'm going mad.
>
> *Mi sembra di stare meglio dopo la cura.*
> I think I feel better after the treatment.

Outbursts about mishaps, too, are quite common:

> *Non sai cosa mi è successo (proprio adesso)!*
> You'll never guess what has just happened to me!

> *Non parlarmene!* < informal >
> Don't talk about it!

> *Vorrei strozzare il mio capo.* < informal >
> I'd like to strangle my boss.

Expressions of one's own feelings about local, national or international events, are also acceptable.

> *Mi fa una rabbia vedere che aumentano ancora la benzina!*
> < coll. >
> I feel so angry that they are putting the petrol prices up again!

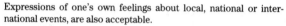

91 Enquiring about other people's feelings

Asking people about their feelings, family, work, is considered an integral part of one's social life, a friendly way of living. Showing no interest, which is called *riservatezza* is usually mistaken for selfishness and lack of human interest. *È un tipo riservato* is usually not a compliment, unless it is related to specific professions. Personal questions are put rather directly to friends, colleagues, acquaintances, even casual acquaintances on holiday or at professional meetings:

> *Che cos' hai? Non ti senti bene?*
> What's the matter? Don't you feel well?

> *Cos'hai da ridere?* What are you laughing at?

> *C'è qualcosa che non va?* Is there something wrong?

> *Che cosa non va?* What's wrong?

> *Non sembri affatto contenta, come mai?*
> You don't seem too happy, how come?

> *Che aria trionfante che hai!*
> You look very pleased with yourself!

> *Mi sembri deluso o è un'impressione?*
> You seem disappointed, or is it my imagination?

> *Ti trovo giù di corda.* You look under the weather.

> *Con chi ce l'hai?* Who are you annoyed with?

In more formal social contexts comments are made on something positive:

> *La trovo allegra!* You look cheerful.
>
> *Si è divertita ieri?* Did you enjoy yourself yesterday?
>
> *Com'è tutta bella abbronzata!* What a wonderful tan you've got!

92 Likes, dislikes and indifference

(i) To express interest one may say:

> *Mi chiedo / domando se / chi / quando . . .*
> I wonder / I would like to know if / who / when . . .
>
> *Uh! M'interessa moltissimo / molto / tanto.*
> I'm very interested in it.
>
> *Non m'interessa proprio / assolutamente.*
> I'm not interested at all.
>
> *L'arte antica mi lascia completamente fredda.*
> Classical art leaves me completely indifferent.
>
> *Mi interesserebbe qualcosa che abbia a che fare con la pittura.*
> I would be interested in something to do with painting.
>
> *È il mio passatempo / programma / sport preferito.*
> It's my favourite hobby / programme / sport.

(ii) To express likes or dislikes:

> *Mi piace molto / moltissimo.* I like it a lot.
>
> *Mi piace un sacco / un mondo.* (literally: a sack, a world) < coll. >
> I'm terribly fond of it.
>
> *Non c'è niente che mi piaccia di più.*
> There is nothing I like more.
>
> *Vado pazza per questa moda / per quel cantante.* < coll. >
> I'm mad about this fashion / that singer.
>
> *Stravede per sua figlia.*
> He is crazy about his daughter. / His daughter is the apple of his eye.
>
> *Mi piace un casino.* < vulgar, youth slang >
> I like it / him very much. (literally: I like it a brothel)

Appreciation and admiration are frequently expressed by changing the ending of nouns with the addition of the diminutive endings *-ino*, *-uccio* (pretty, charming):

> *Che carucci i cuccioli!* Your puppies are lovely!

> *Che tesorini i neonati!*
> Aren't babies lovely! (literally: little treasures)

(iii) To express uncertainty, indifference:

> *Non mi convince.* I'm not taken by it / him.

> *Non mi ha affatto entusiasmato.*
> I haven't found him / it exciting at all.

> *Mi lascia perplessa / indifferente.* It / She has left me indifferent.

> *Diciamo che non ne vado matto.* Let's say I'm not crazy about it.

Lack of interest for something in general:

> *Non m'interessa. / Non m'importa.*
> I don't care. / I couldn't care less.

!! *Me ne sbatto. Me ne frego.* < vulgar > I don't give a damn.

(iv) To express dislike:

che + noun
> *Che banalità!* It's too banal for words!

che + adjective
> *Che sciocco!* How silly!

With understatement:

> *Diciamo che non è il mio giornale preferito.*
> Let's say it's not my favourite newspaper.

> *Non posso dire che mi piaccia.* I can't say I like him / it.

> *Non farei i salti mortali per averlo.*
> I wouldn't go out of my way to get it.
> (literally: I wouldn't do somersaults to have it.)

With frankness: softening expressions such as the English 'I'm afraid' are not commonly used.

> *(Mi dispiace). Lo detesto.* I'm afraid I dislike him.

> *Non lo posso soffrire.* I'm afraid I can't stand him.

To express dislike or disagreement a very frequent, colloquial phrase is:

Ma che cavolo è?
But what on earth is it? (literally: What kind of cauliflower is it?)

Ma che vaccata è? < vulgar, youth slang > Bullshit!

(v) Finding out about other people's interests:

Ti interessi di jazz? Are you interested in / Do you go for jazz?
Ti / Le piace? Ti / Le piacciono? Do you like it? Do you like them?
Ti è piaciuto? Ti piacerebbe? Did you enjoy it? Would you like it?
Trova interessante il pugilato? Do you find boxing interesting?

More formal:

Sono indiscreto se le chiedo qual è la sua banca?
Am I being indiscreet if I ask which is your bank?

Or indirect:

Credevo che le piacesse il violino. I thought you liked the violin.

93 Anxiety, fear and relief

(i) Anxiety because of exams, achievements, people being late, people's behaviour or their health may be expressed by:

Mi sento inquieta. I feel nervous.
Sono in ansia per lui. I am anxious for him.
Non so perché non mi sento tranquilla. I don't know why but I feel res
Non riesco a rilassarmi. I can't relax.
Che tormento! How worrying!
Sono francamente preoccupato. I'm really worried.
La situazione è preoccupante. I find it worrying.
Sono così agitata. I am in a flap.

Forms of indirect admission of anxiety are:

Avrebbe già dovuto telefonare. He ought to have already rung up.
Sarò all'altezza? Will I be up to it (the task)?

(ii) Fear:

Ho paura. I'm afraid. / I'm scared.
Ho una paura folle. I'm worried sick.
Sono terrorizzato al solo pensiero.
I'm scared stiff at the mere thought.
Rabbrividisco all'idea che arrivino in dieci.
It gives me the creeps the idea that there will be ten of them.

Ho i miei dubbi. I have serious misgivings.
Che paura! Che spavento! How frightening!

Che fifa! / Ho una fifa blu. < coll. >
I'm getting cold feet. / I am in a funk.

!!   *Ho caga!* < youth slang > I'm shit scared! (literally: I have shit!)

Common expressions to indicate anxiety for possible unpleasant events are:

Tocca ferro. Touch wood. (literally: touch iron)
Non lo dico per scaramanzia. I don't want to tempt providence.

It has recently become fashionable among young people to keep their fingers crossed, but no verbal expression accompanies the gesture.

(iii) Relief:

Siamo felici di sapere che ha passato gli esami.
We are pleased to hear that he passed his exams.

Meno male! Per fortuna! Thank goodness!
Siamo proprio contenti. We are really glad.
Che sollievo! What a relief!

Mi son tolto un peso dallo stomaco. / Mi son tolto un pensiero.
That's a weight off my mind.

4 Pleasure, satisfaction and enjoyment

Mi fa tanto piacere che siete ritornati amici. < formal >
I'm so pleased to hear that you are friends again.

Urra! Fantastico! Meraviglioso! Tremendo!
Hurrah! Terrific! Fantastic! Fabulous! Great!

Che bella notizia! / Che bellezza! That's good news!

Mi sembra di sognare. / Mi sembra un sogno. < coll. >
It seems like a dream.

Sono al settimo cielo. I'm in seventh heaven! / I'm over the moon!

Mi sembra di toccare il cielo con un dito. < coll. >
I'm overjoyed / as pleased as Punch.

Non mi sembra vero. I can hardly believe it's true.

Sono fuori di me dalla gioia. I'm beside myself with joy.

More formal:

> *Non ho parole per esprimere la gioia per il fidanzamento di sua figlia.*
> I can't say how delighted I am about your daughter's engagement.

> *È con grande piacere che la informo che ha vinto il primo premio.*
> It gives me great pleasure to inform you that you are the first prizewinner.

> *Vorrei esprimerle il mio entusiasmo per la sua performance.*
> I would like to tell you how excited I am about your performance.

> *È la cosa più bella che abbia sentito da tanto tempo.*
> It's the most exciting news I have heard for a long time.

Youth slang:

> *Sei un mito!* Fantastic! (direct congratulations) (literally: You're a myth!)

> *Che mito che è!* He's fantastic! (about a singer or a friend)

> *Che forte!* He's great! (literally: strong)

95 Surprise and hope

(i) Surprise

> *Sono piacevolmente sorpreso.* < formal >
> I am pleasantly surprised.

> *Questa sì che è una sorpresa!* This is a surprise.
> *Sono senza parole.* I am at a loss for words.
> *Veramente! Sul serio! Ma va!* Really?! Fancy that! Never!
> *Cosa mi dice / dici! Scherzi?* < coll. > You're kidding!
> *Che mi venga un colpo!* < coll. > Well! I'm blowed!
> *Trovo la notizia sorprendente.* I find it amazing.
> *Non me l'aspettavo.* I didn't expect it.
> *Mi ha colto di sorpresa.* It has taken me by surprise.

(ii) Hope

The following expressions require the subjunctive in a formal context; in speech the indicative is frequently used.

> *Spero che . . . / Speriamo che . . .* I hope . . . / Let's hope that . . .
> *Siamo sicuri che . . .* We are sure that . . .
> *Mi auguro che . . .* I wish that . . . / I hope that . . .
> *Chissà se potrò . . .* I wonder if I'll be able to . . .

> *Desidero tanto . . .* I really wish . . . / I do so wish . . .
> *Se solo . . .* If only . . .
> *Finché c'è vita c'è speranza.* While there's life there's hope.

Formal expressions are:

> *Sono fiduciosa che venga.*
> I have every confidence that he will come.
>
> *È nostro convincimento che la situazione migliorerà.*
> Our expectation is that the situation will improve.
>
> *Siamo certi che tutto andrà per il meglio.*
> We are confident of every success.

6 Anger, boredom and disappointment

(i) Anger:

Italian people express anger by raising the tone of their voice, even in public. Lowering the voice may be misunderstood as shyness and may not be effective. Irritation and dissatisfaction are formally conveyed with phrases like the following, describing one's own feelings:

> *Mi spiace ma non sono affatto soddisfatta del servizio.*
> I'm sorry I'm not at all satisfied with your service.
>
> *Mi dispiace ma trovo la situazione irritante e offensiva.*
> I'm sorry but this is irritating and offensive.
>
> *Mi spiace ma questo non è accettabile / giusto / vero.*
> I'm sorry I can't accept this. It's not right / true.

It's more likely that a dissatisfied customer will ask to see a senior person:

> *Per cortesia mi faccia parlare con il direttore / il responsabile dell'ufficio.*
> I would like to talk to the director / to the office manager.

Or, simply, that he will let off steam by showing his anger to other people:

> *Ho tanta di quella rabbia in corpo!* I'm hopping mad!
> *Sono furibonda.* I am absolutely furious. / How infuriating!
> *Sono piuttosto seccata.* I'm rather annoyed.
>
> *Ne ho fin sopra i capelli!* < coll. >
> I'm fed up to the back teeth. (literally: I have it up to my hair)

261

> *Sono stufa marcia.* < coll. >
> I'm bored to death. (literally: I am rotten tired)
>
> *Ma guarda che roba!* < coll. >
> But look at this! (literally: But look at this thing / rubbish)
>
> *Che giornata storta!* It's not my day, is it?
>
> *Questa storia mi ha lasciato con l'amaro in bocca.*
> All this has left me with a nasty taste in my mouth.
>
> *Ho proprio perso la pazienza con lui.*
> I have lost patience with him.

Interjections and even swearing as expressions of anger are not uncommon. The first examples given here are the most acceptable though it is still advisable to be able to understand them more than to use them:

> *Accidenti! Porca miseria!*
> Blast! To hell with it! (literally: swine poverty!)
>
> *Ma vada a farsi benedire! Vada a quel paese! All'inferno!*
> *Al diavolo! Vadano . . .* (pl. if referring to institutions)
> Damn! Go to hell!

The following are very frequent interjections, particularly among men, the generation under forty and teenagers. They are very vulgar (the English equivalent might be 'Fuck it!') and newspapers quote them abbreviated.

!! *Non rompere . . .*
!! *Ma che c__ dice!* (sexual metaphors)
!! *Vada via al c__!*
!! *Se lo metta . . .!*

Formal complaints may be expressed as follows:

> *Mi consenta di dire che considero offensiva e inaudita questa soluzione.*
> May I say that I find this solution both offensive and unacceptable.
>
> *Trovo il comportamento del personale inadeguato, per non dire insolente.*
> I must say I find the staff's behaviour inadequate, not to say insolent.
>
> *Sappia che è mia intenzione inoltrare una protesta ufficiale a chi di competenza.*
> I would like to inform you that I intend to make an official complaint to whoever is responsible.

(ii) Boredom

● Describing one's own feelings:

> *Scusa se sbadiglio, ma mi sto annoiando.*
> Sorry I'm yawning, but I'm bored.

> *Non riesco proprio a entusiasmarmi.*
> I can't work up much enthusiasm about it.

> *Sono piuttosto stufa.* I'm fed up.

● Describing the cause of boredom:

> *Non mi sembra molto interessante.* I can't say I find it interesting.

> *È piuttosto noioso.* It's rather boring.

> *Trovo le sue battute noiose da morire.*
> His jokes turn me off / bore me to death.

> *Lo sport mi annoia.* Sport bores me.

● Exclamations:

> *Che barba!* I'm cheesed off! (literally: What a beard! I have grown
> a beard.)

> *Che pizza! Che mattone!* How boring! (literally: What a pizza!
> What a brick!)

> *Che flebo!* < youth slang > What a drip!

> *Che amorfo!* < youth slang >
> How deadly! (literally: colourless, amorphous; of films, people)

(iii) Disappointment

> *Avevo sperato che finisse* (subj.) *in tempo.*
> I had hoped that he would finish on time.

> *Ci contavo proprio invece ha deciso di no.*
> I was counting on it, instead he has decided against it.

> *Sono deluso.* I'm disappointed.
> *È deludente.* That's disappointing.
> *Mi aspettavo di più.* I feel let down.

> *I risultati sono inferiori alle aspettative.*
> The results are not as good as I had expected.

> *Che delusione! / Che sfortuna! / Che disdetta!*
> How disappointing! / Bad luck! / That's too bad.

!!   *Che sfiga che ho avuto!* < sexual metaphor, youth slang >
     I was really unlucky.

‼ *Che sfigato!* < youth slang >
How unlucky!

Che tirapacchi che sei! < youth slang >
You're so unreliable!
(said to someone who has let someone down, e.g. for an appointment)

M'ha dato buca. She / He has let me down. < youth slang >

Devo confessare che l'incontro mi ha deluso. < formal >
I must say the meeting has been disappointing.

Mi dispiace doverle esprimere la mia delusione riguardo al suo progetto. < formal >
I regret to say that your project has come as a great disappointment.

OPINIONS AND DISCUSSIONS

Starting off

Italians adore debating. It's a national sport, the salt and pepper of
social life with friends, acquaintances, strangers at dinner, in coffee
bars, trains, on holidays. Favourite topics are national and
international politics, current events, football and, of course, shared
professional situations. It is a sign of friendliness to ask people's
opinions:

> *Cosa ne pensi / pensa di queste elezioni?*
> What do you think of these elections?

> *Secondo te / voi / lei chi ha ragione?* What's your view? Who is right?

> *Avete sentito / letto di / visto sul giornale di quello scandalo?*
> Have you heard / read about / seen in the newspaper about that
> scandal?

> *Condivide l'opinione del professore sul conto di questo studente?*
> Do you share the teacher's opinion about this student?

> *Concorda che questo bilancio è negativo?*
> Do you agree that this is a negative budget?

> *Sarebbe favorevole o sfavorevole al sistema proporzionale?*
> Would you be in favour of or against proportional representation?

> *La considera una buona idea o no?*
> Do you think it's a good idea or not?

> *Da che parte stai?* Which side are you on?

More formally:

> *Gradirei conoscere il suo pensiero riguardo alla nuova ricercatrice.*
> I'd like to know your opinion in relation to / Would you care to let
> me know your opinion about the new research associate.

> *Mi interesserebbe una sua opinione in merito a questo prodotto.*
> I would be interested in your opinion concerning this product.

Exchanges of opinions also start with someone expressing his / her
own views in the hope of a reaction:

> *Io non so cosa ne pensate voi, ma a me sembra che abbia torto.*
> < formal >
> I don't know what you think, but it seems to me that he is wrong.

A formal debate may be opened with:

> *Dichiaro aperto il dibattito.* The debate is opened.
>
> *Invito il Professor Malletti a prendere la parola / a iniziare la discussione.*
> I invite Professor Malletti to open the discussion.

98 Expressing views

(i) Direct expression of opinion

Italians tend not to preface their opinions with expressions equivalent to the English 'If you don't mind me saying so ...', 'If I may be quite frank ...'. Their approach is more direct:

> *Secondo me / per me ...* In my opinion ...
> *Dal mio punto di vista ...* From my point of view ...
> *A parer mio .../ A mio avviso ...* My own view on the matter is ... / To my mind ...
> *Io sostengo che ...* I think / claim / reckon ...
> *A me sembra che .../ A me pare che ...* It seems to me that ...
> *Per quanto mi riguarda ...* As I see it ...
> *Se volete la mia opinione ...* If you ask me ...
> *Sai che ti dico ...* I'd say ...
> *Ad essere franchi ...* To be perfectly honest ...

(ii) To express opinions one feels confident about

In this case it is not necessary to start a sentence with phrases equivalent to 'I'm afraid', 'I would like to suggest'. It is not considered bad manners to say:

> *Ciò che è certo è che ...* It is certainly true that ...
>
> *Sono sicuro che sbaglia a dimettersi.*
> I think he is wrong to resign. (literally: I'm sure)
>
> *Sono certa che non si amano.*
> I'm convinced they don't love each other. (literally: I'm certain)
>
> *Non ho dubbi in merito.*
> I don't have many doubts about it. (literally: I don't have doubts about it)

(iii) To express opinions with some caution

The most suitable moods of the verbs to express caution are the conditional and the subjunctive:

> *Penserei che / Suggerirei che . . .* I would think / suggest that . . .
>
> *Mi sembrerebbe che . . .* It would seem to me that . . .
>
> *Potrebbe rivelarsi opportuno . . .* It could turn out suitable . . .
>
> *È forse altrettanto / ugualmente giusto . . .* It may be equally right . . .
>
> *Sarei incline a . . .* I would be inclined to . . .

(iv) To express uncertainty, doubts

> *Ma . . .* But . . .
>
> *Chissà! Forse . . .* Who knows! Perhaps . . .
>
> *Non ho un'opinione definitiva in materia.*
> I haven't got strong views on the subject.
>
> *Beato chi non ha dubbi!* I envy anybody who hasn't got doubts.
>
> *Non mi sono formata un'opinione sull'argomento.*
> It's not something I have considered a great deal.
>
> *È più facile a dirsi che a farsi.* It's easier said than done.

(v) Remaining noncommittal

If you wish to avoid giving an opinion you may say:

> *Ah sì?* Really? / Did he? / Has she?
>
> *Eh, sì!* Yes, indeed.
>
> *Però! Ma va!?* < in a querying tone > Fancy that!
>
> *È difficile da dirsi.* It's difficult to say, isn't it?
>
> *Capisco. Eh, dipende da tante cose.*
> I see. It depends on many things.
>
> *Non saprei proprio.* I wouldn't really know.
>
> *È difficile dare una risposta sui due piedi. / Non vorrei
> esprimere un giudizio a caldo.*
> It's difficult to say on the spur of the moment.
>
> *Scusate, ma preferisco non pronunciarmi.*
> I'm sorry but I'd rather not comment.
>
> *Preferisco non entrare nell'argomento.*
> I'd rather not be dragged into the discussion.
>
> *Non spetta a me dare un giudizio.* I'm not in a position to judge.

With a pinch of irony you may say:

> *Come si dice in inglese? 'No comment'?*
> What's the English phrase? 'No comment'?

99 Agreeing and disagreeing

(i) Agreeing

Ah, non ho nulla da eccepire. Well, I have no objection.

Sì, sì, ha ragione. Yes, indeed, I think you're right.

Sono d'accordo con lei / te. I agree.

Ah, è vero. Yes, it's true.

Sembra anche a me così. I think so too.

Ha ragioni da vendere. You are quite right to sell.

Verissimo. / Stravero. It couldn't be more true.

Non posso fare a meno di pensare allo stesso modo.
I'm right behind you.

Sono d'accordissimo. You have my wholehearted support.

Sì, ci sono delle valide ragioni per sostenere che il contratto non è valido, ma anche ragioni altrettanto valide per sostenere il contrario.

Yes, there are excellent reasons to claim that the contract is not valid, but equally valid ones to support the opposite.

And the above sentence could be used to introduce the opposite opinion, tactfully.

(ii) Disagreeing

The whole purpose of Italian discussions lies in disagreeing. Italians find in them the flavour of medieval debates, where people are given the opportunity to show their skill in finding counter-arguments. This element is present even in official board meetings. Expressing an opposite view is often quite acceptable and disagreement can be expressed openly:

Non sono d'accordo. Mi dispiace. I'm sorry, I don't agree.

Non è vero. That's not true.

Ma figurati! I don't think so! / No way!

Mi sbaglierò, ma non credo. I don't think so, I'm afraid.

Non vorrei mettere la mano sul fuoco, però non credo che i fatti siano riportati correttamente.
I wouldn't stake my life on it, but I don't think the facts are correct.

Capisco che tu tiri l'acqua al tuo mulino, tuttavia non sono d'accordo.
I see it's all grist to your mill, but I don't agree.

Scommettiamo che non è così? Do you want to bet?

Or more cautiously introduced:

> *Non vorrei / voglio fare polemica ma . . .*
> I don't want to argue but . . .
>
> *Non per polemizzare ma . . .*
> Not wishing to cause a controversy but . . .
>
> *Per quanto ne so io, invece . . .* On the contrary, as far as I know . . .
> *Lei sostiene che . . . mentre . . .* According to you . . . whereas . . .

With irony:

> *Disturbo se interrompo . . .?* Is one allowed to interrupt?

Disagreement may be expressed more abruptly with:

> *Ma come fai a dire questo!* How can you say that!
>
> *Un momento. Aspetta un attimo. Calma.*
> Hold on a second. Calm down!
>
> *Questo modo di ragionare fa acqua da tutte le parti.*
> I'm afraid this way of thinking is very shaky. (literally: leaking
> everywhere)

!! *Balle! / Storie!* Nonsense!
!! *Ma va a farti benedire, dai!* Go to hell! (literally: But go and be
blessed!)

Or in sophisticated arguments disagreement is introduced by:

> *Se posso fare la parte del diavolo . . .*
> If I can play the devil's advocate . . .
>
> *Ma se si porta questo ragionamento fino in fondo . . .*
> But if one pursues this line of reasoning to its logical conclusion . . .
>
> *Mi è difficile capire come si può sostenere che . . .*
> Isn't it rather difficult to claim that . . .
>
> *I tuoi / vostri / questi ragionamenti mi sembrano sbagliati perché . . .*
> I find your / these arguments rather weak because . . . (literally:
> they seem to me wrong)

Or more formally:

> *Scusatemi, ma vorrei far notare che . . .*
> I do apologize but I would like to point out that . . .
>
> *Mi consenta di contraddirla.*
> Allow me to raise an objection.
>
> *Consentitemi di dissentire / esprimere un diverso punto di vista.*
> I would like to express a different point of view.

Nonostante tutto, credo che lei sia in errore.
Well, I must say I still do not share your view. (literally: you are mistaken)

Mi scusi se insisto, ma a me risulta il contrario.
I am sorry to press the point, but according to my information it is the opposite.

100 Clarifying

(i) Asking for clarification

Allora, dunque . . . So, then . . .
Chiariscimi un punto. Can you clarify one point, please.

Mi spieghi per cortesia come fai a insistere che . . .
Can you tell me, please, how you can insist that . . .

Se . . . come si spiega che . . .
If that's the case . . . how come that . . .

Io vorrei capire come . . .
I would like to understand how . . .

Chi mi dà un esempio di come . . .
Can anyone give me an example of how . . .

Ma non si sottovaluta il fatto che . . .?
But doesn't one underestimate the fact that . . .?

Allora questo significa che . . .?
Then this means that . . .?

Mi son fatta un quadro esatto?
Have I got the correct picture of the situation?

Il che implica, se ho capito bene . . .
Which means, if I have understood you correctly, that . . .

Vorrei chiederle di chiarire un punto.
Could you clarify one point, please?

(ii) Clarifying for others

Cioè . . . That is to say . . .
In altre parole . . . In other words . . .
Ciò che intendo dire è che . . . What I intend to say is that . . .
Per dirla in altri termini . . . To put it differently . . .
O meglio . . . Or rather . . .
Ad esempio . . . For example . . .

Quello che sto cercandoti di dire è che ...
What I'm trying to say is that ...

Per andare al nocciolo della questione ...
To get to the heart of the matter ...

More informally:

Hai capito? Is it clear?
Giusto? OK.?
Messaggio ricevuto? Has the penny dropped?

More formally:

Se sono necessari ulteriori chiarimenti li darò.
If it is felt that further explanations are necessary, I will give them.

Dovrei forse chiarire quello che intendo aggiungendo questo particolare.
I should probably clarify what I mean by adding this detail.

Sarebbe più preciso dire che è scorretto sintatticamente.
It would be more precise to say that it is incorrect syntactically.

Spero di essere stato chiaro.
I trust I made myself clear.

Riformulerei la frase così.
I would reword the sentence like this.

01 Presenting one's reasons

(i) Giving examples

Per esempio ... For example ...
Prendi, ad esempio ... Take for instance ...
Tanto per fare un esempio ... Just to give an example ...

Se consideriamo / prendiamo in considerazione ... < formal >
Let's consider ... / Let's take into consideration ...

Esaminiamo ... Let's examine ...

Non pretendo di essere un esperto ma ...
I'm not an expert but ...

(ii) Taking up a point

A proposito di questo. A questo proposito ... On this subject ...

In relazione proprio a questo suo ultimo argomento ... < formal >
In connection with this last point ...

Quanto dice mi fa ricordare che . . .
What you say reminds me that . . .

Ah! Interessante questo! Oh! That's interesting!

Scusa, fermati su questo punto. Hold on, let's stop at this point.

Scusi, soffermiamoci su questo punto. < formal >
Excuse me, let's pause for a moment to concentrate on this point.

A me sembra una buona idea questa.
I think this is a good idea.

Mi ha colpito una cosa che lei ha detto.
One thing you said has struck me.

(iii) Taking time to think

Mmm . . . sì, sì . . . Ehm . . . yes . . . yes . . .
Ah! sì certo . . . Well, yes . . .
Sì, come posso dire . . . Yes, what can I say . . .
Vorrei pensarci un attimo. Ehm, let me think, well . . .
Ma non saprei. Well, I really wouldn't know.
Dicevo che . . . I was saying that . . .
Come dicevo . . . As I was saying . . .

(iv) Explaining

Beh, perché . . . Well, because . . .
Vedi . . . You see . . .
Il fatto è che . . . The fact is that . . .
Ma scusa . . . Listen . . .
Fondamentalmente . . . Basically . . .

La ragione principale sta nel fatto che è straniero.
The main reason is that he is a foreigner.

Bisogna prendere in considerazione il fatto che . . .
One needs to take into account the fact that . . .

Mi parrebbe che . . . poiché / siccome / in quanto . . .
I would think that . . . because / since / as . . .

È un problema di natura sociale. It's a social problem.

Proviamo ad analizzare questi fatti. Let's analyse these facts.

Ci sarebbe da aggiungere il costo del lavoro.
One should add the labour costs.

Se si inquadra il caso nella situazione politica mondiale . . .
If one looks closely at the issue in the context of the world political
situation . . .

② Conciliatory attitudes

Da un lato sono d'accordo con lei, d'altro canto . . .
On the one hand I agree with you, on the other . . .

Sì, vedo il tuo punto di vista ma fino a un certo punto . . .
Yes, I can see your point but only to a certain extent . . .

In fondo hai ragione ma . . .
There is a lot in what you say but . . .

Ora che ci penso potrebbe darsi che . . .
Thinking about it, it could be that . . .

Se si guarda l'episodio dal punto di vista . . . allora . . ., altrimenti . . .
If one looks at the episode from the viewpoint . . . then . . .,
otherwise . . .

Vediamo quali sono i pro e i contro.
Let's look at the pros and the cons.

Forse dipende se lo si guarda da un punto di vista legale o etico.
Perhaps it depends on whether one looks at it from a legal or an
ethical point of view.

Ma non c'è un frainteso?
But isn't there a misunderstanding?

Ma non dite in fondo la stessa cosa?
But aren't you basically saying the same thing?

Non litigheremo per questo, no?
Well, we are not going to quarrel over it, are we?

OK, d'accordo. OK. Agreed.

SOCIAL STRATEGIES

103 Requests

(i) If you need to remind your flatmate that it's her / his turn to tidy up or do the shopping why not say:

> *A chi tocca far la spesa questa volta?*
> Whose turn is it to go shopping this time?

> *Scusa eh, non mi ricordo se tocca a me andare al supermercato.*
> Sorry but I don't remember whether it's my turn to go to the supermarket.

> *Santo cielo, devo fare la mia camera, è tutta in disordine.*
> Goodness, I have to tidy up my bedroom. It's such a mess.

(ii) To remind a colleague to hurry up and do something you asked for, here is a suggestion:

> *C'è ancora tanta corrispondenza arretrata. Tu a che punto sei?*
> I'm quite behind with the correspondence. What stage are you at?

(iii) To ask someone not to smoke one may say:

> *Mi scusi, credevo fosse riservato ai non fumatori.*
> I'm sorry, I thought it was reserved for non-smokers.

> *Mi scusi, pensavo fosse proibito fumare qui.*
> Excuse me, I thought one couldn't smoke here.

> *Scusate, ho un po' di mal di gola.*
> I'm sorry, I have a sore throat.

If it is a colleague or a young person, smile and ask:

> *Perché hai così premura di andar a trovare San Pietro?*
> Why are you in such a hurry to go and meet St. Peter?

(iv) To ask for a window to be opened or shut:

> *Fa troppo caldo se chiudo la finestra? / il finestrino?*
> Will it be too hot if I close the window? / the train window?

> *Ho paura che mi stia venendo l'influenza / il raffreddore.*
> I think I'm getting flu / catching a cold.

04 Complaints

(i) If your neighbours in a hotel make too much noise coming back at night or keep the TV volume too high, you may greet them next morning and add:

> *Buongiorno. Bella giornata anche oggi. Avete sentito che fracasso stanotte? Siete riusciti a dormire voi?*
> Good morning. What a beautiful day. Did you hear all that noise last night? Did you manage to sleep?

Or in the lounge you may comment:

> *Bel posto, vero? Ambiente simpatico. Peccato che è un po' troppo rumoroso, no?*
> Nice place isn't it? Friendly atmosphere. It's a shame there's a bit too much noise, isn't it?

(ii) Queuing up is not part of Italian culture. The prevailing philosophy is to pretend to ignore the queue. If someone has bypassed you at the post office, in a bank or at the station try saying:

> *Mi scusi, le darei la precedenza volentieri, ma ho premura anch'io.*
> I'm sorry, I would be quite willing to let you go ahead of me, but I'm in a hurry too.

> *Mi dispiace, scusi ma ho premura.*
> I'm sorry, but I'm in a hurry.

> *Scusi, signora / signore, c'era prima lei? / è arrivata prima lei?*
> Excuse me, madam / sir, were you here before I was?

Or quite openly say:

> *Scusi, c'è la coda.* Excuse me, there's a queue.

05 Enquiries

(i) Items in shop windows should, by law, have price tags. But often these are deliberately hidden by the actual garments. Enter and say:

> *Scusi, non riesco a vedere il prezzo di quel vestito.*
> Excuse me, I can't see the price of that dress.

(ii) Asking for professional information without giving the impression of probing into people's personal financial affairs:

> *Hai sentito qualche opinione qualificata sull' aumento di capitale delle Fiat?*
> Have you heard any expert opinion on the capital increase of the Fiat shares?

(iii) To ask a personal question you may introduce your question with:

> *Dirai / Dirà che sono curiosa ma . . .*
> You'll say I am nosy but . . . / Do you mind if I ask a personal question?

106 Refusing

Entertaining people to dinner is considered a very important way to show people they are welcome. Although being on a diet is fashionable, in Italy guests are warmly invited to eat and are expected to indicate their appreciation at being made welcome by showing they enjoy the food. Given the reputation of Italian cuisine that's not usually too much of a sacrifice. However, if you need to refuse, praise the food, then give a convincing explanation:

> *È veramente squisito questo pesce. Ma devo proprio sacrificarmi e prenderne meno. Sono a dieta per ordine del medico.*
> This fish is really excellent. But I'll have to ask you for a smaller portion. I am on a diet on doctor's orders.

A flattering explanation may be equally good if you have been a guest for the weekend:

> *Mi dovete scusare, ne prendo un po' meno. Pago per i peccati di gola di ieri.*
> I'm sorry, I'll have a little less. I over-indulged yesterday and now I'm paying the price.

If you want to indicate that you are not too keen on a dish make it sound like a cultural comparison:

> *La cucina italiana è molto buona anche se usa molto più olio di quella inglese.*
> Italian food is very good even though it uses more oil than we do in English cooking.

7 Tactful solutions

(i) If you want to avoid being dragged into a discussion (see also section 102):

> *Scusatemi se ascolto soltanto, sono stanco morto.*
> I apologize for just listening, but I am dead tired.

(ii) If uncertain whether to write a hand-written or a typed letter you may choose the second and say:

> *La prego di volermi scusare se scrivo a macchina ma non voglio infliggerle la tortura di decifrare la mia pessima calligrafia.*
> I would like to express my apologies for a typed letter but I'd rather not put you through the ordeal of deciphering my handwriting.

(iii) When in company, paying in a restaurant or in a bar is often a tug-of-war in Italy. If you feel that as a foreigner you are at a disadvantage linguistically, here is a solution:

- During the meal pretend you have to go to the toilet:

> *Scusatemi, mi assento un momento.*

Instead go to the cashier and say:

> *Vorrei pagare io il conto. Tenga* (give some money) *poi prenderò il resto.*
> I would like to pay the bill myself. Here is . . . I'll take the change later.

- If you go to the cashier to pay and realize you have left your money at home, go back to your friends or colleagues and say:

> *Scusatemi ero andato per pagare, ma ho solo un pezzo da centomila e non hanno da cambiare!*
> Sorry folks! I went to pay but I've only got a . . . note and they don't have change.

(iv) To end a long telephone conversation, see section 115.

(v) To introduce yourself to a guest speaker, you may make the approach by congratulating him / her on his / her talk:

> *Posso esprimerle le più vive congratulazioni?*
> May I express my warmest congratulations?

> *È stato molto interessante il suo intervento.*
> Your talk was very interesting.

SILENCE AND GESTURES

Silence, gestures, distance between speakers, and clothes are non-verbal codes through which we communicate every day. It is important to understand them, even more than to imitate them, because like words, they may be 'false friends'. Interpreting them correctly is as crucial as understanding a sentence correctly.

108 Silence

In Italy silence is usually considered embarrassing in formal or informal encounters. For instance, when meeting someone after a journey or at the airport, silence is to be avoided during the journey to the hotel or the company offices. It is not seen as a gesture of courtesy to allow people to rest or collect their thoughts. It is seen either as a sign of downright rudeness or as anger or annoyance. Small talk about the journey, the weather, enquiries about likes and dislikes, the country, the town are considered essential to give a polite welcome.

Long silent pauses during meals which are part of a conference or a professional meeting may convey the impression that the silent person has some grievance towards his guests or that he feels it is not worth talking to them. Light conversation is also customary when waiting in a public place for the same meeting. During a meeting or in a seminar, too long a pause before giving one's own opinion or answer is not an indication of courtesy towards potential speakers. On the contrary, it indicates either insecurity or lack of ideas.

Silence is not expected during a public talk or a lecture. Exchanges of opinions with people sitting nearby are considered to be a sign of interest in what the speaker is saying; they are a compliment to his ability to create interest in his subject. Silence is a sign of assent when confronted with a controversial statement during a talk or a discussion. It does not indicate dissent or desire to change the subject. The deafening silence of disapproval may be misunderstood. The Italian proverb says:

Chi tace acconsente. If you keep silent you agree.

Love for words is also apparent in the habit of closing a conversation – professional or personal – by repeating more than once the conclusion reached:

> *Allora abbiamo deciso che . . . Dunque, come ti ho detto . . .*

This repetition is not an indirect insult to the intelligence of the person you are speaking to. It is a way of avoiding an abrupt departure or end to a conversation, even on the phone.

Interrupting or speaking at the same time as the other person shows involvement in the topic. If it is a formal talk, one may say:

> *Scusi se la interrompo, ma . . .* Excuse my interrupting, but . . .

When one of the speakers is looking for the right word, those seconds of silence are often filled by others prompting him with words.

This 'hostile' attitude to silence is evident in attitudes towards noise. Apologies are not conveyed when a loud noise is made by dropping a pan or slamming the door by mistake.

09 Tone of voice

Concern, emotions, sympathy, understanding as well as professional interest must be seen in the eyes and heard in the voice. It is significant that there is no Italian word for self-control. This word borrowed from English is not as highly regarded as in England and can be easily misunderstood for absence of feelings and coldness.

The level of voice is usually fairly high both in private conversations and in public places (trains, bars, meetings, restaurants) where there is usually a good amount of noise. Talking softly is interpreted as whispering and is a sign of secretiveness towards the people nearby. At a formal or informal dinner, the noise made by people talking may sound as if they are quarrelling, but the loud voices are only a sign of participation. At meals it is common to have a discussion with people who are not one's close neighbours at the table.

110 Gestures

If you feel uneasy about gesticulating, it is better to avoid it, or you may risk projecting a caricature of yourself and your personality. Moving one's hands while speaking (obviously without putting a finger in the listener's eyes) has a variety of meanings. It is seen as a sign of spontaneity, openness and friendliness; on a professional level, it indicates keenness to communicate and to establish a friendly relationship.

The following are some of the most frequent gestures to underline a point:

• A denial is often accompanied by shaking of the head. To reinforce the denial the forefinger may be lifted and the hand moved horizontally several times.

• To greet and say goodbye formally, one must shake hands. Informally, *ciao* may be accompanied by waving the arm and the open palm towards the traveller or by closing and opening the hand several times.

• Informally, to ask someone to approach, the right arm may be stretched out and the hand moved downwards several times.

• Walking arm in arm for two women or a man and a woman is not unusual, though not as usual as in the past. Walking hand in hand is typical of young couples.

- While listening to someone, it is common to move the head up and down to show interest in what the speaker is saying.

- Men often express welcome or friendship by putting an arm around another man's shoulders.

- To reinforce a point in a conversation or in the presentation of a report an arm slightly bent at the chest level is moved up and down.

! - Vulgar gestures: forming a 'U' with the forefinger and the little finger as well as placing the right hand against the bent left arm are male gestures of dismissal.

Distance between speakers

Generally Italian people stand fairly close when they speak to each other. As an indication, it is worth noticing that when shaking hands the arm is only bent and not stretched out to reach the counterpart. Stiffening may be misunderstood.

In lifts or similar spaces, people don't shrink into a corner in order to be as far away as possible from each other. Equally, in a corridor, two people talking together get closer to each other to let someone pass. They do not move further apart, because a cast-iron rule of Italian manners says that one does not pass between two people talking.

Clothes

Clothes, hairstyle, etc. play a very important part in all walks of Italian life, and particularly in the world of business and industry. Awareness of the latest trends in fashion and an instinctive skill in adapting them to one's personality is considered very important. These instincts 'tell' about a person's sense of elegance, taste, class and style. All this is summed up as *avere buon gusto* (literally: to have good taste) and is as relevant to one's professional image – for men and women alike – as style and manners for the English. Shabbiness and eccentricity (sometimes associated in Britain or the US with academe) are not understood and only create an impression of lack of money, lack of *buon gusto* and sloppiness. Tourists' individualism is, however, a welcome exception.

THE TELEPHONE

In dealing with people over the telephone it is equally important to recognize standard phrases and be able to use them promptly. To ring from a public place in Italy you may use the telephone card, *la carta telefonica,* money, or special coins called *gettoni.* The *carta* and the *gettoni* are sold in bars, at tobacconists or newsagents.

113 Answering the phone

(i) Private calls

Neither *Ciao* nor the town + telephone number are used to answer the phone. The common reply on lifting the receiver is: *Pronto?* (literally: ready?) The caller's introduction may vary:

- To a friend:

  Buongiorno. / Ciao. Sono Luciano. C'è Cristina?
  Good morning. / Hallo. It's Luciano. May I speak to Cristina?

  Pronto? Sono io. Hallo? It's me.

- More formally:

  Buongiorno signora Gatti. Sono Valentina.
  Good morning Mrs Gatti. This is Valentina.

  Buongiorno. Sono Emilio Fedi della SDS.
  Good morning. I'm Emilio Fedi of the SDS.

(Note the feminine form *della* since the word implied is *ditta* company.

- If you are not sure who has replied, say:

  Buongiorno. Parlo con l'ingegner Dardano?
  Good morning. Am I speaking to Mr Dardano (the engineer)?

(ii) Someone replying on behalf of a family (e.g. an au pair)

  Casa Martini. Desidera? / Chi parla?
  (literally: This is the Martinis' home. Who's calling?)

(iii) Agencies, companies, professional offices

  Studio del notaio Pamfili. Buongiorno.
  Pamfili solicitor's office. Good morning. Can I help you?

> *Qui Elettronica Bresciana. Prego?*
> This is Bresciana Electronics. Can I help you?

(iv) Wrong number

> *Scusi, ho sbagliato numero.*
> I'm sorry. I have got the wrong number.
>
> *Ma scusi non è il 56478?*
> Sorry, but isn't that 56478?

(v) Continuation of a private conversation

> *Mi fa tanto piacere sentirti.*
> How nice to hear from you.
>
> *Scusa se non mi sono fatta viva prima ma . . .*
> I'm sorry I haven't rung up before but . . .
> (literally: I haven't shown myself alive)
>
> *Purtroppo ci si sente così di rado . . . / ogni morte di papa . . .*
> Unfortunately we don't speak often enough . . . / once in a blue moon. (literally: every time a pope dies)

14 Asking to be put through

(i) Private calls

> *C'è Carlo? Sono un suo amico / collega.*
> Can I speak to Charles? I'm a friend / colleague of his.
>
> *Vorrei parlare con la signora Tanzi, se non disturbo.*
> I would like to speak to Mrs Tanzi, if it is convenient.
>
> *Ma se disturbo richiamo più tardi.*
> But if it is inconvenient we can call back later.

(ii) Professional calls

> *Il ragionier Lucchini, per favore.*
> May I speak to Mr Lucchini (the accountant), please.
>
> *Mi passa l'avvocato Lotti, per favore?*
> Could I speak to Mr Lotti (the solicitor), please?

● Asking for an extension:

> *Il 2234 / l'interno 2234 per cortesia.*
> 2234, please. / Can I have extension 2234, please.

- If you do not know whom you need to speak to you may say:

  Vorrei informazioni riguardo a . . . Con chi posso parlare?
  I would like to enquire about . . . Can you put me through to the right person?

  Si tratta di . . . Posso parlare con lei di questo problema?
  It's about . . . Can you help me with this problem?

(iii) Asking and being asked to wait

- Informal:

  Lo / La chiamo subito. Te lo / la chiamo subito.
  I'll call him / her for you.

  Aspetta. Vado a chiamarlo / la.
  Hold on, I'll call him / her.

- Formal:

  Attenda. Glielo / gliela chiamo / passo subito.
  Just a moment. I'll call him / her for you.

- Professional:

  Attenda in linea, prego.
  I'll put you through, hold the line, please.

  Attenda che le passo.
  Hold the line, I'll put you through.

  Può richiamare fra mezz'ora?
  Could you ring back in half an hour?

(iv) Filtering the calls

Scusi, chi lo desidera? Excuse me, may I have your name?
Mi può ripetere il suo nome? Can you repeat your name?
Come si scrive? How do you spell it?
Mi può dire di cosa si tratta? Can you tell me what it is about?
Da dove telefona? Where are you ringing from?

Names are conventionally spelled out with names (mostly of towns) for each letter of the alphabet, e.g. for Giulia, *G come Genova*, or simply *Genova, Imola, Udine* . . .

Ancona	Genova	Londra	Quarto	Vicenza
Bologna	Hotel	Milano	Roma	Vdoppio
Cagliari	Imola	Napoli	Sondrio	X
Domodossola	Jolly	Otranto	Torino	Yugoslavia
Empoli	Kappa	Palermo	Udine	Zagabria
Firenze				

(v) Being asked to call back

● Informal:

> *Senti, non c'è. Puoi richiamare più tardi?*
> Sorry. He isn't in. Can you call later?

> *No. Non so quando torna. Devo lasciarle detto qualcosa?*
> No. I don't know when she'll be back. Do you want me to pass on a message to her?

● Formal:

> *Mi dispiace, non è in casa. Vuole lasciare detto qualcosa?*
> I'm afraid, he / she is not in. Would you like to leave a message?

● Professional:

> *Il dottore Scherpa è sull'altra linea.*
> Dr Scherpa is on the other line.

> *Può attendere o preferisce richiamare?*
> Would you like to hold or will you call back?

> *Mi dispiace, il dottore è fuori sede.*
> I'm sorry, the doctor / Dr. X is not in.

> *È impegnato in una riunione.* He is in a meeting.

● Your replies may be:

> *Chiamo dall' Inghilterra.* I'm calling from England.

> *Attendo, grazie.* I'll wait, / I'll hold, thank you.

> *Sa quando rientra? Quando posso trovarlo?*
> Do you know when he will be in? / When can I get hold of him?

> *Mi sa dire quando è libero?*
> Can you tell me when he will be free?

> *A che ora posso richiamare?* When can I call back?

> *Posso avere un appuntamento telefonico?*
> Can you give me a time to phone?

> *Qual è il momento più opportuno per richiamare?*
> When is the most suitable time to call back?

● The reply may be:

> *Provi a richiamare tra due ore.* Try again in two hours' time.

> *È fuori tutto il giorno.* He is out all day.

> *La faccio richiamare quando rientra.*
> I'll ask him / her to call you when he / she comes back.

Mi lasci il suo recapito telefonico, se crede.
Would you like to leave me your telephone number?

(vi) Leaving a message

- Informal:

    Posso lasciare detto che . . . Can you tell him / her that . . . please . . .

- Formal:

    Posso lasciare un messaggio? Can I leave a message?

- Professional. You may be asked:

    Vuol lasciare detto a me? Can I take a message?

115 Ending the conversation

(i) Informally

Ciao. Grazie della telefonata. Ci risentiamo.
Cheers. / Bye. Thanks for the telephone call. Hear from you soon. /
Speak to you again soon.

(ii) Formally

Grazie e buongiorno. / Grazie a lei.
Thank you and goodbye. Thank you. (literally: Thank you to you.)

Buona sera e grazie. Thank you, good evening.

Mi ha fatto veramente piacere sentirla di nuovo.
It has been nice to hear from you again.

For further forms of farewell see section 71.

(iii) Ending a long conversation

Interjections such as the following may work. They are equivalent
to the English 'em . . . mm . . .', which, on its own, in Italian is rather
impolite:

Eh, . . . sì, . . . sì, . . . già, . . . è vero, . . . ha ragione . . .

- More diplomatically:

    Avvocato, la ringrazio molto, non voglio trattenerla oltre.
    Thank you very much Mr X. I wouldn't really like to keep you any
    further.

    Non voglio abusare oltre del suo tempo.
    I won't take up any more of your time.

● With white lies:

> *Ti devo proprio salutare perché hanno suonato alla porta.*
> I really must go because there is someone at the door.

> *Scusa devo proprio andare perché mio marito / mia figlia è tornata.*
> I'm afraid I have to go because my husband / daughter has arrived.

> *Signora devo salutarla perché ho diversi clienti che mi aspettano. Ho un appuntamento urgente.*
> Mrs . . . it has been nice hearing you. I must go because there are several customers waiting for me. / I have an urgent appointment.

16 The operator, reporting problems, and answering machines

(i) The operator

You are likely to hear something like:

> *Qui è l'operatrice telefonica Torino numero 87. Desidera? / Dica.*
> Can I help you? (literally: Here is the telephone operator number . . .)

You may wish to say:

> *Vorrei un numero a Roma: Società Televisiva Europea, via Corsica 7.*
> I would like a number in Rome . . .

> *Il prefisso di Padova, per piacere.*
> I would like the code for Padua, please.

> *Mi sa dire che ora è in Italia adesso?*
> Can you tell me what time it is in Italy now?

> *Vorrei controllare se questo numero è giusto. Risulta sempre occupato.*
> I would like to check whether this number is right. It's always engaged.

> *Vorrei sapere se questo numero è cambiato. Ha un suono strano.*
> I'd like to know whether this number has changed. I'm getting a strange tone.

(ii) Reporting problems

Buongiorno. Il mio telefono è guasto.
Good morning. My telephone is not working.

C'è qualcosa di strano con il mio telefono. Fa un suono tipo tu . . .
tu . . . tu . . .
There is something odd with my phone. It's making a sound like
this: beep . . . beep . . . beep . . .

Il mio telefono deve essere guasto. È come morto.
My phone must be out of order. The line is dead.

Scusi ma cade continuamente la linea.
We keep getting cut off.

Ma io sento parlare ma loro non mi sentono.
Well, I can hear them talking but they can't hear me.

(iii) Answering machines

You may hear the following standard recorded messages:

Questo è il numero dello studio . . . / della ditta . . . Siamo
momentaneamente assenti.
This is the telephone number of the . . . office / company. There is
nobody in the office at the moment.

L'ufficio è chiuso dalle 12.30 alle 15. / Siamo chiusi per ferie
dal . . . al . . .
The office is closed from . . . to . . . / We are closed (for our annual
holidays) from . . . to . . .

Lasciate il vostro nome, cognome e numero telefonico e vi
richiameremo.
Please leave your name, surname and phone number and we'll call
you back.

Privately, people like to personalize their messages:

Stasera sono fuori con amici. Rientrerò tardi. Non svegliatemi
prima di domani a mezzogiorno.
Tonight I'll be out with friends. I'll be back late. Don't wake me up
before midday tomorrow.

PERSONAL CORRESPONDENCE

7 Capital letters and punctuation

(a) Capital letters

(i) Capital letters <u>are used</u>:

- At the beginning of a sentence.
- After a question or an exclamation mark when a new sentence starts.
- With proper nouns of people, associations, institutions, towns, countries, regions, mountains, lakes, seas. Words such as *mare, lago, monte* are written with a capital letter if they are followed by a proper name: *il Lago di Como*.
- With pronouns *Lei, Loro, Voi, Sua, Vostra, La, Le, Vi*, etc. when addressing people in very formal letters.
- Names of institutions when one refers to their constitutional role:

    la Chiesa the Church

but

    la chiesa qui vicino the church nearby

- Religious words:
    Dio God *la Madonna* the Madonna *la Vergine* the Virgin
- Works of art:
    L'Ultima Cena The Last Supper
- Historical events:
    La Riforma The Reformation
- All other proper nouns.

- Names of centuries:
    Il Duemila the twentieth century

(ii) Unlike in English, capital letters <u>are not used</u> with:

- Titles when followed by a name:
    l'onorevole Andreini (the Honourable . . .)

● The pronoun *io*.

● Names of months and days of the week unless they are solemn dates in Italian history:

> *il 4 Novembre* (end of the First World War)

● With adjectives indicating nationalities:

> *i ragazzi italiani* (the) Italian boys

As a noun, nationalities are written both with and without a capital letter:

> *gli Italiani / gli italiani*

● In titles the capital letter is only used with the first word:

> *La storia del teatro italiano*

(b) Punctuation

Rules are far from being rigidly applied. Italian writers use punctuation as a stylistic device in a very individual way.

(i) Full stop *(il punto fermo)*
It is used to mark the end of a sentence but it is omitted in headlines and listed phrases. A raised full stop is used with figures, to indicate thousands, e.g. 1'500.

(ii) Semi-colon *(il punto e virgola)*
According to tradition, it is used to separate two sentences which are considered part of the same sequence. But it is more and more frequently used to highlight a banal item in a sentence such as *ma* in the following example:

> *Il decreto era emesso in nome del duca di Milano; ma era firmato da Ludovico il Moro.*
> The decree had been issued in the name of the Duke of Milan but had been signed by Ludovico il Moro.

The semi-colon is also used to separate long entries in a list:

> *I personaggi della trama comprendono un morto che tutti vorrebbero suicida; un brigadiere onesto ma senza potere; un pretino un po' simpatico.*
> The characters of the plot include a dead person whom everybody would like to be a suicide; an honest but powerless brigadier; a young and rather pleasant priest.

(iii) Colon *(due punti)*

Traditionally it is used to introduce direct speech, a long quotation, a direct source or a list of words or data, factors, etc.:

> *Nella relazione si legge: 'Il reddito nazionale lordo è di . . .'*
> The report says: 'The national gross income is . . .'

> *Tre sono le ragioni per cui mi oppongo a questa decisione: è legalmente non valida; è controproducente per la nostra espansione; e infine è moralmente discutibile.*
> There are three reasons only why I oppose this decision: it is not legally valid; it is counterproductive for our expansion; and finally it is morally debatable.

More recent uses include:

- Expanding on an introductory statement in order to expand a literary description:

> *La discoteca sembrava impazzita: le luci si rincorrevano sui muri formando disegni da incubo; il latrare del disc-jockey guidava l'ondeggiare dei giovani corpi; le gambe dei ballerini avevano rotto la legge di gravità.*
> The disco seemed completely wild: the lights followed each other along the walls creating nightmarish drawings; the disc-jockey's howling led the swaying of the young bodies; the legs of the dancers had broken the law of gravity.

- To emphasize one piece of information:

> *Della piazza di Vigevano conosciamo con certezza la data: 3 maggio 1442.*
> We know the date of the Vigevano square for certain: 3 May 1442.

- To introduce the consequences of a statement, a device which is frequently employed by the media:

> *Né aerei né treni: è inferno.*
> Neither planes nor trains: it's hell.

- To introduce an explanation and the reasons for a statement:

> *Nessuno piangeva per la morte di un mandarino cinese: un destino e un mondo troppo lontani.*
> No one mourned the death of a Chinese mandarin: a destiny and a world which were too far away.

- To give emphasis to a phrase or to a whole sentence:

  Nel suo film lo stile è: nessuno stile.
  No style is the style of his film.

  Ci si riferisce alla facoltà di architettura di Milano: che è stata, dagli anni sessanta a oggi, la vera e propria fucina dei quadri che hanno creato il made in Italy.
  I refer to the Faculty of Architecture in Milan. From the sixties to the present day, this faculty has been the school (literally: forge) of top Italian designers.

- The graphic impact of the colon is sometimes considered more effective than a full explanation:

  L'Italia potrebbe vedersi affidato il ruolo dei paesi arabi: senza il petrolio.
  Italy could be given the same role as the Arab countries. But we don't have their petrol.

(iv) Comma *(la virgola)*

It is used:

- To introduce a very short quotation:

  Con queste due parole, 'non' e 'ma', l'autore crea il tema del racconto.
  With these two words, 'no' and 'but', the author creates the theme of the story.

- To indicate an interpolated clause:

  Il costo della vita, si sa, è sempre in aumento.
  The cost of living, one knows, is always increasing.

- To separate subordinate clauses from each other and from the main sentence:

  Come forse lei ricorda, segnalai subito l'incidente.
  As you probably remember, I immediately informed you of the accident / incident.

- A comma is placed at the beginning and at the end of a relative clause when this is considered to give additional but not essential information:

  Quell'incontro, che era stato organizzato male, ebbe uno strano successo.
  That meeting, which had been organized so badly, was strangely successful.

- With apposition:

    Federico Fellini, uno dei maggiori registi italiani.
    Federico Fellini, one of the best Italian film directors.

- In a list:

    È in programma un film, uno sceneggiato, un telequiz.
    The programme includes a film, a TV serial, a quiz.

- To separate a sequence of adjectives, including the last one:

    Era una segretaria graziosa, lavoratrice, premurosa.
    She was a pretty, hard-working and attentive secretary.

- After conjunctions such as *inoltre* furthermore, *comunque* still, *eppure* yet, *ma* but, commas are optionally added:

    Eppure, vinse.
    Yet, he won.

- To separate adverbial clauses from the main sentence:

    Sullo sfondo bianco di un Sud abbagliato dal sole, una striscia di sangue lega la sorte di alcuni personaggi.
    Against the white background of the South dazzled by the sun, a trail of blood links the destiny of some of the characters.

- Between two sentences, when in the second the verb is omitted:

    È stato il vostro professore, non il nostro.
    It was your professor, not ours.

(v) Dash *(lineetta)*

Its traditional use is to replace inverted commas in quotations:

    – C'è da impazzire – disse Lorenzo.
    – One must be mad – said Lawrence.

But, under English and American influence, it may now also introduce an additional thought at the end of a sentence.

Full stops, commas and semi-colons go after inverted commas unless they are part of the quotation:

    È quindi accettabile il parere del preside secondo cui 'c'è bisogno di una piscina'.
    We can accept the headmaster's opinion that 'a swimming pool is necessary'.

118 Invitation cards and replies

Traditionally the most elegant cards are white or cream without decorations. It is the paper quality which plays a major role. Except for Christmas and New Year, commercial cards are not part of the Italian tradition, though they are gradually becoming fashionable. However, they are not yet considered refined and it's better to use them for fun and with caution.

(i) Written invitations are mostly used for formal occasions even if the wording is apparently casual. Examples for parties are:

> *Carla e Bruno vi attendono a cena sabato 2 aprile alle ore 20.00.*
>
> *RSVP*
>
> *via Michelangelo 12 – Bergamo*

Carla and Bruno would be delighted if you could come to dinner on Saturday April 2nd at 8.00 p.m.

> *Vi invitiamo a festeggiare con noi il nostro decimo anniversario di matrimonio.*
> *Hotel Grande Parco domenica 8 luglio ore 13.00*

Mr and Mrs Taylor request the pleasure of your company to celebrate the tenth anniversary of their wedding. Hotel Grande Parco Sunday July 8th, 1.00 p.m.

> *Vi aspettiamo a casa nostra per festeggiare il Carnevale.*
> *È di rigore l'abito in maschera!*

Would you care to join us at home for a fancy-dress party to celebrate Carnevale?

(ii) To accept an invitation and thank your host for the evening a note may say:

> *Accettiamo con piacere il vostro invito, felici di passare la serata insieme.*

We are pleased to accept your invitation and will be delighted to spend the evening with you.

One can send a plant with a card saying:

> *Ringraziandovi affettuosamente per la splendida serata, Luisa e Giorgio.*
> Thank you for a lovely evening. Luisa and Giorgio.
>
> *Una breve nota per dirvi come la vostra squisita ospitalità ci ha fatto trascorrere una serata indimenticabile.*
> This is just a short note to thank you for your warm hospitality and a memorable evening in your company.
>
> *Con i ringraziamenti più cari per l'allegro soggiorno e la brillante compagnia. Ogni minuto è stata una festa.*
> I must tell you what a wonderful time we had with you and your charming guests. We enjoyed every minute of it.

19 Best wishes and congratulations

(i) For Christmas, New Year and, less than it used to be, Easter, these are the traditional words:

> *I migliori auguri per un felice Natale e per un Anno Nuovo ricco di soddisfazioni*
> Happy Christmas and a prosperous New Year
>
> *I più affettuosi auguri per il Santo Natale e un Felice Anno Nuovo*
> Best wishes for Christmas and a Happy New Year
>
> *Con i nostri migliori auguri di Buone Feste*
> With our best wishes for Christmas and the New Year
>
> *A tutti una buona fine e un miglior principio*
> All the best for the end of . . . and for next year (literally: A happy end and an even better beginning)

(ii) For birthdays and the *onomastico*, which is the Saint's day corresponding to people's Christian name, e.g. someone called Giuseppe celebrates his *'compleanno'* on Saint Joseph's day, 19 March, one wishes:

> *I migliori auguri di buon compleanno* Happy Birthday
>
> *Buon / felice onomastico* Best wishes
>
> *Affettuosissimi auguri* With fondest good wishes (to a friend, not necessarily with a sentimental overtone, for birthday and name day)
>
> *Cento di questi giorni*
> Many happy returns of the day (literally: One hundred of these days)

(iii) For significant events in people's lives:

Felicitazioni vivissime Congratulations

Le porgo le più vive congratulazioni per . . .
I am writing to congratulate you on your . . .

Partecipiamo alla vostra gioia . . .
We are delighted to hear of your . . . / We are so happy for your . . .

I più cari auguri ai genitori e al piccolo Guglielmo
Fond greetings to the parents and to little William

(iv) To thank someone for a special favour or for help given in difficult circumstances:

Vorremmo porgerle i più sentiti ringraziamenti per il suo interessamento.
Vorrei ringraziarla profondamente per la premura dimostrata nei nostri confronti in un momento difficile.
I am writing to thank you for the help you gave us at a difficult time . . .

120 Condolences

For a bereavement only white cards with handwritten condolences are used. Formal expressions are:

Profondamente addolorato partecipo al vostro sconsolato dolore per la scomparsa di . . .
We were very sorry to hear about the death of . . .

Sgomento per la scomparsa di . . . / Affranto per la morte di . . .
We were shocked to hear of the death of . . .

Partecipo commosso al vostro grande dolore.
Please accept our deepest sympathy.

Vi sono molto vicino / -a in questo tristissimo momento.
We are thinking of you at this sad time.

121 Setting out letters and envelopes

There is no uniformity of style in personal, official or business letters. Beside the traditional layout exemplified below, letters can be written in the 'blocked style', the 'American style' or with a mixture of all three according to the typist's taste or the computer program. The object seems to be to send a clear and aesthetically impressive letter.

(a) Layout of letters

The traditional Italian layout of private and business letters is the following:

- the date is on the top right side: *3/8/92; 3 – 8 – '92; 3 settembre 1992; Roma, 3 – 8 – '92;*
- reference numbers are under the date: *Rif. n.12* Your ref. no.12;
- the recipient's address is placed on the top left side;
- a comma follows the name of the recipient: *Caro Marco;*
- the first line is indented and starts with a small letter;
- subsequent paragraphs are equally indented;
- greetings are placed at the centre of the line and are followed by a comma;
- the signature is placed under the greetings;
- the sender's address, if the letter is not written on headed paper, is placed at the end of the page under the signature;
- at the end on the right: *allegati n.4* 4 enclosures.

(b) Samples of letters

Sample of a private letter:

---

8 gennaio 1993

Caro Marco,
    ti ringrazio delle informazioni speditemi con premura sui corsi di lingua italiana presso la tua università. Leggerò attentamente l'opuscolo e ti farò sapere al più presto le mie decisioni.

        Con i più cordiali saluti anche ai tuoi,

          Clare

My dear Marco,
    Thank you very much for the information you sent me so promptly on the courses in Italian run at your university. I'll read the brochure very carefully and let you know my decisions as soon as possible.

        All the very best to you and your family
          Clare

Sample of a business letter

Savoia Assicurazioni   *5 – 8 – 1992*
via Risorgimento 1   *Rif. 9853*
2345 Lucca

Spett. Compagnia Assicurazioni,

       allego assegno per rinnovo assicurazione auto immatricolata
Fiat CO34687, 7 – 9 – 1988.

               Distinti saluti,
               Rag. Giovanni Gentile

               via Cesare Battisti 89
               5980 Milano

Dear Sir,
       Please find enclosed a cheque to renew the insurance for a Fiat
registration number CO34687, 7 – 9 – 1988.

               Yours faithfully,

(c) Layout of envelopes

(i) Addresses are not punctuated.

● The street number follows the street name.
● The town name is preceded by the postal code; if the town is not
the capital of the province, the name of the province is placed next
to it in brackets. Postal codes and names of provinces are available
from post offices.
● The address may be blocked or indented with this sequence:

Gent. Prof. Francesca Ronzi
via G. Giolitti 92
25015 Sirmione (Brescia)

Gentilissimo Professor
Angelo Lorenzoni
Facoltà di Scienze Naturali
Università di Cosenza

(ii) In addition to the address there may be written:

> *All'attenzione dell' Avvocato Rossi / Alla cortese attenzione*
> *dell'Ingegner Viola*
> For the attention of . . .
>
> *Riservata personale* Private and confidential

● The recipient's name should be preceded by one of these abbreviations:

> *Sig. Federico Dotti*
> Mr F. Dotti
> *Sig.ra Lucia Dotti*
> *Sig.na Clementina Dotti*

A more polite and frequent form is:

> *Egr. Sig. Federico Dotti* (only for men)
>
> *Gent.mo / a Sig. Federico Dotti*
> *Gent.ma Sig.ra Lucia Dotti*
> *Gent.ma Sig.na Clementina Dotti*

For the whole family:

> *Gent. Sig. Dotti* or *Gent. Sig.ra e Sig. Dotti*

There is no equivalent to Ms nor for forms where the woman is given the husband's name and surname.

Officially Italian women keep their maiden name, and in the teaching profession they are addressed both in speech and in writing with their maiden surname.

● The recipient's name must be preceded by the short form of his / her professional qualification:

> *Dott.* (m.) *Dott.essa* (f.) for anyone who has a university degree or is a medical doctor
>
> or, more elaborately,
>
> *Egr. Dott. Viola / Gent. Dott.essa Viola / Preg.mo Prof. Padovani /*
> *Chiar.mo* (for university lecturer)
> *Prof.* for a consultant
> *Avv.* (m.) *Avv.essa* (f.) for a lawyer or a solicitor
> *Arch.* (m. and f.) for an architect
> *Ing.* (m. and f.) for a graduate in engineering (a prestigious title not equivalent to technician)
> *Rag.* (m. and f.) for accountants without a university degree
> *Prof.* (m.) *Prof.essa* (f.) for all teachers from junior school onwards

122 Beginning and ending letters

(a) Beginning a private letter

Formal and informal expressions which can be used in letters can be found in sections 71 – 96.

(i) There are several ways to start a letter to a friend, a relative or a close acquaintance:

> *Caro Franco, Carissima Sandra, Carissima Amanda, Carissimi* (to two or more people)
> Dear . . . / My dear . . ., My very dear . . ., My dearest . . .

(ii) Words of affection or love are:

> *Amore mio, . . . Tesoro . . .*
> My love, . . . My darling . . .

(iii) More formal forms are:

> *Carissima e gentile signora, . . . Gentili signori Bianchi, . . .*
> My dear Mrs . . ., Dear Mr and Mrs . . .

(b) Professional and business letters

(i) Professional and business letters begin as follows:

Gentile signora / dott.essa Giorgi . . ., Egregio Signor / dott. Lucchetti . . .
Egregio is used only for men and is the standard form in business correspondence.

(ii) If the recipient has a professional qualification it must be inserted in small letters, in full or abbreviated. The first name is usually omitted. Initials are not used.

(iii) Possessive or personal pronouns within the letter start with a capital letter in official correspondence. In formal letters this is optional and the use is declining:

> *Egregio Ispettore,*
>   *attendiamo la Sua visita, come convenuto il 18 aprile alle ore 10.*
> Dear Inspector,
>   We are writing to confirm your visit, as agreed, on April 18th at 10 a.m.

(iv) The standard formulas for beginning commercial letters are:

Spett. Ditta, ... Spett. Casa Editrice ... Spett. Compagnia di Assicurazioni.

Spett., the shortened form of *Rispettabile*, is never used in full.

(c) Ending a private letter

(i) Friendly forms are:

> *Tanti cari saluti / affettuosi saluti*
> Love / With much love

> *Ricordandovi con tanta simpatia*
> Kind regards / With best wishes

> *A presto*
> See you soon

> *Cordiali saluti / Le invio i più cordiali saluti*
> Yours,

(ii) More formal endings are:

> *Le porgo distinti saluti ... / Le invio i miei migliori saluti ...*
> Yours sincerely

(d) Ending a business letter

The most common business formula is:

> *Distinti saluti* or *Vogliate gradire distinti saluti*
> Yours sincerely / Yours truly / Yours faithfully

But this ending is often preceded by concluding sentences which make it less abrupt:

> *Nel frattempo, ringraziandovi, porgo distinti saluti*
> Thank you for your kind consideration (literally: Meanwhile we thank you ...)

> *Ponendomi a sua disposizione, le invio i miei migliori saluti ...*
> (literally: I put myself at your disposal ... I send you)

> *In attesa di sue notizie la saluto cordialmente*
> (literally: Waiting for your news ...)

> *Aspettando una vostra risposta ...*
> I / We look forward to hearing from you ... (literally: Waiting for a reply from you ...)

123 Letters concerning employment

(a) Applying for a job as an au pair

Sig.ri Rossi
via Castello 4   27 – 5 – '91
6908 Siena

Gentili signori,
        Catherine James mi ha informato che cercate una ragazza
inglese alla pari. Ho diciotto anni, ho terminato la scuola secondaria
superiore e vorrei imparare l'italiano prima di iscrivermi all'università
qui in Inghilterra. Ho una sorella di otto anni e sono quindi abituata a
trattare con i bambini. Allego il mio, seppur breve, curriculum vitae e i
nomi di due persone disposte a dare delle referenze.
        Se siete interessati ad offrirmi il posto, gradirei conoscere le
condizioni di lavoro e la diaria giornaliera.
        Sperando in una risposta positiva entro breve tempo,
                invio distinti saluti

Dear Mr and Mrs . . .
        Catherine James has told me that you are looking for an English
au pair. I am eighteen years old, I have just passed my A levels and I
would like to learn Italian before going to university in England. I have
an eight-year-old sister and I am therefore accustomed to dealing with
children. I enclose my short C.V. and the names of two people who are
willing to give references.
        If you are interested in offering me the job, please let me know
the conditions of work and the daily allowance you would pay.
        Hoping to receive a favourable reply,
        Yours sincerely,

(b) Applying for a post advertised in the press

Ufficio pubbliche relazioni
Ente Fiera
Piazzale Clodio   *17 – 8 – 1993*
7623 Genova

Spett. Ente Fiera,
      con riferimento all'annuncio del 6 c.m. sul Corriere della Sera
vorrei fare domanda per il posto di traduttrice per inglese e francese.
Come dal curriculum vitae allegato ho quattro anni di esperienza
presso ditte di notevole prestigio in Francia e Gran Bretagna con
relative referenze.
      Nel caso siate interessati ad un colloquio sono a disposizione
tutti i giorni dalle 14 alle 18 del pomeriggio, incluso il sabato.
          Distinti saluti,

Dear Sirs,
      In response to your advertisement in *Il Corriere della Sera* of the
6th, I would like to apply for the post of translator in English and
French. As the enclosed C.V. and referees' names show I have four years'
experience with prestigious companies in France and England.
      Should you be interested in calling me for an interview I am
available every day between two and six o'clock in the afternoon,
including Saturdays.
         Yours faithfully

(c) Seeking a vacation job

Associazione alberghi e discoteche
3476 Rimini (Forlì)

Spett. Associazione,
        cerco un posto di lavoro in Italia per quattro mesi da giugno a
settembre. Scopo del soggiorno è conoscere l'Italia. Vorrei sapere se
c'è la possibilità di lavorare come intrattenitore in una discoteca o
presso un albergo.
        Ho vent' anni e, come potete vedere dal curriculum vitae, ho
una certa esperienza come animatore di programmi musicali presso
Radio Rainbow, una delle radio locali di Manchester. Ho una
profonda conoscenza della musica inglese e americana e sono
aggiornatissimo sull'ultima musica pop. Ho inoltre una personalità
estroversa e un notevole senso dell'umorismo.
        Ho una discreta conoscenza dell'italiano che ho studiato per
un anno e sono sicuro che non avrò problemi a far divertire i vostri
clienti.

        Con i più cordiali saluti

Dear Sirs,
        I am looking for a job in Italy for four months, from June to
September. My aim is to get to know Italy. I would like to know
whether there is a vacancy as a DJ in a local disco or in a hotel.
        I am twenty years old and, as my C.V. shows, I have some
experience as a DJ with a music programme on Radio Rainbow in
Manchester. I have a good knowledge of English and American music
and keep up to date with current trends in modern pop. On Radio
Rainbow I was well known for my extrovert personality and sense of
humour. My Italian is of a reasonable standard as I have been studying
Italian for a year, and I am quite confident that I would have no
problems in entertaining your clients.
                Yours faithfully,

(d) Accepting the offer of a post

Liceo Linguistico Italia
Piazza Mazzini 7
L'Aquila

All'attenzione del preside

Egregio Sig. Preside,
*   la ringrazio della lettera con la quale mi comunica l'offerta*
del posto di assistente di lingua inglese per l'anno scolastico 1992 – 93.
Trovo l'orario e lo stipendio di mio gradimento e sono ansiosa di
venire in Italia al più presto per conoscere lei personalmente e i
colleghi con cui lavorerò.
*   In attesa di un nostro incontro,*
*   le porgo i miei migliori saluti*

For the attention of the Principal

Dear Sir,

Thank you very much for your letter offering me the post of
English language assistant for 1993–94. I find the working hours and
the salary to my satisfaction and I am anxious to come to Italy and get
to know you personally and the colleagues with whom I shall be
working.

Looking forward to meeting you.
Yours sincerely

124 Curriculum vitae

A well-planned and well-typed C.V. is one of the best forms of introduction because, among other things, it saves time for those who have to read it. The example below gives the essential headings.

CURRICULUM VITAE

DATI PERSONALI

COGNOME: *Pirnetti*

NOME: *Giuseppe*

INDIRIZZO: *Piazzale Cavour 8 Pistoia*

TELEFONO: *(02) 7421 casa*
(02) 9632 ufficio

NAZIONALITÀ: *italiano*

DATA E LUOGO DI NASCITA: *23 – 2 – 1965 Grosio (Sondrio)*

STATO DI FAMIGLIA: *celibe* (m.) or *nubile* (f.) / *sposato / divorziato /*
vedovo

DATI PROFESSIONALI

EDUCAZIONE SCOLASTICA E UNIVERSITARIA:
Diploma di ragioniere presso l'Istituto Pascoli di Sondrio (1980 – 85)
Maturità 58
Laurea in Economia e Commercio presso l'Università di Parma (1985
– 90) voti: 110

FORMAZIONE PROFESSIONALE:
Corso di lingua inglese presso la Bell School, Cambridge
Corso di perfezionamento di economia europea, Università Bocconi,
Milano

POSTO DI LAVORO ATTUALE:
Agente di assicurazioni presso Compagnia le Generali sede di
Genova

PRECEDENTI ESPERIENZE:
Cassiere presso la Banca Commerciale di Bergamo

INTERESSI E HOBBY:
Alpinismo e viaggi

CURRICULUM VITAE

SURNAME: Pirnetti

NAME: Giuseppe

ADDRESS: Piazzale Cavour 8 Pistoia

TELEPHONE NUMBER: (02) 7421 home
                                 (02) 9632 work

NATIONALITY: Italian

DATE AND PLACE OF BIRTH: 23 – 2 – 1965 Grosio (Sondrio)

MARITAL STATUS: single / married / divorced / widower

PROFESSIONAL DETAILS

SECONDARY AND HIGHER EDUCATION:
Diploma in Accountancy at the Pascoli Institute, Sondrio (1980 – 85)
School-leaving certificate 58
Degree in Business Studies and Management Science at the
University of Parma (1985 – 90) 110 marks.

PROFESSIONAL TRAINING:
Course in English at the Bell School, Cambridge
Postgraduate course in European Economy at the Bocconi University,
Milan

CURRENT POSITION:
Insurance agent with Compagnia le Generali, Genoa

PREVIOUS EXPERIENCE:
Cashier at the Banca Commerciale in Bergamo

OUTSIDE INTERESTS:
Climbing and travelling

125 Testimonials, references and authorizations

(a) Testimonials

> *23 – 8 – 1990*
>
> *A chi di competenza*
>
> *In qualità di Direttore dell'Istituto di Moda Mare, certifico che Rosa Fini ha svolto l'attività di disegnatrice part-time presso il nostro istituto per due anni (1988 – 90) durante i quali ha svolto la propria attività con intelligente creatività ed entusiasmo.*
> *Arch. Natale Longhi*

To whom it may concern

As a Director of the Institute of Moda Mare, I certify that Rosa Fini has been a part-time art designer at our institute for two years (1988–90) during which time she has worked with intelligence, imagination and enthusiasm.
(Signature of referee)

> *A chi di competenza*   *30 – 1 – 90*
>
> *Università per Stranieri di Perugia*
>
> *Si certifica che John Lambert ha frequentato presso l'Università di Perugia dal 1 gennaio al 30 giugno 1990 il coro semestrale di storia di arte italiana conseguendo 80 / 100 nell'esame finale.*
> *Il direttore d'istituto*

To whom it may concern

This is to certify that John Lambert has attended the University of Perugia from 1st January to 30th June 1990. He successfully completed a six months' course in Italian art, obtaining 80 per cent in the final examination.
The Director

(b) Personal references

(i) Request for a reference:

Luci e Ombre Spa
via Rivoli 10
Salò (Brescia)

Egregio rag.
*conseguentemente all'ampliamento della nostra ditta, stiamo
assumendo nuovo personale. Stiamo perciò prendendo in
considerazione come segretaria bilingue la signora Jenny Smith che
ci ha indicato il Suo nome per una eventuale richiesta di referenze.
Le saremmo quindi grati se potesse indicarci, in assoluta riservatezza,
la sua opinione riguardo alla professionalità della signora.*
In attesa di una sua gentile risposta,
gradisca distinti saluti

Dear Sir
We are expanding our firm and employing new staff. We are
therefore considering Mrs Jenny Smith for the post of bilingual
secretary. Mrs Smith has given us your name as a referee. We would be
most grateful for your opinion, in the strictest confidence, on the
professional qualities of the person in question.
Yours sincerely

(ii) References:

> *Patrizia Scorzoni ha scritto la tesi di laurea 'Teorie del nulla nel Medioevo' sotto la mia guida. Si tratta di una studentessa con una notevole preparazione umanistica. È dotata di intelligenza speculativa, attitudine all'approfondimento di indagini storiche. Carattere riflessivo, quasi introverso è, a mio avviso, più che idonea nel campo della ricerca. La ritengo certamente un'ottima candidata alla borsa di studio per una laurea di perfezionamento in medioevalistica.*
> > *Distinti saluti*
> > *Prof. Carla Gavardi*

Patrizia Scorzoni has written her dissertation on the 'Theories of nothingness in the Middle Ages' under my supervision. She is a student with a remarkable classical background. Endowed with a speculative mind, she has a genuine gift for historical studies. She is thoughtful, almost introverted and, in my opinion, very suitable to carry on with a research project. I consider her an excellent candidate for a PhD grant in Medieval Studies.
> Yours sincerely

> *Leicester, 7th December 1991*
> *Oggetto: Peter Brown: richiesta di referenze*
>
> *Egregio signore,*
> > *Peter Brown ha prestato la sua opera come tecnico, part-time, presso il nostro laboratorio audio-visivo per tre anni mentre era studente presso la facoltà di ingegneria. Lo raccomando caldamente in quanto si tratta di persona giovane ma preparata, interessata al proprio lavoro e con un carattere gioviale, disponibile alla collaborazione con i futuri colleghi.*
> > > *Con i più distinti saluti*

Dear Sir,
> Peter Brown has worked as a part-time technician in our audio-visual department for three years while he was a student at the Faculty of Engineering. I can recommend him wholeheartedly. He is professionally qualified, very interested in his work and has an outgoing personality, which allows him to get on very well with his colleagues.
> Yours sincerely

(iii) Further useful sentences may be:

In risposta alla vostra richiesta di referenze per . . .
In response to your request for a reference for . . .

Conosco . . . da dieci anni / . . . è stata nostra impiegata per quattro anni . . .
I have known . . . for ten years / . . . has been working for us for four years . . .

Si è sempre dimostrata degna della fiducia accordatale.
She has always been a trustworthy person.

Ha sempre eseguito con serietà e precisione le sue mansioni.
She has shown herself capable of working in a responsible manner and with attention to detail.

Posso garantire che si tratta di una persona a cui si possono affidare mansioni amministrative delicate.
I can guarantee that she can be relied upon to carry out confidential administrative work.

(c) Authorizations

(i) Asking permission to use a library:

> 13 – 12 – 1994
>
> *Al Direttore della Biblioteca Comunale di Trento*
>
> *Oggetto: richiesta di accesso sezione mss.*
>
> *Egregio direttore,*
> *la vorrei pregare di acconsentire che la sig.na Patricia Cole, studentessa del 3° anno presso la Facoltà di Storia dell'Università di Warwick abbia accesso ai mss. della vostra biblioteca riguardanti Cesare Battisti. Tale consultazione le è necessaria in quanto la studentessa sta svolgendo ricerche sul patriota italiano per la sua tesi di laurea. Posso assicurare che si tratta di persona affidabile.*
> *Ringraziandola per la sua cortesia,*
> *gradisca distinti saluti*

Dear Sir
        I would like to ask you to authorize Miss Cole to have access to the MSS regarding Cesare Battisti available in your library. Miss Cole is a third-year student in the Department of History at the University of Warwick and needs to read the MSS on the Italian patriot because she is writing a dissertation on him. I can assure you she is a reliable person.
        Yours sincerely

(ii) Authorizing a proxy:

Immobiliare Po   *1 – 1 – 1992*
Via Giovanni da Caminate 7
20141 Milano

All' Amministratore
         Il sottoscritto Ottavio Pinga delega la dott.essa Naomi Yates a
rappresentarla alla Convocazione Straordinaria del Condominio in
via Napoleone 3, riconoscendo sin d'ora per approvato il suo
operato.
                      Firma:

To the Manager
         I, Ottavio Pinga, hereby authorize Doctor Yates to vote on my
behalf at the Extraordinary Assembly of the joint-owners of the
building in 3, Napoleon Street and to accept as valid her decision.
                Signature:

COMMERCIAL CORRESPONDENCE

26 Grammatical features

(i) Unless a letter is addressed to a specific person (e.g. *Egregio Sig. Orsini*), one refers to the company or the agency and therefore uses the second person plural:

> *Questi sono i prezzi netti per voi.*
> These are our net prices for you.

> *Siete pronti a mantenere questi prezzi invariati sino alla fine dell'anno?*
> Are you prepared to keep these prices unchanged until the end of the year?

> *Su questi prezzi vi concediamo una percentuale del 20%.*
> We will give you a 20% discount on these prices.

(ii) The writer refers to his / her company using the first person plural:

> *Siamo spiacenti di inviarvi con ritardo il nostro ultimo catalogo.*
> We are sorry for the delay in sending you our latest catalogue.

(iii) Forms of invitations such as *voglia, vogliate* (the subjunctive of *volere*) are used for 'please':

> *Vogliate cortesemente comunicare la data di consegna.*
> Please let us know the delivery date.

(iv) Dates are written with the contracted preposition before them and the omission of the word 'letter':

> *la vostra del 18 febbraio* your letter dated 18th February

(v) Frequent expressions are:

Alleghiamo . . .	Please find enclosed . . .
Accusiamo ricevuta . . .	We acknowledge receipt . . .
A seguito nostra inchiesta . . .	Following our enquiry . . .
Ci scusiamo . . .	We are sorry . . .
Cogliamo l'occasione . . .	We should like to take this opportunity . . .

Come da vostra richiesta . . .	As requested . . .
Come d'accordo . . .	As agreed . . .
Daremo disposizioni che . . .	We will arrange for . . .
È con piacere che . . .	It is with pleasure that . . .
Effettueremo le spedizioni per nave.	We shall send it by ship.
Entrano in vigore . . .	They come into effect . . .
In risposta a . . .	In reply to . . .
Per il seguente ammontare . . .	For the following amount . . .
Per quanto riguarda . . .	As regards . . .
Scade il . . .	It falls due on . . .
Sono soggetti a . . .	They are subject to . . .
Spese a vostro carico . . .	Expenses to be debited to your account . . .
Uno sconto del 20% . . .	A 20% discount . . .
Verrà addebitato . . .	It will be debited . . .
Vi ringraziamo per . . .	We thank you for . . .
Vi preghiamo di farci sapere . . .	Please let us know . . .

Frequent abbreviations are:

all. (allegato) enclosure	*fatt. (fattura)* invoice
art. (articolo) article	*gg. (giorni)* days
brev. (brevetto) patent	*IVA* VAT
ca. (circa) approximately	*n.to (netto)* net
c.to (conto) account	*Soc. (Società)* Society
ecc. (eccetera) etc.	*S.p.A. (Società per azioni)* Ltd.

(vi) The use of possessives and their shortened forms (*ns. = nostro, vs. = vostro*). See also sections 40b and e.

⓲ Asking for information

For the layout of letters and envelopes see sections 121–122.

(a) Letters of request

> *Spett. Ente Turismo,*
>
> *è nostra intenzione trascorrere tre settimane sul Lago d'Iseo la prossima primavera. Avremmo piacere ricevere un elenco degli alberghi di alcune delle località della zona con relativi prezzi nonchè l'indicazione di quali alberghi accettano cani.*
>
> *In attesa di una vostra risposta vogliate gradire distinti saluti,*

Dear Sir / Madam,

We would like to spend three weeks on Lake Iseo next spring. We would be grateful if you could send us a list of hotels in some small towns in the area with their prices, as well as the names of hotels which accept dogs.

Yours faithfully

> *Spett. Direzione,*
>
> *gradirei ricevere il programma della Fiera dell' Agricoltura che si terrà a Verona dal 10 al 16 maggio c.a. e la lista degli alberghi con voi convenzionati.*
>
> *Distinti saluti*

Dear Sir,

I would like to receive the programme of the Agricultural Fair which will take place in Verona from the 10th to the 16th of May this year and the names of hotels at a discounted rate.

> *Spett. Ufficio Abbonamenti,*
> *vogliate indicarmi la quota di abbonamento annuale de Il*
> *Giornale per l'estero (Gran Bretagna) via aerea e le modalità di*
> *pagamento,*
> *distinti saluti*

Dear Sir,
    Please let me know the annual subscription for *Il Giornale* for
Great Britain air mail and the method of payment.
        Yours faithfully

> *Spett. Casa Editrice,*
> *gradirei ricevere il catalogo delle vostre pubblicazioni*
> *riguardanti la musica italiana nel Novecento. Vogliate inoltre*
> *cortesemente indicare se applicate sconti per istituzioni scolastiche.*
> *In attesa di una gentile risposta,*
> *distinti saluti*

Dear Sir,
    Would you kindly send the catalogue of your publications on
Italian twentieth-century music and let me know if you offer a discount
for schools.
        Yours faithfully

A fax:

> *Vogliate inviarmi via fax le informazioni preliminari per partecipare*
> *all'esposizione internazionale di Genova 'Colombo, la nave e il mare.*
> *Expo 92'. Ringraziando, distinti saluti*

Please send us via fax all the preliminary information necessary for
participation in the international exhibition in Genoa 'Columbus, the
ship and the sea. Expo 92'. Yours faithfully

(b) Letters of reply

> *Egregio signore,*
> *in risposta alla vostra (lettera) del 14 – 9 – '91 inviamo l'elenco*
> *degli alberghi sul Lago con i prezzi aggiornati fino al giugno 1992.*
> *Disponibili per ulteriori informazioni, speriamo di avervi nostri ospiti*
> *sul nostro lago.*
> *Distinti saluti*

Dear Sir,
        In reply to your letter dated 14th September 1991, we enclose
the list of hotels on the Lake of Iseo with the prices valid until June
1992. We would be happy to give you any further information you may
require. Hoping to have you among our guests on the lake.

> *Gentile Signora,*
> *come da lei richiesto, alleghiamo le informazioni sulle*
> *modalità di pagamento per l'abbonamento annuale . . . / alleghiamo*
> *il catalogo delle pubblicazioni d'arte. Purtroppo non è nostra politica*
> *editoriale accordare sconti per istituti scolastici.*

Dear Madam,
        Please find enclosed, as you requested, the relevant information
for an annual subscription to . . . / the art publications catalogue. We
regret it is not our editorial policy to give a discount for schools.

> *Spett. Ditta,*
> *ci dispiace informarvi che non fa parte delle nostre direttive*
> *fornire le informazioni da voi richieste con lettera del 6 – 8 – c.a. Vi*
> *consigliamo di pubblicare direttamente un'inserzione sui due*
> *giornali della città.*
> *Distintamente*

Dear Sirs,
        We regret to inform you that it is not our policy to provide the
information you require. We advise you to put an advertisement in the
two local newspapers.

128 Reservations and bookings

Spett. Direttore Hotel Miramonti,
*   vorrei prenotare una camera doppia con bagno e TV dal 25 –*
12 – c.a. al 6 gennaio. Gradirei una camera con vista sul Monte
Bianco. Tra le varie opzioni abbiamo scelto la mezza pensione con
l'abbonamento allo ski lift. La caparra è stata inviata oggi tramite la
nostra banca.
*   In attesa della vostra conferma ricevuta pagamento,*
*   vogliate gradire distinti saluti*

Dear Sir,
        I would like to book a double room with bathroom and TV from
the 25th December until the 6th January. I would very much like a room
overlooking Mont Blanc. From the various options we have chosen half
board and the subscription to the ski lift. The deposit has been sent
today through our bank. I look forward to your confirmation once you
have received our deposit.
                Yours sincerely

Spett. Campeggio Lungomare,
*   ci piacerebbe prenotare il posto per due tende e una roulotte*
per una settimana a partire dal 15 maggio. Siamo stati nel vostro
campeggio anche l'anno scorso e gradiremmo lo stesso posto
tranquillo vicino al fiume. Vogliate confermare la disponobilità dei
posti, se possibile, a giro di posta.
*   In attesa di una sollecita risposta,*
*   vi salutiamo cordialmente*

Dear Sir,
        We would like to book a place for two tents and one caravan for
a week from May 15th.
        We stayed in your campsite last year and would very much
appreciate the same quiet place near the river. Could you please let us
know whether the places are available, by return of post if possible. I
look forward to hearing from you.
                Yours faithfully,

Egregio signore,
        sono interessato all'annuncio apparso sull' Indipendente del 7 – 3 p. 9, riguardo all'appartamento arredato da affittare per il mese di luglio in Toscana. Gradirei conoscere in dettaglio tutte le spese, oltre all'affitto, e la posizione della casa rispetto all'autostrada.
                In attesa di una gentile risposta,
                        gradisca distinti saluti

Dear Sir,
        I'm interested in the advertisement placed in the *Indipendente* of 7th March, p.9, for a flat to let for the month of July in Tuscany. I would like to know the details of all expenses not included in the rent and the position of the house in relation to the motorway. I look forward to hearing from you.
                Yours faithfully,

Spett. Ufficio Prenotazioni,
        gradiremmo prenotare dieci biglietti per poltroncine per l'opera l'Aida qualsiasi giorno del mese di luglio. Vogliate gentilmente confermare la prenotazione e saperci dire se possiamo ritirare i biglietti pagando la sera stessa all'ingresso.

Dear Sir,
        We would like to book ten seats in the back stalls for *Aida* any day in July. Would you kindly confirm the bookings and inform us whether we can collect the tickets and pay at the box office on the evening of the performance.

Spett. Istituto,
        vorrei iscrivermi al vostro corso di lingua italiana per la durata di tre settimane dal 1 settembre. Mi interessa il livello intermedio con indirizzo commerciale. In attesa di ricevere il modulo per l'iscrizione,
                distinti saluti

Dear Madam,
        I would like to enrol on your three-week Italian course starting September 1st. I am interested in the commercial course at intermediate level. Please send me an enrolment form.
                Yours sincerely

129 Letters of complaint

(a) To an airline / travel agency / airport authority notifying loss of luggage and asking for reimbursement

Domenico Lucini
Studio Legale Lucini
via Monte Rosa 18
8765 Monza (Milano)
Fax 03-9876

Ufficio Bagagli Smarriti
Aereoporto Malpensa
9608 Milano

4 – 6 – 89

Oggetto: smarrimento valigia

Spett. Ufficio
   il giorno 4 – 6 – c.a. è andata smarrita una mia valigia sul volo Dublino Milano AZ948 con partenza da Dublino alle ore 14.00 e arrivo ritardato a Milano alle 17.50. Si tratta di una valigia di pelle nera con bordi rossi, 1.50 m per 70 cm. con inserito il nome e l'indirizzo del proprietario. Poiché, oltre ad effetti personali, la valigia conteneva anche importanti documenti di lavoro, gradirei un vostro sollecito intervento per rintracciarla e, se possibile, una comunicazione via fax.
      In attesa di una vostra risposta, ringraziando per la vostra attenzione vogliate gradire distinti saluti

Lost Property Office
Malpensa Airport
9608 Milan

Dear Sir,
     On the 4th of June my suitcase was lost on the flight Dublin–Milan AZ948 leaving Dublin at 14.00 and arriving late in Milan at 17.50. The lost suitcase is black leather with red stripes, 1.50 m by 70 cm with name and address of the owner on the attached label. Apart from personal objects the suitcase also held important professional documents. I should be grateful if you could make immediate efforts to trace the suitcase and, if possible, send me any communication via fax.
          Thank for your kind attention. I look forward to hearing from you,
          Yours sincerely

Aereoporto Malpensa
Milano   *Oggetto: smarrimento*
                                                           valigia

Spett. Direzione,
        non avendo ottenuto risposta alla mia del 4 – 3 – c.a. inoltro
con questa successiva lettera richiesta di rimborso per l'ammontare di
£ . . .. Allego elenco degli oggetti contenuti con il relativo valore. Mi
auguro un sollecito rimborso,
                distinti saluti

Dear Sir,
        Since I have not received a reply to my letter dated 4 – 3 – '95
I must claim from your airline reimbursement for the total of £ I
enclose a list of the articles contained in the suitcase, with the value of
each. I shall be obliged if you would send me a cheque for this amount
without further delay.
        Yours sincerely

(b) To a travel agency in respect of unsatisfactory accommodation

> *Mondo Intero Viaggi*
> *via Casella 8*
> *345 Valeggio (Mantova)*
>
> *Spett. Agenzia,*
>
> *faccio riferimento al soggiorno pensione completa da voi prenotatoci presso l'albergo 'Il Sole' per il periodo 12 – 24 agosto c.a. Dal vostro dépliant risultava un albergo da quattro stelle. In effetti la camera da letto doppia aveva la dimensione di una singola dove era stato inserito un letto matrimoniale. Era impossibile muoversi. Per quanto riguarda il vitto si trattava di un trattamento da pensione. Le porzioni erano presentate già pronte, scarse, e non si trattava di piatti locali, come indicato nel dépliant, ma di piatti surgelati.*
>
> *L'intenzione di questa lettera non è di chiedere un rimborso ma di portarvi a conoscenza di ciò in quanto l'anno precedente, attraverso voi, avevamo prenotato un albergo che ci aveva pienamente soddisfatto. Avremmo intenzione di servirci ancora di voi ma solo se ci garantite che sarà vostra premura supervisionare gli alberghi che consigliate.*
>
> *In attesa di una vostra cortese risposta,*
> *vi inviamo i più cordiali saluti*

Rosy and John Lily
3 Stratford Road
Kenilworth

Dear Sir,

I am writing to you about the full board accommodation at the hotel 'Il Sole' that we reserved through you from the 12th to the 24th of August this year. According to your brochure it was a four star hotel. In fact the double bedroom was the size of a single room with a double bed in it. It was difficult to move around. As for the food, it was of a quality to be expected in a bed and breakfast establishment. The portions were pre-prepared and small. Contrary to what the brochure said, it was not local, but frozen, food.

It is not my intention to ask for a reimbursement but to bring this to your attention, since, last year, we had booked through you a hotel which was to our complete satisfaction. Could you please assure us that you will check the hotels which you recommend.

(c) Making a complaint for receiving the wrong goods

J. Rashton and Co.
Piccadilly Road
7654 Birmingham

Spett. Ditta,

abbiamo ricevuto le gonne come da nostro ordine (nota di commissione n°1345). Ci dispiace però dovervi comunicare che non corrispondono all'articolo da noi ordinato. Si tratta di gonne di diverso disegno e confezione.

Vi comunichiamo che abbiamo comunque deciso di trattenere la merce allegando la nota di addebito per l'importo di £ . . ., quale differenza di prezzo secondo il vostro listino.

Confidando in una maggiore attenzione da parte vostra in futuro, porgiamo distinti saluti

Dear Sir,

We have received the skirts following our order (ref. n° . . .). Unfortunately we have to inform you that they do not correspond to the items we actually ordered. They are different in pattern and style.

However, we have decided to keep them. We enclose a note of debit for £ . . ., to make up the difference in price according to your price-list.

Hoping for more attention on your part in the future,
Yours sincerely

(d) Complaint on receipt of broken goods

Fuller J. & Sons
41 Winchester Road
Leicester

Spett. Ditta,

vi informiamo della consegna della partita di whisky da noi ordinata il 6 – 9 – '91 (nota commissione n°678). Sfortunatamente un'intera cassa di bottiglie è giunta rotta. Gli spedizionieri, presenti all'apertura di tutte le casse hanno constatato che l'imballaggio era insufficiente.

A seguito di un vostro cenno di accordo, vi spediremo l'importo a mezzo banca come di consueto, detraendo il valore delle bottiglie rotte.

Distinti saluti

Dear Sir,
This is to notify you that we have received the consignment of whisky we ordered on the 6th September 1991 (order n°. 678). Unfortunately a whole box of bottles was broken. The freight agents were present when the crates were opened and they acknowledged that the packing was inadequate.
We shall send the payment through our usual bank, after deducting the value of the broken bottles, as soon as we receive a note of agreement from you.
Yours faithfully

(e) Complaint for a delay in delivering goods

Artigianato Alpestre
via Valleverde 8
6873 Folgaria (Trento)   30 – 10 – 91

Spett. Ditta,

    Non abbiamo ancora ricevuto gli articoli di artigianato che
avevamo ordinato sei mesi fa. Gradiremmo essere informati con
urgenza della ragione di tale ritardo e dei tempi esatti della
consegna. Nel caso che la merce non potesse giungerci entro il
12 – 11, vi preghiamo di considerare l'ordinazione cancellata in
quanto la merce giungerebbe troppo tardi per le vendite natalizie.
    In attesa di una urgente risposta,
      distinti saluti

Dear Sir,
    We haven't yet received the hand-made items which we ordered
six months ago. We would appreciate it if you could inform us by return
of post of the reasons for the delay and the expected date of delivery. If
the goods cannot reach us by 12th November, please consider the order
cancelled as the items would arrive too late for the Christmas market.
    Yours faithfully

130 **Requests for brochures, samples and catalogues**

Radio Sprint
viale Cordova 43   *12 – 3 – 1993*
Arezzo

Spett. ditta,

abbiamo ricevuto la vostra circolare del 3 c.m. Poiché siamo
interessati ai vostri prodotti, vi preghiamo di inviarci il vostro
catalogo unitamente al listino prezzi. Se la qualità e i termini di
consegna saranno favorevoli ci ripromettiamo un ordine di prova.
Nell'attesa di una risposta, distintamente vi salutiamo,

Dear Sir,
          We have received your circular of the 3rd instant. As we are
interested in your products we would like to receive your catalogue
with the price list. If quality and promise of early delivery compare well
with the competition, we shall place a trial order with you.
          Hoping to hear from you shortly, we remain
               Yours faithfully

Sutton & Sons
Leicester Square   5 – 2 – 1994
Coventry CV45

Spett. ditta,

ci affrettiamo ad inviarvi, come da voi richiesto via fax, il
nostro campionario certi che saprete apprezzare la bellezza dei
nostri colori e la resistenza dei tessuti. Siamo interessati a stabilire
rapporti d'affari con voi poiché il nome e la reputazione della vostra
ditta ci sono noti.

I prezzi sono quelli indicati nel listino, imballaggio compreso,
trasporto a parte.

Con i nostri migliori saluti,

Dear Sirs,

As you requested via fax, we are sending you our set of samples.
We are confident that you will appreciate the beauty of the colours and
the quality of the material. We are interested in establishing business
relations with you since the name and reputation of your company is
well-known to us.

The prices are those indicated in the price list. Packing is included,
transport is separate.

Yours faithfully,

Paese d'Arte. Centro per Stranieri.
Vicolo Stretto 5   *25 – 7 – 1998*
Bassano del Grappa (Vicenza)

Spett. direzione,

> *siamo interessati a stabilire un rapporto di cooperazione con la vostra scuola di lingue al fine di poter inviare presso di voi i nostri dirigenti che richiedono corsi intensivi individuali. Gradiremmo perciò ricevere tutte le informazioni necessarie.*
>   *In attesa, vi inviamo distinti saluti*

Dear Sir,
     We are interested in establishing a relationship with your language school with a view to sending some of our executives to follow your intensive individual courses. We should be pleased to receive all necessary information.
         Yours faithfully

The reply could be formulated in this way:

Spett. ditta,

> *la brochure allegata, contiene tutti i dettagli riguardo ai corsi e alle attività culturali e ricreative del nostro Centro. Come le fotografie illustrano il Centro è dotato dei più moderni laboratori linguistici e di una aggiornata videoteca.*
> *I corsi sono tutti programmati per l'apprendimento rapido dell'italiano scritto e parlato appropriato al mondo dell'industria e del commercio.*
>   *Sperando che le informazioni siano di vostro gradimento, vogliate gradire i nostri migliori saluti*

Dear Sir,
     The enclosed brochure includes all the details about our Centre's cultural and recreational activities.
     As the photographs show the Centre has the most sophisticated language laboratories and an up-to-date video library.
     All courses are programmed for the swift learning of spoken and written Italian as it is used in business and industry.
         Hoping the information is to your satisfaction,
         Yours faithfully

Export

(a) Looking for distribution agents

Camera di Commercio di Milano
Viale Venezia 27
Milano

Oggetto: contatti agenti di distribuzione

Spett. Camera di Commercio,

siamo una ditta affermata di articoli di cartoleria e intendiamo introdurci nel mercato italiano. Cerchiamo quindi la vostra collaborazione per contattare agenti di distribuzione. Vi saremmo grati se poteste inviarci dei nominativi di ditte all'ingrosso interessate a cooperare con noi. In caso di preliminare risposta affermativa da parte vostra, sarà nostra premura inviarvi, oltre al già incluso catalogo, informazioni e nominativi per eventuali referenze su di noi.

Ringraziandovi anticipatamente, in attesa di una risposta, vi inviamo distinti saluti

---

Dear Sirs,
      We are a well-established producer of stationery products, interested in entering the Italian market.
      We are therefore looking for distribution agents. We would like to ask you whether you could send us names of wholesale traders interested in cooperating with us. Should we receive a preliminary positive reply from you, we will send you further information about us, together with the names of referees.
            Yours faithfully

(b) Announcing the opening of a branch in Italy

Avv. Cinzia Lorenzoni
Pubbliche Relazioni s.r.l.
via Lamarmora 8
Milano

Gentile avvocatessa,

con la presente mi pregio di confermarle che dal 1 ottobre c.a. apriremo a Milano una filiale della nostra 'Cashmere House'.

La filiale sarà affidata alla signora Lucrezia Gheddi che ha lavorato a Londra con noi per diversi anni e che gode della nostra totale fiducia.

Con questa lettera le confermo che affidiamo a voi la campagna pubblicitaria, come concordato in precedenza.

Nella speranza di incontrarla presto qui a Edinburgo, le invio i miei più cordiali saluti

Dear Madam / Ms 'X',

I am very pleased to inform you that on the 1st October we shall open a branch of 'Cashmere House' in Milan.

The branch will be under the management of Mrs Gheddi who has been working with us for several years in London and who enjoys our full confidence.

I have pleasure in confirming our agreement that you should organize our publicity campaign on this occasion.

I'm looking forward to seeing you in Edinburgh,

Yours

(c) Ordering a market research exercise

Ricerche di Mercato a Tutto Campo
Piazzale Lotto 67
Torino

Spett. Agenzia,

facendo seguito alle precedenti telefonate con il dott. Savoldi e all'intercorsa corrispondenza, desidero comunicarvi che abbiamo accettato le vostre condizioni per farvi condurre una ricerca di mercato sull'uso di elicotteri privati da parte di ditte italiane in base agli indirizzi da noi forniti.

I tempi, i termini e i costi della ricerca rimangono quelli fissati e accettati da entrambe le parti.

Distinti saluti,

Dear Sir,

Following our previous telephone calls with Dr Savoldi and the correspondence exchanged, I am delighted to inform you that we have accepted your conditions to carry out a market research exercise on our behalf on the use of private helicopters by Italian companies, on the basis of the addresses with which we provided you.

The time, the terms and the costs of the research remain those which have been fixed and accepted by both sides.

Yours faithfully,

132 Quotations and orders

(a) Quotation for a set of books

Casa editrice Pace
via Tunisia 8
Perugia   *16 – 1 – 1990*

Spett. Casa editrice,

    gradiremmo ricevere il costo preventivo di 40 copie del corso
di italiano con elaboratore elettronico da voi recentemente
pubblicato Italiano con il computer.
        Distinti saluti

Dear Sir,

    We would like to receive your quotation for 40 copies of *Italiano
con il computer*, the computer-assisted learning course in Italian which
you have recently published.
        Yours faithfully,

Department of Italian
University of Toronto
Toronto   *18 – 4 – 1990*
Canada

Egregio Prof.,

    in risposta alla sua richiesta le inviamo l'inclusa proposta di commissione. Sperando in un suo ordine, voglia gradire distinti saluti,

Allegato: proposta di commissione n° 333

Proposta di commissione

Il corso comprende:
1 libro di testo per studenti	£_____
1 manuale per insegnanti	£_____
2 cassette	£_____
4 dischetti per computer	£_____
Totale	£_____
+ IVA	£_____

Trasporto a carico del destinatario.
Su 50 copie lo sconto applicabile è del 5%. Tali prezzi sono validi fino al 30 – 12 – 1990. Il pagamento è da effettuarsi in lire italiane tramite banca sul nostro c / c. 54987.

Dear Sir,
    In reply to your request, I enclose our quotation.
        Yours faithfully,

Enclosure: quotation no. 333

Quotation

The course includes:
1 student's book	£_____
1 teacher's manual	£_____
2 cassettes	£_____
4 computer disks	£_____
Total	£_____
+ VAT	£_____

Transport to be debited to the customer. On 50 copies the discount is 5%. These prices are valid until 30 – 12 – 1990. Payment is to be made in Italian lire through a bank on our a. / c. 54987.

(b) Requesting a quotation for a package tour

Agenzia Gran Turismo
Largo Augusto 80
4532 Bologna   *7 – 3 – 1990*

Spett. Agente di viaggio,

    gradiremmo ricevere il preventivo per un viaggio in pullman
di sette giorni (6 notti) per 70 persone col seguente itinerario:
Venezia – Dolomiti – Lago di Garda – Verona – Vicenza – Padova –
Venezia nella seconda metà di settembre. Se le vostre condizioni
saranno favorevoli, uno dei nostri manager passerà da voi a definire i
dettagli.

    In attesa vi salutiamo distintamente,

Dear Sir,
    We would like to receive an estimate for a seven-day coach tour
(six nights) for 70 people with the following itinerary: Venice –
Dolomites – Lake Garda – Verona – Vicenza – Padua – Venice, in the
second half of September. If you can offer favourable terms, one of our
managers will visit you to discuss all the details.
            Yours faithfully,

Sunshine Travel Agency
Bull Ring
Birmingham   *10 – 3 – 1990*

Spett. Agenzia,

abbiamo ricevuto con piacere la vostra richiesta del . . .. La proposta allegata evidenzia diverse alternative con relativi costi a seconda del tipo di albergo. Vogliate prendere nota che il deposito minimo per ogni persona è di £ . . . e che il saldo deve essere effettuato 3 settimane prima dell'inizio del viaggio. In caso di rinuncia dopo la conferma della prenotazione il deposito non verrà rimborsato.

Distinti saluti

Dear Sir,
        Thank you for your request for a quotation about . . .. The enclosed proposal includes several alternatives depending on the hotel category.
        Please note that the minimum deposit is £ . . . for each person. Balance of fare is to be paid not later than 4 weeks before departure. In the event of cancellation after the booking has been confirmed the deposit is forfeit.
        Yours faithfully

(c) Complaining about price increases

Società Sistemi Antifurto   *8 – 8 – 1988*
via Barbarossa 10
Siena

Spett. Ditta,

vi ringraziamo della proposta di commissione n° 789 inviataci (oggetto 200 sistemi antifurto tipo 007). Sarebbe nostra intenzione continuare a fornirci presso di voi in quanto abbiamo sempre apprezzato la qualità dei vostri prodotti. Purtroppo i vostri prezzi sono aumentati eccessivamente rispetto ad altri fornitori. Se potessimo addivenire ad un accordo che preveda o una riduzione del 2.50% o il pagamento a 120 giorni dalla scadenza, la nostra collaborazione potrebbe continuare.
Attendiamo con fiducia una vostra positiva risposta, distinti saluti

---

Dear Sir,
        Thank you for the quotation n° 789 (ref. 200 alarm systems type 007). We would very much like to carry on being your customers since we have always appreciated the quality of your products. Unfortunately your prices have increased excessively compared to other manufacturers. If you could offer either a reduction of 2.50% or 120 days' credit from your date of invoice, we feel sure that our collaboration could still be possible.
                Awaiting your reply
                Yours faithfully,

(d) Acknowledgement of order

Istituto Eterna Giovinezza   7 – 7 – 90
Scala Frolli 8
Trieste

Spett. Istituto,

      vi ringraziamo per l'ordinazione ricevuta con data 1 – 7 – 90.
I prodotti saranno spediti entro la fine del c.m.
           Distinti saluti,

Thank you for the order placed with us. The products will be sent by the
end of the current month.
        Yours faithfully,

But other replies could be:

    *Non possiamo procedere alla spedizione dei prodotti da voi
    richiesti (rif . . .) in quanto ci mancano i seguenti dati: . . .*
    We are sorry we cannot process your order because we don't have
    the following data: . . .
    *Ci dispiace comunicarvi che attualmente il materiale richiesto è
    esaurito e che potremo iniziare le consegne a partire dalla fine di
    marzo.*
    We have to inform you that the material you require is out of stock
    and we shall be able to resume delivery from the end of March.

133 Delays in delivery and payment

(a) Informing of late delivery

Supermarket Chains $\quad\quad\quad\quad\quad\quad$ 4 – 6 – '90
Suffolk Road
Cambridge

Spett. Direttore,

dobbiamo purtroppo comunicarle che ci sarà un ritardo nella consegna degli agrumi quest'autunno a causa del clima sfavorevole. Anticipiamo di effettuare la spedizione agli inizi di dicembre.
Confidando nella vostra comprensione
vi salutiamo distintamente

Dear Sir,
We regret to inform you that there will be a delay in the delivery of citrus fruit this autumn because of the unfavourable climate. We foresee being able to start deliveries at the beginning of December.
Yours faithfully,

(b) Apologizing for a delay

International Films Distribution   9 – 4 – 1992
67 Thames Square
Manchester

Spett. casa cinematografica,

vi prego vivamente di scusarci per il ritardo nella consegna
dei film pubblicitari da voi commissionatici. Il progetto si è rivelato
più complesso del previsto a causa della malattia di uno degli attori.
Contiamo di consegnarli entro quindici giorni con la certezza che la
bellezza delle riprese ci farà non solo perdonare ma anche ricevere
ulteriori ordinazioni.

Scusandoci di nuovo per eventuali difficoltà che il nostro
ritardo può avervi causato,

vi porgiamo distinti saluti

Dear Sir,

Please accept our apologies for the delay in delivering the
commercial films. The project has proved more complex than expected
because of the illness of one of the actors. We expect to be able to send
the films within a fortnight, confident that the beauty of the shots will
not only make up for the delay but also lead you to commission further
films from us.

With our apologies,
Yours faithfully

(c) Reminder concerning an overdue account

Oggetto: Sollecito di pagamento

Spett. Prof.
Angela Mainardi
via Raffaello 9
Ravenna   *16 – 8 – 92*

Gentile professoressa,

dal controllo della nostra partita contabile, ci risulta ancora scoperto l'importo di £ . . . a fronte della fattura F.305 del 7 – 5 – 90.
Vi preghiamo di provvedere entro e non oltre 10 gg. dal ricevimento della presente al pagamento di quanto dovutoci.
Nel caso abbiate provveduto nel frattempo, vogliate considerare la presente quale ringraziamento.
Con l'occasione porgiamo distinti saluti,

Dear Madam,

According to our records, the amount of £ . . . is now overdue for payment. Please make arrangements to pay within 10 days from receipt of this reminder. Should you have paid meanwhile, please consider this letter as a note of thanks.

Yours faithfully,

(d) Other expressions of payment reminders are

In attesa di un sollecito pagamento . . .
We look forward to receiving your payment . . .

Se ha delle riserve riguardo al pagamento la preghiamo di mettersi gentilmente in contatto con il nostro ufficio.
If you have any queries concerning your account please do not hesitate to contact our office.

4 Bank and insurance correspondence

(a) Transferring money

> *All'attenzione del direttore*   *9 – 1 – 92*
> *Banca di Rovigo*
> *Rovigo*
>
> *Vogliate cortesemente trasferire £ . . . dal nostro c / c. n° . . . al conto*
> *amministrato n° . . . a partire dalla data odierna.*
>   *Ringraziando*

Please transfer £ . . . from our a/c no. . . . to account no. . . . as from
today.

(b) Making a payment

> *All'attenzione del direttore*
> *Banca di Lecco*
> *Lecco*
>
> *Vogliate fare un bonifico bancario di £ . . . a favore di Luigi Potenza*
> *& Figli – via Giulio Cesare 34 Roma – in data 7 – 9 – 92 addebitando*
> *l'equivalente in sterline sul conto corrente della nostra ditta n° . . .*
>   *Distinti saluti*

Please make a transfer payment of . . . Italian lire in favour of . . .,
debiting it to our company's current account, no . . .
            Yours faithfully,

(c) To extend the cover of an insurance policy

Rag. Tommasi   *7 – 1 – 93*
Savoi Assicurazioni
Viale Giotto 9
Piacenza

Egregio Ragioniere,

*a partire dal 5 dicembre, la nostra casa sulle colline
apenniniche comprenderà una partita di vini di oltre cinquant'anni,
due computer PC, una stampatrice, una fotocopiatrice e una Lancia
2000 oltre a ciò che è attualmente assicurato presso voi. Le
chiediamo di stendere una nuova polizza estendendola agli articoli
indicati.*

*Ringraziandola per la cortese soll ecitudine,
la salutiamo cordialmente*

Dear Sirs,
     As from 5th December our house in the Apennine hills will
include a stock of fifty-year-old wines, two PCs, a printer, a photocopier
and a Lancia 2000 in addition to what is currently insured with you.
Could you please extend our current policy to cover the new items.
                  With thanks,
                    Yours faithfully,

SENTENCE STRUCTURE
AND WORD ORDER

35 Introduction

Word order and sentence structure are intertwined. It is essential for the reader to be aware of how varied and flexible they are in Italian in order to be able to work out the function of words without relying on a fixed pattern (e.g. the subject may be at the end of a sentence) and to appreciate how writers and speakers use this linguistic freedom for stylistic effects.

Today's Italian writing is characterized by a marked search for impact on the reader. The devices chosen to emphasize some specific words or sentences are basically the following:

● the use of punctuation – colon and semi-colon in particular – as graphic highlights to attract the reader's attention to some points of the speech (see section 117);

● the omission of the verb, which is seen as a burden to the sentence, and the omission of which therefore has a striking effect:

> *Perché milioni intorno al Papa di Roma nelle terre dell'Est?*
> Why (did) millions of people in Eastern Europe (gather) around the Pope?
>
> (About a newscaster) *Soprattutto mortalmente serio sul gioco del pallone, disposto a fare un dramma di qualunque cosa accada allo stadio, purché l'indice d'ascolto aumenti.*
> Above all (he is) deadly serious about football. (He is) ready to make a drama out of anything that may happen at the stadium in order to raise the audience rating.

Side by side with these innovations, the following traditional features are still used for emphasis:

● The flexibility of the Italian sentence word order, which allows the writer to place either a single word or a clause in any key position (section 138).

● The typical sentence structure, which is not linear like the English one, but is made up of clauses joined to each other as in carpentry or woven together like straw in a basket.

- The frequent repetition of the linking parts of a sentence (prepositions, adverbs, conjunctions, etc.)

- The accumulation of the same type of clause.

Here are some examples:

È difficile che il tutto esaurito di questi ultimi giorni nei centri sciistici delle Alpi, dopo aver costretto certe stazioni a chiudere le porte ai turisti, sia un fenomeno passeggero che significhi solo che c'è stata nel nostro paese una crescita improvvisa della passione per la montagna.

Skiing resorts in the Alps have registered full booking in these last few days and have been compelled to bar tourists. It is difficult to believe that this is a temporary phenomenon and only a sign of a sudden growth of interest in the mountains.

(Literally: It is difficult that the full booking of these last days in the skiing resorts of the Alps, after having compelled some resorts to bar tourists, is a temporary phenomenon which only indicates that in our country there has been a sudden interest in mountains.)

Niente di meglio di un libro per far viaggiare la fantasia, per dare spazio ai sogni, per aprire gli orizzonti della nostra mente e del nostro cuore.

Nothing better than a book to let our imagination roam, to make room for our dreams, and to open the horizons of our mind and our heart.

Oltre ai ritardi, alle scomodità, all'aumento dei prezzi, ai servizi scadenti, le ferrovie hanno inventato un nuovo sistema per mettere in difficoltà i passeggeri.

Apart from delays, uncomfortable seats, price increases, declining standards of service, the railways have invented a new system to create further difficulties for passengers.

Complete units of meaning

There are expressions which have a complete meaning without being full sentences. For instance:

- *No.* No. *Sì.* Yes. *Ecco.* Here it is. *Giusto!* Right!
  E per che cosa, poi? And what for, then?

- Past participles on their own:
    Preso! Got it! *Toccato!* Touché!

- Colloquial phrases where the verb is omitted:

    Una mano? Want a hand?

(The omission of the subject pronoun would not be enough to form a colloquialism because it is almost the rule to omit it in standard language.)

The simple sentence

For interrogative and negative sentences see sections 39 and 44.

The sentence structure depends on the verb. There are:

(i) verbs like *essere* to be, *sembrare* to seem, *parere* to look like, which may complement the subject with:

- an adjective:

    Questa carne è insipida. This meat is tasteless.

- a noun:

    Mio fratello è un perito agrario. My brother is an agronomist.

- a pronoun:

    Questa biro sembra la mia. This biro looks like mine.

- a comparative word:

    Il tuo computer è come il mio. Your computer is like mine.

(ii) verbs that require an object (transitive verbs):

    Il cane inseguiva il gatto. The dog was pursuing the cat.

(This verb would be meaningless without an object:

    Il cane inseguiva. The dog pursued.)

(iii) verbs that never take a direct object (intransitive verbs). For the correct auxiliary see section 64d.

    Il sole sta tramontando. The sun is setting.

These verbs are often followed by an adjective or an adverb of manner:

    La tragedia accadde rapida(mente).
    The tragedy happened rapidly.

(iv) verbs which can be used with or without an object, i.e. transitively or intransitively:

> *Ho vinto!* I won!
>
> *Ho vinto la scommessa!* I won the bet!

(v) verbs taking nouns or pronouns, both as a direct and an indirect object.

★ Note that, unlike in English, no Italian verb can take two direct objects:

> *Paolo ha regalato alla sua ragazza un micino.*
> Paul has given a kitten to his girlfriend / has given his girlfriend a kitten.
>
> *Gli ho raccontato la trama.*
> I told him the plot. (literally: I told to him the plot.)
>
> *Le ho cucinato una minestra di carote.*
> I cooked a carrot soup for her.
>
> *Gliel' ho portata a casa.*
> I have taken it home to her.

138 Word order

The basic word order of an Italian sentence is: **subject + verb + direct and / or indirect object + adverbial expressions of manner, time and place.** In practice, this sequence is frequently not followed, perhaps because it sounds rather flat in Italian. The overall guiding principle is that the word(s) placed in a different position from the basic one are those which the writer wishes to underline. Here are some examples of common sentence structures:

(a) The position of the subject

(i) The subject always follows these verbs: *c'è* there is, *esistere* to exist, to be, *mancare* to be missing and usually follows these ones: *restare* to remain, to be left, *ergersi* to stand, *spiccare* to stand out, *sorgere* to rise, *spuntare* to rise, to sprout.

> *Mancano tre giorni a Natale.*
> There are three days to Christmas.
>
> *Rimanevano alcune formalità.*
> A few formalities remained.

(ii) With *essere* to be, *sembrare* to seem, *parere* to look like, the subject may be placed at the end of the sentence to emphasize it:

> *È la più bella di tutte quella bambina.*
> That child is the loveliest of them all.

(iii) When the subject is a noun or a pronoun it may have an initial or end position:

> *Claudia ha telefonato.*
> Claudia rang up. Claudia did ring up. (The stress is on the action.)

> *Ha telefonato Claudia.*
> Claudia rang up. (The stress is on the person.)

> *L'ospite è il più risentito.* (unmarked pattern)
> The guest is the most resentful.

> *Il più risentito è l'ospite.*
> It is the guest who is the most resentful. (The stress is on the subject and the general tone of the sentence is more emphatic.)

Similar examples are:

> *Lo sciopero si farà.*
> The strike will be on. (unmarked pattern)

> *Si farà lo sciopero.*
> It will be on. (the strike that had been threatened)

> *Ho telefonato ieri.* I rang up yesterday.

> *Ho telefonato io.*
> I rang up. It was I who rang. (The emphasis is on the subject.)

> *Sono stato io a telefonare.* It was I who rang up.

(iv) In direct questions inversion of the subject is optional.

● Note that unlike in English the adjective cannot be separated from the verb, nor the verb from the object. For example:

> X *Sono queste parole necessarie?* X
> *Queste parole sono necessarie? / Sono necessarie queste parole?*
> Are these words necessary?

● Note that the object is not separated from the verb:

> X *Hai Francesco la carta verde?* X
> *Hai la carta verde Francesco? / Francesco hai la carta verde?*
> Has Francesco got the international insurance card?

> *Paolo ha studiato italiano? / Ha studiato italiano Paolo?*
> Has Paolo studied Italian?

(v) In written texts, the subject usually follows the verb in phrases such as 'he said' placed after direct speech:

> *'Me la pagherete', concluse l'oratore.*
> 'You'll pay for it', said the speaker.

(vi) The subject may follow the direct object:

> *Cercava il rondinotto la rondine.*
> The swallow was looking for its young. (literally: It was searching the young swallow the swallow.)

(vii) The subject is often separated from the verb (see also section 40c):

> *I programmi televisi più dell'editoria possono darci un'idea della situazione culturale del paese.*
> TV programmes, more than the publishing trade, can give us an idea of the cultural situation of the country.

(b) The position of direct and indirect object

(i) The noun functioning as direct object may be placed after the verb (unmarked position) or before the verb (stressed position). In this case an object pronoun agreeing in gender and number must precede the verb or be attached to the end of a gerund, infinitive or imperative (see section 31c):

> *Non vedeva la donna da anni.*
> He hadn't seen the woman for years. (unmarked order)
>
> *La donna non la vedeva da anni.*
> He hadn't seen <u>the woman</u> for years.
>
> *Il cappotto appendilo là.* The coat, hang it over there.

(ii) The direct object may be separated from its adjective:

> *Facciamo le tende rosse.* Our curtains will be red.
> *Le tende le facciamo rosse.* We'll have <u>the curtains</u> red.
> *Le facciamo rosse le tende.* They will be red, the curtains.
> *Rosse le facciamo le tende.* The curtains we are making are red.

(iii) The indirect object can precede the direct object:

> *Pregasi inviare ai nostri clienti il listino dei prezzi.*
> Please send the price list to our customers.

(c) The position of pronouns, conjunctions and adverbs

(i) Other elements such as pronouns may have an initial position:

L'Ucraina è la regione più contigua all'Europa. Di essa ha voluto sempre far parte.

Ukraine is the closest region to Europe. The people have always wanted to be part of it. (literally: Of it it has always wanted to be part.)

(ii) Demonstrative pronouns can have an initial emphatic position:

E queste sono le tue buone maniere!

And these are your good manners!

(iii) Emphatic structures are also achieved by placing an object pronoun in the initial position even if there is also the noun as object (see section 138b):

Li ho già corretti i compiti. (alternative to *I compiti li ho già corretti.*)

I have already corrected the homework.

Ne leggi molti di gialli? Do you read many thrillers?

(iv) Conjunctions such as *però* but, *tuttavia* however, *nonostante* despite tend to have a medial (middle) position, even between two parts of a verb:

Pare infatti che gli scienziati stiano nonostante tutto rompendosi il capo per capirne l'essenza.

Despite this it seems that scientists are racking their brains to understand the essence of it.

Intanto, però, il risparmio continua.

Meanwhile, however, savings continue.

(v) Conjunctions and adverbs may separate two elements of a verb:

Abbiamo raramente sostenuto l'economia con tanto vigore.

We have rarely supported the economy with so much vigour.

(vi) Adverbial phrases and adverbs may have an initial, medial or end position:

Di straordinario interesse sono i suoi diarii.

His diaries are of extraordinary interest.

Il Ministro degli Interni, intanto, ha ordinato l'uso della benzina senza piombo.

The Home Secretary, meanwhile, has ordered the use of unleaded petrol.

I giapponesi hanno importato gli scioperi all'europea in questi giorni.

The Japanese have imported European-style strikes these days.

(d) 'Split up' sentences

(i) A frequent device is to begin sentences with *è / è stato / era* (it is / it has been / it was) + subject + *che* (that / who) to emphasize the word or phrase that follows. This type of sentence is called a 'cleft sentence':

È stato il rappresentante della banca che ha rilasciato un'intervista esplosiva.

It has been the bank representative who has given an explosive interview.

(ii) Literary writers imitate the liveliness of conversational style by introducing the anacoluthon, a structure where the subject has no grammatical relationship with the rest of the sentence.

Casanova, era la sua caratteristica sedurre le donne.

(literally: Casanova, it was his characteristic to seduce women.)

(e) Adjectives and adverbs

For the position of adjectives and adverbs, see sections 23 and 29c.

139 Compound sentences

Clauses may be joined either with commas or with conjunctions. The following are the most common types of co-ordinating conjunctions. These conjunctions do not affect the tense or the mood of the verb:

- listing:

    dapprima first of all
    secondo in the second place
    per ultimo, infine finally

- addition:

  e, ed and   *inoltre* besides that, moreover
  anche also   *per di più* furthermore
  e anche and also   *nè, neppure, nemmeno, neanche*
  altresì, parimenti likewise   neither. . .(nor)

- appositional:

  così thus   *tra parentesi* in brackets

- continuation:

  e poi and then   *poi* then

- alternative:

  o, oppure, ovvero, ossia or
  d'altra parte, d'altro canto on the other hand

- contrast:

  ma but   *sennonché* but, otherwise
  però yet   *anzi* on the contrary
  peraltro what is more   *tuttavia* however
  altrimenti otherwise   *eppure* and yet
  nondimeno however   *piuttosto* rather
  invece whereas   *pure* and yet

- consequence:

  perciò, dunque consequently   *pertanto* therefore
  ebbene well   *di conseguenza* hence

- explanations:

  cioè, vale a dire that is to say

- correlations:

  sia . . . sia . . . both . . . and . . .
  non solo . . . ma anche . . . not only . . . but also . . .

- summarizing:

  nel complesso all together   *in breve* to sum up

E (and) is not traditionally used to start a sentence. However, newspapers tend to disregard this for stylistic effects:

  I magistrati proclamano lo sciopero. E attaccano chi li attacca.
  Magistrates declare a strike attacking those who attack them.

> *L'autore conobbe la diva; e aggiungerei che la conobbe abbastanza bene.*
> The author knew the star and I should add he knew her rather well.

140 Complex sentences and the order of clauses

A complex sentence is formed by one main or independent clause and one or more subordinate or dependent clauses.

(i) In Italian, dependent clauses may be placed either before or after the main clause or between the subject of the main clause and its verb:

> *Quando la polizia arrivò c'era una gran folla.*
> *C'era una gran folla quando la polizia arrivò.*
> *C'era, quando la polizia arrivò, una gran folla.*
> When the police arrived there was a large crowd.

(ii) A subordinate clause may split another subordinate clause:

> *La clamorosa vittoria del generale che, in quanto convertito alla causa del nemico, era stato duramente criticato, non ha infranto l'unità nazionale.*
> The resounding victory of the general, who had been severely criticized because he had been converted to the enemy's cause, did not damage national unity.

(iii) There may be more than one dependent clause before or after the main one:

> *Riacutizzatasi la malattia, dopo aver tentato un'altra terapia, si decise di sottoporlo a intervento.*
> Since the illness had become more acute, a different therapy was tried. After that it was decided to operate on him.

(iv) The main clause governing a subordinate clause may be separated from it by an adverbial phrase:

> *C'è chi sostiene, con abbondanti argomentazioni, che il mondo del libro ha poco a che fare con la cultura.*
> There are those who claim, with plenty of arguments, that the world of books has nothing to do with culture.

The following are dependent clauses:

(a) Noun clauses governed by statements or verbs of reporting

(i) They may be introduced by:

- verbs like *credere* to believe, *sapere* to know, *dichiarare* to declare, *dire* to tell:

    Mi hai sempre detto che ti trovi bene con me.
    You always told me that you like my company.

- impersonal forms like *si dice che . . .* it is said that . . . or *è* + *sicuro, ovvio, risaputo* it is well known that:

    È noto che gli ecologisti non vogliono una funivia sul Cervino.
    It's well known that ecologists do not want a cableway on the Matterhorn.

- nouns:

    Era peccato che fossero avanzate tutte quelle aragoste.
    It was a shame that all those lobsters had been left over.

★ **(ii)** Noun clauses must be linked to the main clause with *che* and take the indicative or the subjunctive depending on the verb. But if the subject of the main clause is the same as the subject of the subordinate clause, the *che* construction is usually replaced by the infinitive construction or *di* + infinitive (for verbs requiring *di* see section 17):

    Era convinto di essere stato l'innovatore della pittura italiana.
    He was convinced he had been the innovator of Italian painting.

    I critici d'oggi sostengono che è stato l'innovatore della pittura italiana.
    Today's critics claim he was the innovator of Italian painting.

(iii) The main verb and *che* may be separated:

    Il Ministro rilevava ieri amaramente in un'intervista a una TV locale che le cinture di sicurezza non sono mai messe.
    Yesterday, in an interview on a local TV station, the minister remarked that safety belts are never worn.

(iv) Noun clauses may follow or precede the main clause. When it is in the initial position the noun clause has more emphasis:

> *È ovvio che non parli. / Che non parli è ovvio.*
> It's obvious he doesn't speak.

With the stressed position, if the subject of the main clause is different from that of the subordinate clause the sequence is: subordinate clause + pronoun *lo* + main sentence (verb + subject):

> *Che ci sarà una tregua lo hanno anticipato le agenzie di stampa.*
> Press agencies have anticipated that there will be a truce.
> That there will be a truce has been anticipated by press agencies.

(b) Indirect questions

(i) They are introduced by:

● verbs like *chiedersi, domandarsi* to wonder, *voler sapere* to wish to know, followed by interrogative adjectives, pronouns and adverbs (see also section 39):

se if, whether	*quando* when	*quale* which
come how	*dove* where	*che cosa* what
perché, come mai why	*quanto* how much	*chi* who, etc.

Indirect questions take the indicative if the events are given as certain and the subjunctive if the facts are considered possible or probable. For verbs requiring the subjunctive, see sections 58 and 59b.

> *Mi domando chi venga* I wonder who may be coming.
> *So chi viene.* I know who is coming.

● words such as *domanda, questione* demand, request, question:

> *La domanda che ci si poneva era: come intervenire per prevenire altri incidenti gravi?*
> We were asking each other this question: what could be done to prevent other serious accidents?

(ii) The interrogative clause usually follows the main one but may also precede it. In this case, the pronoun *lo* is inserted:

> *Non si saprà mai quali siano state le cause.*
> *Quali siano state le cause non lo si saprà mai.*
> One will never know what were the causes. / What the causes were will never be known.

(iii) There may be one or more subordinate clauses:

Ci si chiede se ci sarà il libero mercato o se ci sarà il mercato nero.
People wonder whether there will be the free or the black market.

(c) Relative clauses

(i) Relative clauses are linked to the main clause by means of relative pronouns (see section 38).

Scelsero lo studente che aveva maggiori necessità finanziarie.
They chose the student who had more financial difficulties.

Chi volesse fare politica attiva incontrerebbe numerosi ostacoli.
Those interested in a political career would encounter many obstacles.

(ii) Past participles and infinitives may function as relative clauses:

A causa dell'agitazione iniziatasi ieri e conclusasi questa sera non posso partire.
Because of the strike which started yesterday and is ending tonight I cannot leave.

Era stato Francesco a protestare. / A protestare era stato Francesco.
It was Frank who had protested / protested.

(d) Temporal clauses

(i) Temporal clauses are introduced by:

allorché, allorquando < literary > when	*dal tempo che* since
appena che as soon as	*finché* until
dopo che after that	*ogni volta che* each time that
mentre while	*quando* when

These conjunctions are followed by the indicative mode. *Che* too may be used with the meaning of 'when':

Sono arrivati sul binario che il treno partiva.
They arrived on the platform when the train was leaving.

Mentre controllavo il mio conto corrente mi vennero i sudori freddi.
While I was checking my current account I broke out into a cold sweat.

Il suo sguardo era triste anche quando sorrideva.
His look was sad even when he smiled.

Andava, dal tempo del primo divorzio, sempre vestita di rosso.
Since the time of her first divorce she always dressed in red.

(ii) Temporal clauses may also be expressed by:

- the gerund when the action in both sentences takes place at the same time
- *nel* + infinitive
- *prima di* + infinitive
- *dopo* + past infinitive
- the past participle, when the action precedes that of the main verb

> *Baciandola le fece gli auguri.*
> Kissing her he wished her all the best.

> *Nel risalire la corrente, la barca si capovolse.*
> In going upstream the boat overturned.

> *Lo citò in giudizio prima di valutare le conseguenze.*
> He sued him before assessing the consequences.

> *Respirò a fondo dopo essersi seduto e rispose con calma.*
> He took a deep breath after sitting down and answered calmly.

> *Pentitosi, le inviò delle rose.*
> After regretting his action, he sent her some roses.

(e) Clauses of manner

(i) They are introduced by:

come as	*nel senso che* in the sense that
come se (+ subj.) as if	*senza che* ... without ...
come quando like when	

> *Era bionda come quando era ragazza.*
> She was as blonde as when she was a girl.

(ii) They can be expressed by:

- the gerund
- *senza* + the infinitive
- *con il* + infinitive

> *Minacciava, urlando, di andare dal direttore.*
> He was shouting and threatening to go to the director.

> *Senza preoccuparsi della porta aperta, cominciò a litigare.*
> Without worrying that the door was open he started to argue.

> *Con l'allenarsi si migliora.* With training one improves.

(f) Clauses of purpose

(i) They may be introduced by: *affinché, acciocché* < formal >, *cosicché* < formal > so that, *che, perché* in order that – all requiring the subjunctive:

> *Era chiaro che lo avevano pagato affinché tacesse.*
> It was clear they had paid him so that he would keep silent.

(ii) When the subject is the same as that of the main verb, clauses of purpose may also be expressed with *per, allo scopo di, al fine di* + infinitive in order to:

> *Si erano trasferiti al fine di stare vicini alla figlia handicappata.*
> They moved house in order to be close to their handicapped daughter.

(g) Clauses of reason

(i) They are introduced by:

a seguito di because of	*siccome* since
ché because	*per il fatto che* given that
giacché in as much as	*visto che* seeing that
perché because	*sapendo che* knowing that

These all take the indicative. Clauses of reason are also introduced by verbs such as *dolersi* to regret, *essere dispiaciuto* to be sorry, *godere* to be delighted, *rallegrarsi* to rejoice, *rammaricarsi* to regret + *che*, which generally require the subjunctive:

> *Ha usato la lana perché non aveva il cotone.*
> She used wool since she did not have cotton.

> *Per il fatto che il premio fu dato al suo avversario, si ubriacò.*
> Because the prize was given to his adversary he got drunk.

(ii) They may also be expressed by:

- *per* + present or past infinitive
- present or past gerund
- past participle

> *Stanno costruendo una diga per fermare la lava dall'Etna.*
> They are building a dam to stop the lava from Etna.

> *Il programma fu respinto essendo basato su nuove banalità.*
> The programme was rejected as it was based on new banalities.

> *È una capitale invivibile, inquinata dai rumori e dallo smog.*
> It is a capital where it is impossible to live, because it is polluted by noise and smog.

(h) Result clauses

(i) They may be introduced by:

così / tanto / talmente . . . che so much that
tanto / tale / siffatto + noun such . . .
sicché so that (requiring the indicative or the conditional)
abbastanza / troppo / poco / . . . perché + subjunctive enough /
too much / too little . . . to
al punto che to the point that
in modo che + subjunctive in such a way that

> *Era mosso da siffatta curiosità che non si curò di apparire indiscreto.*
> He was moved by such curiosity that he did not care about being indiscreet.

(ii) They may also be expressed with *così . . . da* + infinitive:

> *Tende a essere così poco obbiettivo da rendere i suoi giudizi inaccettabili.*
> He tends to be so subjective that his opinions are unacceptable.

(i) Concessive clauses

(i) Conjunctions introducing them are:

ancorché < formal >
benché, sebbene although
malgrado despite the fact that
nonostante, seppure, quantunque although
tanto più che all the more so
qualunque + noun no matter
per / per quanto + adjective whatever

They all require the subjunctive:

> *Benché il freddo fosse pungente, era in camicia.*
> Despite the piercing cold, he was only wearing a shirt.
>
> *Il rapporto di lavoro, qualunque fosse stata la risposta, era finito.*
> Whatever his answer, the working relationship had finished.

(ii) As the above examples show, these clauses usually precede the main sentence though they may also follow it, or divide its subject and object.

(iii) Clauses of concession are also expressed by:

- one of the conjunctions listed above and a past participle
- *pur* + gerund

> *Ancorché risentito, tacque.*
> Though he was angry he kept quiet.

> *Pur essendo in confidenza, temeva di essere invadente.*
> Although they were on friendly terms, he was afraid of being intrusive.

(j) Clauses of contrast

(i) They are usually introduced by *laddove* < formal > whilst, *mentre* while + indicative or conditional:

> *Mentre lui avrebbe dato l'anima per vincere il concorso, l'altro era indifferente.*
> While he would give his life (literally: soul) to win the competition, the other was indifferent.

(ii) They may also be expressed with *invece di* + infinitive, *in luogo di* + infinitive < formal > instead of:

> *Invece di tranquillizzarla, la spaventò.*
> Instead of calming her down, he frightened her.

(k) The hypothetical or conditional sentence

(i) Hypothetical sentences are introduced by:

a condizione di on condition that	*a meno che* unless
nel caso che in the event that	*premesso che* given that
purché provided that	*sempre che* provided that
qualora, posto che, posto il caso che in case that	*se* if

If the hypothesis is presented as real it requires the indicative; if it is considered possible it requires the subjunctive. If it is unrealizable in the present, the hypothetical sentence uses the imperfect subjunctive, if it is unrealizable in the past it takes the pluperfect subjunctive:

> *Avrebbe fatto quadrare il bilancio, sempre che fossero state rispettate le direttive.*
> The accounts would have balanced had they respected the directives.

(ii) They may also be introduced by a verb of thought, or declaration:

> *Puoi immaginare che se avessi avuto un figlio lo avrei adorato.*
> You may imagine that if I had had a son I would have adored him.

(iii) Or be expressed by:

- the gerund
- *a* + the infinitive

> *Mangiando una mela al giorno si tiene lontano il medico, dice il proverbio.*
> An apple a day keeps the doctor away, according to the proverb.

> *A pensarci bene, non mi è mai piaciuto.*
> Thinking about it, I never liked her.

(l) Comparative clauses

(i) They may be introduced by comparative words (see section 24).

(ii) Comparative clauses may also be expressed with *piuttosto che* + infinitive:

> *Più che di evitare la bancarotta, è esistito l'intento di salvare i propri capitali.*
> More than avoiding bankruptcy, the aim was to save one's own capital.

> *Piuttosto che stirare tutta quella biancheria taglierei l'erba dieci volte.*
> Rather than iron all that linen I would cut the grass ten times.

WRITING AN ESSAY

The success of an essay depends primarily on these prerequisites: well-informed and pertinent content; a well-developed and cogent argument; language which is grammatically correct, with well-chosen words and idiomatic structures. For sentence structure and word order see sections 135–140.

41 Preparatory stages: the plan and the vocabulary

● It is vital to analyse the title carefully, evaluating the meaning or meanings of each word, both individually and in relation to the whole sentence. Special attention needs to be given to 'false friends'. A list of them is given in section 167.

● Depending on the title, the essay may require reading a book in depth, studying secondary sources or / and collecting information and data.

● An initial step to start off thoughts is to be guided by some basic questions, even if in a very loose way: *Who* are the agents or the protagonists of the essay? *What* are the issues under discussion? *Why* are they controversial? Why is it felt necessary to write about them? *When* do the issues arise? On what occasions? *What* is the background? *Where?* e.g. Where are the experiments taking place?

● At this stage it is useful to write down thoughts at random as they occur.

● The next step is to detect and work out the thread linking the various ideas. A useful device for those who find it difficult to organize their thoughts is the drawing of the traditional tree with the title of the essay standing out on the trunk as a reminder, with each branch stemming directly from the trunk, highlighting the main themes and with their respective twigs indicating secondary issues. In addition, one could write the examples or evidence in support of the themes in a different colour.

● Data and thoughts may be related to each other through one of the following links: addition, comparison, alternatives, contrast, explanation, time, place, manner, purpose, cause, result, concession, condition. For conjunctions see section 139.

● The last task is to write the sequence which will be followed to present and discuss the various items. This sequence, or *scaletta* (small ladder) as it is called in Italian, must indicate the order of headings and sub-headings, according to their level of importance, e.g. for an essay on Italian fashion:

1.	Current boom of Italian stylists abroad
1.a	The top names
1.b	Their individual styles
2.	Fashion magazines
2.a	Their commercial functions:
2.a(i)	As publicity instruments
2.a(ii)	As opinion makers, etc.

(a) The plan

Most essays develop along the following stages:
i.   Introduction to the subject.
ii. Aim of the essay.
iii. Outline of the plan.
iv. The main body (e.g. presentation of the thesis and of the antithesis of an issue or presentation of the negative and positive aspects of a situation plus one's own proposals for a solution).
v.   Summing up and conclusion.

(b) The vocabulary

(i) Assembling the skeletal vocabulary for a specific topic has two functions. First it helps to 'warm up' the mind; secondly it avoids interrupting the thread of one's thoughts by looking up words in a dictionary too many times.

(ii) In order to expand the initial list of words and expressions one is already familiar with here are some suggestions:

● with the help of a bilingual dictionary compile a list of words with similar and opposite meanings;

● create a 'family' from a word by adding adjectives, verbs, adverbs, e.g. *la moda, creare la moda, lanciare la moda, di moda, la modella, il modello, modellare*;

● prepare a list of words related to the main theme by looking up the definitions of some key words given by monolingual dictionaries. This helps in preparing a pool of words and idiomatic sentences to use as synonyms or for paraphrasing. Furthermore the examples given may suggest historical, artistic and sociological associations – and stimulate further ideas, e.g. *moda: comportamento e immagine di una comunità sociale secondo il gusto particolare del momento, specialmente in relazione all'abbigliamento.*

For lists of words for specific topics, see sections 169–184.

42 Introduction

(i) An essay may be started by introducing the state of the art or the current situation using:

● One word:

È una tragedia.
It's a tragedy. (e.g. referring to recent political events)

● A sequence of nouns, adjectives or verbs to give a general picture of the situation and perhaps the causes:

Abbiamo vari tipi di sciopero: selvaggio, a scacchiera, a singhiozzo, bianco.
We have various kinds of strikes: wildcat, staggered, intermittent, sit-down.

La fuga precipitosa . . . il rifiuto . . . il vagabondare . . . determinano un quadro sconvolgente.
The precipitous flight . . . the refusal . . . the roaming about . . . paint a perturbing picture.

Sollevata, perplessa, prudente, l'America affronta l'URSS dopo il golpe.
Relieved, perplexed, cautious, the USA faces the USSR after the *coup d'état.*

Sognare, ridere, scherzare. Io sono così.
Dreaming, laughing, joking – that's me.

● Presenting a set of figures:

Sono ventiduemila e cinquecento le persone già condannate per spaccio di droga oggi in Europa.
22.500 people have already been charged for selling drugs in Europe today.

(ii) Alternatively, one may come straight to the point:

> *Va subito detto che . . .*
> First of all it must be said that . . .
>
> *Questo tema riguarda il linguaggio di / tratta del . . .*
> This essay deals with the language of / is about . . .
>
> *Faccio subito il punto della situazione.*
> I will come immediately to the point.

(iii) Or warn of a simple or complex situation:

> *Lo scenario è sempre quello.*
> The situation / background is always the same.
>
> *Molto si è detto e molto si è scritto su Alberto Moravia.*
> A lot has been said and written about Alberto Moravia.

(iv) Or commenting on the title:

> *È essenziale accordarci subito sul significato da dare alla parola chiave di questo titolo, 'ecologia'.*
> In the first instance it is essential to agree on the meaning of the key word of this title, 'ecology'.
>
> *Svolgere questo tema significa affrontare il problema dei rapporti fra letteratura e giornalismo.*
> Writing this essay involves dealing with the problem of the relationship between literature and journalism.

(v) A quotation may open the essay followed by one or two words of comments:

> *'. . . . . .', è un pensiero di Platone la prima citazione del nuovo Primo Ministro.*
> '. . . . . .', the first quotation of the new Prime Minister is taken from Plato.
>
> *'. . . . . .', affermazioni pesanti queste. Sono state dette ieri da . . .*
> '. . . . . .', are heavy statements. They were said yesterday by . . .

Stating the aim of the essay

(i) A personal interpretation may be proposed:

Vorrei proporre in questo saggio una nuova interpretazione di . . .
I would like to propose in this essay a new interpretation of . . .

(ii) The aim of the essay may be explained as a reply to a set of questions:

Scopo di questo saggio è rispondere alle seguenti domande.
The aim of this essay is to answer the following questions.

Ci si chiede: '. . . . . .?'. I dati in possesso rispondono che . . .
One asks: '. . . . . .?'. The data available lead us to reply that . . .

Pier Paolo Pasolini, controverso autore italiano, parla ancora all'Italia di oggi? Questa domanda se la stanno ponendo molti critici.
Does Pier Paolo Pasolini, the / a controversial Italian author, still speak to today's Italy? Many critics are asking this question today.

(iii) The aim may be the denial of an accepted truth:

(Scopo di questo tema è dimostrare come) Non è vero che Giuseppe Mazzini non fosse favorevole alla monarchia.
(The aim of this essay is to show that) It is not true that Giuseppe Mazzini was against the monarchy.

44 Outlining the plan

(i) How one intends to proceed may be announced directly:

Cominciamo da . . . Let's start with . . .

Prima di tutto . . . / Innanzi tutto . . . First of all . . .

Incominciamo a analizzare l'uso dei cosmetici.
Let's start by analysing the use of cosmetics.

Diamo la parola alle nude cifre.
Let's look at the figures. (literally: Let's speak the naked figures.)

La conferma di ciò arriva dalle analisi seguenti.
This is confirmed by the following analyses.

Intendo suddividere il tema secondo il seguente schema.
I intend to divide the essay according to the following plan.

Il tema sarà strutturato secondo il seguente schema.
The essay will be structured in the following way.

Gli argomenti saranno così suddivisi.
The arguments will be divided in the following way.

(ii) Or in various phases presented at intervals wth these phrases:

Primo . . . Secondo . . . Terzo . . .
First of all . . . Secondly . . . Thirdly . . .

Prima osservazione: . . . La seconda osservazione riguarda . . . Il legame che corre tra la prima e la seconda è . . .
The first observation concerns . . . The second is about . . . The link between the first and the second is formed by . . .

Questo presenta un duplice, anzi triplice problema: politico, umano, organizzativo. Per quanto riguarda il primo . . . Il secondo, invece, . . . Venendo ora al terzo problema . . .
This presents two or rather three problems: a political, a humane and an organizational one. As for the first . . . The second, on the contrary, . . . Coming to the third problem . . .

Numerosi sono i motivi per cui ho esaminato questo. Il primo motivo è che . . . Il secondo nasce da . . .
I chose to examine this for several reasons. The first is that . . . The second reason stems from . . .

(iii) Discussing specific elements of literature, history of art, etc.

Vediamo la prima stanza / immagine.
Let's look at the first stanza / image.

Di questo poema ne esistono due versioni. La prima è quella che accredita . . .
There are two versions of this poem. The first is the one which proves .

(iv) To present the existing variety of opinions before discussing one's own:

Potrei dire che i responsabili sono . . . Potrei ricordare che . . . Ma potrei anche sostenere che . . .
I could say that the responsibility lies with . . . I could also recall that . . . But I could equally claim that . . .

Tra i critici c'è chi pensa che . . ., chi sostiene che . . ., e chi è convinto che . . .
There are critics who think that . . ., those claiming that . . ., and those who are convinced that . . .

(v) To present the range of the arguments of the essay:

> *L'analisi del quadro copre la tecnica del colore, l'uso dello spazio, il tema del tempo.*
> The analysis of the picture covers the technique of colour, the use of space, the theme of time.

> *Questo saggio va dall'esame dei personaggi principali a quello dei personaggi minori, dall'esame della struttura a quello della lingua.*
> This essay ranges from the examination of the main characters to those of the minor ones, from the examination of the structure to that of the language.

45 The main body

(a) Contrasting opinions

(i) Opposing one's own opinions to other writers' views:

> *Gli esperti concordano sul fatto che . . . ma, secondo me non tengono conto di . . .*
> Experts agree on the fact that . . . but, in my opinion, they do not take into account that . . .

> *È opinione comune che . . . Ed è proprio questo luogo comune che intendo mettere in discussione.*
> It's a common opinion that . . . And it is precisely this commonplace that I intend to dispute.

> *Sarà il film più stimolante, sarà il cast più sensazionale, sarà la regia più innovativa, ma il risultato finale è deludente.*
> It may be the most exciting film, it may be the most sensational cast, he may be the most innovative director but the final result is disappointing.

(ii) Contrasting past with present opinions:

> *Fino a ieri si riteneva che* Othello *fosse opera di Shakespeare, oggi ciò è messo in discussione.*
> Until yesterday *Othello* was thought to be Shakespeare's work; today this is questioned.

> *È chiuso il periodo in cui si credeva che l'Europa non avrebbe più visto una guerra. Ora si spara in Jugoslavia.*
> The time when it was thought that Europe would never again see a war has ended. Now there is fighting in Yugoslavia.

> *La tesi prevalente è oggi quella che vuole che tutti possano andare all'università.*
> Today the prevailing thesis claims that everybody should be able to go to university.

(iii) Juxtaposing two words with opposite meanings to present a conflicting situation:

> *Città bella e crudele, guscio che conforta e devasta.*
> A beautiful and cruel city, a shell which provides comfort at the same time as it lays waste.

(iv) Presenting a contrasting situation:

> *In contrasto con la solitudine delle grandi città, la campagna riacquista il suo fascino.*
> In contrast with the loneliness of large cities, the countryside is regaining its charm.

(b) Placing the topic in context

> *Nel quadro degli studi sui gerghi quello della malavita ha suscitato particolare interesse.*
> Within the work done on jargon that of the underworld has generated special interest.

> *Quest'opera si presenta come un'eccezione nell'ambito della produzione seicentesca.*
> This work is to be seen as an exception within the context of the production of the seventeenth century.

(c) Introducing one's own or other people's opinions

> *Secondo . . .* According to . . .

> *Da un punto di vista strettamente storico . . .*
> From a strictly historical point of view . . .

> *Per quanto riguarda questo studioso, egli è dell'opinione che . . .*
> As for this scholar, he is of the opinion that . . .

(d) Presenting the evidence in support of one's views

> *A dimostrazione di ciò / di quanto detto . . .*
> To prove this / what I said . . .

> *Infatti, . . .* Evidence of this is . . .

Infatti solo questo elemento ci prova che . . .
As it is, only this element proves that . . .

(e) Guiding the reader

Si consideri che . . .	One must consider that . . .
Si badi che . . .	One should pay attention to the fact that . . .
Vi è da notare che . . .	One should notice that . . .
Vediamo adesso che . . .	We shall see now that . . .
Veniamo al punto, al dunque . . .	Coming to the most important point . . .
A questo proposito . . .	In relation to this . . .
In questa prospettiva / ottica . . .	Against this background . . .
Da questo punto di vista . . .	From this point of view . . .

Il problema andrebbe valutato in un'ottica meno limitata.
The problem should be assessed from a less petty point of view.

(f) Introducing examples

. . . Verdi, Puccini, Mascagni, fra gli altri.
. . . Verdi, Puccini, Mascagni, among others.

Si pensi, ad esempio, alle idee femministe.
Let's think for example of feminist ideas.

Un esempio fra molti è la crescita caotica delle periferie.
One example among many others is the chaotic growth of the suburbs.

Prendiamo un altro esempio: i viaggi organizzati.
Let's use another example: package tours.

Esempi analoghi sono numerosissimi.
Similar examples are very frequent.

Per comprendere l'origine di questa teoria basta un esempio.
One example is enough to understand the origin of this theory.

Cito un esempio di estrema attualità.
I quote an example particularly relevant at the moment.

(g) Clarifying one's own words

Uso la parola nel senso di . . .
I use the word in the sense of . . .

Ho usato il termine secondo la definizione di . . .
I have used the term according to the definition of . . .

Il termine va interpretato nell'accezione di . . .
The term must be interpreted in the sense of . . .

Il decreto, 'la grida', secondo la terminologia italiana di allora.
The decree, the *'grida'*, according to the Italian terminology of the time.

La franchigia, per dirla con un termine più specialistico . . .
The franchise, to use a more specialized word . . .

Trovo utile spiegare questo esempio con un'analogia.
I find it useful to explain this example by an analogy.

(h) Referring to a quotation

Come dovrebbe risultare dall'esempio sopra citato . . .
As it should be evident from the example quoted above . . .

Come è facile notare nelle cifre elencate . . .
As it is easy to see in the figures listed . . .

(i) Pointing out the reasons

È per le seguenti ragioni che . . .
It is for the following reasons that . . .

La risposta è in una legge fondamentale di fisica.
The answer lies in a fundamental law of physics.

Ecco perchè non è facile capire che . . .
That is why it is not easy to understand that . . .

È questo che rende il problema . . .
It is this which makes the problem . . .

(j) Pre-empting an objection and counter-arguing

Ovviamente / naturalmente / va da sè che . . . tuttavia
Obviously / naturally / it goes without saying that . . . however

Certo, il tema principale dell'epistolario è che . . . Ma questo non significa che . . .
Certainly, the main theme of the letters is that . . . But this does not mean that . . .

D'altro canto / D'altronde / Di contro / Per contro . . .
On the other hand . . .

Se da un lato ci sono questi aspetti negativi, dall'altro ve ne sono altri positivi.
If, on the one hand, there are these negative aspects, on the other hand there are positive ones.

(k) Underlining a topic

Sottolineiamo che la conseguenza più grave è l'incomunicabilità.
We must underline that the most severe consequence is the lack of communication.

Ci soffermeremo sul problema delle armi nucleari.
We'll scrutinize the nuclear arms problem.

(l) Referring back to a point

Come si è precedentemente accennato . . .
As has been previously mentioned . . .

Richiamandoci a quanto precedentemente detto . . .
Going back to what has been said previously . . .

Tornando al problema degli asili nido . . .
Going back to the problem of crèches . . .

46 Summarizing and concluding

(a) Summing up

Eccovi in poche righe . . . Here in a few lines are . . .
Fin qui si è detto che . . . Up to this point it has been said that . . .
In precedenza si è detto che . . . It has previously been said that . . .
Abbiamo fin qui esaminato . . . Up to now we have examined . . .
Come abbiamo detto . . . As we said . . .
Facciamo il punto della situazione. Up to this point . . .
Ricapitolando / riassumendo . . . Summing up . . .

Riassumendo brevemente quanto fin qui detto . . .
Summing up briefly what has been said up to now . . .

(b) Reinforcing the comparison with the summary

Un utile e significativo confronto potrebbe essere fatto, infine, con le tecniche audiovisive per comprovare che . . .
Finally, a useful and meaningful comparison could be made with audiovisual techniques to prove that . . .

A confronto, l'apprendimento con questo metodo risulta . . .
By comparison, learning with this method turns out to be . . .

Anche questi, come i primi, non sono . . .
These two, like the first, are not . . .

Di un simile esperimento racconta Dante nella Divina Commedia.
Dante, in the *Divine Comedy*, tells of a similar experiment.

Come allora, anche oggi . . .
Like yesterday, today too . . .

Una simile interpretazione . . .
Such an interpretation . . .

(c) Drawing a conclusion

Con ciò non vogliamo sminuire il valore di queste sperimentazioni.
In saying this, we do not want to disparage the value of these experiments.

Da quanto si è detto si deduce che . . .
From what has been said, the conclusion to draw is . . .

Tutto ciò dimostra che . . .
All this shows that . . .

A questo punto è utile trarre le prime conclusioni.
At this point it is quite useful to draw initial conclusions.

Alla luce di queste considerazioni . . .
In the light of these observations . . .

Fatto il punto della situazione, procediamo ora a trarre alcune conclusioni.
Having assessed the situation, let's draw some conclusions.

La breve / dettagliata analisi di questo fenomeno ha evidenziato che . . .
The short / detailed analysis of this phenomenon has highlighted that . . .

Per concludere . . . / Concludendo . . .
To sum up . . .

Playing with words may also be an effective way of closing an essay:

> *Non è finito un golpe. È finita la politica dei golpe.*
> It is not one *coup d'état* that has failed. It is the end of politics based on *coups*.

> *In quest'opera è l'erotismo a diventare arte e non l'arte a diventare erotismo.*
> In this work it is eroticism which becomes art and not art which becomes eroticism.

> *Sta alla ricerca linguistica diventare uno strumento stimolatore e non devastatore.*
> It's the task of linguistics to become a challenge and not a tool of destruction.

FORMAL REPORTS AND ADDRESSES

This section provides an outline for writing research papers and business reports. The register of language is appropriate for written papers as well as verbal presentations to a board or a conference. For further specific vocabularies, see sections 169–184.

Reports are usually written in the first person singular if there is one author and the paper is addressed to one specific person or a restricted committee. If the work is the result of a team or the paper is intended for an audience or a wider readership the most suitable form is the impersonal *si*, the passive form or the first person plural.

A report structure may comprise: a summary, a statement of the aims and objectives of the research project, the findings, the background to the project, the methods adopted, information related to past, present and future situations, statistical evidence, a description of changes in progress, suggestions for provisions, conclusion and recommendations. The following are some examples of how to present some of these points.

147 Summary

La presente relazione comprende l'analisi dell'attuale politica del governo circa l'insegnamento delle lingue straniere nelle scuole; il resoconto dell'indagine effettuata in 100 scuole; lo studio di un piano di lavoro per attuare una politica diversa.
The following report includes an analysis of the Government's current policy on foreign language teaching in schools; an account of the survey carried out in 100 schools; a study for a working plan to implement a different policy.

Questo, in estrema sintesi, il senso del documento che verrà qui presentato.
In a nutshell, this is the sense of the document that I will present now.

È stato vivisezionato settore per settore; sono stati valutati i punti di forza e di debolezza; sono state soppesate le conoscenze tecnologiche acquisite; la consistenza patrimoniale del gruppo.
We have examined in detail each sector, we have assessed the strengths and weaknesses, the acquired know-how and the financial strength of the group.

La ricerca è stata impostata secondo le direttive della riunione dell'
8 – 1 – 1993. Si sono identificati alcuni aspetti del problema. Si sono
ipotizzate le possibili cause del fenomeno. Si sono, di conseguenza,
formulate delle proposte raccomandando una revisione della situazione
tra sei mesi.

The research project has been organized according to the directives of
the meeting held on the 8th of January 1993. We have identified some
aspects of the problem, the possible causes of the issues in question. As
a result some proposals have been put forward with the
recommendation of a review of the situation in six months' time.

48 Aims and objectives

Il nostro studio ha preso l'avvio dalla consapevolezza che l'azienda,
opportunamente riorganizzata avrebbe potuto continuare a
competere sul mercato internazionale.

Our study has been inspired by the awareness that the company, if
suitably reorganized, would be able to continue competing in
international markets.

Lo scopo dell'analisi qui presentata è quello di fare un quadro dell'uso
dei fondi agricoli CEE.

This analysis aims to provide information about the use of EC
agricultural funds.

La nostra ricerca si era proposta di evidenziare quali sono i problemi
dell'infanzia di competenza del governo, degli educatori e delle
famiglie.

The objective of our research project was to highlight children's
problems which are the responsibility of the government, educators
and families.

Attraverso questo studio ci siamo proposti di fornire un'ampia
panoramica delle opinioni di singoli e di istituzioni circa le strategie
necessarie per far fronte al problema del traffico urbano.

The main objective of this study was to provide a comprehensive picture
of perceptions and views from individuals and institutions about the
necessary strategies to deal with traffic problems in urban areas.

Ci si è proposti un duplice scopo: identificare i punti chiave della politica
del settore e avanzare delle proposte per un intervento.

Our aim was twofold: to identify key policy issues and make
recommendations for action.

*L'obbiettivo più specifico era quello di rafforzare gli scambi
commerciali e culturali con il Medio Oriente.*
Its specific scope was to strengthen our commercial and cultural
exchanges with the Middle East.

 Findings

*Le risultanze principali riguardano la concorrenza, vista la vertiginosa
caduta dei prezzi dei prodotti.*
The main findings concern our competitors in the light of the dramatic
fall in the prices of our products.

*Si è riscontrata un'accentuata consapevolezza della necessità di risolvere
il problema.*
There is a heightened awareness of the need to solve the problem.

*Gli aspetti rilevanti della questione che sono stati identificati sono i
seguenti.*
The following relevant aspects of the issue have been identified.

*Si sono messi a fuoco i fattori distinti fra loro ma interconnessi che
determinano i cambiamenti in corso.*
We have focused on a number of distinct but interrelated factors which
are seen to influence the changes already taking place.

*Le rilevazioni statistiche mostrano che la qualità dell'assistenza sanitaria
è in regresso.*
Statistical findings show that there is a decline in the quality of health
care.

Risulta che la domanda supera l'offerta di case di riposo per anziani.
It has proved that the demand for rest homes for the elderly exceeds
the supply.

*I grafici dimostrano come vi sia stata un'accelerazione nella tendenza ad
acquistare giocattoli da guerra.*
Our graphics show that there has been an increasing tendency to buy
war toys.

*Ma segnala anche un crescente interesse in altre aree, anche se il loro
numero rimane limitato.*
But it equally points to signs of growing interest in other areas though
the number remains small.

Il quadro complessivo ottenuto conferma che vi è stato un calo sproporzionato di pubblico teatrale negli ultimi cinque anni.
The overall picture confirms that there has been a disproportionate drop in theatre audiences in the last five years.

50 Background and methodology

Questo studio è la continuazione di una ricerca preliminare richiesta dall'Istituto di medicina legale.
This study is the continuation of a preliminary investigation commissioned by the Institute of Legal Medicine.

L'interesse iniziale per questa ricerca d'archivio sul teatro napoletano è stato ispirato da un articolo pubblicato sulla rivista internazionale . . .
My initial interest for this archival research on the Neapolitan theatre was inspired by an article published in the international review . . .

Parte di questa ricerca attinge a fonti orali.
This research project partly draws on oral sources.

È stata utilizzata la banca dati del Consiglio Nazionale delle Ricerche.
We have used the data bank of the CNR.

Si è preceduto con un sondaggio.
We proceeded with a survey.

Si basa su un corpus di spogli elettronici di 100'000 parole tratte da articoli di chimica industriale.
It is based on a computer analysis of 100,000 words taken from articles on industrial chemistry.

I risultati sono stati compilati sulla base di interviste e di inchieste sul posto di lavoro.
The results have been compiled on the basis of interviews and fieldwork.

I questionari, i formulari e le schede di rilevazione dati sono stati compilati secondo i seguenti criteri.
The questionnaires, the forms and statistical cards have been filled in according to the following criteria.

Le fonti dell'inchiesta sono state suddivise in tabulati.
The sources of our investigation have been tabulated.

Lo studio analizza nei minimi dettagli, con l'aiuto di modelli di simulazione, le possibili applicazioni del metodo psicologico di Roberto Roberti.
With the aid of simulated models our study analyses in the greatest detail the potential applications of Robert Roberti's psychological method.

Tutta la documentazione originale è stata allegata in appendice.
All the original documents have been included in the appendix.

151 Changing attitudes

Le quotazioni qui presentate illustrano un'ampia gamma di opinioni contrastanti.
The following quotations illustrate a wide spectrum of contrasting views.

Le cifre denotano un netto cambiamento nell'atteggiamento verso il divorzio.
Our figures show a clear change in attitudes towards divorce.

I cambiamenti nelle strategie d'intervento aziendale sono viste come frutto di pressioni del mercato europeo.
The changes in the company's strategy are seen as the result of pressure from the European market.

In contrasto con l'attuale situazione si prevede una diminuzione della spesa pubblica.
In contrast with the current situation a decline in public expenditure is foreseen.

Dagli ultimi sondaggi trapela una netta opposizione a ulteriori rinvii e si notano precise aspettative.
The most recent surveys indicate a clear opposition to further postponements as well as clear expectations.

Lo spostamento di opinione degli intervistati è percepito come un fenomeno transitorio.
The shift in attitudes of the people interviewed is perceived as a temporary one.

52 Statistical evidence

Per questa relazione si sono usate le statistiche dell'ISTAT.
To write this report I have used the ISTAT statistics.

La cifra nel 1988 era di 28·000·000 e rappresentava l'11% del bilancio totale.
The number in 1988 was 28,000,000 and it represented 11% of the total budget.

L'incremento complessivo sull'arco di un anno nasconde una effettiva diminuzione.
The overall increase over a year hides an effective reduction.

C'è stata una costante espansione.
There has been a steady growth.

Le cifre riguardanti il settore tecnico non prendono in considerazione i nuovi sviluppi.
The figures for the technical sector do not take into account the new developments.

Da quanto detto emergono tre quadri diversi.
From what has been said three different pictures emerge.

L'indice di natalità è indicativo.
The birth rate is significant.

For vocabulary related to statistics and numbers see section 170f.

53 Changing practice and provisions

Si propone un cambiamento.
A shift should be considered.

Dei cambiamenti sono già in atto nel settore della biochimica.
Changes are already under way in biochemistry.

I provvedimenti proposti sono di vario tipo: licenziamento del personale, chiusura delle linee improduttive, concentrazione in pochi stabilimenti molto efficienti.
Different provisions have been proposed: staff reduction, closures of production lines, concentration on a few very efficient plants.

È opinione di chi scrive che si debba attuare una riorganizzazione strutturale.
It is my opinion that a structural change must be implemented.

Le misure proposte vanno estese.
The proposed measures must be extended.

*La nostra proposta tiene conto che il nostro mercato è in espansione,
che la linea fin qui seguita ha avuto successo e suggerisce perciò che
continui a prevalere.*
Our proposal takes into account that our market is expanding, that
our policy has been successful. We therefore suggest that we carry on
with it.

Issues and policies

*Guardiamo dapprima alla gamma di problemi legati agli investimenti
per 500 miliardi nelle scienze biologiche.*
Let's first look at the range of problems concerning the investment of
500 billion in biological sciences.

*Le problematiche manageriali saranno trattate nella seconda parte
della relazione.*
Managerial proposals will be treated in the second part of the report.

Si pongono i seguenti problemi:
– la professionalità del personale
– il rinnovamento technologico
– le ore lavorative
– maggiore efficienza
The issues arising include:
– staff qualification and training
– the technological turnover
– working hours
– greater efficiency

*Il contenuto di questo studio va considerato in relazione alla
distribuzione geografica.*
The contents of this study must be considered in relation to the
geographical distribution.

Si tratta di una pianificazione da attuarsi a livello nazionale.
Planning needs to be addressed at national level.

55 Conclusion and recommendations

Le conclusioni raggiunte in questa ricerca e le proposte suggerite esprimono il punto di vista dei ricercatori e non rappresentano necessariamente quelle dell'Istituto.
The conclusions of this research and the suggested proposals reflect the researchers' point of view and do not necessarily represent those of the Institute.

Dopo aver espresso il mio disaccordo con il piano anti-crisi del Gruppo, lascio la decisione all'assemblea.
After expressing my disagreement with the Corporation's plan to fight the recession, I leave the decision to the assembly.

Sulla base di queste informazioni vengono avanzate le seguenti proposte circa la programmazione per il prossimo quinquennio.
On the basis of these data, we present the following proposals for the five-year plan.

Ne risulta che il reparto esportazioni deve mettere alla base del suo piano di sviluppo due obbiettivi.
It transpires that the development plan of the export section must be based on two objectives.

Le proposte suggerite comprendono:
– la diversificazione dei mercati
– licenziamenti
– investimenti nella ricerca.
The recommended proposals include:
– diversification of markets
– redundancies
– research investments.

A livello operativo si richiede l'impianto di un adeguato sistema per la raccolta di dati statistici.
At a technical level there is a strong recommendation for the provision of an appropriate data collection system.

Si propone, per ultimo, ma non come ultima misura, che vengano presi ulteriori provvedimenti per la sicurezza dei passeggeri.
Last but not least, it is suggested that the agency should take further measures for the safety of passengers.

PART 3

Word power

SELECTIVE GLOSSARIES

56 Building on verbs: idioms

Verbs are a good starting point to expand your knowledge of Italian. This section includes the most frequent idiomatic uses of some basic verbs and their compound forms. Section 157 shows how one verb can acquire further meanings depending on the preposition following it. Section 158 indicates how new meanings can be obtained by adding suffixes.

Irregular verbs are marked *. For their forms see Appendix 1. Compound tenses follow the same irregular pattern as the basic verb.

When the auxiliary *essere* is required in compound tenses, this is indicated in brackets.

alzare to lift (up), to raise

alzare la bandiera to hoist the flag
alzare le carte to cut the cards
alzare la cresta to get cocky
alzare il gomito to have a drop too much
alzare le mani to surrender
alzare le mani su qualcuno to lay hands on somebody
alzare i prezzi to raise prices
alzare le spalle to shrug one's shoulders
alzare una statua to erect a statue
alzare i tacchi to take to one's heels
alzare il tiro < fig. > to intensify the attack
alzare le vele to set sail
alzare la voce to shout
alzare il volume to turn up the sound

alzarsi to get up, to stand up, to raise oneself, to rise (*essere*)

rialzare to lift up again

rialzare la casa di due piani to make a house two floors higher

rialzarsi to get up (after a fall); < fig. > to rise again (*essere*)

andare* to go (*essere*)

andare in bestia to fly into a rage
andare a cavallo to ride
andare a donne < coll. > to chase after women
andare a genio a qualcuno to be to someone's liking
andare a gonfie vele to be under full sail; < fig. > to be very successful
andare a monte to come to nothing
andare a passeggio to go for a walk
andare a pennello to suit to a 't'
andare a pezzi < fig. > to fall to pieces
andare a rotoli to go bust

> *Ma va!* Come on now! Come off it!
> *Va bene!* That's fine.
> *Questo articolo va molto.* < commercially > This item sells well.
> *Le gonne corte andavano anni fa.* Short skirts were fashionable
>   years ago.
> *La tua giacca non mi va bene.* Your jacket doesn't suit me.
> *La cravatta non va con il vestito.* The tie doesn't match the suit.
> *Va da sé che . . .* It goes without saying that . . .
>
> PROVERBS:
> *Dimmi con chi vai e ti dirò chi sei.*
> You can tell a man by the company he keeps.
>
> *Chi va con lo zoppo impara a zoppicare.*
> He that dwells with a cripple, will learn to limp.

andarsene to go away (*essere*)

andarsene al creatore < coll. > to die

attaccare to attach, to fasten, to hitch up, to tie, to attack

attaccare bottone a qualcuno to buttonhole someone
attaccare un bottone to sew on a button
attaccare il cappotto to hang up a coat
attaccare a chiacchierare < coll. > to start talking
attaccare discorso con qualcuno to strike up a conversation with
  someone
attaccare un francobollo to stick on a stamp
attaccare lite to pick a quarrel

> *Mi ha attaccato l'influenza.* She passed his flu on to me.
> *Queste teorie non attaccano.* These ideas don't catch on.
> *Non attacca!* < coll. > It's no use!
> *Mi dispiace, con me non attacca.* I'm sorry. I'm not taken in.

contrattaccare to counter-attack

riattaccare to attack again, to join again, to resume

staccare to take off, to detach, to separate

staccare un assegno to pay by cheque
staccare la batteria to disconnect the battery
staccare bene le parole to utter each word clearly
staccare i cavalli to unharness the horses
staccare i concorrenti to leave the other competitors behind
non staccare gli occhi da qualcuno not to take one's eyes off someone
staccare presto dal lavoro to finish work early
staccarsi dagli altri to stand head and shoulders above the rest (*essere*)

> *La nave si staccava dal porto.* The ship was pulling away from the port.
> *Non riesco a staccarmi da quell'uomo.* I can't tear myself away from that man.

battere* to beat, to hit, to defeat

battere una lettera to type a letter
battere bandiera italiana to fly the Italian flag
battere cassa to ask for money
battere il marciapiedi < coll. > to walk the streets
battere sullo stesso tasto to harp on about something
non battere ciglio not to bat an eyelid

> *Batteva i denti dal freddo.* His teeth were chattering.
> *L'orologio ha battuto le dieci.* The clock struck ten o'clock.

> PROVERB:
> *battere il ferro finch'è caldo* to strike while the iron is hot

battersi to fight (*essere*)

battersi fino all'ultimo to fight to the finish
battersela to take to one's heels

abbattere to knock down, to demolish, to fell, to shoot down

combattere to fight

dibattere to discuss

dibattersi to wriggle, to be torn between (*essere*)

imbattersi to run into somebody (*essere*)

cadere* to fall, to fall down, to drop; < fig. > to sink, to fail (*essere*)

cadere ammalato to fall ill

cadere a proposito to come in handy

cadere dalle nuvole to be dumbfounded

cadere dalla padella alla brace to jump out of the frying pan into the fire

cadere dal sonno to be dropping with sleep

cadere di mano to drop

cadere in disgrazia to fall out of favour

cadere in disuso to become obsolete

cadere in miseria to fall upon evil days

cadere in piedi < fig. > to fall on one's feet

cadere lungo disteso < literally > to fall flat

cadere nelle mani di gente di pochi scrupoli to fall into the hands of
   unscrupulous people

cadere nel volgare to lapse into vulgarity

> *I lunghi capelli le cadevano sulle spalle.* Her long hair hung down
>   to her shoulders.
>
> *Il mio compleanno cade di sabato.* My birthday falls on a Saturday.
>
> *Questo cappotto cade proprio bene.* This coat hangs well.
>
> *Mi caddero le braccia.* I felt my heart in my boots.
>
> *Mi cadde l'occhio su quel bambino.* My eye fell on that child.
>
> *Il discorso era caduto sulla pornografia.* The conversation had
>   turned to pornography.
>
> *Le sue parole caddero nell'indifferenza generale.* Her words fell
>   on deaf ears.
>
> *Il vento è caduto.* The wind has dropped.
>
> *Ogni sospetto cadde.* Every suspicion disappeared.

far cadere qualcuno to knock someone down (*avere*)

lasciar cadere la forchetta to drop a fork (*avere*)

lasciarsi cadere sulla poltrona to sink into the armchair

lasciar cadere l'argomento to drop the subject

lasciar cadere la cosa to let the matter rest

accadere to happen

decadere to decline, to decay; < legal > to forfeit

ricadere < also fig. > to fall again, to relapse

> *Le colpe dei padri non devono ricadere sui figli.*
> The sins of the fathers should not be visited upon the children.

scadere to decline, to decrease

> *Questa cambiale scade tra due giorni.* This bill is due in two days.
> *Il suo incarico scade tra un anno.* His term of office expires in a
>   year.
> *Il contratto scade tra un mese.* The contract runs out in a month.

cercare to look for, to seek, to try to find

cercare un ago nel pagliaio to look for a needle in a haystack
cercare fortuna to seek one's fortune
cercare guai to be looking for trouble
cercare per mare e per terra / per mare e per monti to look high and low
cercare una parola nel vocabolario to look up a word in the dictionary
cercare il pelo nell'uovo to split hairs
cercare una via d'uscita < also fig. > to look for a way out
cercare una via di scampo to seek safety
cercasi appartamento < commercial > flat / apartment wanted

> PROVERB:
> *Chi cerca trova.* Seek and you shall find.

cercare di (+ infinitive) to try, to endeavour

andare a cercare to go and get

mandare a cercare to send for

venire a cercare qualcuno to call for someone

ricercare to look for something again

essere ricercato dalla polizia to be wanted by the police

cogliere* to pick, to gather

essere colti dal temporale to be caught in a storm
cogliere in flagrante to catch someone red-handed
cogliere l'occasione to take the opportunity, to seize one's chance
cogliere qualcuno di sorpresa to take someone by surprise
cogliere nel segno to hit the target
cogliere il senso to gather the meaning
cogliere alla sprovvista to catch someone unawares
cogliere al volo to catch; < fig. > to understand quickly

accogliere to welcome, to have someone as a guest

accogliere a braccia aperte to receive with open arms
accogliere qualcuno da trionfatore to welcome someone as a hero
accogliere una richiesta to grant a request
accogliere un ricorso to admit a claim

389

raccogliere to gather, to pick up

raccogliere un'allusione to take a hint
raccogliere applausi to be applauded
raccogliere i capelli in una treccia to gather one's hair in a plait
raccogliere dati to collect data
raccogliere francobolli to collect stamps
raccogliere i frutti del proprio lavoro to reap the fruits of one's labour
raccogliere il grano to harvest
raccogliere pettegolezzi to believe in idle gossip
raccogliere profughi to shelter refugees
raccogliere i propri pensieri to collect one's thoughts
raccogliere successi to be very successful
raccogliere le vele to furl the sails
raccogliere voti to win / receive votes

PROVERBS:

Chi semina vento raccoglie tempesta. As you sow so you shall
    reap.
Chi parla semina chi tace raccoglie. All talk no action.

raccogliersi to assemble, to gather (*essere*)

raccogliersi in preghiera to pray

La folla si raccolse nella piazza. The crowd gathered in the square.

comperare / *comprare* to buy

comprare in contanti to buy for cash / to pay cash
comprare i giudici to bribe the court
comprare a occhi chiusi to buy with your eyes closed
comprare qualcosa a qualcuno / *per qualcuno* to buy someone
    something / something for someone
comprare qualcosa da qualcuno to buy something from someone
comprare a rate to buy by instalments

comprarsi to buy something for oneself (*essere*)

correre* to run, to rush, to speed, to flow (*avere* and *essere*; see
    section 64d)

correre in aiuto di qualcuno to run to help someone
correre a chiamare qualcuno to go to fetch someone
correre dietro a qualcuno < also fig. > to run after someone
correre pericolo to be in danger
correre a gambe levate to take to one's heels
correre ai ripari to take measures

> *coi tempi che corrono*   as things are at present
> *Corrono voci strane sul suo conto.*   Rumours run wild about him.
> *Tra lui e lei ci corre un abisso.*   They are poles apart.
> *Il loro pensiero corse alla famiglia.*   Their thoughts went straight to the family.
> *Il tempo corre veloce.*   Time flies.

far correre un cavallo   to race a horse

far correre una voce   to spread rumours

lasciar correre   to turn a blind eye

accorrere   to run, to rush (*essere*)

discorrere   to talk, to chat

incorrere   to run into, to incur (*essere*)

occorrere   to need, must (*essere*)

> *Occorre amare la natura.*   One should love nature.
> *Occorrono più uova.*   More eggs are needed.
>
> with time: *Sono occorse tre ore.*   It took three hours.

percorrere   to walk along, to run through

percorrere in lungo e in largo   to travel throughout

percorrere molti chilometri   to cover many kilometres

percorrere tutto un paese   to travel all over a country

percorrere velocemente con l'occhio   to scan

> *C'è molta strada da percorrere.*   There is a long way to go.

precorrere   to anticipate

precorrere i tempi   to be ahead of one's time

soccorrere   to help, to aid

trascorrere   to spend time, to pass time

dare*   to give

dare qualcosa a qualcuno   to give someone something

dare atto di qualcosa   to acknowledge something

dare ascolto a qualcuno   to pay attention to somebody

dare il benvenuto   to welcome someone

dare un calcio   to kick someone

dare la colpa a qualcuno   to blame someone

dare del lei / dare del tu   to address someone formally or informally

dare un esame to take an examination
dare una festa to give a party
dare in affitto to rent
darle a qualcuno to hit somebody
dargliele tutte vinte to give in to someone along the line
dare nell'occhio to be conspicuous
dare ragione to say someone is right
dare sui nervi to get on one's nerves
dare a intendere che . . . / bere che . . . to make somebody believe that . . .
dare il permesso di fare qualcosa to give permission to do something
dare un premio to give a prize
dare alla testa < fig. > to go to one's head
dare del cretino a qualcuno to call somebody a cretin
darci dentro / sotto < coll. > to pitch in

> *Dai!* Come on!
> *Ti ha dato di volta il cervello?* Have you gone off your head?
> *È un azzurro che dà sul verde.* It's a pale blue with a touch of green.
> *Quanti anni le dai?* How old do you think he is?
> *Questa storia mi dà da pensare.* I smell a rat.
> *Questi titoli danno il 7%.* These shares yield 7%.
> *Questa finestra dà sulla strada.* This window overlooks the street.

darsi to devote oneself to (*essere*)

darsela a gambe to take to one's heels
darsi delle arie to give oneself airs
darsi da fare to do everything in one's power
darsi un gran daffare to put on a big show
darsi al tennis to pick up tennis
darsi al bere to take up drinking
darsi per vinto to give in

> *Può darsi che sia vero.* It may be true.

dire* to say, to tell

dire di sì, dire di no to say yes, to say no
dire bugie to tell lies
dire bene / male di qualcuno to speak highly / badly of someone
dirne un sacco e una sporta to hurl insults at somebody
avere da dire su qualcuno to find fault with someone
dire pane pane vino al vino to call a spade a spade
dire peste e corna to paint someone black

Di' un po' ehi! I say!

Dica dica! Go ahead!

Lascialo dire! Take no notice of him!

Dici sul serio? Are you serious?

E dire che doveva essere una bella serata. To think that it was meant to be a nice evening.

Te lo dicevo io! I told you so!

Si ha un bel dire ma . . . It's easy to say but . . .

vale a dire that is to say

È tutto dire! What more can you say!

a dir poco to put it mildly

Chi mi dice che . . . How do I know that . . .

come si suol dire as they say

inutile dire che needless to say that

per così dire as it were

detto fatto no sooner said than done

PROVERBS:

Dimmi con chi vai e ti dirò chi sei.
Birds of a feather flock together.

Non dire gatto finché non l'hai nel sacco.
Don't count your chickens until they are hatched.

Tra il dire e il fare c'è di mezzo il mare.
It's easier said than done.

mandare a dire to send word that

sentir dire to hear

voler dire to mean

disdire to rescind, to cancel

disdire la prenotazione to cancel the booking
disdire un abbonamento to discontinue a subscription

contraddire to contradict, to be contrary to

contraddirsi to contradict oneself, to contradict each other

predire to foretell, to predict

predire il futuro to tell somebody's fortune
predire una disgrazia to predict a disaster

ridire to repeat, to say again

Trova sempre da ridire su tutto. He is always finding fault.
Hai qualcosa da ridire? Have you any objection?

dormire to sleep, to be asleep

dormire supino to sleep lying on one's back
dormire della grossa to sleep soundly
dormire come un ghiro to sleep like a log / top
dormire sugli allori to rest on one's laurels
dormire tra due guanciali to rest easy
dormire ventiquattr'ore di fila to sleep the clock round
dormirci sopra to sleep on it

> *Dormi?* Are you asleep?

> PROVERB:
> *Chi dorme non piglia pesci.* The early bird catches the worm.

andare a dormire to go to bed

mettere / mandare qualcuno a dormire to send someone to sleep

entrare to enter, to come in, to get through (*essere*)

entrare in argomento to get on to the main subject
entrare in azione to go into action
entrare in campo to come into play
entrare nei particolari to go into details
entrare nel vivo della questione to get to the heart of the matter

> *Il decreto è entrato in vigore.* The decree has become effective.
> *Giove entra nei Pesci.* < zodiac > Jupiter enters Pisces.
> *Mi è entrato addosso un freddo.* I suddenly feel cold.
> *Questi nomi non mi vogliono entrare in testa.* I can't get these names into my head.
> *Ti entrano quei pantaloni?* Do those trousers fit you?
> *Cosa c'entra?* What's that got to do with it?
> *Mi è entrato qualcosa in un occhio.* I've got something in my eye.
> *Io non c'entro.* It's nothing to do with me. / It's no business of mine.

fare entrare to let / show someone in (*avere*)

rientrare to come back, to re-enter, to return (*essere*)

rientrare alla base to return to one's base
rientrare in gioco < fig. > to be back in the race
non rientrare nel programma not to be part of the programme
far rientrare to indent

> *Scopare non rientra nei suoi obblighi.* Sweeping is not part of his duties.

Il mare rientrava in quel punto. The sea curved inward at that point.

La minaccia è rientrata. The threat has been called off.

subentrare to take the place of someone, to replace something, to take over from someone (*essere*)

È subentrato a suo padre. He took over from his father.

fare* to do, to make

fare all'amore to make love

fare un bagno to take a bath

far caldo / freddo to be hot / cold

fare una bella figura to cut a dash

fare una brutta figura to cut a poor figure

fare le camere to clean the rooms

fare del bene / del male a qualcuno to do something good to / to harm someone

fare un errore to make a mistake

fare un esame to take an examination

fare finta to pretend

farla franca to get away with it

fare una gita to take a trip

fare l'ingenua to pretend to be naive

far male a qualcuno to hurt someone

fare a meno di qualcosa to do without something

fare il pieno to fill up

fare del proprio meglio to do one's best

fare un sogno to have a dream

fare di tutto per . . . to do one's best to . . .

fare le vacanze to spend one's holidays

farne di tutti i colori to cause havoc

Fa bel tempo. The weather is fine.

Hanno fatto molta strada. They got on in the world.

Fa lo stesso. It's all the same.

Non fa per lui. It's not for him.

Ha fatto per uscire ma . . . He was on the point of going out but . . .

Il ragionamento faceva acqua da tutte le parti. The argument was not watertight / was full of loopholes.

Non mi fa né caldo né freddo. It's all the same to me.

È ora di farla finita. It's high time all this came to an end.

PROVERBS:

Chi fa da sè fa per tre. If you want something done do it yourself.
Chi la fa l'aspetti. We reap as we sow.

farsi to become, to grow (*essere*)

farsi prete to become a priest
farsi più alto to grow taller
farsi la barba to shave
farsi bello to smarten oneself up
farsi coraggio to pluck up courage
farsi in quattro to do one's utmost
farsi male to hurt oneself
farsene una ragione to come to terms with someone

fare (+ infinitive) (see section 68 for the grammatical construction)

disfare to undo, to unmake, to unpack

disfare le valigie to unpack the suitcases

disfarsi to melt (*essere*)

disfarsi di qualcuno to get rid of someone

    Il gelato si è disfatto. The ice-cream has melted.

rifare to do again, to remake

rifare di sana pianta to do it all over again
far rifare to have something done again

sopraffare to overwhelm, to overcome, to overpower

essere sopraffatto dalla disperazione to be overwhelmed with grief

fidarsi to entrust, to trust (*essere*)

    Mi fido della loro esperienza. I trust their experience.
    Ci si può fidare di lui? Is he a man you can depend on?

PROVERB:
Fidarsi è bene, non fidarsi è meglio.
To trust is wise, not to trust is wiser.

fidarsi a (+ infinitive) to dare (*essere*)

    Non mi fido a uscire senza ombrello. I don't dare go out without
an umbrella.

affidarsi to place one's trust (*essere*)

affidarsi alla fortuna to trust to chance

Si è affidato al banchiere di famiglia. He placed his trust in the family's banker.

confidare to put one's trust

Confido nella sua abilità. I trust his skill.
Confido che ritornerai. I trust you'll return.

confidarsi to confide, to open one's heart (*essere*)

La donna si confidò col prete. The woman confided in the priest.

sfidare to challenge, to dare, to defy

sfidare i colleghi a tennis to challenge one's colleagues at tennis
sfidare un pericolo to defy a danger

gettare to throw away

gettare indietro la testa con civetteria to toss one's head coquettishly
gettare in faccia un errore a qualcuno to cast a mistake in somebody's teeth
gettare le fondamenta to lay the foundations
gettare polvere negli occhi < fig. > to throw dust in somebody's eyes
gettare le reti to cast / haul in the nets
gettare i soldi dalla finestra to throw one's money out of the window
gettare a terra to throw something to the ground
gettare la tonaca alle ortiche to give up the cowl / veil
gettare via tempo e denaro to throw away time and money

I geranei stanno gettando. Geraniums are budding.

gettarsi to throw oneself (*essere*)

gettarsi sul nemico to hurl oneself at the enemy
gettarsi a capofitto nel lavoro to throw oneself into one's work
gettarsi al collo di qualcuno to embrace someone

Quel fiume si getta nel mare. That river flows into the sea.

aggettare < architecture > to jut out

Il tetto di quella casa aggetta di venti centimetri. That house roof juts out twenty centimetres.

assoggettare to subdue, to subject

progettare to plan

rigettare to throw again, to throw back, to repel, to reject
rigettare il pasto < coll. > to vomit

giocare to play

giocare a palla, tennis, calcio, etc. to play ball, tennis, football
giocare agli indiani to play at being Indians
giocare a guardie e ladri to play cops and robbers
giocare sulle parole to play with words
giocare un tiro a qualcuno to play a trick on somebody
giocare in borsa to deal in stocks and shares

> *Ma a che gioco giochi?* What is your game? / What are you up to?
> *È stato giocato.* He has been tricked.

giocarsi (*essere*)

giocarsi il posto to lose one's job
giocarsi la reputazione to gamble one's reputation
giocarsi la camicia to bet one's shirt

lasciare to leave, to let

lasciar correre to forget about it
lasciare detto a qualcuno to leave word with someone
lasciare qualcuno a bocca asciutta to disappoint somebody
lasciare qualcuno in asso to leave someone high and dry
prendere o lasciare to take it or leave it

> *Ma lasciami andare.* Let me go.
> *Lasciami entrare.* Let me come in.
> *Lascialo parlare.* Let him speak.
> *Lascialo dire.* Let him say.
> *Lasciami stare.* Leave me alone.
> *Lascia andare!* Forget it!
> *Vivi e lascia vivere!* Live and let live!
> *Lascia fare a me!* Leave it to me!
> *Lasciamo stare!* Let's drop it!

> PROVERB:
> *Chi lascia la via vecchia per la nuova sa quel che lascia ma non sa quel che trova.* (literally: Whoever leaves the old road for a new one knows what he is leaving but does not know what he will find.) Better the devil you know than the devil you don't.

lasciarsi (+ infinitive) (*essere*) (See section 68.)

lasciarsi andare to let oneself go

> *Questa carne si lascia a mala pena mangiare.* This meat is barely edible.
> *Ci lasciammo dopo una lite.* We parted after a quarrel.

rilasciare to leave again, to release

rilasciare la merce to deliver the goods
rilasciare un permesso to grant permission
rilasciare un documento to issue a document
rilasciare una ricevuta to make out a receipt
essere rilasciato dalla polizia to be released by the police

tralasciare to omit, to interrupt

levare to take away, to remove

Levo il disturbo. It's time for me to go now.
Me l'hai levato di bocca. You have taken the words out of my mouth.
È una vista da levare il fiato. It's a sight which takes the breath away.
Se si leva quello studente, il resto della classe non è male. Except for that student, the rest of the class is not bad.

levarsi to rise, get up, get out (*essere*)

Mi sono levata un capriccio. I satisfied a whim.
Mi sono levata la voglia di una pizza. I satisfied my longing for a pizza.
Levati dalla testa di andare in discoteca. You can forget about going to a disco.
Si è levato un venticello. A light wind has risen.
Levati di torno. Get out of the way.

prelevare to withdraw

prelevare denaro da una banca to withdraw money from a bank
prelevare sangue < medical > to take blood

sollevare to raise, to lift

sollevare la popolazione contro il tiranno to stir up people against a tyrant
sollevare una questione to bring up a matter, raise a question
sollevare un dubbio to raise a doubt
sollevare un putiferio to raise hell

sollevarsi to arise, to rise, to get up (*essere*)

mancare to lack (*essere*) For the impersonal construction see section 64.

mancare di rispetto to be offensive
mancare di parola to break one's word
mancare di un venerdì < coll. > to have a screw loose

Ti manca molto? Will it take you long to finish?

Mancano venti minuti a mezzanotte. It's twenty minutes to midnight.

Non mancherò di scriverle. < formal > I shall not fail to write to you.

Gli vennero a mancare le forze. His strength failed him.

Ci mancò poco che non andassi sotto un auto. I nearly ran under a car.

Mi mancano i miei genitori. I miss my parents.

È mancata la luce. The light went out.

Ci mancava solo questo. This is the last straw.

Mancavano voti sufficienti. There were not enough votes.

Mancava da un mese. He had been away for a month.

mandare to send, to forward, to dispatch, to transmit

mandare avanti la baracca to keep one's business going

mandare un bacio to throw a kiss / to send a kiss

mandare la palla in rete to score a goal

mandare per le lunghe to procrastinate

mandare due righe to drop two lines

mandare in rovina / a rotoli to bring to ruin

mandare via to send away

È dura da mandar giù. That's hard to swallow.

Che Dio gliela mandi buona. God help him.

Pioveva che Dio la mandava. It was coming down in buckets.

Non gliele ha mandate a dire. He told him his opinion to his face.

Questo fiore manda un buon profumo. This flower smells nice.

PROVERB:

Chi vuole vada, e chi non vuole mandi.
If you want something done do it yourself.

mandare a chiamare qualcuno to send for someone

mandare a dire to send word to someone

mandare a prendere qualcuno to send someone for something

rimandare to send again, to send back, to return, to postpone

rimandare alle calende greche to put off till doomsday

rimandare a un'altra pagina to refer to another page

rimandare all'ultimo momento to leave something to the last minute

Giorgio è stato rimandato in matematica.
George has had to repeat his maths exam.

PROVERB:

Non rimandare a domani ciò che puoi fare oggi.
Never put off till tomorrow what can be done today.

tramandare to hand down

tramandare di generazione in generazione to hand down from father
  to son

mettere* to put, to place

mettere al corrente to inform
mettere la mano sul fuoco to stake one's life
mettere a frutto la propria esperienza. to make use of one's own
  experience
mettere a fuoco < also fig. > to focus
mettere a ferro e a fuoco to put to fire and sword
mettere in chiaro to clarify
mettere in dubbio to put in doubt
mettere la testa a partito to turn over a new leaf
mettere al mondo to give birth to
mettere gli occhi addosso a qualcuno to fancy someone
mettere alla prova to put to the test
mettere la testa a partito to settle down
mettere a soqquadro to turn topsy-turvy
mettere ai voti to put to the vote
mettere una mano sulla spalla to lay a hand on somebody's shoulder
mettere la mani su qualcuno to beat someone

  Mettiamoci una pietra sopra. Let's think no more about it.
  Metti che nevichi. < coll. > Suppose it snows?
  Quanto ti hanno messo di affitto? How much did they charge you
    for rent?
  Quanto tempo ci metti? How long will it take?
  Vediamo come si mettono le cose. Let's see how things develop.

mettersi (*essere*)

mettersi in libertà to make oneself comfortable
mettersi in mente to convince oneself (that)
mettersi all'opera to start working
mettersi di buzzo buono to get down to work with gusto
mettersi il cuore in pace to put one's mind at rest
mettercela tutta to bend over backwards

  PROVERB:
  Mettere il carro davanti ai buoi.
  To put the cart before the horse.

mettersi a (+ infinitive) to start (*essere*)

> *Si mise a cantare.* He started to sing.

dimettersi to resign, to retire, to step down (*essere*)

emettere to utter, to give out, to issue

emettere un assegno to issue a cheque
emettere un gemito to groan

immettere to put in, to introduce

immetere un prodotto sul mercato to put a product on the market

immettersi to get into (*essere*)

immettersi in autostrada to get on to the motorway

omettere to omit

omettere di firmare to omit signing

rimettere to put again, to put back, < coll. > to vomit

rimettere a nuovo to restore / to remove
rimettere al giudizio di qualcuno to submit to somebody's arbitration
rimettere in uso to make something work again

rimetterci to lose, to ruin

rimetterci la reputazione to lose one's reputation
rimetterci la salute to ruin one's health
rimetterci le penne to lose

scommettere to bet

scommettere sui cavalli to bet on horses

> *Ci scommetterei non so che cosa!* I'll bet my soul!

smettere to stop

smettere di leggere to stop reading

> *Smettila!* Stop it!
> *La smetti una buona volta!* Will you stop once and for all?

trasmettere to hand on, to transmit, to send

trasmettere un telegramma to send a telegram
trasmettere un programma to broadcast a programme
trasmettere un'ordinazione to pass an order to somebody

partire to leave, to go away, to set out, to set off (*essere*)

partire in treno / in aereo to leave by train / by plane

a partire da oggi . . . starting from today . . .
a partire dall'8 luglio as from the 8th of July
a partire da questa pagina starting from this page

PROVERB:
Partire è un po' morire.
To part is to die a little.

ripartire to set off again, to distribute

Il peso è ripartito sulle quattro ruote. The weight is distributed on
four wheels.

spartire to share, to divide

Non ho niente da spartire con lui. I have nothing in common with
him.
Abbiamo spartito qualche parola. We exchanged a few words.

perdere to lose

perdere i contatti con qualcuno to lose contact with someone
perdere del tempo to waste time
perdere l'abitudine di fare qualcosa to lose the habit of doing
something
saper perdere to be a good loser

Al confronto ci perde. It comes off worst in comparison.
Ci perdo così This way I lose out.
Questa bottiglia perde. This bottle leaks.

PROVERB:
Chi perde al gioco vince in amore. Unlucky at cards lucky in love.

perdersi to lose oneself, to get lost, to lose one's way (*essere*)

perdersi d'animo to lose heart
perdersi in un bicchiere d'acqua to drown in an inch of water

disperdere to scatter, to dispel, to waste

disperdere le proprie energie to waste one's energies

disperdersi (*essere*)

I dimostranti si dispersero. The demonstrators dispersed.

portare to bring, to take, to fetch

portare bene gli anni to look young for one's years / to carry one's age
well
portare in braccio to carry somebody in one's arms

portare i capelli corti to have short hair
portare al cinema to take someone to the cinema
portare collant francesi to wear French tights
portare il cognome della madre to carry the surname of the mother
portare alla disperazione to drive to despair
portare delle prove to bring proof
portare i segni della malattia to carry / bear the signs of the disease
portare via tempo to take up time

    un autobus che porta in centro a bus going to the centre

portarsi to go, to come (*essere*)

portarsi bene to carry one's age well

apportare to bring

apportare cambiamenti to introduce changes
apportare tagli al bilancio to introduce cuts to the budget

comportare to involve

comportare un grosso sforzo to involve a great effort

comportarsi to behave, to act

deportare to deport

esportare to export

importare to import

riportare to bring something again

riportare una sgradevole impressione to receive an unpleasant
  impression
riportare ferite to suffer injuries
riportare il totale su un'altra pagina to carry a total forward to the next
  page

sopportare to tolerate, to bear

sopportare un danno to sustain damage

trasportare to transport, to carry, to transfer

lasciarsi trasportare dalla felicità to be transported with happiness

prendere* to take, to catch, to seize, to collect

prendere o lasciare to take it or leave it
prenderla con spirito to take it easy
prendere le vacanze to take one's holidays

essere preso dalla paura to be seized by fear
prendere una brutta piega to take a turn for the worse
prendere la laurea to take a degree
prendere il primo premio to take the first prize
prendere un buon stipendio to earn a good salary
prendere qualcuno per un'altra persona to take / mistake someone for
   another person
prendere qualcuno con le buone to treat someone tactfully
prendera a calci to kick someone
prendere le cose come vengono to take things as they come
prendere lucciole per lanterne to get hold of the wrong end of the
   stick
prendere dalla mamma to take after the mother
prendere la palla al balzo to seize an opportunity
prendere il sole to sunbathe
prendere il toro per le corna to take the bull by the horns

   Che ti prende? What's the matter with you?

prendersi to take upon oneself

prendersi la responsabilità to take the responsibility
prendersela to take offence
prendersela con comodo to take it easy
prendersela con qualcuno to be angry with someone

   Per chi mi prendi? Who do you take me for?
   Come l'ha presa? How did he take it?

apprendere to learn

comprendere to understand (*avere*), to include (*essere*)

comprendèrsi to understand each other (*essere*)

riprendere to catch again, to take again

riprendere fiato to get one's breath back again
riprendere il discorso to resume the talk
riprendere qualcuno con fermezza to reproach someone

   Il bambino è stato ripreso bene in quel quadro. The child is well
      portrayed in that painting.

riprendere a (+ infinitive) to start again

riprendersi to recover, to collect oneself (*essere*)

ridere* to laugh

ridere come un matto to laugh one's head off

ridere a crepapelle to split one's sides with laughter
ridere fino alle lacrime to laugh till one cries
ridere sotto i baffi to laugh up one's sleeve
scoppiare a ridere to burst out laughing, to break into laughter

> *Rideva delle sue parole.* He laughed at his words.
> *Non c'è nulla da ridere.* There is nothing to laugh at.
> *Cosa c'è da ridere?* What's there to laugh about?
> *Me ne rido delle tue accuse.* I don't care about your accusations.

far ridere qualcuno to make someone laugh

far ridere i sassi to make a cat laugh

> PROVERBS:
> *Chi ride il venerdì piange la domenica.*
> He that sings on Friday will weep on Sunday.
>
> *Ride bene chi ride ultimo.*
> He who laughs last laughs longest.
>
> *Ridi e il mondo ride con te; piangi e piangerai solo.*
> Laugh and the world laughs with you; cry and you cry alone.

arridere to smile on, to be propitious

> PROVERB:
> *La fortuna arride agli audaci.* Fortune smiles upon the brave.

deridere to deride, to mock, to jeer

irridere to mock

sorridere to smile

> *Quell'idea mi sorride.* I like that idea.

stare* to stay, be (*essere*)

star a cuore to have something at heart
stare sulle generali to be vague
stare in montagna to live in the mountains
stare in punta di piedi to stand on tiptoe
stare allo scherzo to be able to take a joke
stare sulle sue to keep aloof
non stare in sè dalla gioia to be beside oneself with joy

> *Sta a loro decidere.* It's up to them to decide.
> *Le cose stanno così.* That is how things are.
> *Stammi a sentire!* Listen!
> *Ti sta bene!* It serves you right!
> *Se stesse in me . . .* If it were left to me . . .

tenere* to hold, to keep

tenere qualcuno per mano to hold someone by the hand
tenere in braccio to hold in one's arms
tenere un consiglio di guerra to hold a council of war
tenere i conti to keep the accounts
tenere una festa to give / hold a party
tenere presente qualcosa to bear something in mind

> *Questa bottiglia tiene meno di due litri.* This bottle holds less than two litres.
> *Questa colla tiene.* This glue sticks.
> *Quest'auto tiene bene la strada.* This car holds the road well.
> *Ci tengo alla mia reputazione.* I think my reputation is very important.
> *Se proprio ci tieni!* If you really want it!
> *Non c'è scusa che tenga.* There is no excuse for it.
> *Non riesco a tenermi dal ridere.* I can't help laughing.

tenersi to keep to oneself (*essere*)

tenersi in esercizio to keep in training

attenersi to follow, to stick to

attenersi alle prescrizioni del medico to follow the doctor's prescriptions

contenere to include, to comprise, to contain

detenere to hold, to possess

ritenere to believe

sostenere to support

trattenere to hold, to restrain, to check

tirare to pull, to draw

tirare l'acqua al proprio mulino to bring grist to one's own mill
tirare avanti la baracca < coll. > to make both ends meet
tirare in ballo qualcuno / qualcosa to involve someone / to bring something up
tirare in lungo to drag on
tirare un sospiro to heave a sigh
tirarsi su le maniche to tuck up one's sleeves
tirare sul prezzo to haggle

> *La mia auto non tira in salita.* My car has difficulty going uphill.
> *Le tirano i pantaloni.* Those trousers are tight.

attirare to attract

attirarsi l'invidia dei colleghi to earn one's colleagues' envy / respect

ritirare to withdraw, to take back, to retract

ritirarsi in camera to retire to one's room

> *Il cotone si ritira dopo la prima lavata.* Cotton shrinks after the first wash.

uscire* to go out (*essere*)

uscire di cervello to go out of one's mind
uscire sano e salvo to come out safe and sound
uscire di scena to leave the stage / scene

> *Mi è uscito di mente.* It slipped my mind.
> *Mi esce dagli occhi.* I'm fed up with it.
> *Esce dai miei compiti.* It is beyond my duties.
> *Che non ti esca una parola di bocca.* Don't let a word escape you.

vedere* to see

vedere di fare qualcosa to try to do something
non vedere di buon occhio to take a dim view of something
avere a che vedere con qualcuno to have something to do with someone
essere ben visto to have a good reputation
farsi vedere to show oneself
far vedere to show (*essere*)

> *Che cos'ha questo a che vedere con me?* What has this got to do with me?
> *Ci vedo poco chiaro.* There's something fishy here.
> *Cose mai viste!* Things unheard of!
> *Gliela farò vedere io!* I'll show him!
> *Non vediamo l'ora di arrivare.* We are looking forward to seeing you.
> *Non ci ho visto più.* I saw red.
> *Non posso vedere quella donna.* I can't stand that woman.
> *Non ci vedevano più dalla fame.* < fig. > They were dying of hunger.
> *Se l'era vista brutta.* They had a narrow escape.
> *Stai a vedere che perdiamo l'aereo.* I bet we are going to miss the plane.
> *Chi s'è visto s'è visto.* He took the money and disappeared into the blue.

Voglio vederci chiaro. I want to get to the bottom of this.
Voglio vedere come va a finire. I want to see how it ends up.

PROVERB:
Occhio non vede cuore non duole.
What the eye doesn't see the heart doesn't grieve over.

vedersi to see oneself (*essere*)

vedersi nello specchio to see oneself in the mirror
vedersi costretto a fare qualcosa to find oneself compelled to do
  something

> *Non mi ci vedo a fare l'astronauta* I don't see myself being an
>   astronaut.
> *Veditela tu!* You deal with it!

prevedere to foresee, to forecast, to predict

provvedere to provide, to supply

rivedere to see again, to revise

venire* to come (*essere*)

venire alle mani to come to blows
venire al mondo to come into the world
venire al sodo to come to the point

> *Se ne venne fuori con una storia incredibile.* He came out with an
>   incredible story.
> *Vengono su bene quei fiori.* Those flowers are coming on well.
> *Cosa ti viene in mente?* You must be mad!
> *Veniamo ai fatti.* Let's get down to facts.
> *Le venivano le lacrime agli occhi.* Tears rose to his eyes.
> *Viene bene il tuo giardino.* Your garden is coming on well.
> *Mi viene da starnutire.* I feel like sneezing.

avvenire to happen, to take place

convenire to suit, to be worthwhile, to agree

divenire to become

pervenire to reach, to achieve

prevenire to prevent, to precede, to anticipate

provenire to derive, to arise, to be caused

sovvenire < literary > to remember

volere * to want, to wish (see section 59)

> *senza volerlo* without wishing it
>
> *Se l'è voluta!* He asked for it!
>
> *Non volermene.* Don't hold it against me.
>
> *Volere o volare bisogna farlo.* He has to do it willy-nilly.
>
> *Questo freddo non vuol passare.* This cold doesn't seem to go
>   away.
>
> *Qui ti voglio!* There is the rub!
>
> *Se Dio vuole siamo arrivati.* Thank heavens we have arrived.
>
> *C'è voluto del bello e del buono per convincerlo.* It took a lot of
>   doing to convince him.
>
> *Ce n'è voluto del tempo.* You took your time.

PROVERBS:

> *Non fare agli altri quello che non vorresti fosse fatto a te.*
>   Don't do to others what you wouldn't want them to do to you.
>
> *Volere è potere.* Where there is a will there is a way.
>
> *Chi troppo vuole nulla stringe.* Grasp all, lose all.
>
> *Chi vuole vada chi non vuole mandi.* If you want something done
>   do it yourself.

157 Building on verbs: adding prepositions

This section lists prepositions which give a different meaning when
they follow certain verbs. Traditionally, formal and literary Italian
considered these prepositional phrases inappropriate for written
style and preferred the synonyms listed in the second column. The
current attitude, under the influence of mass media, has largely
changed and these prepositional phrases are now also used in the
written language.

INFORMAL / SPOKEN	FORMAL / LITERARY	
avanti before		
andare avanti	*procedere*	to carry on
essere avanti negli anni	*essere anziani*	to be well on in years
essere avanti di 10 punti	*sopravanzare di 10 punti*	to be ten points ahead
farsi avanti nella vita	*affermarsi nella vita*	to get on in life
mandare avanti la famiglia	*provvedere alla famiglia*	to support the family

INFORMAL / SPOKEN   FORMAL / LITERARY

mettere avanti scuse	*addurre scuse*	to make excuses
mettere le mani avanti	*prendere precauzioni*	to take precautions
venire avanti	*avanzare*	to come forward
tirare avanti	*vivere stentatamente*	to scrape along

dentro within, inside

andare dentro < fig. >	*andare in prigione*	to be put in clink
covare dentro propositi di vendetta	*meditare vendetta*	to brood on vengeance
dar dentro a qualcosa	*urtare qualcosa*	to knock something
darci dentro	*impegnarsi*	to do something with determination
essere dentro e.g. alla politica	*essere addentro a . . .*	to have inside knowledge
essere dentro la parte	*immedesimarsi*	to identify oneself with

dietro back, backwards, behind

andare dietro alla moda	*imitare la moda*	to follow fashion
andare dietro a qualcuno	*1. corteggiare*	to court
	2. seguire i consigli di	to listen to somebody
buttare il passato dietro le spalle	*dimenticare*	to put the past behind
correre dietro al successo	*inseguire il successo*	to seek success
dire dietro a qualcuno	*sparlare di qualcuno*	to talk behind someone's back
essere dietro a fare qualcosa < coll. >	*stare facendo qualcosa*	to be doing something
farsi correre dietro < coll. >	*farsi desiderare*	to wait to be asked twice
farsi ridere dietro	*farsi prendere in giro*	to make a fool of oneself
gridare dietro parolacce	*insultare*	to shout insults after someone
lasciarsi dietro i rivali	*superare i rivali*	to outrun / outstrip one's rivals
perdersi dietro a sciocchezze < coll. >	*attribuire importanza a*	to waste time on
portarsi dietro	*portare con sè*	to take something with oneself
ridere dietro a qualcuno	*ridere alle spalle di*	to laugh at somebody
star dietro a qualcuno	*sorvegliare / curare*	to watch over / to take care of someone
tenere dietro a qualcuno	*stare al passo di qualcuno*	to keep up with someone
tirarsi dietro	*attirare, coinvolgere*	to attract, to involve

INFORMAL / SPOKEN	FORMAL / LITERARY	
tirar dietro la merce < coll. >	*vendere a prezzi stracciati*	to sell very cheaply

di mezzo in the middle

andarci di mezzo	*patire le consequence*	to be a loser
mettercisi di mezzo	*interferire*	to interfere
togliere di mezzo	*spostare / uccidere*	to remove / to kill

fuori out, outside, without, abroad

avere fuori 10 miliardi	*essere esposto per 10 miliardi*	to have 10 billion outstanding
buttar fuori la cena < coll. >	*vomitare la cena*	to throw up
chiamarsi fuori	*dichiararsi estraneo*	to have nothing to do with
dar fuori di testa < coll. >	*impazzire*	to go mad < fig. >
far fuori qualcuno	*ammazzare qualcuno*	to bump off someone
far fuori il capitale	*dilapidare*	to squander a fortune
lasciar fuori	*omettere*	to leave out
mettere fuori una notizia	*diffondere una notizia*	to spread a piece of news
mettere fuori denaro	*sborsare denaro*	to spend money
restare fuori	*essere escluso*	to be left out
saltare fuori con una battuta	*uscire con una battuta*	to come out with a wisecrack
tagliar fuori	*isolare*	to cut off
tirar fuori una nuova canzone	*lanciare una nuova canzone*	to bring out a new song
tirare fuori la pistola	*estrarre la pistola*	to take out the revolver
tirar fuori delle storie	*cercare scusanti*	to find excuses

giù down, below, downwards

INFORMAL / SPOKEN	FORMAL / LITERARY	
andar giù	*deperire*	to be run down
andar giù di valore	*deprezzarsi*	to go down in value
non mi va giù	*non lo tollero*	I can't stand it
buttar giù un articolo	*compilare un articolo*	to write an article
il caldo mi butta giù	*il caldo mi deprime*	the heat depresses me
essere giù di spirito	*essere depresso*	to be down in the dumps
gettare giù degli appunti	*prendere appunti*	to jot down some notes
gettare giù da cavallo	*disarcionare*	to unsaddle
mandare giù un caffè / un'offesa	*ingoiare un caffè / un'offesa*	to swallow a coffee / offence

INFORMAL / SPOKEN	FORMAL / LITERARY	
mettere giù le mani	ritrarre le mani	to take one's hands off
tirarne giù (Ne ha tirate giù!)	imprecare	to swear heavily
tirar giù un lavoro < coll. >	lavorare senza attenzione	to work carelessly
venir giù a catinelle	piovere forte	to rain heavily

indietro back, backwards, behind

tirarsi indietro	venir meno a un impegno	to give up / withdraw from an engagement

su on, upon, over, above, about, after

avercela su con	essere indignati con	to be angry with
i prezzi vanno su	i prezzi salgono	prices go up
mettere su (la minestra)	cominciare a cucinare (la minestra)	to start cooking (the soup)
mettere su contro qualcuno	istigare contro qualcuno	to turn against someone / incite against
mettere su un negozio	impiantare un negozio	to set up a shop
pensarci su	ponderare	to brood over
saltare su	arrabbiarsi	to get angry
tenere su il morale a qualcuno	sostenere / incoraggiare qualcuno	to boost somebody's morale
tirare su	riprendere le forze	to buck oneself up
tirare su i figli	allevare i figli	to raise one's children
tirare su una gamba	sollevare	to lift
venire su bene (bambini / piante)	crescere bene	to grow (up) well (children, plants)

via away, off

andar via	allontanarsi	to go away
buttar via } gettar via }	disfarsi di	to throw away
buttar via tempo	sprecare	to waste time
cacciar via	allontanare	to send somebody packing
essere via	essere assente	to be away / absent
portare via	rubare	to take away / to steal

Building on verbs: adding suffixes

Italian is characterized by a rich use of suffixes which permit the creation of new verbs, adjectives and nouns.

The following suffixes can be added to verbs with the infinitive ending in -*are*. To add a touch of nonchalance, cheerfulness or liveliness one may use:

-erellare

cantare to sing	*canterellare* to sing cheerfully
giocare to play	*giocherellare* to toy, to fiddle playfully
trottare to trot	*trotterellare* to trot briskly

To convey nuances in the sound indicated by the verb one may add:

-ettare, -ottare

fischiare to whistle	*fischiettare* to whistle with joy
parlare to talk	*parlottare* to speak furtively
picchiare to beat	*picchiettare* to tap, to patter
scoppiare to blow	*scoppiettare* to crackle

The following endings convey the idea of something done in a leisurely or cursory manner:

-icchiare, -acchiare, -ucchiare

guardare to watch	*guardicchiare* to watch without too much attention
leggere to read	*leggiucchiare* to read cursorily
ridere to laugh	*ridacchiare* to snigger

Building on nouns: idioms

In Italian, nouns can be created from adjectives and verbs (see sections 22 and 63). Equally, like verbs, nouns too acquire in Italian a variety of meanings when they are used idiomatically and when they are modified by prefixes or suffixes.

affare (m.) business deal

> *Che si interessi degli affari suoi!*
> I wish he would mind his own business!

> *Che affare è che hai in mano?*
> What's that thing you have in your hand?

È stato proprio un affare quest'auto usata.
It has really been a bargain, this second-hand car.

È un'azienda a conduzione familiare ma con un giro d'affari di centinaia di miliardi.
It's a family-run firm with a turnover of hundreds of billions.

Affare fatto! That's agreed.

Con l'invenzione degli Swatch hanno fatto affari d'oro.
The invention of the Swatch turned out to be a gold mine.

PROVERB:
Gli affari sono affari. Business is business.

amore (m.) love

Imparò l'italiano per amore dei figli.
He learned Italian for his children's sake.

Il film narra degli amori di Don Giovanni.
The film tells of Don Juan's love affairs.

L'amor proprio non è un difetto, è una qualità.
Self-respect is not a short-coming, it's a quality.

Va d'amore e d'accordo con la matrigna.
She gets on like a house on fire with her stepmother.

Per amore o per forza le tasse vanno pagate.
Income taxes must be paid by hook or by crook.

base (f.) basis

Con quell'incontro hanno gettato le basi per una nuova politica.
That meeting has laid the foundations for a new policy.

Metto sempre una base di crema prima del trucco.
I always use a foundation cream before make-up.

Imparerà presto perché ha buone basi in scienze.
He will learn quickly because he has a good grounding in sciences.

La verdura è un elemento base della dieta mediterranea.
Vegetables are a basic element of the Mediterranean diet.

Parte da un buon stipendio base.
He starts with a good basic salary.

battuta (f.) beating, beat

Hai sempre la battuta pronta.
You are never lost for an answer.

Peccato. Con quella sconfitta ha subito una battuta d'arresto.
What a shame. That defeat has brought him to a standstill.

Quante battute fai al minuto con la nuova macchina da scrivere?
How many words per minute do you do with the new typewriter?

Ha sempre delle battute simpatiche.
He always makes funny quips.

Sei mai stato a una battuta di caccia?
Have you ever been hunting?

Che splendida battuta! < tennis >
What a splendid service!

bocca (f.) mouth

Acqua in bocca!
Not a word about it!

In bocca al lupo!
Fingers crossed!

Non sono riuscita a cavargli una parola di bocca.
I have not been able to get a word out of him.

I miei sono tutti di buona bocca.
My family all enjoy their food.

Scusa, mi è scappato di bocca.
I'm sorry, it just slipped out.

La sua reputazione è sulla bocca di tutti.
His reputation is the talk of the town.

Rimango a bocca aperta a sentir questo.
Hearing this leaves me speechless.

Non mi ricordo dal naso alla bocca.
I have no memory at all.

corpo (m.) body

Questa analisi si basa su un corpo di 50'000 parole.
This analysis is based on a corpus of 50,000 words.

La polizia ha comunicato che ha trovato il corpo del reato.
The police have announced they found material evidence.

L'ONU ha inviato un corpo di pace internazionale.
The UN sent an international peace force.

La scuola dove insegno ha un corpo insegnante multi etnico.
The school where I teach has a multi-ethnic teaching staff.

Sei in grado di dare corpo alle tue accuse?
Can you give substance to your allegations?

La brochure va stampata in corpo 10.
The brochure must be printed in 10-point type.

Dottore, vorrei qualcosa per andare di corpo.
Doctor, I would like a laxative.

Non sta mai fermo. È come se avesse il diavolo in corpo.
He is never still. He is on the go all the time.

Non vorrei che tu dessi corpo alle ombre.
I think you are letting your imagination run wild.

Il progetto di un centro sportivo sta prendendo corpo.
The project for a sports centre is taking shape.

Ha deciso di darsi anima e corpo alla pittura.
He has decided to throw himself body and soul into painting.

cosa (f.) thing

Senti, dimmi una cosa . . .
Listen, tell me one thing . . .

Lascia stare il canarino, per prima cosa.
Leave the canary alone, to start with.

Fra una cosa e l'altra mi sono dimenticata il pane.
What with one thing and another I forgot to buy the bread.

Promettimi che la cosa rimanga tra noi.
Promise me that the matter remains between us.

È proprio una cosa da ridere!
It's really a laughing matter!

A cose fatte ti racconterò tutto.
When it's all over and done with I'll tell you everything.

Devi imparare a prendere le cose per il verso giusto.
I must learn to put a brave face on things.

Sta facendo troppe cose: finirà con un esaurimento.
He has taken on too much: he will end up with a nervous
breakdown.

Lascia perdere, cosa vuoi, è giovane.
Forget about it, after all he is young.

PROVERBS:
Cosa fatta capo ha. What is done can't be undone.

Da cosa nasce cosa. One thing leads to another.

cuore (m.) heart

> *Con che cuore puoi rifiutarmi quest'aiuto?*
> How can you refuse me that?
>
> *Il rinnovo di quel contratto mi sta molto a cuore.*
> I care very much about the renewal of that contract.
>
> *Sarà meglio che mi metta il cuore in pace.*
> I'd better set my mind at rest.
>
> *L'ho sempre conosciuto come persona di buon cuore.*
> I have always known him as a good-hearted man.
>
> *Mi hai fatto proprio ridere di cuore.*
> You have really made me laugh heartily.
>
> *Mettiti una mano sul cuore e fagli quel favore.*
> Be generous and do that favour for him.
>
> PROVERBS:
> *Mano fredda, cuore caldo.*
> Cold hands, warm heart.
>
> *Lontano dagli occhi lontano dal cuore.*
> Out of sight out of mind.
>
> *Il cuore ha delle ragioni che la ragione non conosce.*
> The heart has reasons that reason doesn't know.

dente (m.) tooth

> *Ha il dente avvelenato contro quella collega.*
> She has got a grudge against that colleague.
>
> *Agli italiani piacciono gli spaghetti al dente.*
> Italian people like their spaghetti slightly undercooked.
>
> *I banditi che assaltarono quel camion erano armati fino ai denti.*
> The robbers which attacked that lorry were armed to the teeth.
>
> *Vorrei mettere qualcosa sotto i denti prima di partire.*
> I would like to grab a bite before leaving.
>
> *Parlando fuori dai denti, considero questa vendita un disastro.*
> Frankly, I think this sale is a disaster.
>
> *Sembrava che reggesse l'anima coi denti.*
> He looked as if he was hanging on to life by the skin of his teeth.
>
> *Si vedeva che sorrideva a denti stretti.*
> One could see that he was smiling tight-lipped.
>
> PROVERBS:
> *La lingua batte dove il dente duole.*
> The tongue ever turns to the aching tooth.

Non è pane per i tuoi denti.
You have bitten off more than you can chew.

disegno (m.) drawing

Il disegno di legge sulla riforma costituzionale non è stato ancora presentato alla Camera.
The bill on the reform of the constitution has not yet been presented in Parliament.

Mi piace il disegno di questa tovaglia.
I like the pattern of this tablecloth.

Va a lezione di disegno perchè vuole iscriversi a architettura.
He is taking private lessons in draftsmanship because he wants to do architecture at university.

Lavora nel campo del disegno industriale.
He is working in the field of industrial design.

dito (m.) finger *dita* (f.pl.)

Non alzò un dito per aiutarlo.
He didn't lift a finger to help him.

Le persone al concerto si potevano contare sulle dita.
One could count the people at the concert on one's fingers.

È il tipo che se gli dai un dito ti prende un braccio.
He is the kind of person that if you give him an inch he'll take a mile.

Quella frase se l'è legata al dito.
He will bear a grudge because of what was said.

Hai messo il dito sulla piaga.
You have touched on a sore point.

Appena ho parlato, mi sarei morso le dita.
As soon as I spoke, I regretted saying that.

Chiedilo a lui, ha la pratica sulla punta delle dita.
Ask him, he knows that file like the back of his hand.

Ho toccato il cielo con un dito dalla gioia.
I was in seventh heaven with joy.

PROVERB:
Tra moglie e marito non mettere il dito.
Don't interfere in a quarrel between husband and wife.

faccia (f.) face

Che faccia da schiaffi che ha!
You've got a nerve!

Che faccia tosta che hai!
You've got a nerve! / What a cheek!

Mi piace dire le cose in faccia alla gente.
I like to tell people things to their face.

Non sa guardare in faccia la realtà. Questo è il suo problema.
He doesn't know how to face up to things. That is his problem.

Non negarlo. Te lo si legge in faccia.
Don't deny it. It's written all over your face.

Va dritto per la sua strada senza guardare in faccia a nessuno.
He goes straight ahead without caring about what people think.

Esaminiamo le due facce della medaglia.
Let's look at both sides of the question.

Bello questo tessuto a due facce.
This reversible material is nice.

Vorrei fare la faccia. < at a beauty therapist >
I would like to have a facial.

fatto (m.) fact

Perchè non badi ai fatti tuoi?
Why don't you mind your own business?

Purtroppo l'hanno colto sul fatto.
Unfortunately he has been caught red-handed.

Caro mio, i fatti sono maschi le parole sono femmine.
My dear, actions speak louder than words.

Sei in gamba. Sai il fatto tuo.
You are great. You certainly know what you want.

Lascia stare le opinioni, vieni ai fatti.
Leave out opinions, come to the point.

Ho cercato dappertutto. Fatto sta che il documento non si trova.
I have looked everywhere. The fact is I can't find the document.

Nel suo diario descrive i fatti di quei giorni di guerra.
In his diaries he describes the events of those wartime days.

I fatti di cronaca li trovi a pagina quattro del giornale.
The news items are found on page four of the newspaper.

Di quel fatto di sangue se ne parla ancora dopo quarant'anni.
People still talk about that murder forty years later.

Se non lo fermavano, passava a vie di fatto.
Had they not stopped him, he would have come to blows.

gamba (f.) leg

> *Sono scivolata sul ghiaccio e sono finita a gambe all'aria.*
> I slipped on the ice and went head over heels.

> *Sono ragazze in gamba.*
> They are smart girls.

> *Non prendere le cose sotto gamba!*
> Don't underestimate things!

> *Ho camminato così tanto che non mi reggo sulle gambe.*
> I walked so much that I can hardly stand up.

> *Corse via a gambe levate dalla paura.*
> Out of fear he ran away like the wind.

> *Sono carichi di debiti perché fanno il passo più lungo della gamba.*
> They are up to their eyes in debt because they are too big for their
>   boots.

PROVERBS:
> *Le bugie hanno le gambe corte.*
> Truth will out. (literally: Lies have short legs.)

> *Chi non ha testa abbia gambe.*
> If you don't use your head, you'll have to use your legs.

idea (f.) idea

> *Che idea!*
> What a ridiculous thing! < or, depending on the intonation > Brilliant!

> *Erano tutti della stessa idea gli elettori.*
> The voters were all of a mind.

> *Mi sto facendo un'idea della vita in Italia.*
> I'm getting to know life in Italy.

> *Nemmeno per idea. Non ti metti il rossetto.*
> Not on your life. You're not putting on lipstick.

> *Ho idea che dovrò portare a far revisionare l'auto.*
> I suspect I shall have to take the car in for a service.

> *È un'idea fissa di mia suocera.*
> My mother-in-law has this bee in her bonnet.

lingua (f.) language, tongue

> *È pettegola. Non sa tenere a freno la lingua.*
> She's a gossip. She can't hold her tongue.

> *Aveva sulla punta della lingua il nome della città.*
> He had the name of the town on the tip of his tongue.

Il test ha rivelato che ha una vera attitudine per le lingue.
The test has revealed his real aptitude for languages.

Entrò ansimante con la lingua fuori.
He entered puffing and panting.

Non si può dire che non abbia la lingua sciolta.
One can't say he hasn't got the gift of the gab.

Parla proprio perché ha la lingua in bocca.
He talks just for the sake of talking.

Viaggia molto nei paesi di lingua inglese.
He travels a lot in English-speaking countries.

PROVERBS:

Ferisce più la lingua che la spada.
The pen is mightier than the sword.

La lingua batte dove il dente duole.
The tongue ever turns to the aching tooth.

linea (f.) line

Tra qui e la cattedrale ci sono due chilometri in linea d'aria.
It is two kilometres as the crow flies between here and the cathedral.

Il tema era sulle grandi linee di comunicazione.
The essay was on the great travel routes.

In linea di massima, allora, ci vediamo venerdì.
Tentatively, let's say that we'll see each other on Friday.

Una valanga aveva interrotto la linea ferroviaria.
An avalanche had blocked the railway line.

È una nuova linea di prodotti per mantenere la linea.
It's a new line of products to keep one's figure trim.

Era in prima linea nella battaglia per i diritti civili.
He was in the front line in the civil rights battle.

Ho solo tracciato il programma a grandi linee.
I have only outlined the programme.

mezzo (m.) means, half

Sto cercando con tutti i mezzi di convincerlo a andare dal dentista.
I'm trying by any means to make him go to the dentist.

Sei d'accordo che il fine giustifica i mezzi?
Do you agree that the end justifies the means?

Ha sposato una persona che ha mezzi.
He has married someone who has means.

I mezzi pubblici di questa città sono troppo scomodi.
The public transport in this town is too inconvenient.

Vuoi una pera intera o la facciamo a mezzo?
Do you want a whole pear or do we have half each?

Togliti di mezzo, per favore.
Can you get out of the way, please?

naso (m.) nose

Che rabbia! Mi hanno portato via il portafoglio da sotto il naso.
How infuriating! They have taken my purse from under my nose.

Lo conosci. È quel tipo che parla col naso.
You know him. He is that chap who speaks through his nose.

Non mi piace perché ficca il naso negli affari altrui.
I don't like him because he pokes his nose into other people's
    business.

Vedo che arricci il naso. Non ti piace?
I see you've turned up your nose at it. Don't you like it?

L'ha preso per il naso perché è troppo ingenua.
He has led him by the nose because he is too naïve.

A sentire quelle parole gli montò la mosca al naso.
When he heard those words he flew into a rage.

oro (m.) gold

Non uscirei con lui per tutto l'oro del mondo.
I wouldn't go out with him for all the money in the world.

A non comprare quell'orologio ho perso un'occasione d'oro.
I lost a golden opportunity by not purchasing that watch.

È gente che nuota nell'oro.
They are people rolling in money.

Ho un amico che vale tanto oro quanto pesa.
I have a friend who is worth his weight in gold.

Ricordavano la fata dai capelli d'oro.
They remembered the fairy with golden hair.

Non prendere per oro colato tutto quello che dicono i giornali.
Don't take for gospel truth whatever the newspapers say.

PROVERB:
Non è tutto oro quel che riluce. All that glitters is not gold.

passo (m.) step

> *Facciamo due passi visto che è una bella sera.*
> Let's go for a walk since it is a nice evening.
>
> *Se non allunghiamo il passo arriveremo col buio.*
> If we don't hurry up we'll arrive in the dark.
>
> *Al sabato sera si va sempre a passo d'uomo.*
> On Saturday evening we have to inch along.
>
> *Aspettavano solo che facesse un passo falso per licenziarlo.*
> They were waiting for him to step out of line to sack him.
>
> *La ricerca del vaccino contro l'AIDS segna il passo.*
> Research into the vaccine against AIDS is marking time.
>
> *Faccio due passi avanti e due indietro con questo lavoro a maglia.*
> I'm taking two steps forward and two steps back with my knitting.
>
> *Procedevano di buon passo quando si sentì male.*
> They were walking at a good pace when he felt ill.
>
> *Nel mondo del commercio bisogna stare al passo con le esigenze dei clienti.*
> In the business world one has to keep pace with the customers' requirements.
>
> *Parlava di questo e di quello e via di questo passo.*
> He was talking of this and that and so on.

presa (f.) taking, grasp, plug / socket

> *Con la presa di Porta Pia Roma diventò capitale d'Italia.*
> With the seizure of Porta Pia Rome became the capital of Italy.
>
> *D'inverno la valle Padana è alle prese con la fitta nebbia.*
> In winter the Po valley faces the problem of thick fog.
>
> *Lo sceriffo abbandonò la presa solo quando arrivò la polizia.*
> The sheriff let go his hold only when the police arrived.
>
> *Come politico aveva una forte presa sulle masse.*
> As a political man he has a strong hold on the masses.
>
> *Ho comprato questa presa di corrente internazionale all'aereoporto.*
> I bought this international plug at the airport.
>
> *Con l'aiuto di un intermediario fu stabilita una prima presa di contatto.*
> With the help of an intermediary a first contact was established.

In questi ultimi anni c'è stata una presa di coscienza dei problemi dell'immigrazione in Italia.
In recent years people have become aware of the problems of immigration in Italy.

Le tue moine non fanno presa su di me.
Your blandishments don't have any effect on me.

Mi piacerebbe trovarmi una volta dietro la macchina da presa.
I would like to find myself behind the movie camera for once.

questione (f.) question, issue, problem

Bisogna risolvere questa questione.
We have to resolve this question.

Alla prossima riunione intendo sollevare la questione del parcheggio.
At the next meeting I intend to raise the parking issue.

Qual è il nocciolo della questione?
What is at the heart of the matter?

Non è una questione di mia competenza.
It's not a question under my jurisdiction.

Ho una questione coi vicini di casa per via del bidone della spazzatura.
I have a dispute with my neighbours because of the dustbin.

spirito (m.) spirit, mind

Si è salvato grazie alla sua prontezza di spirito.
He saved himself thanks to his presence of mind.

Tu credi negli spiriti?
Do you believe in ghosts?

Lo fa solo per spirito di contraddizione non perché è convinto.
He does it only for the pleasure of contradicting, not because he is convinced.

Vincono perché sono uniti da un forte spirito di squadra.
They win because they are united by a strong team spirit.

Bisogna guardare lo spirito della legge.
One must follow the spirit of the law.

Mi affascina perché è una persona di spirito.
I'm fascinated by his sense of humour.

Se la cavò con una battuta di spirito.
He got away with a witty remark.

testa (f.) head

> *Era un'attrice che ha fatto perdere la testa a molti colleghi.*
> She was an actress who made several colleagues lose their heads.

> *Abbiamo pagato dieci sterline a testa per la cena.*
> We paid ten pounds each for the dinner.

> *Questi verbi non mi entrano in testa.*
> I can't get these verbs into my head.

> *Quelle teste calde danneggiano la causa.*
> Those hot-headed people do damage to the cause.

> *Garibaldi si mise alla testa dei Mille.*
> Garibaldi put himself at the head of the Thousand.

> *Se solo avesse la testa meno dura.*
> If only he was less obstinate.

> *A quell'età vogliono fare di testa propria.*
> At this age they want to decide for themselves.

> *Non fasciarti la testa prima di essersela rotta.*
> Cross that bridge when you come to it.

> *Dopo tanti amori ha messo la testa a partito.*
> After so many love affairs he settled down.

> *È timido ma ha tenuto testa all'esaminatore con sicurezza.*
> He is shy but he argued against the examiner with confidence.

160 Building on nouns with suffixes and prefixes

There are many suffixes which can be attached to nouns to add a nuance to their basic meanings and the Italians use this device with zest. The last vowel is dropped before suffixes are added. Usually the gender of the original noun remains the same. The suffix changes its last vowel to form the feminine singular and the plural (like an adjective ending in *-o*: *-o / -a / -i / -e*).

(a) Suffixes

-ino is by far the most frequent. It indicates something small but with a tone of affection. It is often used for things relating to children:

regalo (m.) *regalino*

> *Le ho fatto un bel regalino per il suo compleanno.*
> I gave her a nice little present for her birthday.

pensiero (m.) *pensierino*

> *Ecco il quaderno dei pensierini della mia bambina.*
> Here are the first sentences my daughter wrote in her exercise
> book.

-etto and **-ello** also denote something pretty and endearing:

giardino (m.) *giardinetto*
casa (f.) *casetta*

> *Dall'aereo le città inglesi sembrano formate da tante casette
> ognuna con un giardinetto.*
> From the air English towns seem to be made up of many pretty
> houses, each one with a small garden.

Sometimes -*ino* and -*etto* or -*ello* are used together:

rosa (f.) *rosellina*

> *È un disegno con tante roselline di vari colori.*
> It's a pattern with many pretty little roses of various colours.

-uccio may indicate something small and nice or something
mediocre depending on which noun it is added to:

cosa (f.) *cosuccia*

> *Era una cosuccia di poco valore ma le ero affezionata.*
> It was a little thing of no great value but I was fond of it.

cappello (m.) *cappelluccio*

> *Portava un vecchio cappelluccio sdrucito.*
> He was wearing an old ragged little hat.

-ucolo, **-uolo**, **-attolo** belittle something and often add a derogatory
touch:

insegnante (m.) *insegnantucolo*

> *Per me è solo un insegnantucolo che si dà molte arie.*
> To me he is only a poor teacher who gives himself airs.

faccenda (f.) *faccenduola*

> *Stiamo perdendo tempo su una faccenduola da niente.*
> We are wasting time on a pretty irrelevant matter.

febbre (f.) *febbriciattola*

> *Da un po' di tempo ho una febbriciattola che non mi piace.*
> For some time I have had a slight temperature which I'm not happy
> about.

-one, -ona, on the other hand, are used instead of 'big' or 'huge'. Some feminine words take *-one* as a suffix and become masculine. These words tend to be derogatory:

ragazzo (m.) boy	*un ragazzone* (m.) a big boy
parola (f.) word	*una parolona* (f.) a big word
finestra (f.) window	*un finestrone* (m.) a large window
donna (f.) woman	*un donnone* (m.) a big woman
faccia (f.) face	*un faccione* (m.) a large fat face

-accio, -astro and *-azzo* give the idea of something negative and unpleasant and even despicable:

una ragazza (f.) a girl	*una ragazzaccia* (f.) a bad girl
un medico (m.) a doctor	*un medicastro* (m.) a worthless doctor

Notice that in some cases the suffix has lost its additional function and some words have acquired a totally different meaning from that of the original noun:

i capelli (m.pl.) hair	*un cappellone* (m.sg.) a long-haired man
la maglia (f.sg.) a jersey	*un maglione* (m.sg.) a heavy jumper
una caserma (f.sg.) barracks	*un casermone* (m.sg.) an ugly block of flats
una piuma (f.sg.) a feather	*un piumone* (m.sg.) a duvet
uno straccio (m.) a rag	*uno straccione* (m.sg.) a down-and-out (man)

(b) Prefixes

In an age of mass communication, the need for hyperbolic messages has led to the continuous creation of new words by means of prefixes which either magnify or minimize. The most common are:

iper-

ipertensione (f.) hypertension
ipernutrizione (f.) hypernutrition

macro-

macrostruttura (f.) macrostructure
macroorganizzazione (f.) macro-organization

maxi-

maxilitigata (f.) a gigantic quarrel
maxiraduno (m.) a gigantic gathering

super-

supercampionato di calcio (m.) football championship
supersaldi (m.pl.) monster sales

pluri-

pluricoltura (f.) diversified farming
plurimilionario (m.) multimillionaire

ultra-

ultracentrifuga (f.) ultracentrifuge
ultrasuoni (m.pl.) ultrasounds

ipo-

ipotensione (f.) hypotension

micro-

microsaggio (m.) mini-essay
forno a microonde (m.) microwave oven
microcriminalità (f.) petty crimes

mini-

minigonna (f.) miniskirt
minigolf (m.) minigolf

61 Two-word nouns

(i) The juxtaposition of two nouns – a basic pattern in English – is becoming increasingly popular in Italian. There is, however, a fundamental difference between the two languages. Unlike English, in Italian it is the second noun which has the function of adjective. Some are well-established, i.e. *la borsa valori* the Stock Exchange, others are made up daily like the following examples:

> *Il giornalismo spazzatura indigna sempre di più.*
> The gutter press fills people with more and more indignation.
>
> *Ci sarà una multa record per il calciatore trovato ubriaco.*
> There will be a record fine for the footballer who was found drunk.

(ii) The use of the hyphen is optional:

> *Una video-discoteca è l'ultima novità per attrarre il turismo giovanile.*
> A video-discotheque is the latest innovation to attract young tourists.

(iii) The two nouns may be of different genders and number:

> *Ha minacciato una rivelazione-bomba.*
> He has threatened to make an explosive revelation.
>
> *Hanno vietato l'accesso alle auto nella zona centro.*
> They have made the town centre a car-free zone.
>
> *Le vacanze-avventura sono molto di moda quest'estate.*
> Adventure holidays are very popular this summer.
>
> *L'informazione-farsa di questo telegiornale.*
> That TV news is a farce.

(iv) The second noun, if masculine, remains masculine singular even if the first noun is feminine or plural:

> *Le inchieste-spettacolo dividono l'opinione pubblica.*
> Investigative TV shows divide public opinion.

(v) The second noun may be followed by an adjective which agrees with it:

> *La sua autobiografia-manifesto politico*
> His autobiography is no more than a political manifesto.

(vi) New words are also coined using *tutto* as an invariable masculine singular noun:

> *il tutto legno* the woodcraft shop
> *Rimini ha fatto il tutto esaurito.* Rimini was fully booked.

162 Building on adjectives

In section 22 we saw how adjectives can be and frequently are turned into nouns in Italian:

> *Contro l'elaborato, l'impegnativo, l'artificiale vinceranno l'autentico, il semplice, il naturale.*
> What is authentic, simple and natural prevails over what is elaborate, exacting and artificial.

Furthermore, traditionally, more adjectives can be created from a simple adjective by adding either a prefix or a suffix. More recent and fashionable is the vogue of coining a new adjective by juxtaposing two adjectives.

(a) The use of prefixes (see also section 26)

The following are the most common prefixes. They all help to describe the highest degree of a quality.

arci-

> *Erano arcicommossi alla cerimonia.*
> They were extremely moved at the ceremony.
>
> *È una categoria arcipagata.*
> It is an overpaid category.

iper-

> *i nostri ipersensibili uomini politici*
> our deeply sensitive politicians

ipo-

> *Si sta sottoponendo a una dieta ipocalorica.*
> He is following a low-calorie diet.

extra-

> *I lavoratori extracomunitari non godono dei vantaggi CEE.*
> Workers not belonging to the EC countries do not enjoy EC benefits.

pluri-

> *Già pluridivorziato, si è sposato per la sesta volta.*
> He has already been divorced several times and got married for the sixth time.

stra-

> *Si discute di un fenomeno straconosciuto e stradenunciato da anni e da molti.*
> We are debating an issue which has been widely known by many people for years and denounced countless times.

super-

> *Offrono vacanze superavventurose a prezzi superstracciati.*
> They offer super-adventurous holidays at incredibly reduced prices.

ultra-

> *Al congresso nazionale hanno vinto gli ultraconservatori.*
> At the national conference the right-wing conservatives won.

(b) The use of suffixes

Suffixes are joined to the adjective after dropping its last vowel.

They agree in gender and number with the noun they refer to, e.g.
-ino / -a / -i / -e:

-ino is the most frequent and often refers to the world of children. It
expresses smallness:

sciocco fool

> *Non fare lo sciocchino.* Don't be silly.

-icino, -olino This suffix expresses smallness and reduces the
meaning of the original adjective:

fresco cold

> *Fa frescolino.* It's pretty cold.

magro thin

> *La sorella è più magrolina di lui.*
> Her sister is rather thinner than he is.

-etto, -ello, -uccio This suffix indicates smallness and a sympathetic
attitude on the part of the speaker:

piccolo small

> *Rascel, comico famoso, era soprannominato il Piccoletto.*
> Rascel, the famous comedian, was nicknamed the Charmingly
> Small One.

pazzo mad

> *Quei ragazzini facevano i pazzerelli.*
> Those boys were a little madcap.

caldo warm, hot

> *Che bel calduccio che c'è qui dentro.*
> How nice and warm it is here.

-one (m.), **-ona** (f.) This suffix gives the idea of something unpleasantly large:

bello good-looking

> *Era una bellona.* She was a showy beauty.

-ognolo, -iccio, -occio These convey a sense of repulsiveness:

verde green

> *Lavata male, la gonna era diventata verdognola.*
> As it had been washed wrongly, the skirt had become a sort of
> yellow-green colour.

sudato wet with perspiration

> *Aveva le mani sudaticce.*
> His hands were sweating.

grasso fat

> *È grassoccia.* She is rather plump.

(c) Juxtaposing two adjectives

This popular trend is particularly used with adjectives related to subject-matters and nationalities.

(i) The first adjective remains in the masculine form while the second agrees in gender and number with the noun it refers to. The two adjectives are linked with a hyphen.

> *È un programma fisico-matematico.*
> It is a physico-mathematical programme.

> *È sostenuto dai più potenti gruppi politico-finanziari.*
> He is supported by the most powerful political and financial
> groups.

> *Ha appena scritto una autobiografia politico-sentimentale.*
> He has just written a political and sentimental autobiography.

> *Ha presentato una valutazione tecnico-giuridica.*
> He has presented a technical and legal assessment.

(ii) Adjectives of nationalities and others such as *biologico, socio-logico* or *agricolo* are abbreviated in the following way:

> *Si tratta di problemi biochimici.*
> They are bio-chemical problems.
>
> *Le sue sorelle sono italo-brasiliane.*
> Her sisters are half-Italian and half-Brazilian.
>
> *Tutto si basa sull'accordo franco-inglese.*
> Everything is based on the Anglo-French agreement.
>
> *Si tratta di studi socio-economici.*
> They are social and economic studies / studies in socio-economics.
>
> *Entriamo in una regione agro-turistica.*
> We are entering a region characterized by country tourism.

(iii) The first adjective often drops its last vowel:

> *Sono programmi TV nazional-popolari.*
> They are TV programmes which appeal to popular tastes.
>
> *Questo nuovo giornale è un settimanal-quotidiano.*
> This new daily newspaper has the features of a weekly magazine.
>
> *Apparteneva alla società mondan-rivoluzionaria di Roma.*
> He belonged to the revolutionary jet set of Rome.

163 Idioms with colours

Colours are often used figuratively in Italian expressions. Let's start with the word 'colour' itself:

colore colour

I turisti sono attratti dal colore locale.
Tourists are attracted by the local colour.

Dopo un week-end al mare ha ripreso colore.
After a weekend at the seaside his cheeks have more colour.

Se ne sentono proprio di tutti i colori.
One really hears all kinds of colourful stories.

È una classe dove se ne fanno di tutti i colori.
It's a class where there is always a lot of mischief.

È diventato di tutti i colori dalla vergogna.
He turned scarlet with shame.

Gliene disse di tutti i colori.
He covered him with insults.

Avevo una mano dello stesso colore. < at cards >
I had a hand of cards of the same suit.

azzurro sky-blue

Il Principe Azzurro svegliò la Bella Addormentata.
Prince Charming awoke the Sleeping Beauty.

Gli italiani fanno sempre un grande tifo per gli Azzurri.
The Italians are always great supporters of their national sports teams.

bianco white

i colletti bianchi white-collar workers

Era talmente spaventato che era bianco come un ciencio.
He was so frightened that he was as white as a sheet.

È raro come una mosca bianca vedere oggi un uomo con la bombetta.
Nowadays you only see a man wearing a bowler hat once in a blue moon. (literally: It is as rare as a white fly . . .)

Ha sonno perché ha passato una notte in bianco.
He is sleepy because he has spent a sleepless night.

Quel caso di corruzione ha causato una polemica al calor bianco.
That corruption case has caused a white-hot controversy.

Preferisco che l'accordo venga messo nero su bianco.
I prefer that the agreement is put down in black and white.

Attenta a non lasciare in giro assegni in bianco.
Don't leave blank cheques lying around.

Gli ho dato carta bianca per organizzare la mostra.
I gave him a free hand / *carte blanche* to organize the exhibition.

All'esame ha lasciato il foglio in bianco.
In the examination he left the sheet blank.

Devo mangiare in bianco dopo l'operazione.
I have to eat boiled food after the operation.

Di punto in bianco mi chiese di prestarle i soldi.
Out of the blue I was asked to lend her some money.

blu blue

le tute blu blue-collar workers

celeste light blue

D'estate la volta celeste è uno spettacolo.
The blue of a summer sky is magnificent.

giallo yellow

In treno leggo sempre un giallo.
I always read a thriller on the train.

Perché non cerca sulle pagine gialle?
Why don't you look it up in the yellow pages?

grigio grey

Previsioni in grigio per l'economia < headline >
Gloomy forecasts for the economy

Conduceva una vita molto grigia.
He led a monotonous life.

Non c'è niente da fare se non c'è la materia grigia.
There is nothing one can do if there are no grey cells there.

Ha molto successo perché ha il fascino delle tempie grigie.
He is very successful because his grey hair adds to his charm.

nero black

i Neri the Fascists

Giornata nera per la Borsa < headline >
Black day for the Stock Exchange

Era una notte senza luna nera come la pece.
It was a pitch-black night without a moon.

Il latino è stato la bestia nera di molti studenti.
Latin has been the bugbear / bête noire of many students.

Porta ancora il nero dopo venti anni di vedovanza.
She is still dressed in black twenty years after her husband's death.

Durante la guerra c'era il mercato nero.
During the war there was a black market.

Non parlarmene nemmeno. Sono nero.
Don't even mention it. I'm in a foul mood.

L'economia di molti paesi si basa sul lavoro nero.
The economy of many countries is based on unofficial employment.

Non leggo mai la cronaca nera.
I never read the crime page.

La magia nera mi fa paura.
Black magic frightens me.

Era sempre stato considerato la pecora nera della famiglia.
He was always considered the black sheep of the family.

Da un po' di tempo vedo tutto nero.
I've been looking on the black side for some time.

Coraggio! Il diavolo non è nero come lo si dipinge.
Come on! The devil is not as black as he is painted.

Dopo lo scontro in auto è caduta nella disperazione più nera.
After the car crash she fell into a deep despair.

La famiglia viveva nella miseria più nera.
The family lived in the most abject poverty.

Perché sei di umore nero?
Why are you in a black mood?

Quella non è una segretaria, è un'anima nera.
She is not a secretary, she is an evil soul.

rosa pink

È un ottimista. Vede la vita in rosa.
He is an optimist. He sees life through rose-coloured glasses.

Legge solo i rotocalchi con la cronaca rosa.
He only reads tabloids with news of love affairs.

Applausi per la giovane bacchetta rosa.
Applause greeted the young woman director.

Lo scandalo dei balletti rosa era su tutti i giornali.
The scandal of the porno-parties hit the headlines.

rosso red

i Rossi the Reds

Non so se era rosso di rabbia o di vergogna.
I don't know if she blushed with anger or shame.

Guarda quei turisti al sole rossi come gamberi.
Look at those tourists as red as beetroots in the sun.

Il bilancio nazionale è in rosso.
The national budget is in the red.

Il rosso '91 è a 16'028 miliardi.
The '91 trade deficit is 16,028 billion.

È una regione rossa.
It's a largely communist region.

Quando dice così vedo rosso.
When he speaks like this I see red.

PROVERBS:

> *Rosso di sera bel tempo si spera.*
> Red sky at night, shepherd's delight.

> *Rosso di mattina brutto tempo si avvicina.*
> Red sky in the morning, sailor's warning.

verde green

È verde d'invidia.
She is green with envy.

Era un uomo aitante nei suoi anni verdi.
He was a handsome man in his youth.

È una città che non ha più un filo di verde. Ecco perché i verdi hanno vinto le elezioni.
It's a town without a blade of grass. That's why the Greens have won the elections.

Allora era nel verde degli anni.
In those days he was young and green.

Quel gruppo industriale diventa più verde. < headline >
That industrial group is acquiring an agricultural products company.

Sta per diventare obbligatoria la benzina verde.
Unleaded petrol is about to become compulsory.

Social variations: colloquialisms and slang

As in other languages, Italian too is characterized by social variations which depend on the speaker's regional origin, education, age and sex. We saw in Part 2 that the use of language includes technical and professional registers and informal slang and jargon.

As for slang, it is said that today's slang is tomorrow's formal language. It is interesting to notice that in Italian there is really no equivalent of the word 'slang'. There is *gergo,* which is clearly a translation of 'jargon'. So the idea of slang is conveyed by *linguaggio colloquiale.* The examples given in this section cover expressions which are today widely used in spoken Italian in everyday life but which are also occasionally found in quality newspapers, where journalists scatter them to pep up their articles. They are, however, not yet part of the language of professional reports or essays. If one really wishes to insert them, it is advisable to put them in inverted commas.

In the following examples the slang phrase (underlined) is followed by the equivalent in standard Italian and in brackets the literal meaning when traceable:

Il suo principale l'ha lasciato a bagno. (literally: *lasciare a bagno* to leave in the wet) *L'ha lasciato nei guai.*
His boss has left him in deep trouble.

I mass media oggi sono tutto un bla bla bla di dibattiti. dibattiti irrilevanti
Today's mass media only indulge in irrelevant debate.

L'hanno beccata sul fatto. (literally: *beccare* to peck up) *colta sul fatto*
They have caught her red-handed.

È una bomba! (literally: he is a bomb) *È fantastico!*
He's great!

Purtroppo si bucava. (literally: *bucarsi* to prick oneself) *si drogava*
Unfortunately he took drugs.

Quella notizia era una bufala. (literally: a cow buffalo) *era un errore madornale.*
That piece of news was an enormous blunder.

Ciccia! (literally: fat) *Non m'importa.*
I don't care.

Costa duemila lire a cranio. (literally: skull) a head

È un drago nel suo campo. (literally: He is a dragon.) *È capace*
He is a genius in his field.

Hanno fatto un colpo in banca ieri qui. (literally: *fare un colpo* to strike
a blow) *Hanno fatto una rapina.*
There was a bank robbery here yesterday.

Mi sono fiondata al supermercato. (literally: I catapulted myself) *Sono
corsa.*
I darted off to the supermarket.

Non capisco come una persona così sensibile possa farsi. (literally: to do
himself) *drogarsi*
I don't understand how such a sensitive person can take drugs.

Sono tutte fesserie! sciocchezze.
They are all silly words!

È una delle storie d'amore più gettonate. (literally: *gettonare* to select
with coins) *richieste*
This love story is one of the hits of all time.

Tra invitati e imbucati saranno stati trecento. (literally: posted) *intrusi*
Between guests and gate-crashers there must have been three
hundred there.

Quella bugia l'ha fatto imbufalire. (literally: to be as angry as a buffalo)
infuriare
That lie has infuriated him.

Quelle rivelazioni hanno incastrato il candidato. (literally: *incastrare* to
mortise) *messo in posizione inaccettabile*
Those revelations have trapped the candidate.

È bravo a fare manfrina. (literally: to drag on the dance) *tirare per le
lunghe*
He's good at avoiding the issue.

Questa versione è tutta un'altra minestra. (literally: a different soup)
offre un altro punto di vista
This version is a completly different kettle of fish.

È stata piantata senza una spiegazione. (literally: planted) *lasciata*
She has been jilted without an explanation.

La sua recitazione è un pianto! (literally: a cry) *deludente*
His performance is disappointing.

Negando il regalo ha fatto una pitoccata. (literally: *fare una pitoccata* to behave like a skinflint) *gesto meschino*
He was a real Scrooge not to buy her a present.

È un tipo pizzoso. È noioso.
He's bore / a drag.

Quel romanzo è un polpettone. (literally: meat-loaf) *senza omogeneità*
That novel is heavy going.

Ha una faccia da puttaniere. (literally: from whore) *un volgare dongiovanni*
He is a cheap womanizer.

Piacciono i suoi occhi rapinosi (literally: women like his robbing eyes) *occhi seducenti*
His bedroom eyes make him very attractive.

Questo resoconto è una sbrodolata. (literally: long broth) *prolisso*
This report is tediously long.

Mi sono sbolognata mia suocera. mi sono liberata
I got rid of my mother-in-law.

L'hanno scippata mezzo minuto fa. L'hanno derubata della borsetta.
They have snatched her handbag.

Quella nuova auto è uno schianto! (literally: a crash) *stupenda*
That new car is a beauty.

Ho dovuto sciropparmi il discorso del preside. (literally: *sciropparsi* to drink a syrup) *ho dovuto sopportare*
I had to digest the headmaster's talk.

È un tipo che se la sfanga se necessario. (literally: *sfangarsela* to clean from the mud) *se la cava*
He is a bloke who finds a solution, if necessary.

Gli piace smanettare con le moto.
He likes to muck about with his motorbikes.

Hanno silurato anche il vice direttore. (literally: torpedoed) *hanno licenziato*
They have fired the deputy director as well.

Smamma! Vattene!
Clear off!

L'hanno catturato grazie a una soffiata. (literally: a whisper) *a una spiata*
They caught him thanks to a tip-off.

Le hanno soffiato l'affare. (literally: blown away) *sottratto*
They have beaten her to it.

Con quel saggio sputtana le intenzioni del suo partito. (literally:
sputtanare to deal with a whore) *screditare*
He discredits his party's intentions with that essay.

Sono stufa marcia di questo posto. (literally: stewed rotten)
profondamente stanca
I'm heartily fed up with this place.

L'opinione pubblica ne ha le tasche piene. (literally: full pockets)
< vulgar > *È molto insoddisfatta*
Public opinion has had enough of this.

In tribunale ha tirato in ballo il suo socio. (literally: brought into the
dance) *ha chiamato in causa*
In court he dragged his partner into the affair.

Tra tante trombonate la sua è una proposta seria. (literally: sounds of
trumpets) *smargiassate*
In spite of his bragging his proposal is a serious one.

Zitto e mosca. (literally: silent and a fly) *silenzio assoluto*
Don't mention a word.

Social variations: youth jargon

A recent national survey organized by the Italian publisher UTET
showed that young Italians use great imagination in creating their rich
jargon. It is a language influenced by TV (*quizzare* to ask), cartoons
(*slurpare* to enjoy), recent events such as the Gulf War (*spezzare uno
Scud a favore di un amico* to help a friend), regional usage
(*strambio* strange from Trieste becomes *strambicciato*). Above all
teenagers love to invent their own words to describe their own
feelings or to talk to people. This need to invent one's own language
has been confirmed by boys and girls during my own smaller
survey. Here are some popular examples with the standard Italian
next to them (further expressions are presented in sections 71–96).

YOUTH	STANDARD	
l'arterios	*mio papà / mio padre*	dad / father
è la tipa di Pippo	*è la ragazza di Pippo*	it is Pippo's girlfriend
è il tipo della Chiara	*è il ragazzo di Chiara*	it is Chiara's boyfriend
che sballo!	*che divertimento!*	how enjoyable!

YOUTH	STANDARD	
che secchia che sei!	*che sgobbone / a che sei!*	what a swot you are! (for both sexes)
mi dà addosso	*mi dà fastidio*	it annoys me / pisses me off
ha delle storie tese	*ha dei problemi*	he has got problems
è un po' schizzato	*è un po' matto*	he is a little mad
che sfiga! < vulgar >	*che sfortuna!*	what bad luck!
è una divata	*è un successo*	it's great (of a performance)
fanno le vasche	*passeggiare in centro*	to stroll in the city centre
è mondiale!	*è favoloso!*	it's fabulous
è un cesso (literally: a lavatory)	*è brutta*	she is ugly
mi becca bene	*mi piace*	I like it
mi becca male	*non mi piace*	I don't like it
mi sono scazzato < vulgar >	*mi sono annoiato*	I got bored
smolla	*dammi*	give me (e.g. a beer)
schiodiamoci / diamoci una mossa	*decidiamoci*	let's go / let's do it
gli sbarbi / le sbarbi	*i ragazzi / le ragazze*	the boys / the girls
che tirapacchi che sei	*non sei stato di parola*	you let me down
m'ha dato buca	*non è stato di parola*	he hasn't kept his word to me
è un tossico	*è un tossico-dipendente*	he is a druggie

66 Neologisms

Some people's dream of a common universal language (perhaps based on English!) certainly won't come true in the near future. As this and the following sections illustrate, despite infiltrations from other languages, Italian is alive and kicking and new words are coined every day. Hundreds of words are simply made up by means of some basic prefixes such as *ri-, neo-* and *pre-*, as the recently published second volume of the *Vocabolario Treccani* edited by Aldo Duro, 1992, has made evident. Publicity and the media are the two main producers and consumers; some words live only for the duration of an event, others are likely to remain for generations.

Leaving aside specialized terms in specific scientific and medical fields, the following terms have been chosen to reflect the wide range of changes and innovations in the last few decades. See also sections 177–183 on computers, cars, mass media, fashion, design, etc.

(a) Food

i cibi integrali (m.pl.)	wholemeal food
i cibi precotti (m.pl.)	pre-cooked meals
grapperia (f.s.)	bar (its speciality being a selection of eaux-de-vie)
kiwi (m.)	kiwi fruit
paninoteca (f.)	snack bar offering a variety of sandwiches
i piatti pronti (m.pl.)	cooked meals
rosticceria (f.) / *gastronomia*	take-away
spaghetteria (f.)	snack bar offering a variety of spaghetti dishes
spuntino (m.)	snack
surgelati (m.pl.)	frozen food
tavola calda (f.)	snack bar
vinoteca (f.)	a pub for wine-tasting
whiskyteca (f.)	a pub offering a large selection of whiskeys

(b) Gadgets, household and technological objects

adesivo (m.)	sticker
bianchetto (m.)	correction fluid
calcolatore (m.) *calcolatrice* (f.)	pocket calculator
carta magnetica (f.)	magnetic card
carta telefonica (f.)	phone card
cinepresa (f.)	video camera, cinecamera
evidenziatore (m.)	felt-tip pen, highlighter
forno a microonde (m.)	microwave oven
fotocopia (f.)	photocopy
fotocopiatrice (f.)	photocopier
fotocopiare	to photocopy
frigo congelatore (m.)	freezer
lavapiatti / lavastoviglie (f.)	dishwasher
nastro trasportatore (m.)	conveyor belt
numero verde	free phone number
personalizzare	to personalize e.g.
agenda personalizzata	personalized diary
portatile	portable
quaderno a fogli estraibili (m.)	loose-leaf pad
registratore (m.)	recorder
sacca (f.)	school satchel
segreteria telefonica (f.)	answering machine
telecamera (f.)	video-camera
telecomando (m.)	remote control
telefono cellulare (m.)	car phone / cellular phone
teleobiettivo (m.)	telephoto lens
televisione via cavo (f.)	cable TV
televisione via satellite (f.)	satellite TV
video proiettore (m.)	video projector
videoregistratore (m.)	video recorder

(c) Beauty products

bagnoschiuma (m.)	bubble bath
balsamo (m.)	conditioner
cipria compatta / sciolta (f.)	compact / loose powder
cosmetici (m.pl.)	cosmetics
crema antirughe	anti-wrinkle cream
crema idratante	moisturizing cream
crema nutriente	nourishing cream
fard (m.)	blusher
fondotinta (f.)	foundation
idromassaggio (m.)	hydromassage
lacca per capelli (f.)	hairspray

latte detergente(m.)	face cleanser
linea di prodotti (f.)	line of products
lucida labbra (m.)	lip gloss
mascara (m.)	mascara
ombretto (m.)	eye-shadow
pulizia del viso (f.)	face cleansing
riflessante (m.)	shader
schiuma (f.)	mousse, foam
shampoo colorante (m.)	colour shampoo
tonico (m.)	toner

(d) Political and social topics

(See also the mass media, section 180.)

ambientalisti (m.pl.)	environmentalists
analfabetismo di ritorno (m.)	semi-literate adults
animalisti (m.pl.)	animal rights activists
audiolesi (m.pl.)	hard of hearing
contraccettivi (m.pl.)	contraceptives
criminalità organizzata (f.)	organized crime
degrado ambientale (m.)	run-down areas
donne di carriera (f.pl.)	career women
droga (f.)	drugs
drogato (m.)	a drug addict
ecologia (f.)	ecology
ecologisti (m.pl.)	ecologists
emergente (adj.) e.g.	
attore emergente	up-and-coming actor
paesi emergenti	developing countries
estraniazione (f.)	marginalization
europarlamentare (m. and f.)	Euro MP
i falchi (m.pl.) *e le*	hawks and doves
colombe (f.pl.)	
fruire	to make use of
garantismo (m.)	right of protection by law
ingegneria genetica (f.)	genetic engineering
lottizzare	to appoint people according to their political party and not their professional ability
mammografia (f.)	mammograph
di massa e.g. *società di massa*	mass society
multifunzionale (adj.)	multifunctional
narcodollari (m.pl.)	drug money
narcotrafficanti (m.pl)	drug barons
nonvedenti (m.pl.)	visually impaired

nullologo	an ignorant commentator
opinionista (m.)	mass media commentator
pendolare (m. and f.)	commuter
i pidiessini	members of the reformed Communist party (*PDS Partito Democratico Socialista*)
politicante (m.and f.)	someone belonging to the political underworld
progressista (adj.)	liberal
pubbliche relazioni (f.pl.)	public relations
rampante (adj.) e.g. *manager rampante*	yuppie
sessuologo (m.)	sexologist
sieropositivo / a (adj.)	HIV-positive
spacciatore (m.)	small-time drug dealer
riciclare denaro sporco	to launder dirty money
tangente < coll. >	under-the-counter money
tecnologia applicata (f.)	applied technology
tempo reale (m.)	real time
terziario (m.)	tertiary sectors
tossicodipendente (m. and f.)	drug-dependent
totalizzante (adj.), e.g. *un amore totalizzante*	total
trasgressivo / a (adj.)	transgressive
tuttologo (m.)	mass media commentator expert on all subjects
vacanzieri (m.pl.)	holiday crowds
villaggio globale (m.)	global village
volontariato (m.)	voluntary service workers
zona pedonale (f.)	pedestrian precinct / car-free area

67 *Faux amis*

The number of words which look very similar in the two languages (Italian and English) but differ in meaning is rather extensive and not easy to classify. The following is therefore a selection of these 'false friends' which can cause misunderstandings.

È una casa abusiva. (abusive *offensivo*)	It's a house built illegally.
Ti sei annoiata alla cerimonia? (to annoy *irritare*)	Did you get bored at the ceremony?

È un argomento interessante. (argument *discussione*, f.)	It's an interesting issue.
Sai arrangiarti a aggiustarlo? (to arrange *organizzare*)	Can you manage to mend it?
È stato assunto come interprete all'UNESCO. (to assume *presumere*)	He has been appointed as a UNESCO interpreter.
Attualmente il prodotto non è in vendita. (actually *in realtà*)	At present the product is not on sale.
È un bar famoso per i suoi gelati. (bar *spaccio* (m.) *di bibite*)	It's a place famous for its ice-cream.
Portava le bestie al pascolo. (beast *bestione*, m.)	He used to take the animals to graze.
È un bravo attore. (brave *coraggioso*)	He is a good actor.
Questa biancheria non è candida. (candid *franco*)	This linen is not pure white.
Ha una cantina piena di vini. (canteen *mensa*, f.)	He has a cellar full of wines.
È stato un incontro casuale. (casual *fortuito*)	It was a chance meeting.
Non tirare la coda al cane. (queue *coda*, f.)	Don't pull the dog's tail.
Ho visto le foto con commozione. (commotion *trambusto* m.)	I saw the photos with emotion.
È un albergo con tutte le comodità. (commodity *merce*, f.)	It's a hotel with all the comforts.
È un giudice comprensivo. (comprehensive *completo*)	He is an understanding judge.
La cifra è comprensiva dei costi.	The figure includes the costs.
Ha tenuto una conferenza sulla religione. (conference *convegno*)	He gave a lecture on religion.
Confronta i due testi. (to confront *affrontare*)	Compare the two texts.

È carta consistente. (consistent *coerente*)	It's a thick paper.
Sono contento del risultato. (content *soddisfatto*)	I am happy with the results.
È un prezzo conveniente. (convenient *utile*)	It's good value for money.
in data 3 ottobre 1997 (date *appuntamento* m.)	on 3 October 1997
Il suo comportamento è deludente. (to delude *illudere*)	Her behaviour is disappointing.
È una domanda difficile. (demand *richiesta*, f.)	It's a difficult question.
Quando ha fatto domanda di lavoro?	When did she send in her application?
Dispone di un parco automobili. (to dispose *sbarazzarsi*)	He has a fleet of cars.
Poche persone sono distratte come lui. (distracted *confuso*)	Few people are as absent-minded as he is.
Vi siete divertiti a teatro? (to divert *dirottare*)	Did you enjoy yourselves at the theatre?
È un piccolo editore. (editor *curatore*, m.)	He is a small publisher.
Mi piace perché è ben educato. (educated *istruito*)	I like him because he is well-mannered.
Sei troppo emotivo. (emotive *impressionabile*)	You are too emotional.
Eventualmente lo tagliamo. (eventually *alla fine*)	If it happens we cut it.
Lavora in una fattoria. (factory *fabbrica*, f.)	He works on a farm.
Il fine giustifica i mezzi. (fine *sottile*)	The end justifies the means.
Aveva dei modi molto fini.	She was a real lady.
Metta qui la firma. (firm *ditta*, f.)	Please sign here.
Ha dei lineamenti gentili. (gentle *fine*)	He has delicate features.

449

Era un uomo grande in tutti e due i sensi. (grand grandioso)	He was a big man in both senses of the word.
L'ingresso è gratuito. (gratuitous ingiustificato)	Entrance is free.
È un'accusa gratuita.	It's a groundless accusation.
È un micio grosso. (gross grossolano)	It's a large cat.
Guarda che cielo stellato. (to guard custodire)	Look — what a starry sky!
Era un cammino impervio. (impervious impenetrabile)	It was an inaccessible path.
Era una strada impraticabile. (impracticable inattuabile)	It was an unusable road.
Non farti impressionare dal racconto. (to impress colpire)	Don't be shocked by the tale.
Il suo ragionamento è incoerente. (incoherent sconnesso)	His reasoning is inconsistent.
Smettila di ingiuriare. (to injure ferire)	Stop being insulting.
È un uomo invidioso. (invidious irritante)	He is envious of other people.
È una libreria ben fornita. (library biblioteca, f.)	It's a well-equipped bookshop.
È un tipo lunatico. (lunatic matto)	He is moody.
Tutta la merce è in magazzino. (magazine rivista, f.)	All the goods are in the store / warehouse.
Ha svolto una missione importante. (mission mandato, m.)	He has carried out an important task.
Ho messo la gonna marrone. (maroon castano rossastro)	I put on the brown skirt.
La lana era morbida. (morbid morboso)	The wool was soft.
È una notizia segreta. (notice avviso, m.)	It's secret information.

Mi occorrono gli occhiali. (to occur *accadere*)	I need glasses.
È un mio parente. (parents *genitori*, m.pl.)	He is a relative of mine.
È un pavimento di marmo. (pavement *marciapiede*, m.)	It's a marble floor.
Sono navi cariche di petrolio. (petrol *benzina*, f.)	They are ships loaded with crude oil.
È stato processato per un delitto. (to process *elaborare*)	He has been brought to trial for murder.
la professoressa di economia domestica (professor *professore universitario*)	the teacher of home economics
Ognuno si interessa del proprio futuro. (proper *corretto*)	Everybody is interested in his or her own future.
È una questione irrilevante. (question *domanda*, f.)	It's an irrelevant problem.
Come cucini le rape? (rape *stupro*, m.)	How do you cook turnips?
Lo vendono a rate. (rate *tassa*, f.)	It can be paid for by instalments.
Ricordami di comprare il pane. (to record *registrare*)	Remind me to buy the bread.
È stato ricoverato in clinica. (to recover *guarire*)	He has been admitted to hospital.
La folla si è riversata in piazza. (folly *follia*)	The crowd swarmed into the square.
Ho riversato i miei problemi sui di lui. (to reverse *rovesciare*)	I poured out my problems to him.
Quella lavatrice fa troppo rumore. (rumour *diceria*, f.)	That washing-machine makes too much noise.
È un bambino sano. (sane *sano di mente*)	He is a healthy child.
Lo scopo è dimenticare. (scope *ambito*, m.)	The aim is to forget.
Sono alberi secolari. (secular *secolare*)	They are centuries-old trees.

È gente sensibile. (sensible *equilibrato*)	They are sensitive people.
È stato un bello spettacolo. (spectacles *occhiali*, m.pl.)	It has been a good show.
È simpatico e spiritoso. (sympathetic *comprensivo*)	He is charming and with a sense of humour.
Sembrava uno spiritato. (spirited *brioso*)	He looked wild (e.g with fear).
Che stolido! (stolid *impassibile*)	How stupid of him!
Si ammirava una vista suggestiva. (suggestive *insinuante*)	One could admire a charming view.
Faccio fatica a sopportare i suoi capricci. (to support *sostenere*)	I find it difficult to put up with his whims.
La conferenza stampa è finita. (stamp *francobollo*, m.)	The press conference is over.
Tasta questa coperta, per favore. (to taste *assaggiare*)	Can you feel this blanket, please?
Ho schiacciato il tasto sbagliato. (taste *sapore*, m.)	I've pressed the wrong key.
Non ha nessun titolo di studio. (title *titolo* m.)	He has no qualifications.
È un'espressione triviale. (trivial *di poco conto*)	It's a coarse expression.
C'è un ulteriore motivo. (ulterior *nascosto*)	There is a further motive.
Ultimamente si è tinta i capelli. (ultimately *in ultima analisi*)	Recently she dyed her hair.
L'affluenza alle urne è stata ampia. (urn *urna*, f.)	The turn-out of people at the polls has been large.
Ha urtato un altro sciatore. (to hurt *ferire*)	He bumped into another skier.
Si sono comportati da vili. (vile *meschino*)	They behaved like cowards.

È un villano. (villain *farabutto*)	He is rude.
È un ambiente vizioso. (vicious *malvagio*)	It's a vice-ridden environment.
È un carattere volubile. (voluble *loquace*)	He has a fickle temperament.

68 Foreign borrowings (*forestierismi*)

As well as the occasional word of Spanish (e.g. *pibe de oro* golden boy, imported for the football champion Maradona) or German (e.g. *Blitz, Putsch*), modern Italian still uses some Latin expressions, so frequent as to be almost proverbs, and a good cluster of French ones. Nowadays, however, most imported words come from England and the USA. This section gives examples of well-established borrowings, as well as recent acquisitions; it also shows how some of them have changed their meanings after becoming part of the Italian language and how they have been adapted to Italian grammar and structure. When the Italian word occurs as frequently as the foreign borrowing, it has been indicated here next to the English. Grammatically, it is important to remember that English words are pronounced according to Italian pronunciation rules, i.e. *gas = gaass*. The following example appeared as a newspaper headline when the protagonist of the soap opera 'Dallas', J.R., visited Mantua: *Gei Ar è arrivato a Mantova!*

(a) Well-established words

For further borrowings in the language of commerce, finance, computers, technology, fashion, etc., see sections 173–183. Notice that, when words are absorbed in Italian, they acquire a gender. The English 's' for the plural is usually omitted. The article preceding them here indicates whether they are feminine or masculine:

il boom	*il gas*	*un party* (entertainment)	*il setter*
il camping	*l'hotel* (m.)	*un playboy*	*lo shock*
il cocker	*l'identikit* (m.)	*la privacy*	*lo sport*
il cocktail	*i jeans*	*il rayon*	*lo stand*
il clown	*un leader*	*il sandwich*	*il taxi*
il cow-boy	*un manager*	*lo shampoo*	*il week-end*
il fair-play	*il nylon*	*il self-control*	*il western*
un film		*il sense of humour*	

453

(b) More recently imported words

The following are a few examples of some more recent acquisitions from a variety of areas:

la baby-sitter	*il lifting*
il / la caravan	*la lobby*
il charter	*il make-up*
l'establishment (m.)	*il partner* (in business and private life)
il fax	*il promoter*
il flash	*il racket*
il freezer	*il self-service*
la gang	*lo shopping*
i gay	*gli skin-heads*
il grill	*lo status symbol*
l'hamburger (m.)	*il summit*
gli hooligan	*i teen-agers*
il killer	*il telefax*
il jet-set	*lo zapping*

(c) Old and recent acquisitions from the world of music

Notice in the following words that the gender is sometimes still uncertain.

un album	*l'hifi* (m.)
la band	*il jazz; il soul jazz*
i blues	*la hall* (in a hotel)
un compact disc	*un pop group*
la country music	*il poster*
il dee-jay	*il rap*
la disco music	*il rock and roll*
un elle pi (LP)	*la rock star* (man or woman)
i fan / fans	*lo slogan*
la hit parade	*il soundtrack la colonna sonora*
la hostess	*un / una videoclip*

(d) From the world of entertainment

l'anchorman (m.)	*lo scoop*
un best-seller	*un serial*
la fiction	*un / una sex symbol*
un flash	*la soap opera*
un home video	*uno special*
un network / una rete televisiva	*il talk-show*

(e) From the world of sport

il baseball	il poker
il basket	il polo
il bob	la pole-position
il cricket	un round; vincere un round (to win a
il fairway	round)
il golf	il rugby
l'hockey (m.); l'hockey su ghiaccio	lo sparring partner
(ice hockey)	lo skate-board
il motocross	lo squash
la mountain-bike	il volleyball

(f) From the world of commerce

(See also sections 173–174.)

il budget	il leasing
l'executive (m.)	il manager
la holding	il marketing
una joint venture	il trading; l'insider trading

(g) Commonly used technical words

(See also section 177.)

il compact-disc	lo scanner
il gap	il test
il know-how	il walkie-talkie
il laser	

(h) English words with Italian prefixes and suffixes

il cocker / il cockerino	a small cocker spaniel
il minitour di Frank Sinatra	Frank Sinatra's minitour

(i) Italian words and phrases based on English

As the examples show, Italian verbs modelled on English ones belong to the 1st conjugation:

acculturation > *acculturazione, deculturazione*

to assemble > *assembleare*

> *I viveri sono stati assembleati sull'aereo.*
> The supplies have been assembled on the plane.

determined > *determinato*

> *Va bene in determinate condizioni.*
> It is all right in certain conditions. (traditional meaning)
> *È un tipo determinato.* (anglicism)
> He is a determined person.

dribbling > *dribblare*

> *Hanno dribblato le sue obbiezioni.*
> They have bypassed his objections.

fax > *faxare*

> *Ho faxato la risposta stamane.*
> I sent the reply by fax this morning.

flirt > *flirtare*

> *A sua madre non piace che flirti con quella ragazza.*
> His mother doesn't like him flirting with that girl.

hobby > *l'hobbistica* (f.)

> *L'hobbistica è diventata un'industria.*
> Hobby-related goods have become an industry.

interface > *interfaccia* (f.)

> *L'interfaccia non funziona.*
> The interface isn't working.

to intrigue > *intrigare*

> *Questo ruolo mi intriga.* (standard Italian: *mi incuriosisce*).
> This role intrigues me.

jazz > *il jazzista*

> *Per me è il jazzista più grande di tutti i tempi.*
> For me he is the greatest jazzman of all time.

jazz > *jazzistico*

> *Era un concerto jazzistico.*
> It was a jazz concert.

lobby > *il lobbista*

> *Sta diffondendosi la professione del lobbista.*
> Lobbyism as a profession is growing.

made > *il made in Italy*

> *Il made in Italy è una delle nostre industrie trainanti.*
> Italian fashion and design is one of our leading industries.

manager > *manageriale*
>
> *È entrato con il suo fare manageriale.*
> He entered with his managerial air.

marked > *marcato* < linguistics >
>
> La parola si trova in posizione marcata.
> The word is in a stressed position. (a position with emphasis)

to mix > *mixare*
>
> *È una musica mixata.*
> It is remixed music.

modals > *modali*
>
> *I verbi modali sono irregolari in italiano.*
> Modal verbs are irregular in Italian.

playboy > *playgirl*
>
> *Nel bar sedevano playboy e playgirl.*
> In the bar playboys and girls were sitting around.

to realize > *realizzare*
>
> *Ha realizzato una bella impresa.*
> He has achieved an important goal. (traditional meaning)
>
> *Ha realizzato che non aveva capito niente.* (anglicism)
> He realized he hadn't understood a thing.

rock > *rockettaro, rock 'n' roller*
>
> *È un bar frequentato da rockettari.*
> It's a bar popular with rock 'n' rollers.

to shock > *scioccare*
>
> *La sua volgarità mi ha scioccato.*
> His vulgar manners have shocked me.

shocking > *scioccante*
>
> *È stata un'esperienza scioccante.*
> It has been a shocking experience.

to shop > *fare lo shopping*
>
> *Sono andata a Londra a fare dello shopping.*
> I went to London to do some shopping.

snobbery > *lo snobismo*
>
> *Quelle vacanze sono una nuova forma di snobismo.*
> Those holidays are a new form of snobbery.

to be a snob > *snobbare*
>
> *Snobbare tutti è la sua arma.*
> Snobbery towards everybody is his weapon.

to sponsor > *sponsorizzare*

> *Il concerto è stato sponsorizzato da un privato.*
> The concert has been sponsored by a private citizen.

sponsor > *la sponsorizzazione*

> *È stata una sponsorizzazione.* (literally: sponsorization)
> It has been sponsored.

stock > *lo stockista*

> *In italiano lo stockista è un negozio dove si vendono vestiti d'alta moda a prezzi ridotti alla fine della stagione.*
> In Italian the *stockista* is a shop where high fashion clothes are sold at reduced prices at the end of the season.

to stop > *stoppare* < sporting slang >

> *Gli ha stoppato la via alla Casa Bianca.*
> He has momentarily stopped him on his way to the White House.

to stress > *stressare*

> *Mi sento proprio stressata.*
> I really feel stressed.

stressful > *stressante*

> *È una realtà stressante.*
> It is a stressful situation.

to test > *testare*

> *Hanno testato un nuovo farmaco per i trapianti.*
> They have tested a new product for transplants.

topic > *topicalizzazione* < linguistics >

> *La topicalizzazione dell'oggetto è frequente in italiano.*
> The topicalization of the object is frequent in Italian.

zoom > *una zoomata*

> *Sto facendo una zoomata di quel cervo.*
> I'm zooming in on that deer.

(j) English words which have acquired a different meaning in Italian

Sometimes the different meaning originates from a figurative use of the English word, as indicated.

l'audience (f.) the audience rating

> *Oggi l'audience è l'unico fine dei produttori TV.*
> Today reaching a high audience rating is the only aim of TV producers.

il bar coffee bar; ice cream shop

> *Andiamo al bar?*
> Shall we go to an ice-cream shop?

il basket basketball

> *Giochi a basket?* Do you play basketball?

i big the big shots < fig. >

> *I big della finanza si sono incontrati in Germania.*
> The big shots of the financial world have met in Germany.

un box garage

> *È una villetta a schiera con due box.*
> It's a semi-detached with two garages.

il bunker < also fig. >

> *Il Torino nel bunker* < headline >
> Turin on the defence

il casual refined, expensive, casual-looking fashion

> *L'uomo d'oggi veste casual.*
> Today's man dresses in expensive casual clothes.

casual (adj.)

> *Ha giocato una Juventus casual.*
> Juventus played a sloppy game.

il cocktail < fig. >

> *Eccovi un cocktail di idee per le feste di Pasqua.*
> Here is a cocktail of ideas for your Easter holidays.

salvarsi in corner < fig. >

> *Il ministro si è salvato in corner.*
> The minister saved himself by the skin of his teeth.

il derby football match between two teams of the same city

> *L'ultimo derby è stato vinto dal Torino.*
> The last football match between Juventus and Turin was won by Turin.

un fast food fast-food shop / take away

> *Hanno aperto un fast food nel centro storico.*
> A fast-food shop has been opened in the city centre.

il fast food

> *Il fast food rende bene.*
> The fast-food industry pays well.

un festival a music competition

> *Il Festival di San Remo è ormai un evento nazionale.*
> The San Remo Festival is now a national event.

il green golf course

> *Potrete giocare sul nostro prestigioso green.*
> You'll be able to play on our prestigious golf course.

il meeting conference

> *Il Papa è venuto al Meeting di Rimini.*
> The Pope has come to the Rimini Conference.

il network consortium of private TV channels

> *I network privati fanno valida concorrenza alla RAI.*
> Private TV channels are valid competitors of RAI channels.

il night night-club

> *A Parigi sono andati in un night.*
> In Paris they went to a night club.

gli optional car accessories

> *I cristalli atermici sono tra gli optional.*
> Heated windows are among the extras.

poker < fig. >

> *La Roma ha realizzato un poker di reti.*
> The Roma team has realized a full set (as in a game of poker) of scores.

lo speaker newscaster

> *È lo speaker più popolare.*
> He is the most popular newscaster.

lo spot TV commercial

> *La legge italiana permette tre spot ogni film.*
> Italian law allows three commercials in every TV film.

il ticket the cost of a prescription

> *Il costo del ticket è aumentato anche per gli anziani.*
> The cost of prescriptions has increased even for the elderly.

il toast or *tost* (Italian spelling) a hot sandwich with cheese and ham

> *Ti preparo un tost?*
> Shall I make you a toasted sandwich?

(k) English words acting as adjectives

The English word in this case follows the Italian one according to the Italian basic rule on adjective position (see sections 23 and 161).

> *L'architetto dice: vivere country.*
> Architects say: live country style.

> *Oggi impiegano gli spacciatori baby per vendere la droga.*
> Nowadays they employ drug-dealers who are practically babies.

Vado matta per la musica pop.
I'm crazy about pop music.

Gli hanno dato un ultimatum soft.
They gave him an easy ultimatum.

Per i compleanni va di moda il libro-gadget.
For birthdays the 'gadget book' is fashionable.

(l) Full English construction

Sometimes the full English construction is adopted in headlines or publicity slogans.

È stato l'organizzatore del Pavarotti-day.
Italian form: *È stato l'organizzatore del giorno di Pavarotti.*
He was the organizer of the Pavarotti day.

Il Barcellona business per le Olimpiadi è già cominciato.
Italian form: *Il giro di affari a Barcellona per le Olimpiadi è già cominciato.*
The business for the Olympic games has started in Barcelona.

La Club Tenco Story
Italian form: *La storia del club dedicato a Tenco*
The history of the club named after Tenco (an Italian singer)

(m) English word order and structures in Italian

Attempts to introduce English word order are still rare. This first sentence shows a well-established two-word noun in the English word order.

Il calciomercato è oggi un turbine di miliardi.
Traditional form: *il mercato del calcio*
The football market is today a whirlwind of billions.

This case is a journalist showing off and was probably not understood by a large number of readers:

Ecco in poche righe il conte-pensiero.
Traditional form: *il pensiero del conte*
Here is the earl's thought in a few lines.

The third example – with the preposition *alla* not followed by a noun – would normally be considered a typical howler in a foreign student's essay, but in this case it is to be read as poetic licence.

'Di fatto è un testo essenziale non solo per introdurre alla, ma per arricchire, sfumare la conoscenza di Calasso ...'

Traditional form: *'Di fatto è un testo essenziale non solo per introdurre*
                alla conoscenza di Calasso ma anche per arricchirne e
                sfumarne la lettura . . .'

                'In fact, it is an essential text not only as an introduction
                to, but as a means of enriching and deepening,
                knowledge of his writings . . .'

This example shows a well-established mixture of English and Italian word order:

                È cominciata la tre giorni di dibattito.
Traditional form: *Il dibattito di tre giorni è cominciato.*
                The three-day debate has started.

(n) French borrowings

(i) To the world of fashion belong:

l'atelier fashion house (m.)	*il foulard* scarf
la boutique	*la griffe* trade-mark
chic	*il satin*
double-face	

(ii) To the world of food:

la brioche	*i marrons glacés*
lo champagne	*l'omelette* (f.)
il cognac	*il purée*
il consommé	*il ragù*
il frappé	*il soufflé*

(iii) Words from other areas include:

il battage pubblicitario publicity campaign	*una reclame* advertisement
il bidet	*un reportage* special report
il cabaret	*una roulotte* caravan
il cliché	*il tour*
i collant tights	*una tournée* tour
il dossier	*una vedette* film star
l'élite (f.)	*la verve* liveliness
un'équipe (f.) team	

(o) Latin expressions

The following are only some of the expressions which are used in everyday spoken and written language. They are so common that even headlines in the sports pages display them, as in this case:

    In casa della Fiorentina si recita il mea culpa.
    At the Fiorentina football club they confess their own sins.

Even a new occasional tax was given a Latin name: *la una tantum* (the 'once in a while' tax). Other expressions are:

> *Era il factotum della ditta.*
> She was the factotum of the company.

> *È stato preparato ad hoc per lui.*
> It has been prepared to suit him perfectly.

> *Ha avuto l'imprimatur del segretario del suo partito.*
> He had the permission of his party's secretary.

> *Hanno accettato lo status quo.*
> They have accepted the situation as it is at the moment.

> *Il reddito pro capite è tra i più alti in Europa.*
> The individual income is among the highest in Europe.

> *Ipso facto gli diede i soldi.*
> He gave him the money immediately.

> *Ecco il vademecum del buon turista.*
> Here is the good tourist's guide.

> *È l'habitat naturale degli scoiattoli.*
> It's the squirrel's natural habitat.

SPECIAL VOCABULARIES

 Travel

(a) Roads

l'autostrada a pagamento (f.)	motorway with toll
un'autostrada a quattro corsie	dual carriageway
la circonvalazione	ring road
un ingorgo	traffic jam
il pedaggio	toll
una sopraelevata	flyover
uno spartitraffico	roundabout
un tamponamento a catena	pile-up
la tangenziale	bypass

Road conditions are given on the radio and on TV. It is also possible to telephone the local police station or *l'ACI* (*Automobil Club Italiano*).

(b) Public transport

Buses, coaches and underground

Bus tickets are usually purchased in advance in bars or at a tobacconist's or a newsagent's and must be stamped in a machine when getting on. The same applies to tramways, which still exist in Milan for instance.

In some cities a ticket lasts for one hour and allows one to change buses. Since each town seems to have its own rules it is best to ask.

l'abbonamento (m.)	season ticket
l'autobus	bus
il biglietto	ticket
un blocchetto di biglietti	book of tickets
convalidare il biglietto	to stamp the ticket
la corriera	coach
la fermata	stop
la fermata facoltativa / obbligatoria	request / regular stop
l'orario (m.)	timetable

Trains

Train tickets can be purchased in advance at the station or from agencies. On some trains reservation is not compulsory but there is a charge for it. Return tickets must be stamped on the day of return. Elderly people get a reduction with *la carta d'argento* (the silver card) and so do children under five. There are also special reductions for teenagers. Tickets are stamped on the train by ticket collectors.

un biglietto andata e ritorno	return ticket
il controllore	ticket collector
feriale	only weekdays
festivo	only on Sunday
un intercity	fast train
un locale	slow train
in orario	on time
prenotare	to book
in ritardo	late

Planes

un aereo	plane
atterrare	to land
la carta d'imbarco	boarding card
il controllo passaporti	passport control
decollare	to take off
il deposito bagagli smarriti	lost luggage
fare il check in	to check in
la navetta	shuttle
il negozio esente da dazio	duty free shop
il ritiro dei bagagli	luggage reclaim

70 Numbers and statistics

(a) Cardinal numbers

1	*un / uno / una*	12	*dodici*
2	*due*	13	*tredici*
3	*tre*	14	*quattordici*
4	*quattro*	15	*quindici*
5	*cinque*	16	*sedici*
6	*sei*	17	*diciassette*
7	*sette*	18	*diciotto*
8	*otto*	19	*diciannove*
9	*nove*	20	*venti*
10	*dieci*	21	*ventuno*
11	*undici*	22	*ventidue*

30 *trenta*	500 *cinque cento*
40 *quaranta*	600 *sei cento*
50 *cinquanta*	700 *sette cento*
60 *sessanta*	800 *otto cento*
70 *settanta*	900 *nove cento*
80 *ottanta*	1000 *mille*
90 *novanta*	1100 *mille e cento* (etc.)
100 *cento*	2000 *duemila*
101 *cento uno*	10.000 *dieci mila*
200 *due cento*	100.000 *cento mila*
300 *tre cento*	*un milione* a million
400 *quattro cento*	*un miliardo* a billion

(b) Ordinal numbers

These numbers take the singular / plural / feminine / masculine form according to the noun they refer to:

1st *il primo / la prima*	9th *il nono*
2nd *il secondo*	10th *il decimo*
3rd *il terzo*	11th *l'undicesimo*
4th *il quarto*	12th *il dodicesimo*
5th *il quinto*	13th *il tredicesimo*
6th *il sesto*	14th *il quattordicesimo* (etc.)
7th *il settimo*	100th *il centesimo*
8th *l'ottavo*	1000th *il millesimo*

(c) Dates

★ **(i)** For dates, Italian uses the ordinal number only for the first day of the month. For other dates, it uses the cardinal numbers:

> *Compie gli anni il primo gennaio.* His birthday is the 1st of January.

> *Partiamo il 10 di questo mese.* We leave on the 10th of this month.

(ii) For dates in letters see section 121.

(iii) To ask the date, there is a choice between two equally common ways:

> *Che data è oggi? / Quanti ne abbiamo oggi?*
> What's the date today?

(iv) Other expressions referring to dates are:

> *Finiranno i lavori nell'anno in corso.*
> The works will be finished in the current year.

> *Negli anni venti ci fu una seria recessione.*
> In the twenties there was a serious recession.

> *Il cinema italiano ebbe grandi registi tra gli anni cinquanta e sessanta.*
> Italian cinema had great directors during the fifties and the sixties.

(d) Approximate numbers

To give an approximate figure, the suffix *-ina* may be added to some numbers between 10 and 90:

una decina	about 10	*una quindicina*	about fifteen
una dozzina	a dozen	*una ventina*	about twenty (etc.)

Note:

un centinaio	about a hundred	*centinaia*	hundreds
un migliaio	about a thousand	*migliaia*	thousands

(e) Numbers in idioms

contare come il due di briscola	to be worth a farthing
essere al settimo cielo	to be over the moon / in seventh heaven
fare due passi	to take a stroll
fare due salti in discoteca	to go for a dance at a disco
fare quattro chiacchiere	to have a nice chat
farsi in quattro per fare qualcosa	to go out of one's way to help
piegarsi in due dal ridere	to double up with laughter
spaccare il capello in quattro	to split hairs
uno sì e uno no	every other one
parlare a quattr'occhi	to talk in private
fare quattro passi	to go for a walk
in quattro e quattr'otto	right away
È a due passi da casa.	It's only a few steps from home.
Non c'è due senza tre.	It never rains but it pours.
Oggi otto cominciano le vacanze.	A week today holidays start.
Uno per uno non fa male a nessuno.	Some for each is good for all.
Gliene ha dette quattro.	He gave him a piece of his mind.
È partito in quarta.	He took off like a bat out of hell. (literally: in fourth gear)

(f) Statistics and percentages

For statistics in reports see also section 152.

Il tasso di scolarità è del 97%.
The number of children going to school is 97%.

Il novanta per cento della popolazione è turca.
Ninety per cent of the population is Turkish.

Un abitante su venti lascia la grande città.
One inhabitant in twenty leaves the city.

Una crescente percentuale dei giovani italiani sceglie di non sposarsi.
An increasing percentage of young Italians chooses not to marry.

L'età media dei laureati italiani è di ventisei anni.
The average age at which Italians take their degree is twenty-six.

La casistica parla di 400 casi all'anno.
There are 400 hundred cases a year.

Le statistiche dicono che il numero dei malati aumenta / diminuisce in autunno.
According to statistics the number of ill people increases / decreases in the autumn.

Il numero dei passeggeri è passato da 3000 a 4000 unità nel giro di una settimana.
The number of passengers rose from 3000 to 4000 within a week.

Si otterrà un risparmio fino al 20%.
There will be a 20% saving.

71 Times, dates, age, and temporal expressions

(a) Giving the time

In official timetables (public transport, working hours, radio / TV programmes) the 24-hour clock is commonly used:

> *Il telegiornale delle venti è il più seguito.*
> The eight o'clock TV news is the most popular.

> *Bisogna essere all'aereoporto alle 19.55.*
> We have to be at the airport at 7.55 p.m.

To ask the time you may say:

> *Che ora è? / Che ore sono? / Che ore fai?* < familiar >
> What time is it? What time do you make it?

In conversation there are abbreviated forms for giving the time:

> *Manca cinque (alle sette).* It's five to (seven).

> *È la mezza.* It's half past.

To give an approximate time:

> *Saranno le sette meno dieci.* It's probably ten to seven.

(b) Referring to the past

ieri	yesterday
il mese scorso	last month
il mese prossimo	next month
allora	at that time
in precedenza	previously
nel passato	in the past
tempo addietro	formerly
una volta	once

(c) Referring to the present

al momento presente	currently
finora	up to now
oggi	today
coi tempi che corrono	in this day and age
di questi giorni	these days
oggigiorno	nowadays

(d) Referring to the future

a partire da oggi	from today
d'ora in avanti	from now on
domani	tomorrow
dopodomani	the day after tomorrow
in futuro	in future
in un prossimo futuro	in the near future
l'indomani < literary >	the next day
tra pochi giorni	in a few days' time

(e) Age

sono adolescenti	they are in their teens
gli anni pesano	age weighs on him
un bambino di tre anni	a three-year-old boy
compie trent'anni	he is thirty years old
è avanti con gli anni	he is an elderly person
è un quarantenne	he is about forty / he is in his early forties
ha diciotto anni	he is eighteen years old
ha cinquantacinque anni suonati	he is well into his fifties
in tenera età	in one's earliest years
non dimostra gli anni che ha	he doesn't look his age
col passare degli anni	as years go by
una persona di mezza età	a middle-aged person
porta bene gli anni	he is young for his years
la terza età	over sixty
la quarta età	over eighty
va per gli ottanta	to be getting on for eighty

172 The weather

For common expressions about the weather conveyed with impersonal verbs (e.g. *piove* it is raining), see section 67.

(a) Expressions common in conversation

Quali sono le previsioni del tempo? What is the weather forecast?

Soffri molto il caldo? Do you suffer from the heat?

C'è stata un'ondata di caldo. There has been a heatwave.

Faceva un freddo cane stamattina. It was freezing this morning.
   (literally: a cold dog)

Tirava un vento che portava via. There was such a wind that it blew one away.

C'è un nebbione che non si vede da qui a lì. The fog is a real pea-souper.

Sembra che venga bello. It seems to be brightening up.

(b) Expressions used in weather reports

Cielo sereno o poco nuvoloso sulle regioni settentrionali.
In the north clear sky or with little cloud.

Ci saranno addensamenti nelle zone Alpine. Clouds will increase on the Alps.

In serata locali precipitazioni. There will be occasional showers.

Si annunciano foschie durante le ore diurne. It will be misty during the day.

La temperatura è in lieve aumento. The temperature is rising.

Sulle isole cielo sereno. It will be sunny on the islands.

Si prevedono brevi nevicate sulle zone appenniniche.
Light snowfalls are forecast on the Appenines.

(c) Long-term changes in the climate

La prolungata siccità provoca l'avanzata dei deserti.
Because of the prolonged drought more land is becoming desert.

Da pochi anni si parla dell'effetto serra.
There has been talk of the greenhouse effect for some years.

C'è chi teme una nuova era glaciale e chi un surriscaldamento della terra.
Some fear a new ice age, others global warming.

Il problema più immediato è quello del buco dell'ozono.
The most immediate problem is that of the ozone layer.

173 Commerce

(a) Selling points

una boutique	boutique
un centro commerciale	shopping centre
una città mercato	hypermarket / a superstore
una concessionaria import / export	import / export agent
il concessionario d'auto	car distributor
il concessionario esclusivo	sole agent
la fiera / mostra / rassegna	trade fair
un grande magazzino	department store
la macchina automatica	automatic vending machine
un mercato all'aperto	open market
un mercato coperto	covered market
un negozio	shop
un supermercato	supermarket
la vendita per corrispondenza	mail-order shopping
la vendita promozionale	promotional sale

(b) Sales and reductions

una liquidazione	clearance sale
i saldi	sales
saldi di fine stagione	end of season sales
uno sconto del 4%	4% reduction
settimana del bianco	sale of bed linen
la stagione dei saldi	sales season
una svendita	selling off / clearance sale
la vendita al dettaglio	retail sale
la vendita all'ingrosso	wholesaler
la vendita per chiusura totale	closing-down sale

(c) Methods of payment

l'assegno da viaggio (m.)	traveller's cheque
il conguaglio	settlement / balance
in contanti	cash
dare lo scontrino	to give the till receipt
emettere una fattura	to send an invoice

Non ha moneta per caso?
You don't have the right change, do you?

effettuare un versamento	to make a payment
firmare un assegno	to write a cheque
l'importo totale (m.)	total amount

pagare a rate	to pay in instalments
pagare con la carta di credito	to pay by credit card
pagare contrassegno	to pay cash on delivery
pagare fino all'ultimo centesimo	to pay to the last farthing
pagare sull'unghia	to pay cash down
la ricevuta	receipt
rimborsare	to refund
ritirare dal conto corrente	to withdraw from the current account
saldare il conto	to settle an account
scadenza	expiry date
un vaglia	money order
versare / lasciare un acconto	to pay a deposit
versare sul conto	to make a deposit

(d) Costs

gli aumenti	increases
costare circa / oltre / meno di / più di	to cost about / over / less than / more than
fissare il prezzo	to fix the price
IVA compresa / esclusa	including / excluding VAT
il prezzo si aggira sui . . .	the price is about . . .
a proposito di prezzi	still in relation to prices
le tariffe postali	postal rates
vendere sottocosto	to sell below cost

(e) Selling

la campagna promozionale	promotional sale
il campionario	sample collection / sample case
il catalogo	catalogue
le condizioni di vendita	terms of sale
il contratto di vendita	sale contract
immettere sul mercato	to come onto the market
in locazione	on hire / on lease
in vendita	for sale / on sale
mettere in vendita	to put up for sale / to offer for sale
puntare a vendere	aiming at selling
i punti di vendita	selling points
la vendita all'asta	auction sale
vendere a credito	to sell on credit
la vendita a domicilio	door-to-door selling
la vendita all'ingrosso	wholesale
la vendita al minuto	retail

174 Finance

(a) The state's role

abbassare i tassi	to lower interest rates
l'amministrazione pubblica	public administration
la bilancia commerciale	balance of trade
la burocrazia	bureaucracy
i contribuenti	taxpayers
la denuncia delle imposte	tax return
la detrazione fiscale	tax relief
evasore fiscale (m.)	tax dodger
il fisco	Inland Revenue / tax system
l'imposta fondiaria (f.)	land tax
l'imposta sul reddito (f.)	income tax
l'imposta sul valore dei beni immobili (f.)	property tax
l'inflazione (f.)	inflation
il Ministro del Tesoro	Chancellor of the Exchequer
le misure restrittive	restrictive measures
gli oneri fiscali	tax burden
il paradiso fiscale	tax haven
le partecipazioni statali	state-controlled bodies
il prelievo fiscale	deduction at source
i tagli alla spesa pubblica	cuts to public expenditure
le tasse di successione	death duties
i tributi locali	local taxes / rates
Servizio Sanitario Nazionale	National Health Service
il bilancio dello stato	government budget
il disavanzo della bilancia commerciale	balance of trade deficit
la finanza pubblica	public expenditure
il fondo pensioni	pension fund
i fondi pubblici	public funds
gli interventi statali	state intervention
una lira forte	strong lira
una manovra di politica economica	economic policy manoeuvre
una moneta stabile	stable currency
operare una stretta creditizia	to restrict government funding
la politica monetaria	monetary policy
una politica protezionistica	protectionist policy
una politica dei redditi	incomes policy
privatizzare enti statali	to privatize state-owned companies
la riduzione del disavanzo pubblico	reduction in the public deficit
il settore pubblico / privato	public / private sector
sovvenzionare un ente pubblico	to subsidize a nationalized industry
la spesa pubblica	public spending

una svalutazione del 3%	3% devaluation
il tasso di sconto	the base rate
il terziario	tertiary sector
i titoli pubblici	bonds / government stocks

(b) Salaries and income

When talking about salaries and wages Italian people refer to their monthly salary. They may also refer to *la tredicesima* (literally: the thirteenth). This is an extra month's salary which is given in December both in the public and private sector, to part-time and full-time employees. It is compulsory by law.

(i) Basic words

gli assegni familiari	family allowances
la cassa integrazione	unemployment benefits to workers temporarily laid off
impiego a tempo pieno	full-time job / post
lavorare in proprio	to be self-employed
il lavoro a ore	hourly-paid job
il lavoro part-time	part-time job
la pensione	pension
la minima < familiar >	occupational pension after 15 years' service
una pensione integrativa	occupational pension
la pensione sociale	state pension
il prepensionamento	early retirement
un premio / una gratifica	bonus
il reddito	income
il reddito fisso	fixed income
il salario	wages
la scala mobile	index-linked wage increase
lo stipendio	salary

(ii) Other factors concerning salaries

l'anzianità (f.)	length of service with employer
il blocco dei salari	freezing of wages
il contratto nazionale di lavoro	national contract
un contratto esteso a . . .	contract extended to . . .
un contratto valido fino a . . .	contract valid until . . .
i datori di lavoro	employer
la disoccupazione	unemployment
la manodopera qualificata	qualified manpower
il mercato del lavoro	labour market
il Ministero del Lavoro	Secretary of State for Employment and Social Security

un mutuo	mortgage
persi 4000 posti di lavoro	4000 jobs to go
la piena occupazione	full employment
il pubblico impiego	civil servants
la riduzione del salario	wage / salary cut
il rinnovo del contratto	renewal of the contract
lo sciopero	strike
i sindacati	trade unions
la soluzione della vertenza sindacale	solution of a labour dispute
le trattative	negotiations

(iii) Other forms of income:

le azioni	shares
le fonti di reddito	sources of income
i fondi di investimento	unit trusts
le obbligazioni	bonds / debentures
le plusvalenze	capital gain (the English word is also used in Italian)
rendite immobiliari	rent income
rendita vitalizia	life annuity
il risparmio	savings
i risparmiatori	savers

(c) The private sector

(i) The market situation

aggiudicarsi un appalto	to win a tender
l'andamento del mercato	market trend
conquistare i mercati	to conquer the markets
i consumatori	consumers
correzione di rotta del mercato	to change the market's course
la crescita / diminuzione della domanda	growth / reduction of demand
le esportazioni	exports
una fascia di mercato	market segment
un giro di affari di . . .	turnover / total sales of . . .
le importazioni	imports
il mercato dell'auto	car market
un mercato in continua evoluzione	market in constant evolution
un mercato inesplorato	unexplored market
un mercato in lenta ripresa	slow recovery of the market
l'offerta rimane bassa	the supply stays low
l'orientamento della domanda	orientation of the demand
perdere terreno	to lose ground
un recupero del mercato interno / estero	recapture of the domestic / foreign market

una ricerca di mercato	market research project
fare una ricerca di mercato	to carry out market research
il rilancio delle esportazioni	relaunching exports
ottenere un subappalto	to obtain a subcontract
strategie aziendali	business administration strategies
una tendenza che alimenta l'acquisto di . . .	trend that increases the demand for . . .

(ii) Production and management policies

adottare soluzioni	to adopt solutions
l'aumento di capitale	increase of capital
un'azienda	firm
le barriere doganali	customs and excise barriers
mantenere la competitività	to maintain one's competitiveness
misurarsi con la concorrenza internazionale	to compete internationally
la Confindustria	CBI
la congiuntura negativa	slump
il contenimento delle spese	control of expenditure
il costo del denaro	cost of money
il costo del lavoro	cost of labour
la creazione di strutture	creation of infrastructures
una crescita superiore al 20%	growth of more than 20%
i dati economici	financial data
una ditta	firm / company
una fabbrica	factory
la gestione di una ditta	company management
un gruppo industriale	industrial group
gli imprenditori	industrialists / businessmen
un'impresa	firm
gli investimenti	investments
investire a breve / lungo termine	short- / long-term investment
gli oneri sociali	welfare contributions
il quadro della finanza negli anni '90	the financial picture of the '90s
la politica degli investimenti	investment policy
la recessione	recession
il rendimento nominale / reale	nominal / real income
pianificare un take over	to plan a take-over
la pianificazione della produzione	production planning
la produzione	production
realizzare un fatturato di 100 miliardi	to realize a turnover of 100 billion
il rendimento	performance
la ripresa economica	economic recovery
le strategie industriali	industrial strategies
lo sviluppo aziendale	company development

(d) Banking and the Stock Exchange

(i) Terms related to banking include the following:

un assegno circolare	banker's draft
un assegno (sbarrato)	a (crossed) cheque
una banca	bank
un conto amministrato	administered portfolio
un conto corrente	current account
l'estratto conto (m.)	statement of account
un prelievo	withdrawal of money
il prelievo automatico	cashpoint machine
un prestito bancario	bank loan
il rendimento annuale	yearly interest
il saldo	balance (of bank account)
l'utile netto (m.)	net profit
un versamento	paying in

(ii) Shares referred to by the name of their company are feminine plural: *le (azioni) Fiat, le Pirelli*. If they are referred to in terms of their trading product, they are masculine plural: *gli assicurativi* (*i titoli assicurativi*) insurance securities, *i chimici, i bancari*.

un agente di cambio	stockbroker
le azioni	shares
le azioni quotate in Borsa	Stock Exchange listing
gli azionisti	shareholders
i piccoli azionisti	small investors
le blue chips	blue-chip stocks
la Borsa Valori	Stock Exchange
il cambio	exchange rates
le divise straniere	foreign currencies
giocare in Borsa	to buy and sell on the Stock Exchange
guadagnare	to earn
il mercato dei cambi	foreign exchange market
gli operatori di Borsa	Stock Exchange dealers
le operazioni di Borsa	Stock Exchange transactions
perdere	to lose
Piazza Affari	the Stock Exchange headquarters in Milan
Piazza Affari brilla	the stock market is buoyant
un portafoglio	portfolio
le quotazioni in chiusura	closing prices
realizzare in Borsa	to make a profit on the Stock Exchange
il rendimento dei titoli a tasso fisso	stocks with fixed return
SIM società di intermediazione immobiliare	(from 1992 it substitutes for the traditional dealer)

sono stati effettuati notevoli scambi	there has been a high volume of trading
gli tassi d'interesse delle eurodivise	interest rate of Eurocurrencies
gli titoli indicizzati	index-linked stocks
gli titoli in rialzo	rising share prices
gli titoli in ribasso	falling share prices
i valori	stocks, securities

 ## Insurance

assicurare / assicurarsi	to insure / to insure oneself
l'assicurato (m.)	the insured
l'assicurazione (f.)	insurance
un'assicurazione sulla casa	home insurance
un'assicurazione contro gli infortuni	accident insurance
una compagnia di assicurazioni	insurance company
essere assicurato contro	to be insured against
essere assicurato per	to be insured for
il premio	premium
la polizza	insurance policy
una polizza antifurto	policy against theft
una polizza antincendio	fire insurance policy
una polizza vita / sulla vita	life insurance policy
stipulare una polizza	to take out a policy

 ## Institutions

The legal profession and procedures are profoundly different in Italy and Great Britain. In some cases, therefore, there is no straightforward translation.

(a) The state

la Camera dei Deputati	lower house of parliament
il Capo dello Stato	Head of State
il consiglio comunale	town / city council
la costituzione	constitution
il Gabinetto / il Consiglio dei ministri	Cabinet
il governo	Government
un ministero	ministry
il Ministro degli Affari Esteri	Foreign Secretary

il Ministro delle Finanze	Chancellor of the Exchequer
il Ministro dell'Interno	Home Secretary
la monarchia	monarchy
Palazzo Chigi	residence of the head of the Government (used by the media to indicate the Prime Minister)
il parlamento	parliament
il prefetto	government representative in a province (county)
la prefettura	headquarters of the *prefetto*
il Presidente del consiglio / il Primo Ministro	Prime Minister
il Presidente della Repubblica	President of the Republic
il questore	Home Secretary's representative in charge of the police force in a county
la questura	residence of the *questore*
il Quirinale	official residence of the President of the Republic (used by the media to indicate the President, e.g. '*Il Quirinale conferma che...*' cf. 'Downing Street said . . .')
la Regione	regional council
la repubblica	republic
il Senato	upper house of parliament
un senatore / un deputato	Member of Parliament
il servizio militare / la naia < coll. >	military service
il sindaco	mayor
il sistema costituzionale	constitutional system
uno stato totalitario	totalitarian state

(b) Elections

andare alle urne	to go to the polls
la base	grassroots militants
la campagna elettorale	election campaign
un candidato	a candidate
una circoscrizione elettorale	a constituency
la coalizione	coalition
la destra	the right
eleggere	to elect
gli elettori	voters
le elezioni	general election
le elezioni europee	elections for the European Parliament
essere di destra	to be right wing
essere di sinistra	to be left wing

formare il governo	to form a government
indire le elezioni	to call an election
gli iscritti	party members
le liste elettorali	lists of candidates
la maggioranza	majority
i militanti	militants
l'opposizione	opposition
l'opposizione ombra	shadow cabinet
un partito politico	political party
il programma elettorale	election programme
la propaganda elettorale	electioneering
raccogliere le firme per il referendum	to collect the signatures for the referendum
il referendum	referendum
le riforme	reforms
i risultati elettorali	poll results
la scheda elettorale	ballot paper
il segretario del partito	party secretary
la sinistra	the left
il sistema proporzionale	proportional representation
un sondaggio	opinion poll
le urne	ballot-boxes
votare	to vote

(c) The law and legal matters

(i) Government

adottare un progetto / una proposta di legge	to vote a bill through
approvare un progetto di legge	to vote a bill through
una commissione parlamentare	a parliamentary committee
discutere una legge in commissione	to debate a bill
legge passata a maggioranza / all'unanimità	the bill has passed by a majority / unanimously
la legge respinta	rejected bill
presentare una legge	to introduce a bill
respingere una legge	to reject a bill
votare a favore / contro una legge	to vote in favour of / against a bill

(ii) The legal system

accusare qualcuno di	to charge someone with
archiviare l'indagine	to leave a case open
assolvere l'imputato	to acquit a defendant
avviso di garanzia	caution
l'avvocato difensore	defending solicitor / barrister

l'avvocato di parte civile	counsel for the prosecution
il banco degli imputati	dock
un caso non risolto	case which has not been solved
comparire davanti ai giudici	to appear in court
Corte d'Appello	Criminal Court of Appeal / Divisional Court
Corte d'Assise	Assize Court (i.e. Crown Court)
Corte di Cassazione	Court of Appeal (court which quashes sentences)
condannare a sette anni	to sentence to seven years' imprisonment
dichiarare colpevole	to find guilty
emettere un verdetto	to return a verdict
un giurista	lawyer
la giustizia civile e penale	civil and criminal law
il gp / giudice istruttore	magistrate in charge of investigations
le indagini	investigations
interrogare	to examine / to cross examine
la magistratura	the Bench / the Court
il non luogo a procedere	verdict of non-proven
il palazzo di giustizia	the law courts
il pretore	lower court judge
il procuratore (della repubblica)	public attorney / prosecutor
rimangono degli interrogativi inquietanti	disquieting questions remain
una vertenza giudiziaria	judicial controversy

(iii) Crime

aggredire / assalire	to mug
un'aggressione armata	armed robbery
un attentato	political assassination attempt
un bandito	(armed) robber
un caso di corruzione	case of corruption
chiedere un riscatto	to ask for a ransom
il contrabbando	contraband
una contravvenzione / multa	fine
un criminale	criminal
un crimine	crime
un delitto	murder
un detenuto	prisoner
dirottare un aereo	to hijack a plane
un dirottatore / pirata dell'aria	hijacker
un'infrazione al codice della strada	infringement of the highway code
per legge	by law
la polizia	police

il racket del vizio	vice racket
un raid	raid
rapire	to kidnap
i rapitori	kidnappers
la sofisticazione alimentare	food contamination
il traffico di stupefacenti	drug trafficking

The three anti-crime institutions are:

I carabinieri   La polizia   La Guardia di Finanza

I carabinieri come under the Ministry of Defence, *la polizia* under the Home Office and *la Guardia di Finanza* the Exchequer. Their responsibilities vary according to the ministries they report to, although they are intertwined.

77 Computers

The language of computer technology is rich with words imported from English, although it is curious that the word itself comes from the Latin *computare* (to count). In the following glossary, when the Italian word is used just as frequently as the English word, both terms are given.

le applicazioni del PC	PC functions
una banca dati	a data bank
binario	binary
i bit	bit
i byte / i megabyte	byte / megabyte
CAD	CAD
una cartuccia	cartridge
un chip	chip
circuito	circuit
compatibile	compatible
la computerizzazione	computerization
conservare un file	to save a file
una copia pirata	a pirate copy
il cursore	cursor
desktop publishing	desktop publishing
digitale	digital
il dischetto / un floppy	floppy disk
il disco rigido / hard disk	hard disk
l'elaborazione testi (f.)	text processing
un file	file
formattare	to format
la gestione dati	data

un gioco elettronico	a computer game
la grafica	graphics
l'hardware (m.)	hardware
l'informatica	computer science
inserire	to insert
il joystick / la leva di comando	joystick
un laptop	laptop
LCD	LCD
un linguaggio di programmazione	a program language
la mailbox	mailbox
un main frame	main frame
il manuale	manual
la memoria	memory
memorizzare	to store
il menù	menu
modificare	to modify
MODEM	MODEM
il monitor	monitor
MS-DOS	MS-DOS
il mouse	mouse
i pacchetti software integrati	integrated software packages
un personal	personal computer
il plotter	plotter
un portatile	portable computer
un programma	program
un programma di gestione dati	spreadsheet program
un programma per la contabilità	budget management program
programmare	to program
un programmatore	programmer
richiamare dei dati	to recall data
ROM	ROM
lo schermo	screen
il sistema operativo	operating system
lo scanner	scanner
lo shareware	shareware
il software	software
la stampante	printer
la stampante laser	laser printer
la stampante a margherita	daisy wheel
la tastiera	keyboard
il terminale	terminal
versatile	versatile
la video scrittura / il word processor	word processor
il video	video

78 Cars

(a) Describing a car

Common adjectives describing cars are:

dolce	pleasant
equipaggiata con . . .	equipped with . . .
esclusiva	a model
ineguagliabile	matchless
morbida	soft
potente	powerful
raffinata	refined
sobria	serious

and these adjectives are often linked up with nouns like:

il confort	comfort
l'eleganza (f.)	elegance
la linea sportiva	sports style
il piacere di guida	driving sensation
la potenza	power
la prestazione elevata	high performance
la qualità	quality
la sicurezza	safety

and verbs such as:

esporre alla mostra	to show at the exhibition / exhibit
guidare	to drive
immettere sul mercato	to launch on the market
presentare il nuovo modello	to present the new model
provare	to try

(b) Parts of the vehicle

gli alzacristalli	electric windows
a quattro posti	with four seats
aria condizionata	air-conditioning
la carrozzeria	car body / bodyshell / bodywork
la chiusura centralizzata	central locking
le cinture di sicurezza	safety-belts
un'auto di grossa cilindrata	high-performance vehicle
i cristalli atermici	heated windows
il costo su strada	on-the-road price
il cruscotto	dashboard
decappotabile	convertible
una fuoristrada	off-road vehicle
l'insonorizzazione (f.)	soundproofing

l'interno (m.)	interior
il lavacristalli	windscreen washer
il lunotto	rear window
la marmitta catalitica	catalytic converter
il motore a diesel	diesel engine
il motore verde	environmentally friendly engine
il portabagagli	roof rack
il portellone	boot door
i proiettori	headlights
il sedile anteriore / posteriore	front / back seat
il serbatoio	petrol tank
il servosterzo	quiet engine
le tendine parasole	blinds
la tenuta di strada	road-holding
la trazione anteriore	front-wheel drive
la velocità	speed
un veicolo commerciale	commercial vehicle
il volante in pelle	leather steering wheel

179 Sport

accedere alla finale	to reach the final
allenarsi	to train
l'allenatore (m.) / il coach	trainer
un / un'atleta	athlete
l'atletica (f.)	athletics
l'automobilismo (m.)	motor-racing
la barca a vela	sailboat
il bob	bobsleigh
il campione del mondo	world champion
il campionato (e.g. di tennis)	(tennis) cup / championship
un campo di calcio	football field
un campo da tennis	tennis court
un campo da golf	golf course
una classe di ginnastica	keep-fit class
il centometrista	hundred-metre runner
il ciclismo	cycling
la corsa a ostacoli	obstacle-race
il discesista	downhill skier
disputare una gara	to take part in a race / competition
il doping	drug-taking
il doppio	a double
un / un'escursionista	excursionist
essere in testa / in vantaggio	to be in front

la finale maschile / femminile	the men's / women's final
la formazione	formation / team
una gara	race / competition
i giochi olimpici	Olympic Games
un game (tennis)	game (tennis)
un incontro di pugilato /	boxing match
un match di boxe	
il lancio del giavellotto	javelin throwing
la medaglia d'oro / argento	gold / silver medal
navigatore	navigator
un open di tennis	open tournament
un ostacolista	obstacle-race runner
una partita	match
un peso massimo	a heavy weight
il pesista	weight lifter
la pista	ski-run
il pattinaggio artistico	figure-skating
il pattinaggio su ghiaccio	ice-skating
la prestazione	performance
qualificarsi	to qualify
la qualificazione	qualification
il quattrocentista	four-hundred-metre runner
la regata	regatta; sailing race
regatare	to compete in a sailing race
rimontare	to work one's way up / to catch up
il / la rivale	rival
il salto con l'asta	pole-jump / pole-vault
lo sci d'acqua	water-ski
lo sci di fondo	cross-country skiing
la semifinale	semifinal
il servizio (tennis)	service
il set (tennis)	set
lo skipper	skipper
il singolare di tennis	singles
lo slalom / slalom gigante	slalom / giant slalom
il sollevamento pesi	weightlifting
la squadra rivale	the opposing team / the opposition
la staffetta	relay race
il tie-break	tie-break
tifoso	fan
il torneo	tournament
vincere	to win
la volata finale	final sprint

Mass media

l'alta definizione	high definition
l'anteprima (f.)	preview
l'articolista (m.)	columnist
un collegamento televisivo con	hook-up
condurre una trasmissione	to present a programme
un conduttore televisivo	anchorman
un corrispondente	correspondent
un dibattito	debate
la diretta / in diretta	live broadcast
una differita / in differita	pre-recorded programme
esteri (newspaper page)	foreign news
fare l'abbonamento a	to take out a subscription to
un filmato	TV film
un fotoreporter	press photographer
il giornale	newspaper
i giornalisti	journalists / newsmen
l'immagine (f.)	image
l'inchiesta (f.)	coverage
l'indice di ascolto (m.)	the audience rating
un'intervista	interview
un inviato speciale	special correspondent
interni (newspaper page)	home news
mandare in onda	to broadcast
i mezzi di comunicazione di massa /	mass media
i mass media	
un mezzobusto < coll. >	newscaster
la moviola	replay (in slow motion)
notizie sportive	sports news
un opinionista	opinion maker
in programma	to be on
il pubblico	audience
il quotidiano	daily
una recensione	review
un recital	recital
la redazione	editorial office
un reporter	reporter
una rete televisiva	TV network
il rotocalco	tabloid
uno sceneggiato	screenplay
uno scrittore ombra	ghost-writer
il settimanale	weekly
la stampa	press
uno studio televisivo	TV studio
una testata	newspaper

trasmettere uno sceneggiato a puntate	to serialize a programme on TV
una valletta	showgirl
una videocassetta	video cassette

181 Cinema

(i) Key nouns, verbs and phrases

i cartoni animati	cartoons
il cast	cast
è in cartellone da due mesi	it has been running for two months
il cinema d'arte	experimental films
un cineasta	film enthusiast
la colonna sonora	soundtrack
un colossal	epic
un cortometraggio	short documentary film
la distribuzione	distribution
il doppiaggio	dubbing
un festival cinematografico	film festival
film in versione originale	not dubbed, original language version
la fotografia	camera work
girare un film	to shoot a film
inquadrare	to frame
interpretare	to interpret
l'interpretazione (f.)	interpretation
l'industria cinematografica (f.)	film industry
gli interpreti	interpreters
il mixaggio	sound editing
il montaggio	editing
produrre un film	to produce a film
il produttore	producer
recitare	to play
la recitazione	playing
la regia	direction
il regista	director
una retrospettiva cinematografica	film retrospective
un ruolo	role
le sequenze	sequences
il set	filmset
la sceneggiatura	screenplay
la scenografia	setting
il sottofondo musicale	background music

(ii) Adjectives describing films:

amaro	bitter
crudo	harsh
divertente	amusing
drammatico	dramatic
elaborato	elaborate
sensazionale	sensational
passionale	passionate
sensuale	sensual
stilizzato	stylized

 Fashion

The language of fashion is constantly updated with new words, a revival of classical ones, both adjectives and verbs used to create a sense of glamour and to stimulate interest. This section gives examples of the names of some of the most recent and up-to-date items of clothing which have now become part of today's life, and a sample of some of the sentences likely to be found in journals and magazines.

(a) Items of clothing

l'abbigliamento	clothing
l'abbigliamento per bambini (m.)	children's wear
l'abbigliamento intimo (m.)	underwear
l'abbigliamento in pelle (m.)	leatherwear
l'abbigliamento sportivo (m.)	sportswear
gli accessori	accessories
aderente / aderentissimo	tight / tight-fitting
gli anfibi	Doc Marten's
le bermuda	bermudas
il bikini	bikini
il blazer	blazer
il body	leotard
la calzamaglia	thick / opaque tights
la camiceria	assortment of shirts
la canotta (*la canottiera* is out)	vest
i coordinati	matching outfits / a two-piece / coordinates
una dolce vita	polo-neck sweater
la firma / la griffe	designer label

la felpa	sweatshirt
i fuseaux	leggings
il giaccone	heavy coat above knees
il giaccone trapuntato	quilted coat
le grandi case di moda	fashion houses
il jersey	jersey
il look	look
la maglieria	knitwear / hosiery
la minigonna / la microgonna	miniskirt / microskirt
la moda pronta / il prêt-à-porter	off-the-peg clothes
il montgomery	dufflecoat (It takes its name from General Montgomery who wore one during the Second World War.)
il pantalone a staffa	skipants
la polo	polo shirt
profilato in pelliccia	fur trimming
il pull	pullover
pura lana vergine	100% pure wool
le scarpe da ginnastica	trainers
lo scozzese classico	classic tartan
gli shorts	shorts
la sfilata	fashion show
lo swatch	swatch watch
gli stilisti / i grandi sarti	fashion designers
il tailleur	a lady's suit / costume
il tessuto stretch	stretch fabric
la T shirt	T-shirt
topless	topless
la top model	top model
la tuta	tracksuit
unisex	unisex
lo zainetto	rucksack for girls

(b) Key phrases

The implied subject is occasionally 'that fashion designer'.

la geometria raffinata e i quadri scozzesi	elegant geometric designs and tartan checks
le grandi novità della stagione	the season's latest innovations
Conferma il suo stile versatile.	He confirms his versatile style.
Esalta l'alta qualità.	He enhances top quality.
È evidente il filone innovatore.	The innovatory trend is evident.
Gioca sui tessuti fluorescenti.	He creates effects with fluorescent fabrics.
Lancia i colori accesi.	He is launching brilliant colours.

La moda capta tendenze e propone le novità.	Fashion captures the trends and proposes the changes.
Da notare l'ottima confezione.	Notice the excellent tailoring.
Porta una sfrenata fantasia.	He has let his imagination run wild.
Preferisce il taglio rigoroso.	He prefers a strict, traditional cut.
Presenta una creatività esasperata.	He presents a heightened creativity.
Le proposte sono proiettate verso il futuro.	The proposals are aimed towards the future.
Privilegia i dettagli ricercati.	He gives merit to refined details.
Propone l'eleganza inappuntabile.	He suggests impeccable elegance.
Punta sui tessuti pregiati.	He has a tendency to use expensive fabric.
Ritorna il taglio morbido.	The loose-fitting style returns.
Sfilano le collezioni primavera-estate.	The Spring-Summer collections are presented.
Sfondano le mini audaci.	Daring minis are all the rage.
Sono di gran moda i verdi intensi.	Deepest shades of green are the latest fashion.
Stupisce per le scollature profonde.	He amazes people with plunging necklines.
Trionfano i gialli decisi.	Brilliant yellows prevail.

183 Interior design

Italian houses have changed a great deal in the last few decades. Italian interior design and furniture have become famous all over the world. New words have appeared to describe these changes. Here are some of the most important:

(i) Key nouns

l'angolo studio (m.)	study area
l'armadio ad ante scorrevoli (m.)	wardrobe with sliding doors
l'architetto (m.)	architect / designer
l'architettura per giardini (m.)	landscape gardening
l'arredamento (m.)	interior design
l'arredamento di classe (m.)	exclusive furnishing
l'attico (m.)	penthouse
un bilocale	two-roomed apartment
una bifamiliare	semi-detached house
il cancello elettrico	remote-controlled gate
il citofono	intercom
il condominio	apartment building / block of apartments

il divano letto	sofa bed
il legno laccato	varnished wood
la mansarda	attic room
i materiali	materials
un monolocale	a studio flat / apartment
le lampade alogene	halogen lamp
le lampade a stelo	standard lamp
il locale disimpegno	boxroom
un negozio ristrutturato	renovated shop
il piano cottura	kitchen work surface
le piastrelle firmate	exclusive floor tiles
la poltrona letto	sofa bed
la sedia pieghevole	folding chair
il soggiorno-pranzo	living-room
la taverna	games room / family room
le tendenze casa	trends for home furnishing
le tendenze colore	trendy colours
la zona pranzo / ufficio	dining / work area
la zona giorno / notte	living / sleeping area
villette a schiera	modern terraced homes

(ii) Some phrases describing a house and its interior design:

l'aspetto gioioso e vivace della stanza	a room's bright and cheerful look
un arredo studiato su misura	custom-made furniture
il bagno elegante nel design	the elegantly designed bath
la cucina di grande attualità	the very latest kitchen
idee innovative per ampliare un locale	fresh ideas to enlarge a room
sul fondo spiccano colori vivaci la poltrona firmata dal famoso architetto	brilliant colours show up against the background
il progetto ricercato nei dettagli	an elaborately detailed plan
raffinate soluzioni per ricavare un vano	stylish solutions to create a new room
la ricercata risoluzione dei problemi logistici	solutions to logistical problems
la sala accessoriata in prestigiosa pelle	a room with finishing touches in luxurious leather
le tende sono pennellate di colori	the curtains with splashes of colours
le ultime novità per arredare lo studio	the very latest in furnishing a study

Literature

(a) Writers

For writers in the mass media, see section 180. For the gender of words ending in *-ore* see section 2.

un autore / un'autrice	author
un biografo	biographer
un correttore di copie	proofreader
un critico	critic
un drammaturgo	playwright
un lettore / una lettrice	reader
un poeta / una poetessa	poet
un redattore / una redattrice	editor
un romanziere	novelist (for serious novelists the word *scrittore di romanzi* is preferred)
un saggista	essayist
uno scrittore / una scrittrice	writer
comporre	to compose
creare	to create
delineare	to outline
dipingere	to paint / depict
disegnare	to draw
evocare	to evoke
redigere (e.g. articolo, resoconto)	to write up
scrivere	to write
stendere (e.g. la brutta copia)	to make a rough draft
tratteggiare	to sketch

(b) Prose

un articolo in terza pagina	an article in the prestigious literary page of a daily newspaper
un'autobiografia	autobiography
una biografia	biography
un capolavoro	masterpiece
una composizione	composition
una fiaba	fable / fairy tale
una favola	fairy tale
i fumetti	cartoons
la letteratura	literature / narrative
un libro in edizione economica	paperback
la narrativa	literature / fiction
una novella	short story
un'opera	literary work (prose, theatre, poem)

un pamphlet	pamphlet
la prosa	prose
una raccolta (e.g. di racconti)	collection (e.g. of short stories)
un racconto	contemporary short story
una recensione	critical review
un romanzo	novel
un romanzo d'evasione	escapist novel
un romanzo poliziesco	detective story
un romanzo rosa	romantic novel
un saggio	essay

(c) Theatre

un allestimento teatrale	theatre production
un atto	act
un atto unico	one-act play
una commedia	comedy
i dialoghi	dialogues
un dramma	dramatic play
la commedia dell'arte	commedia dell'arte
l'intervallo (m.)	interval
un monologo	monologue
un musical	musical
un'opera lirica	opera
un'opera (di teatro)	play
la parte	role
una pastorale	pastoral play
i personaggi	characters
uno spettacolo	performance, play
gli spettatori	the public
il teatro	the theatre / the drama
una tragedia	tragedy
la trama	plot
i costumi	costumes
le luci	footlights
il palcoscenico	stage
il suggeritore	prompter
interpretare un ruolo	to play a role
mettere in scena	to produce
recitare	to play

(d) Poetry

l'allitterazione (f.)	alliteration
una ballata	ballad
una figura poetica	poetic figure
la lirica	lyric poetry / lyrical poem

l'onomatopoeia (f.)	onomatopoeia
un poema epico	epic poem
una poesia	short poem
la rima	rhyme
il ritmo	rhythm
la strofa	strophe
un verso	a line of poetry

(e) Other elements

l'atmosfera (f.)	atmosphere
l'argomento (m.)	topic
l'azione (f.)	action
la caratterizzazione	characterization
la critica letteraria	literary criticism
l'espressione (f.)	expression
un eufemismo	euphemism
una figura retorica	rhetorical figure
la forma	form
la funzione	function
i generi letterari	literary genres
l'imitazione (f.)	imitation
le immagini	imagery
l'iperbole (f.)	hyperbole
la lettura	reading
il linguaggio	language
una metafora	metaphor
i piani della narrativa	levels of the narrative
il protagonista	protagonist
la pubblicistica	literature (brochures, leaflets)
la retorica	rhetoric
la semiotica	semiotics
un simbolo	symbol
la similitudine	simile
il soggetto	topic
lo stile	style
la stilistica	stylistics
la struttura dell'opera	the work's structure
la struttura letteraria	literary structure
lo strutturalismo	structuralism
il tema	theme
la tematica	main theme
la tradizione letteraria	literary tradition
un tratto distintivo	distinctive trait
il valore espressivo	expressive force

Appendix 1
Common irregular verbs

The section below summarizes the conjugation of the most frequent irregular verbs. Only the irregular forms are listed and these should be used as the basis for forming the entire tense. For an explanation on how to form the various tenses see sections 45–61; for the reflexive verbs see section 37.

andare to go

PRESENT INDICATIVE
io vado I go
tu vai you go
lui va he goes

noi andiamo we go
voi andate you go
loro vanno they go

FUTURE INDICATIVE
io andrò I shall go (etc.)

CONDITIONAL
io andrei I would go (etc.)

PERFECT INDICATIVE
io sono andato I went / I have been (etc.)

PRESENT SUBJUNCTIVE
io / tu / lui vada I / you / he may go
noi andiamo we may go

voi andiate you may go
loro vadano they may go (etc.)

IMPERATIVE
va / va' / vai! go!

andiamo! let's go!
andate! go!

apparire to appear

PRESENT INDICATIVE
io appaio I appear
tu appari you appear
lui appare he appears

noi appariamo we appear
voi apparite you appear
loro appaiono they appear

FUTURE INDICATIVE
io apparirò I shall appear (etc.)

CONDITIONAL
io apparirei I should appear (etc.)

PAST HISTORIC
io apparvi I appeared
tu apparisti you appeared (etc.)

PRESENT SUBJUNCTIVE
io appaia I may appear

PERFECT INDICATIVE
io sono apparso I appeared / have appeared

bere to drink

PRESENT INDICATIVE

io bevo I drink
tu bevi you drink
lui beve he drinks

noi beviamo we drink
voi bevete you drink
loro bevono they drink

FUTURE INDICATIVE
io berrò I shall drink (etc.)

CONDITIONAL
io berrei I would drink (etc.)

PAST HISTORIC
io bevvi I drank
tu bevesti you drank (etc.)

PERFECT INDICATIVE
io ho bevuto I drank / have drunk

PRESENT SUBJUNCTIVE

io beva I may drink
tu beva you may drink
lui beva he may drink

noi beviamo we may drink
voi beviate you may drink
loro bevano they may drink

IMPERATIVE
bevi! drink ! (etc.)

cadere to fall

FUTURE INDICATIVE
io cadrò I shall fall (etc.)

CONDITIONAL
io cadrei I would fall (etc.)

PAST HISTORIC
io caddi I fell
tu cadesti you fell (etc.)

PERFECT INDICATIVE
io sono caduto I have fallen

chiedere to ask

PAST HISTORIC
io chiesi I asked
tu chiedesti you asked (etc.)

PERFECT INDICATIVE
io ho chiesto I have asked

chiudere to close

PAST HISTORIC
io chiusi I closed
tu chiudesti you closed (etc.)

PERFECT INDICATIVE
io ho chiuso I closed / have closed

correre to run

PAST HISTORIC
io corsi I ran
tu corresti you ran (etc.)

PERFECT INDICATIVE
io ho corso / sono corso I ran / have run (see section 61)

crescere to grow up

PAST HISTORIC
io crebbi I grew up
tu crescesti you grew up (etc.)

PERFECT INDICATIVE
io ho cresciuto / sono cresciuto I
   have grown up (see section 61)

dare to give

PRESENT INDICATIVE
io do / dò I give
tu dai you give
lui dà he gives

noi diamo we give
voi date you give
loro danno they give

FUTURE INDICATIVE
io darò I shall give (etc.)

PRESENT SUBJUNCTIVE
io dia I may give (etc.)

CONDITIONAL
io darei I would give (etc.)

IMPERFECT SUBJUNCTIVE
io dessi I might give (etc.)

PAST HISTORIC
io diedi I gave
tu desti you gave (etc.)

IMPERATIVE
da / dai / da'! give!
diamo! let's give!
date! give!

PERFECT INDICATIVE
io ho dato I gave / have given

decidere to decide

PAST HISTORIC
io decisi I decided
tu decidesti you decided (etc.)

PERFECT INDICATIVE
io ho deciso I decided / have decided

difendere to defend

PAST HISTORIC
io difesi I defended
tu difendesti you defended (etc.)

PERFECT INDICATIVE
io ho difeso I defended / have
   defended

dipingere to paint

PAST HISTORIC
io dipinsi I painted
tu dipingesti you painted (etc.)

PERFECT INDICATIVE
io ho dipinto I have painted

dire to say / to tell

PRESENT INDICATIVE
io dico I say
tu dici to say
lui dice he says

noi diciamo we say
voi dite you say
loro dicono they say

FUTURE INDICATIVE
io dirò I shall say (etc.)

CONDITIONAL
io direi I would say (etc.)

PERFECT INDICATIVE
io ho detto I said / have said

PRESENT SUBJUNCTIVE
io dica I may say	*noi diciamo* we may say
tu dica you may say	*voi diciate* you may say
lui dica he may say	*loro dicano* they may say

IMPERATIVE
di' / dì! say!	*diciamo!* let's say!
	dite! say!

PAST HISTORIC
io dissi I said
tu dicesti you said (etc.)

dirigere to direct

PAST HISTORIC
io diressi I directed
tu dirigesti you directed (etc.)

PERFECT INDICATIVE
io ho diretto I directed / have directed

discutere to discuss

PAST HISTORIC
io discussi I discussed
tu discutesti you discussed (etc.)

PERFECT INDICATIVE
io ho discusso I discussed / have discussed

dividere to divide

PAST HISTORIC
io divisi I divided
tu dividesti you divided (etc.)

PERFECT INDICATIVE
io ho diviso I divided / have divided

dovere to have to / must / owe (see section 59)

PRESENT INDICATIVE
io devo / debbo I have to	*noi dobbiamo* we have to
tu devi you have to	*voi dovete* you have to
lui deve he has to	*loro devono / debbono* they have to

FUTURE INDICATIVE
io dovrò I shall have to (etc.)

CONDITIONAL
io dovrei I would have to (etc.)

PRESENT SUBJUNCTIVE
io debba I may have to	*noi dobbiamo* we may have to
tu debba you may have to	*voi dobbiate* you may have to
lui debba he may have to	*loro debbano* they may have to

esistere to exist

PERFECT INDICATIVE
lui è esistito he existed / has existed

fare to do / make

PRESENT INDICATIVE
io faccio I do
tu fai you do
lui fa he does

noi facciamo we do
voi fate you do
loro fanno they do

FUTURE INDICATIVE
io farò I shall do (etc.)

PRESENT SUBJUNCTIVE
io faccia I may do (etc.)

CONDITIONAL
io farei I would do (etc.)

IMPERFECT SUBJUNCTIVE
io facessi I might do (etc.)

PAST HISTORIC
io feci I did
tu facesti you did (etc.)

IMPERATIVE
fa / fa' / fai! do!
facciamo! let's do!
fate! do!

PERFECT INDICATIVE
io ho fatto I did / have done

fingere to pretend

PAST HISTORIC
io finsi I pretended
tu fingesti you pretended (etc.)

PERFECT INDICATIVE
io ho finto I pretended / have
    pretended

leggere to read

PAST HISTORIC
io lessi I read
tu leggesti you read (etc.)

PERFECT INDICATIVE
io ho letto I read / have read

mettere to put

PAST HISTORIC
io misi I put
tu mettesti you put (etc.)

PERFECT INDICATIVE
io ho messo I put / have put

morire to die

PRESENT INDICATIVE
io muoio I die
tu muori you die
lui muore he dies

noi moriamo we died
voi morite you die
loro muoiono they die

FUTURE INDICATIVE
io morrò (morirò regular) I shall
  die (etc.)

CONDITIONAL
io morrei (morirei regular) I would
  die

PAST HISTORIC
io morii I died
tu moristi you died (etc.)

PERFECT INDICATIVE
io sono morto I died / have died

PRESENT SUBJUNCTIVE
io muoia I may die (etc.)

muovere to move

PAST HISTORIC
io mossi I moved
tu muovesti you moved (etc.)

PERFECT INDICATIVE
io ho mosso I moved / have moved

nascere to be born

PAST HISTORIC
io nacqui I was born

PERFECT INDICATIVE
io sono nato I was born / have
  been born

offrire to offer

PAST HISTORIC
io offersi (offrii regular) I offered
tu offristi you offered (etc.)

PERFECT INDICATIVE
io ho offerto I offered / have
  offered

perdere to lose

PAST HISTORIC
io persi I lost
tu perdesti you lost (etc.)

PERFECT INDICATIVE
io ho perso (perduto regular)
  I lost / have lost

potere to be able / can (see section 59)

PRESENT INDICATIVE
io posso I can
tu puoi you can
lui può he can

noi possiamo we can
voi potete you can
loro possono they can

FUTURE INDICATIVE
io potrò I shall be able (etc.)

CONDITIONAL
io potrei I would be able / could
  (etc.)

PRESENT SUBJUNCTIVE
io / tu / lui possa I / you / he can
  (etc.)

prendere to take

PAST HISTORIC
io presi I took
tu prendesti you took

PERFECT INDICATIVE
io ho preso I took / have taken

rendere to give back

PAST HISTORIC
io resi I gave back
tu rendesti you gave back (etc.)

PERFECT INDICATIVE
io ho reso I gave back / have given
back

ridere to laugh

PAST HISTORIC
io risi I laughed
tu ridesti you laughed (etc.)

PERFECT INDICATIVE
io ho riso I laughed / have laughed

rimanere to remain

PRESENT INDICATIVE
io rimango I remain
tu rimani you remain
lui rimane he remains

noi rimaniamo we remain
voi rimanete you remain
loro rimangono they remain

FUTURE INDICATIVE
io rimarrò I shall remain (etc.)

CONDITIONAL
io rimarrei I would remain (etc.)

PAST HISTORIC
io rimasi I remained
tu rimanesti you remained (etc.)

PERFECT INDICATIVE
io sono rimasto I remained /
have remained

PRESENT SUBJUNCTIVE
io rimanga I may remain
tu rimanga you may remain
lui rimanga he may remain

noi rimaniamo we may remain
voi rimaniate you may remain
loro rimangano they may remain

rompere to break

PAST HISTORIC
io ruppi I broke
tu rompesti you broke (etc.)

PERFECT INDICATIVE
io ho rotto I broke / have broken

salire to go up / climb

PRESENT INDICATIVE
io salgo I go up
tu sali you go up
lui sale he goes up

noi saliamo we go up
voi salite you go up
loro salgono they go up

PRESENT SUBJUNCTIVE
io salga I may go up

noi saliamo we may go up
tu salga you may go up

voi saliate you may go up
lui salga he may go up

loro salgano they may go up

IMPERATIVE
sali! go up!

saliamo! let's go up!
salite! go up!

sapere to know

PRESENT INDICATIVE
io so I know

noi sappiamo we know
tu sai you know

voi sapete you know
lui sa he knows

loro sanno they know

FUTURE INDICATIVE
io saprò I shall know (etc.)

PERFECT INDICATIVE
io ho saputo I knew / have known

CONDITIONAL
io saprei I would know (etc.)

PRESENT SUBJUNCTIVE
io sappia I may know (etc.)

PAST HISTORIC
io seppi I knew
tu sapesti you knew (etc.)

IMPERATIVE
sappi che . . . know / be aware that . . .
sappiate! know / be aware!

scegliere to choose

PRESENT INDICATIVE
io scelgo I choose

noi scegliamo we choose
tu scegli you choose

voi scegliete you choose
lui sceglie he chooses

loro scelgono they choose

PAST HISTORIC
io scelsi I chose
tu scegliesti you chose (etc.)

PERFECT INDICATIVE
io ho scelto I chose / have chosen

PRESENT SUBJUNCTIVE
io scelga I may choose

noi scegliamo we may choose
tu scelga you may choose

voi scegliate you may choose
lui scelga he may choose

loro scelgano they may choose

scendere to come down

PAST HISTORIC
io scesi I came down
tu scendesti you came down (etc.)

scrivere to write

PAST HISTORIC
io scrissi I wrote
tu scrivesti you wrote (etc.)

PERFECT INDICATIVE
io ho scritto I wrote / I have written

sedersi to sit down

PRESENT INDICATIVE
io mi siedo I sit down
tu ti siedi you sit down
lui si siede he sits down

noi ci sediamo we sit down
voi vi sedete you sit down
loro si siedono they sit down

PRESENT SUBJUNCTIVE
io mi sieda I may sit down (etc.)

IMPERATIVE
siediti! sit down!
sediamoci! let's sit down!
sedetevi! sit down!

stare to stay

PRESENT INDICATIVE
io sto I stay
tu stai you stay
lui sta he stays

noi stiamo we stay
voi state you stay
loro stanno they stay

FUTURE INDICATIVE
io starò I shall stay (etc.)

CONDITIONAL
io starei I would stay (etc.)

PAST HISTORIC
io stetti I stayed
tu stesti you stayed (etc.)

IMPERFECT SUBJUNCTIVE
io stessi (etc) I might stay

PERFECT INDICATIVE
io sono stato I stayed / have stayed

IMPERATIVE
sta / sta' / stai! stay!
stiamo! let's stay!
state! stay!

PRESENT SUBJUNCTIVE
io stia (etc.) I may stay

tenere to hold

PRESENT INDICATIVE
io tengo I hold
tu tieni you hold
lui tiene he holds

noi teniamo we hold
voi tenete you hold
loro tengono they hold

FUTURE INDICATIVE
io terrò I shall hold (etc.)

PERFECT INDICATIVE
io ho tenuto I held / have held

CONDITIONAL
io terrei I would hold (etc.)

IMPERATIVE
tieni! hold!
teniamo! let's hold!
tenete! hold!

PAST HISTORIC
io tenni I held
tu tenesti you held (etc.)

PRESENT SUBJUNCTIVE
io / tu / lui tenga I / you / he may hold   *noi teniamo* we may hold
voi tenete you hold   *loro tengono* they may hold

togliere to remove

PRESENT INDICATIVE
io tolgo I remove   *noi togliamo* we remove
tu togli you remove   *voi togliete* you remove
lui toglie he removes   *loro tolgono* they remove

PAST HISTORIC
io tolsi I removed   IMPERATIVE
tu togliesti you removed (etc.)   *togli!* remove!
          togliamo! let's remove!
PERFECT INDICATIVE   *togliete!* remove!
io ho tolto I removed / have
  removed

PRESENT SUBJUNCTIVE
io tolga I may remove   *noi togliamo* we may remove
tu tolga you may remove   *voi togliate* you may remove
lui tolga he may remove   *loro tolgano* they may remove

uscire to go out

PRESENT INDICATIVE
io esco I go out   *noi usciamo* we go out
tu esci you go out   *voi uscite* you go out
lui esce he goes out   *loro escono* they go out

PAST HISTORIC   PERFECT INDICATIVE
io uscii I went out   *io sono uscito* I went out / have
tu uscisti you went out (etc.)   gone out

PRESENT SUBJUNCTIVE
io esca I may go out   *noi usciamo* we may go out
tu esca you may go out   *voi usciate* you may go out
lui esca he may go out   *loro escono* they may go out

IMPERATIVE
esci! go out!

vedere to see

FUTURE INDICATIVE   PAST HISTORIC
io vedrò I shall see (etc.)   *io vidi* I saw
          tu vedesti you saw (etc.)

CONDITIONAL
io vedrei I would see (etc.)

PERFECT INDICATIVE
io ho visto I saw / have seen

venire to come

PRESENT INDICATIVE
io vengo I come
tu vieni you come
lui viene he comes

noi veniamo we come
voi venite you come
loro vengono they come

FUTURE INDICATIVE
io verrò I shall come (etc.)

CONDITIONAL
io verrei I would come (etc.)

PAST HISTORIC
io venni I came
tu venisti you came (etc.)

PERFECT INDICATIVE
io sono venuto I came / have come

PRESENT SUBJUNCTIVE
io venga I may come
tu venga you may come
lui venga he may come

noi veniamo we may come
voi venite you may come
loro vengono they may come

IMPERATIVE
vieni! come!

vivere to live

FUTURE INDICATIVE
io vivrò I shall live (etc.)

CONDITIONAL
io vivrei I would live (etc.)

PAST HISTORIC
io vissi I lived
tu vivesti you lived (etc.)

PERFECT INDICATIVE
io ho vissuto I lived / have lived

volere to want (see section 59)

PRESENT INDICATIVE
io voglio I want
tu vuoi you want
lui vuole he wants

noi vogliamo we want
voi volete you want
loro vogliono they want

FUTURE INDICATIVE
io vorrò I shall want (etc.)

CONDITIONAL
io vorrei I would want (etc.)

PAST HISTORIC
io volli I wanted
tu volesti you wanted (etc.)

PERFECT INDICATIVE
io ho voluto I wanted / have wanted

PRESENT SUBJUNCTIVE

io voglia I may want	*noi vogliamo* we may want
tu voglia you may want	*voi vogliate* you may want
lui voglia he may want	*loro vogliano* they want

Appendix 2
Tense sequence with the subjunctive

It is important to remember that the dependent sentence must be connected with the main one with *che* if there is no other connector such as *se* or interrogative indirect pronouns or adverbs.

MAIN SENTENCE TENSE	DEPENDENT SENTENCE TIME OF ACTION IN RELATION TO THE MAIN SENTENCE	DEPENDENT SENTENCE TENSE
PRESENT *penso* I think	concurrent	PRESENT SUBJ.: *che capisca* that she may understand
	concurrent	CONDITIONAL: *che capirebbe* that she would understand
	precedent	PERFECT SUBJ.: *che abbia capito* that she has understood
	precedent	CONDITIONAL: *che avrebbe capito* that she would have understood
	subsequent	PRESENT SUBJ.: *che capisca* that she may understand
	subsequent	FUTURE: *che capirà* that she will understand
IMPERATIVE *chiedi* ask	concurrent	PRESENT SUBJ.: *che venga* that she comes
FUTURE *pregherò* I'll pray	concurrent	PRESENT SUBJ.: *che capisca* that she may understand
	precedent	PERFECT SUBJ.: *che abbia capito* that she may have understood
PAST FUTURE *avrà pregato* she will have prayed	concurrent	IMPERFECT SUBJ.: *che capisse* that she might understand
	precedent	PERFECT SUBJ.: *che abbia capito* that she may have understood
avrà sperato she will have hoped	precedent	PLUPERFECT SUBJ.: *che avesse capito* that she would have understood
	subsequent	PAST CONDITIONAL: *che avrebbe capito* that she would understand

The following tenses take the same sequence:

**PERFECT AND
PAST HISTORIC**

ho pensato / pensai I have thought / I thought	concurrent precedent subsequent	IMPERFECT SUBJ. *che capisse* that she understood PLUPERFECT SUBJ.: *che avesse capito* that she had understood PAST CONDITIONAL: *che avrebbe capito* that she would understand / that she would have understood

IMPERFECT

pensavo I thought / I used to think / I was thinking	concurrent precedent subsequent	IMPERFECT SUBJ. *che capisse* that she understood PLUPERFECT SUBJ.: *che avesse capito* that she had understood PAST CONDITIONAL: *che avrebbe capito* that she would understand / that she would have understood

PLUPERFECT

avevo pensato I had thought	concurrent precedent subsequent	IMPERFECT SUBJ. *che capisse* that she understood PLUPERFECT SUBJ.: *che avesse capito* that she had understood PAST CONDITIONAL: *che avrebbe capito* that she would understand / that she would have understood

CONDITIONAL

mi piacerebbe I would like	concurrent precedent subsequent	IMPERFECT SUBJ.: *che capisse* her to understand (lit. that she understood) PLUPERFECT SUBJ.: *che avesse capito* her to have understood IMPERFECT SUBJ.: *che capisse* her to understand

PAST CONDITIONAL

mi sarebbe piaciuto I would have liked	concurrent precedent	IMPERFECT SUBJ.: *che capisse* her to understand PLUPERFECT SUBJ.: *che avesse capito* her to have understood

Suggestions for further reading

(1) Dictionaries

Devoto, G., and Oli, G.C., *Dizionario della lingua italiana*, Le Monnier, Florence (1989)

Enriques, L., and Suvero, A., *Dizionario enciclopedico scientifico e tecnico*, McGraw-Hill Zanichelli (1991)

Langenscheidt Universal Italian Dictionary, Berlin and Munich (1982)

Picchi, F., *Economics and Business. Dizionario enciclopedico economico e commerciale inglese-italiano italiano-inglese*, Zanichelli (1988)

Rossi, G., *Il Nuovo Ragazzini, dizionario inglese-italiano, italiano-inglese*, Zanichelli, Bologna, 2nd edition (1987)

The Cambridge Italian-English English-Italian Dictionary, C.U.P. Signorelli, Milan (1981)

The Collins Sansoni Dictionary Italian-English English-Italian, Macchi, V. (ed), Florence, 3rd edition (1988)

(2) Reference grammars

Altieri Biagi, M.A., *La grammatica del testo*, Mursia, Milan (1986)

Bordoni Di Trapani, A., *Dentro la lingua*, La Scuola, Brescia (1986)

Brunet, J., *Grammaire critique de l'italien*, Université de Vincennes, Paris (1978-86), 8 vols.

Dardano, M., and Trifone, P., *Grammatica italiana*, Zanichelli, Bologna (1989)

Lepschy, A., and Lepschy, G., *The Italian Language Today*, Hutchinson (1977)

Renzi L. (ed.), *Grande grammatica italiana di consultazione*, Il Mulino, Bologna (1988), vol. 1.

Sensini M., *La grammatica della lingua italiana*, Oscar Mondadori, Milan (1990)

(3) Contemporary usage and word power

Banfi, E. and Sobrero, A.A. *Il linguaggio giovanile degli anni novanta*, Laterza, Bari (1992)

Brini, A., Cappannelli, C., and Fontana, F., *Lettere commerciali italiano-inglese*, Pancaldi G. (ed.), Capitol CEB (1989)

Browne, V., and Natali, G., *Bugs and Bugbears. Dizionario delle insidie e dei tranelli nelle traduzioni fra inglese e italiano*, Zanichelli, Bologna (1989)

Browne, V., *Odd Pairs & False Friends. Dizionario di false analogie e ambigue affinità fra inglese e italiano*, Zanichelli, Bologna (1987)

Dardano, M., *La formazione delle parole nell'italiano di oggi*, Bulzoni, Roma (1978)

De Felice, E., *Le parole d'oggi*, Mondadori, Milan (1984)

Diadori, D., *Senza parole. 100 gesti degli italiani*, Bonacci, Roma (1991)

Duse, A., *Lettere commerciali italiano-inglese*, Bignami (1986)

Forconi, A., *La Mala Lingua. Dizionario dello << slang >> italiano*, Sugarco, Milan (1987)

Forconi, A., *Dizionario delle nuove parole italiane*, Sugarco, Milan (1990)

Giaveri, M., *Parlare e scrivere oggi*, Fabbri, Milano (1985), 5 vols.

Giongo, M.C., *La frase giusta per ogni circostanza*, De Vecchi Editore, Milan (1987)

Maury, P., *Caro amore ti scrivo. Lettere d'amore serie e scherzose*, Pan Libri, Milan (1989)

Sephton, D., *Tick Tack. Language Guide for Business, Italian-English*, Primrose Publishing (1982)

Sotis, L., *Bon Ton. Il nuovo dizionario delle buone maniere*, Mondadori, Milan (1986)

Vassalli, S., *Le parole italiane degli anni Ottanta*, Zanichelli, Bologna, 1989

Index